Building a European Identity

BERGHAHN MONOGRAPHS IN FRENCH STUDIES

Editor: **Irwin Wall,** Professor Emeritus, University of California, Riverside
Visiting Scholar, Center for European Studies, New York University

The study of the French past has always functioned as a kind of template for the great historical movements in European history, whether the Renaissance, Absolutism, Enlightenment, 'Nationalism, Democracy, or Imperialism, while the Great French Revolution still stands as a model for revolution worldwide and evokes debate over the central questions of historiography. And France and French society continue to serve as a laboratory for academic innovation in the study of history and other disciplines. Centralization provides easy access to well-preserved and rich documentary collections in Paris and provinces and departments for all periods; it is no accident that studies of local and social history were pioneered by French historians in the writings of the Annales school. France, the former French Empire, and contemporary Francophonie continue to provide models for modern studies in Imperialism, Postcolonialism, and Multiculturalism.

BUILDING A EUROPEAN IDENTITY

*France, the United States, and
the Oil Shock, 1973–1974*

Aurélie Élisa Gfeller

Berghahn Books
New York • Oxford

Published by
Berghahn Books
www.berghahnbooks.com

© 2012 Aurélie Élisa Gfeller

Library of congress cataloging-in-publication data

Gfeller, Aurélie Elisa, 1977-
  Building a European identity : France, the United States, and the oil shock,
1973–1974 / Aurélie Élisa Gfeller.
    p. cm. — (Berghahn monographs in French studies ; v. 12)
  Includes bibliographical references and index.
  ISBN 978-0-85745-225-2 (hardback : alk. paper) — ISBN 978-0-85745-227-6
(e-book)
    1. European Union countries—Foreign relations—United States. 2. United
States—Foreign relations—European Union countries. 3. France—Foreign
relations—United States. 4. United States—Foreign relations—France.
5. Political culture—European Union countries. 6. Group identity—
European Union countries. 7. National characteristics, European. I. Title.
  D1065.U5G45 2012
  327.407309'047—dc23

                                                              2012001272

British Library cataloguing in publication data

A catalogue record for this book is available from the British Library.

Printed in the United States on acid-free paper

ISBN 978-0-85745-225-2 (hardback)
ISBN 978-0-85745-227-6 (ebook)

CONTENTS

ACKNOWLEDGMENTS

I want to acknowledge, first, Philip Nord, who has offered guidance and constructive commentary throughout this project. I have benefited immensely from his suggestions and ceaseless encouragement. I am also indebted to Harold James for his valuable advice and ideas. Robert Darnton, Anthony Grafton, Daniel Rodgers, and Maurice Vaïsse all inspired me along the path of learning, pushing me to think about history in broad, comparative terms.

All books need critical readers. From those who engaged with this manuscript, I have received important ideas, qualifications, and counsel. Matthew Connelly and John Ikenberry read a preliminary version of this text. Piers Ludlow and John Kim Munholland commented on the final manuscript, offering useful corrections and suggestions.

I have had the chance to present or publish pieces of my research in other venues and formats. My thanks go to Anne Deighton, Jussi Hanhimäki, Johnny Laursen, Kiran Patel, Morten Rasmussen, Federico Romero, and Antonio Varsori, who issued invitations, organized conferences, or provided much-needed editorial criticism.

While preparing this book, I accumulated debts to the many colleagues who directed me to archives, suggested useful texts and resources, and shared their own work. I wish to mention in particular Gérard Bossuat, Eric Bussière, Wilfried Loth, Guia Migani, Emmanuel Mourlon-Druol, Luke Nichter, Matthieu Osmont, Emilia Robin-Hivert, Angela Romano, Frédérique Schillo, Matthias Schulz, and Christian Wenkel.

A number of archivists gave me helpful assistance. Pascal Geneste at the Archives nationales and Grégoire Eldin, Dominique Vondrus-Reissner, and Françoise Watel at the Quai d'Orsay worked to make new sources available. The staff at the Bibliothèque nationale de France, the U.S. National Archives, the Historical Archives of the European Union, and the Fondation Jean Monnet pour l'Europe patiently answered all my queries. The late Henri Rieben shared his memories of Jean Monnet, while several historical actors, notably Valéry Giscard d'Estaing and François de Rose, were kind enough to grant me interviews.

Support has come not only from individuals, but also from institutions. The Graduate School and History Department at Princeton University and the Swiss National Science Foundation provided essential fellowship support. I spent fruitful months at the Institut d'études politiques in Paris, where I began research for this project, and at the Robert Schuman Center for Advanced Studies at the European University Institute in Florence, where I prepared the manuscript for publication.

I am very thankful to Marion Berghahn at Berghahn Books for trusting the manuscript. I was also extremely fortunate to have Irwin Wall as an editor. His suggestions and close attention to the details of the book improved it immensely.

Among the friends and colleagues who opened their homes during my research trips, a special mention goes to David and Manuela Doeller-Hauner. Laura Weinrib has been a most generous friend and demanding reader, always making time in a busy schedule to offer advice and editorial comments.

My deepest gratitude goes to my parents. They instilled in me a thirst for knowledge and gave me unwavering support, often from afar.

Acronyms and Abbreviations

ACUSE	Action Committee for the United States of Europe
Ambafrance	Ambassade de France
AO	Archives orales
AP	Archives privées
BP	British Petroleum
CHAN	Centre historique des archives nationales, Paris, France
CEE	Communauté économique européenne
CFPF	Central Foreign Policy Files
COREPER	Comité des représentants permanents (Committee of Permanent Representatives)
COREU	Correspondence européenne
CSCE	Conference on Security and Cooperation in Europe
C20	Committee of Twenty
EAG	Energy Action Group
EDC	European Defence Community
EC	European Community
ECG	Energy Coordinating Group
ECSC	European Coal and Steel Community
EN	Fonds Emile Noël
EP	European Parliament

EPC	European Political Cooperation
EU	European Union
FCO	Foreign and Commonwealth Office
FJM	Fondation Jean Monnet pour l'Europe, Lausanne, Switzerland
GATT	General Agreement on Tariffs and Trade
GFPL	Gerald Ford Presidential Library
G5	Group of Five
G7	Group of Seven
G77	Group of Seventy-Seven
HAEU	Historical Archives of the European Union, European University Institute, Florence, Italy
HAK	Henry A. Kissinger
IEA	International Energy Agency
IMF	International Monetary Fund
JM	Jean Monnet
KM	Fonds Klaus Meyer
MAE	Ministère des affaires étrangères, Paris, France
mbd	million barrels per day
MBFR	Mutual and Balanced Force Reductions
Memcon	Memorandum of conversation
NAC	North Atlantic Council
NARA	National Archives and Records Administration, College Park, MD
NATO	North Atlantic Treaty Organization
NPM	Nixon Presidential Materials (currently at NARA, College Park, MD)
NSA	National Security Advisor
NSC	National Security Council

NSSM	National Security Study Memorandum
OAPEC	Organization of Arab Petroleum Exporting Countries
OECD	Organization for Economic Cooperation and Development
OPEC	Organization of Petroleum Exporting Countries
PCF	Parti communiste français
PLO	Palestine Liberation Organization
RG	Record Group
SALT	Strategic Arms Limitation Talks
SD	Records of the State Department
SU	Soviet Union
Telcon	Telephone conversation
UDR	Union des démocrates pour la République
UN	United Nations
UNSC	United Nations Security Council
VH	Jacques van Helmont
WEU	Western European Union

Introduction

"This presidency [of the European Union] has taught me much over the past six months," French President Nicolas Sarkozy told the European Parliament in 2008. "When you have the chance to learn about, and decide on, issues from twenty-seven member states," Sarkozy went on to say, "you understand that Europe is probably the most beautiful idea that was ever conceived during the twentieth century, and that we need Europe more than ever."[1] However, any attempt to build Europe against the will of "nations," he warned, would be "a historical mistake."[2] These statements provide an appropriate introduction to a book on France's European project. Sarkozy's words illustrate a lasting feature of French views on Europe, namely, ambivalence.[3] France has been one of the major actors of European integration. Starting in the 1950s, governments supported unification because it helped to create a stable structure of peace in Western Europe while fostering economic growth and modernization. Over time they delegated, however reluctantly, more powers to the supranational institutions of the European Community (EC) and, subsequently, of the European Union (EU). This process encroached upon the nation-state and hence upon the political self-understanding of political actors, thus causing anxiety among French political elites, who were concerned with maintaining sovereignty. The result was an enduring uneasiness about European integration.

This lasting ambivalence should not obscure the real changes that have taken place in the intervening decades. By the 1960s, Charles de Gaulle's design for national regeneration and restored grandeur had come to shape the political debate. De Gaulle's views left virtually no room for progress toward European unity except within a strictly intergovernmental framework. De Gaulle died in 1970, but his legacy lived on. Nevertheless, the early 1970s saw a readjustment. In 1969, President Georges

Notes for this section begin on page 13.

Pompidou helped to give new impetus to European integration through his famous triptych "completion, deepening, enlargement." Pompidou's lifting of the French veto to Britain's EC membership laid the basis for the 1973 enlargement to include Britain, Denmark, and Ireland. Pompidou also grudgingly agreed to meet his EC partners' request to grant limited budgetary powers to the European Parliament as part of a new funding system for the EC budget—the EC's own resources as opposed to national contributions. The most important shift, however, occurred in 1973 and 1974. In the context of renewed transatlantic tensions and the first oil crisis, Pompidou's government set out to assert the nascent European entity as a world actor vis-à-vis the United States and the Arab world. The French political elites also invented a new language of a politically, rather than culturally, defined "European identity." Last but not least, centrist leader Valéry Giscard d'Estaing, Pompidou's successor to the presidency, fleshed out this new notion of European identity by spurring reforms that strengthened the institutional architecture of the European polity along both intergovernmental and supranational lines. How did these moves come about? Which short- and long-term geopolitical, economic, and cultural factors made them possible? Combining a study of French foreign policy–making within a multilateral framework with an analysis of political discourse, I offer an answer to these questions, one that points to broad political and economic forces, contingency, and change of political leadership. I suggest that this unprecedented emphasis on common European action on the global stage, combined with Giscard's willingness to embrace supranational reforms, marked a new recognition of the need for a political Europe.

Shifts in the geopolitical and economic context made this reconfiguration possible. By the early 1970s, U.S. power appeared to be on the wane, providing an auspicious background for the EC countries to assert themselves on the global stage. The United States had lost its nuclear supremacy. Its gross national product had fallen from 40 percent of the world's total in 1950 to 25 percent in 1975. Its share of world monetary reserves had declined from 50 percent in 1950 to 16 percent in 1970.[4] The U.S. economy was on shaky ground. Rising foreign defense spending in the mid and late 1960s, together with Lyndon B. Johnson's "Great Society" domestic reform agenda, had produced growing budget and balance-of-payments deficits.[5] Above all, the Vietnam quagmire had tarnished America's image abroad. Yet "even without that purgatory," former U.S. Secretary of State Henry A. Kissinger reflected, "a major reassessment of American foreign policy would have been in order, for the age of America's nearly total dominance of the world stage was drawing to a close."[6]

Talk of decline, which was not uncommon in U.S. policy circles at the time,[7] seems exaggerated with the benefit of hindsight. This narrative was challenged as early as the 1970s. Leading French intellectual Raymond Aron insisted that in absolute terms, the United States remained "the wealthiest and most powerful country on earth," even if its relative power had declined, turning it into "a first among equals [*primus inter pares*]."[8] In an era when neorealist thinking still held sway in U.S. policy circles, however, U.S. political actors and commentators focused more on absolute power than on the country's relative position in the international system.[9]

This pervasive sense of decline influenced U.S. policy thinking and policy making toward both friends and foes. Beginning in the 1960s, the U.S. government had grown increasingly reluctant to assume the largest share of the cost of Western European defense. Responding to domestic pressure, the first Nixon administration had intensified its calls for fairer burden-sharing.[10] A number of U.S. political figures—prominent among them Democratic Senator Mike Mansfield—favored halving U.S. troops in Europe. In 1971, the U.S. Senate rejected the Mansfield amendment by a 61 to 36 majority, but the Montana senator and majority leader would introduce it again in subsequent years. Détente with the Soviet Union was also a response to such concerns over decline.[11] Efforts to surpass the Soviet Union in military capabilities had been costly and had only triggered comparable efforts on the Soviet part. Richard Nixon's first foreign policy report sounded the alarm bell: "An inescapable reality of the 1970s is the Soviet Union's possession of powerful and sophisticated strategic forces approaching, and in some categories, exceeding our own in numbers and capability."[12] Nixon and National Security Advisor Kissinger concluded that mutual restraint would best serve U.S. interests. In shifting U.S. strategic thinking from "superiority" to "sufficiency," the Nixon administration remained committed to the principle of "containment."[13] The goal was to integrate the Soviet Union into a structure of peace and hence stabilize the international order on U.S. terms. The Sino-Soviet split of 1969 worked in favor of this policy. Engaging in triangular diplomacy, the U.S. government achieved major breakthroughs. The "opening" to China culminated in Nixon's 1972 trip to Beijing—a first essential step toward mutual recognition in 1979. The first round of U.S.-Soviet Strategic Arms Limitation Talks (SALT) ended in 1972 with an agreement to freeze strategic missile launchers at existing levels. One year later, the United States and the Soviet Union would sign a groundbreaking Agreement on the Prevention of Nuclear War.

East-West détente was another factor encouraging Western European countries to escape the U.S. shadow. It had begun as a predominantly European phenomenon in the 1960s. Gaullist France had been the first to travel that path. After the 1962 failure of his Fouchet Plan—an intergovernmental "union of [Western European] states"—de Gaulle had revived his 1950 concept of a "Europe from the Atlantic to the Urals."[14] This concept subsumed a security order resting on Franco-Soviet "entente" and largely excluding the United States.[15] By the time de Gaulle left office in 1969, France and the Soviet Union had created a "small" and a "large" committee designed to foster bilateral exchanges and engaged in a dialogue spanning scientific, technological, economic, and political cooperation.[16]

Meanwhile, in 1963, Social Democrat Berlin Mayor Willy Brandt and his trusted adviser, Egon Bahr, had made groundbreaking programmatic statements on relations with Eastern Europe. Bahr had coined the phrase "change through rapprochement [*Wandel durch Annäherung*]," while Brandt had referred to "the transformation of the other side [*Transformation der anderen Seite*]."[17] Their proclaimed objective was to lay the foundation of peaceful East-West coexistence. Christian Democrat Konrad Adenauer, West German chancellor from 1949 to 1963, had insisted on German reunification as a precondition for any progress toward peaceful relations with the Eastern bloc.[18] Students of West German foreign policy have argued that Brandt and Bahr remained committed to reunification.[19] Their proposed *Ostpolitik* was designed to attain German unity through different means. Medium- or long-term changes in the postwar order would result from temporary acceptance of the status quo.

In 1966, Brandt was appointed foreign minister in the "great coalition" government formed by Christian Democrat Chancellor Kurt Kiesinger. Kiesinger's government moved cautiously toward détente with the Eastern bloc. Its plan was to conclude a nonaggression treaty with the Soviet Union based on existing borders and, subsequently, a treaty on "regulated coexistence [*geregeltes Nebeneinander*]" with East Germany—one in which the West German state would grant "temporary power [*befristete Geschäftsfähigkeit*]" to its Eastern counterpart pending reunification.[20] Whether Soviet opposition or disagreements within the coalition blocked the implementation of this policy is a matter of debate.[21] The Christian Democrats certainly remained reluctant to take any radical departure from past policies.[22]

Brandt's 1969 election as chancellor and his forming of a coalition government with the Free Democrats gave him significantly more room to maneuver. Events had set the stage for his *Ostpolitik*. In 1968, the United States had implicitly acquiesced to the Soviet crushing of the "Prague Spring," a movement of political liberalization in Czechoslovakia. Leonid Brezhnev, general secretary of the Soviet Communist Party, had subsequently justified military intervention whenever a country's development toward socialism was under threat. The Soviet show of force and the "Brezhnev doctrine" meant that any effort at lessening East-West tensions would have to reckon with Soviet dominance in Eastern Europe.[23] Johnson, moreover, had made it clear that the United States would no longer consider a resolution of the so-called German problem a prerequisite for progress in East-West relations.[24] Finally, U.S. debates on troop reduction fueled concerns in Bonn about unilateral U.S. action and the resurgence of isolationism. Détente was clearly a necessity if the United States was to leave the continent of Europe. *Ostpolitik* would become a hallmark of Brandt's government,[25] leading to three major treaties: the 1970 Moscow Treaty, a non-aggression pact with the Soviet Union; the 1970 Warsaw Treaty, a border recognition treaty with Poland; and the 1972 Basic Treaty, a mutual recognition agreement between the two halves of divided Germany.

Engaging in its own "bridge-building" policy, the Johnson administration tried to counteract these centrifugal forces within the Atlantic Alliance by multilateralizing the détente process. The 1967 Harmel Report established the basis for the dual approach of the North Atlantic Treaty Organization (NATO) to East-West relations, that is, "maintain adequate military strength ... to deter aggression and pursue a policy of 'détente.'"[26] In 1968 in Reykjavik, the members of NATO's command structure—all except for France—declared their intention to initiate Mutual and Balanced Force Reductions (MBFR) discussions with the Warsaw Pact.[27] The "Reykjavik signal" paved the way for the launch of MBFR negotiations five years later.

Although the Nixon administration took détente a significant step farther than its predecessor had, it was uneasy about Brandt's *Ostpolitik.* Would West Germany's commitment to the Atlantic Alliance "be gradually eroded by Herr Brandt's new policy of promoting better relations with Eastern Europe?" Nixon asked British Prime Minister Harold Wilson in 1970.[28] Kissinger expressed fears that this policy would gain its own momentum and "lead Brandt into dangerous concessions."[29] "Brandt is sincere," he told former U.S. Secretary of State Dean Acheson in December 1970, "but there are a lot of sincere fools in the world."[30] The specter of the past also loomed large in U.S. thinking. "The problem," Kissinger had warned at a 1969 State Department seminar, "is the counteraction which may set in ... a resurgence of Nazism."[31] Nonetheless, the Nixon administration tacitly backed *Ostpolitik* as it became entwined with its own détente policy. Nixon hailed the September 1971 Four-Power Agreement on Berlin as a major step in U.S.-Soviet relations, publicly claiming credit for it. The Soviet Union, in turn, made implementation of the agreement conditional upon West German parliamentary ratification of the Eastern treaties.[32] In Kissinger's words, "Brandt has maneuvered the situation so that we have been pushed into the position of being responsible both for Berlin and for the success of his Eastern initiatives."[33]

Whether *Ostpolitik* contradicted U.S. policy is a matter of debate. The Brandt government had no intention of breaking away from NATO. Quite the opposite, it was determined to keep West Germany firmly anchored in the West.[34] Since the early 1960s, however, U.S. officials had worried

that the Soviet Union might successfully advance its own agenda by playing on divisions within NATO. When he was appointed national security
advisor, Kissinger warned that *Ostpolitik* might help the Soviets achieve
this objective: "the Soviets ... may then confront the F[ederal]R[epublic
of]G[ermany] with the proposition that a real and lasting improvement in
the FRG's relations with the G[erman]D[democratic]R[epublic] and other
Eastern countries can only be achieved if Bonn loosens its Western ties."[35]
Jussi Hanhimäki has thus argued that Kissinger's problem "was not with
the Germans," but with the Soviets.[36] This was not the whole story, however. *Ostpolitik* signaled a new assertiveness that fueled concerns about a
revival of German nationalist impulses.[37] There was also an inherent contradiction between America's détente policy and *Ostpolitik,* even if they
were both designed to diffuse East-West tensions. U.S. policy was essentially conservative in nature, whereas *Ostpolitik* was ultimately aimed at
changing the territorial status quo.[38]

   Ostpolitik also raised concerns in France. Pompidou had obtained what
he wanted in Berlin. The 1971 agreement maintained strict quadripartite
control over the divided city. West Berlin did not become a constituent
part of West Germany, and the Soviet Union remained exclusively responsible for regulating access to it.[39] Pompidou had resisted the Soviet request
to share access control with East Germany. To the French president, the
Western rights over Berlin were the most effective tool to control Germany.[40] The *Ostpolitik* treaties were broadly congruent with French policy
objectives.[41] Since the 1964–1965 period, the French government had advocated East-West reconciliation and Germany's discarding of its claims over
the territories east of the Oder-Neisse line. Nonetheless, French officials
feared that *Ostpolitik* could backfire. This policy line, they argued, could
encourage West Germany to drift toward the Soviet Union and hence
result in its "Finlandization."[42] Pompidou also worried about a possible
Soviet-German agreement or "condominium" based on the reunification
and even the nuclearization of Germany.[43]

   These fears influenced French policy toward the East, the United States,
and Western Europe, prompting Pompidou to foster a cautious and incremental approach to détente with the Soviet Union—as opposed to
de Gaulle's design of a pan-European order under Franco-Soviet leadership.[44] Many high-level Franco-Soviet meetings took place during Pompidou's presidency, but the French government resisted the Soviet wish
for a bilateral treaty.[45] Such concerns also shaped Pompidou's geopolitical vision of Europe, particularly his emphasis on transatlantic entente
and enhanced Western European cohesion, notably among EC countries.
Combined with U.S. military support, a cohesive Western Europe would
ensure French security against the Soviet threat while keeping German
ambitions in check.[46]

Overall, the relaxation of East-West tensions encouraged Western European governments to pursue a policy line more independent from the United States. EC states did so individually, but also collectively. They availed themselves of the mechanisms for European Political Cooperation (EPC), created in 1970, in order to forge common positions toward the Conference on Security and Cooperation in Europe (CSCE). Collective European diplomacy was influential in the inclusion of human rights in the 1975 CSCE Helsinki Final Act.[47] The U.S.-Soviet dialogue also triggered anxiety over the credibility of U.S. nuclear deterrence. Concerns over a U.S.-Soviet agreement at Europe's expense compelled Western European decision makers to think of their security interests as possibly conflicting with those of the United States.[48] In France in particular, such fears were often articulated in terms of a U.S.-Soviet "condominium." They would play an important role in Pompidou's reassessment of EPC in the fall of 1973.[49]

Transatlantic divisions were also fueled by economic transformations. In 1971, a rising U.S. balance-of-payments deficit precipitated the fall of the Bretton Woods monetary order. In a unilateral move on 15 August, Nixon suspended the convertibility of the dollar into gold, the cornerstone of Bretton Woods. Ensuing talks within the International Monetary Fund (IMF) brought transatlantic differences into sharp focus.[50] The U.S. government wanted to establish an automatic mechanism placing the burden of adjustment on countries that ran permanent balance-of-payments surpluses, notably West Germany and Japan.[51] Its Western European counterparts insisted on the need to reduce the U.S. deficit and to set up an asset settlement mechanism through which the world's large dollar reserves could be converted into gold, foreign exchange, or the IMF's special drawing rights.[52] Significantly, EC countries did not wait until the March 1973 move to floating exchange rates between the U.S. dollar and the world's major currencies to work out a solution of their own. In April 1972, they settled on narrower bands of fluctuation between their currencies than what the December 1971 Smithsonian Agreement—a short-lived attempt to establish a system of fixed exchange rates without the backing of gold— had allowed. In March 1973, they established a joint currency float, the so-called "snake."

Trade was similarly divisive. Western Europe had enjoyed unprecedented growth rates during the 1950s and the 1960s, with an average of 4 percent between 1950 and 1970, against 1 percent between 1913 and 1950.[53] Rising European prosperity, combined with a declining U.S. trade balance that turned into deficit in 1971, fueled U.S. resentment against EC protectionism and the Common Agricultural Policy in particular. Faced with the prospect of the EC's enlargement, the U.S. government departed from its unqualified support for European integration.[54] Adopting a belligerent stance, it sought compensation under the General Agreement on Tariffs and Trade (GATT).[55] Despite reduced industrial tariffs, Britain's EC membership meant an overall higher level of protection. In 1974, the EC would have to accept a $45 million compensation settlement.[56] But EC countries also used the GATT framework to pursue their own ends. They had negotiated as a single entity during the Kennedy GATT round of trade liberalization (1964–1967). In the early 1970s, they jointly opposed the U.S. request to include agriculture in a new liberalization round.[57] The September 1973 agreement that launched the Tokyo round reflected their economic strength, as it provided for the "specificity" of agricultural trade.[58]

Last but not least, the rise of the Third World also encouraged greater assertiveness on the part of EC states. It highlighted European dependence upon raw material producers while opening a field of independent diplomatic opportunity for EC countries. The use of oil as a political weapon in the October 1973 Arab-Israeli war emboldened the Organization of Petroleum Exporting Countries (OPEC) to quadruple the posted price of oil. This move took place against the background of a tightening oil market and a world commodity price surge caused by an accelerated rise in the world's money supply.[59] Western economies had become so reliant on cheap imported oil that the fourfold increase in its price caused both a demand and a supply shock. By undermining consumer and investor confidence, the price rise weakened demand. Higher input prices squeezed profitability, reducing firms' demand for labor. Monetary factors magnified these twin shocks. Taking its cue from the United States, Western Europe had pursued loose monetary policies since the early 1970s. Once inflation began accelerating, Western central banks resorted to monetary tightening, which further depressed demand.[60] The resulting 1974 recession proved particularly painful in Western Europe because it marked the end of the *trente glorieuses.* Signs of structural change were already emerging in the early 1970s, but the first oil crisis accelerated the day of reckoning.[61]

The oil shock threw light on a shifting balance of power between advanced and developing countries. It showed that the Third World was now in a position to enact huge wealth transfers between the industrialized "North" and the developing "South." From 1973 to 1974 the balance-of-payments deficit of advanced countries rose from $7,279 million to $22,530 million. The surpluses registered by oil producers, by contrast, increased from $3.6 billion in 1973 to $38.5 billion in 1974.[62] There were concerns that other raw material producers might follow suit, especially since only two to four countries supplied key raw materials like copper, aluminum, rubber, and bauxite.[63] Energy-saving measures quickly brought home to Western consumers the new strength of the developing world.[64] Reduced heating, the cancellation of Christmas illuminations or late-night movie shows, and car-less Sundays became potent symbols of this power shift.

At the same time, the oil producers' assertiveness created openings for EPC. In signaling the end of European dominance over the Third World, it made Western European decision makers more apprehensive about America's *imperium*. Western European governments would not challenge the paradigm of the "'Empire' by invitation" which had been the dominant mode since World War II.[65] But they would grow increasingly uneasy about U.S. supremacy. The French in particular were "pathologically sensitive about any possible implication that Europe is in any sense subordinate to or dependent upon the United States. It is strangely like a sort of Third World psychosis towards the colonial power."[66] By spurring the rise of U.S. influence in the Middle East, the fourth Arab-Israeli war, also known as the Yom Kippur War, exacerbated such feelings. In fostering the use of oil as a political weapon, it also narrowed the gap between pro-Israeli and pro-Arab EC states, providing the basis for common action.

These events encouraged the EC countries to adopt a stance that was more independent of U.S. policy—which, of course, suited the Gaullist establishment just fine. Drawing on a long tradition of cultural and political anti-Americanism, de Gaulle had begun to move France away from tight cooperation with the United States.[67] His battle against the "exorbitant" privilege of the U.S. dollar, his ambiguous appeal for a "free" Quebec, and the French withdrawal from the military arm of NATO had all been attempts at asserting French independence from the United States. Early in his presidency, Pompidou had cultivated friendlier relations with the United States, hoping to strengthen France's influence in Europe through close ties with its American ally. Top French and U.S. officials had even started talks on defense, including nuclear cooperation.[68] But U.S. security and monetary policy had subsequently triggered renewed strains in bilateral ties.[69] At the December 1971 Franco-American Azores summit, Pompidou had negotiated an agreement on devaluing the U.S. dollar. Although French officials recognized that the ensuing Smithsonian Agreement rested on shaky ground, the demise of the Bretton Woods monetary system in 1972–1973 caused frustration in Paris. So did the ensuing IMF talks. Pompidou remained committed to a system of fixed exchange rates based on gold, special drawing rights, or both.[70] The U.S. government, by contrast, was happy to live with a floating rate regime. Given de Gaulle's legacy and French misgivings about U.S. security and monetary policy, it is not surprising that Kissinger's April 1973 call for a new "Atlantic charter" sparked a negative reaction.

What was unexpected was the nature of the French response to Kissinger's "Year of Europe" initiative. Pompidou's government signaled a new willingness to play by EPC's rules in accepting a coordinated EPC stance so long as it asserted the distinctiveness of the European entity.

Soon thereafter, having reappraised the value of EPC in the Mediterranean world in light of the Yom Kippur War, French officials helped to forge the Declaration on the Middle East, published by EC countries in November 1973. They also played a leading role in devising the so-called "Euro-Arab dialogue," a mechanism to promote cooperation between the nine EC countries (EC Nine) and the League of Arab States.

Moreover, the new concept of European identity, popularized in this context, brought an added layer of complexity to French political discourse. Clearly, the notion of a European identity was not designed to undermine the nation-state as the paramount category of French political life. Nevertheless, it appealed to a supranational political entity that could function as a unit of political legitimacy alongside—and potentially in opposition to—the French nation. The EC institutional reform Giscard initiated in 1974 may seem unrelated to this new language or to the French emphasis on EPC during the final year of Pompidou's presidency. By supporting the creation of the European Council, however, Giscard followed in Pompidou's footsteps. Pompidou had called for institutionalized summitry in the aftermath of the Yom Kippur War in order to strengthen European political leadership. Interestingly, Giscard's government combined this intergovernmental reform with supranational measures, and in so doing broke with de Gaulle's strict intergovernmental paradigm.

Together, these various steps contributed to the rise of a reconfigured political ideal for the French elites during the last decades of the twentieth century—an ideal that persists today. This ideal features a European entity acting as a world power in lieu of the French nation. It also involves the recognition that sovereignty can be divided between the nation-state and a European polity. The concept of European identity now has pride of place alongside that of French identity in French political thought and discourse.

This book is a sequence of interrelated stories, each revolving around an event that got the nascent European Union involved in world politics. Some of these episodes testify to the then-EC states' ability to speak with one voice on the global stage. The EC Nine jointly drafted a statement in response to Kissinger's plea for an "Atlantic charter." Despite U.S. objections, they held their ground, rejecting the proposed amendments of the Nixon administration. They also issued a pioneering Declaration on European Identity. The Yom Kippur War and its aftermath compelled them to devise a common position on the Arab-Israeli conflict. Their Declaration on the Middle East was a historical novelty: never before had EC states jointly expressed their opinion on a high-level foreign policy issue. Nonetheless, there was another side to the story. The contentious EC-U.S. statement was discarded in spring 1974, and all NATO members—France included—subsequently came around to what the Nixon administration wanted, signing a NATO declaration that asserted the importance of transatlantic consultation. Most importantly, France and its EC partners clashed over the proposed U.S. international energy plan. The dominant scholarly narrative is therefore one of disappointment.[71]

Drawing on French, U.S., British, and German archival records, this study offers a different interpretation. Rather than stressing failure, I underscore EPC's achievements at such an early stage in its history. Analyzing EPC's 1974 vicissitudes as the normal pangs of birth, I underscore the longer-term implications of what the EC Nine succeeded in doing during this two-year period. By carrying the analysis through December 1974—as opposed to March or June 1974, the conventional endpoints—I show that the oil shock did not halt the EC Nine's quest for political unification. Rather, the emphasis shifted away from foreign policy cooperation and toward institutional engineering. These were two sides of the same coin; at least, French decision-makers certainly saw them as such. Both Pompidou and Giscard's government fostered institutional reform as a way of building an internationally influential Europe.

Furthermore, this book fills a gap in the literature on the Year of Europe and the 1973 Middle East crisis by investigating French policy-making. These events have mostly been explored from a British and a U.S. perspective.[72] More broadly, the nascent scholarship on transatlantic relations in the 1970s has tended to focus on the United States, Britain, and West Germany.[73] One notable exception is Daniel Möckli's monograph on EPC's early history,[74] which examines the triangular diplomacy between Britain, France, and West Germany with an emphasis on key decision-makers (president/prime minister and foreign minister). By contrast, this book is mainly, though not exclusively, about France. It also encompasses a wider range of actors, including named and unnamed senior and medium-rank officials as well as press commentators. By making greater use of French sources and probing a broader spectrum of views, I offer a more complex account of France's policy making and show the responses of the French press as the shaper, if not the mouthpiece, of elite public opinion. I also challenge Möckli's interpretation of a sharp break between France's pursuit of a "European Europe" during Pompidou's final year in office and Giscard's reassertion of the "transatlantic prerogative."[75] I demonstrate that although Giscard placed renewed emphasis on the transatlantic relationship at the beginning of his presidency, he nevertheless sought to foster the rise of a political Europe.

While being a piece of international historical research, this book is a national study at heart. The historical study of French foreign relations during the 1970s remains in its early stages, but a few trends are now apparent. Although the president and the ministry of foreign affairs (hereafter Quai d'Orsay) shared—as they still do today—responsibility for foreign-policy making, this history is primarily told through a presidential lens.[76] The Association Georges Pompidou has contributed to this trend by sponsoring a series of conferences and edited volumes exploring Pompidou's views and policies on various domestic and foreign-policy topics.[77] Reflecting de Gaulle's historic prominence, this history also gives pride of place to issues of change and continuity, with an emphasis on continuity in French policy from the 1960s to the 1970s.[78] Finally, some topics, such as Brandt's *Ostpolitik,* have received far greater attention than others. Despite the Arab world's centrality to France's foreign policy, a paucity of studies treat France's Arab policy not only in the 1970s but more generally during the postwar era.

This book makes a threefold contribution to French diplomatic history. First, by considering a more comprehensive set of actors, I provide a deeper understanding of the policy-making process. Second, I offer a rare archival-based account of French policy-making in the Arab world during the Fifth Republic. Third, I refine the dominant historiographical narrative of continuity. It is my contention that the concept of a European identity went beyond de Gaulle's early 1960s notion of a "European Europe." Both terms were originally coined to assert European independence from the United States. The notion of a European Europe referred to a "union of nation-states," whereas the concept of a European identity conjured up the vision of a European polity. De Gaulle's Fouchet Plan never materialized. By 1973, EPC was in place, and French officials used it as de Gaulle might have used his proposed union of states, namely, as a device to assert French influence. Their very use of EPC, however, went beyond de Gaulle's vision of a "concert of powers."[79] Through their willingness to compromise in particular, French officials signaled a new commitment to collective action. In 1974, Giscard's plan for institutional reform confirmed that the era of hard-line intergovernmental Gaullism had definitely come to an end.

As much as this book is about policy making, it is also about political language. Language's significance for diplomacy cannot be overstated. Diplomats use it to interact and negotiate, and language is also a key tool in shaping international policy agendas. Surprisingly, however, diplomatic historians seldom give it the emphasis it deserves. The Year of Europe and its aftermath are no exception. Historians have paid little attention to its discursive dimension, even though it was central to the story.[80] Kissinger's call for a new charter spawned a battle of words and ideas. This feud sheds light on the interconnections between words and power. Political actors on both sides of the Atlantic perceived words as a window into power relations. Words also served as weapons against the powerful, and the French in particular used them to try to reduce U.S. influence over Western Europe. The debate was not confined to government circles. The leading French press institutions were at one with the government in rejecting wording that appealed, implicitly or explicitly, to a U.S.-dominated Euro-American community. They also contributed to popularizing the new concept of a politically defined European identity.

Finally, in charting these intertwined histories, this book contributes to the ongoing scholarly reappraisal of the 1970s in European history. The dominant interpretation is a tale of political and economic difficulties, with an emphasis on the end of the "growth miracle," the twin woes of inflation and unemployment, and the unprecedented wave of domestic terrorism in Italy and West Germany.[81] The words "malaise" and "crisis" have been used over and over to describe this decade.[82] Students of European unification have long contributed to this pessimistic appraisal, portraying the 1970s as an era of stagnation and euro-skepticism before the *relance* of the mid 1980s.[83] New research has cast doubt on this narrative.[84] There was perhaps no major leap forward toward a united Europe. Nevertheless, EC countries initiated reforms that involved both widening, as in the successful conclusion of the enlargement negotiations with Greece in 1979, and deepening, as in the 1978 European Monetary System and new common policies in the regional, social, and environmental fields.[85] In so doing, they set out new dynamics that would shape European integration in subsequent decades. This study provides grist for the revisionist mill. By revisiting the traditional interpretation of EPC's early history and examining it jointly with institutional reform, it shows that during the 1970s, the EC Nine took steps toward a political Europe.[86]

Notes

All translations of quotations from untranslated sources are by the author.
1. Nicolas Sarkozy, "Allocution prononcée le 16 décembre 2008 au Parlement européen de Strasbourg à l'occasion de la fin de la présidence française de l'Union européenne," http://www.ambafrance-cn.org/Discours-de-Nicolas-Sarkozy-au-Parlement-Europeen.html; Frédérique Schillo, *France-Israël, 1948–1959* (Paris: André Versaille, 2012).
2. Sarkozy, "Allocution prononcée le 16 décembre 2008." See also Gérard Bossuat, *Faire l'Europe sans défaire la France. 60 ans de politique d'unité européenne des gouvernements et des présidents de la République française (1943–2003)* (Brussels: P.I.E. Peter Lang, 2005).
3. Anne Dulphy and Christine Manigand, *La France au risque de l'Europe* (Paris: Armand Colin, 2006), 278.
4. Geir Lundestad, *The United States and Western Europe since 1945: From "Empire" By Invitation to Transatlantic Drift* (Oxford and New York: Oxford University Press, 2003), 189.
5. Harold James, *International Monetary Cooperation since Bretton Woods* (Washington, D.C., and New York: International Monetary Fund and Oxford University Press, 1996), 208–9.

6. Henry A. Kissinger, *Diplomacy* (New York: Simon & Schuster, 1994), 703–4.
7. Lundestad, *The United States and Western Europe since 1945*, 193.
8. Raymond Aron, *Les articles de politique internationale dans Le Figaro de 1947 à 1977*, ed. Georges-Henri Soutou, 3 vols. (Paris: Editions de Fallois, 1990–1997), vol. 3, 1214.
9. On "balancing" versus "power maximization," see the book by neorealist scholar Kenneth N. Waltz, *Theory of International Politics* (New York: McGraw-Hill, Inc, 1979), 126.
10. Matthias Schulz and Thomas A. Schwartz, "The Superpower and the Union in the Making: U.S.-European Relations, 1969–1980," in *The Strained Alliance: U.S.-European Relations from Nixon to Carter*, ed. Matthias Schulz and Thomas A. Schwartz (New York: Cambridge University Press, 2009), 358–59.
11. Robert D. Schulzinger, "Détente in the Nixon-Ford Years, 1969–1976," in *The Cambridge History of the Cold War*, ed. Melvyn P. Leffler and Odd Arne Westad (Cambridge and New York: Cambridge University Press, 2010), 374.
12. Quoted in John Lewis Gaddis, *Strategies of Containment: A Critical Appraisal of American National Security Policy During the Cold War*, 2nd ed. (New York: Oxford University Press, 2005), 319.
13. Ibid., 281, 87; Jussi M. Hanhimäki, "Détente: A Three-Way Discussion. Conservative Goals, Revolutionary Outcomes: The Paradox of Détente," *Cold War History* 8, no. 4 (2008): 503–12.
14. Marie-Pierre Rey, *La tentation du rapprochement. France et URSS à l'heure de la détente (1964–1974)* (Paris: Publications de la Sorbonne, 1991), 17.
15. Georges-Henri Soutou, "The Linkage between European Integration and Détente: The Contrasting Approaches of De Gaulle and Pompidou, 1965–1974," in *European Integration and the Cold War: Ostpolitik-Westpolitik, 1965–1973*, ed. N. Piers Ludlow (London: Routledge, 2007), 11–35; Maurice Vaïsse, ed., *De Gaulle et la Russie* (Paris: CNRS Editions, 2006).
16. Rey, *La tentation du rapprochement*, 40–55.
17. Gottfried Niedhart, "U.S. Détente and West German *Ostpolitik*," in Schulz and Schwartz, *The Strained Alliance*, 41.
18. Ibid.
19. Ibid.; David C. Geyer and Bernd Schaefer, "American Détente and German Ostpolitik, 1969–1972: Preface," *German Historical Institute, Washington, D.C., Bulletin Supplement* (2004): 143–46. See also Gottfried Niedhart, "Revisionistische Elemente und die Initiierung friedlichen. Wandels in der neuen Ostpolitik 1967–1974," *Geschichte und Gesellschaft*, no. 28 (2002): 233–66.
20. Quoted in Werner Link, "Ostpolitik: Détente German-Style and Adapting to America," in *The United States and Germany in the Era of the Cold War, 1945–1990: A Handbook*, ed. Detlef Junker et al. (New York: Cambridge University Press, 2004), 35.
21. Ibid.
22. Bernd Schaefer, "The Nixon Administration and West German *Ostpolitik*, 1969–1973," in Schulz and Schwartz, *The Strained Alliance*, 45.
23. Gottfried Niedhart, "Ostpolitik: The Role of the Federal Republic of Germany in the Process of Détente," in *1968: The World Transformed*, ed. Carole Fink, Philipp Gassert, and Detlef Junker (Cambridge and New York: Cambridge University Press, 1998), 177.
24. Ibid., 176.
25. Niedhart, "U.S. Détente and West German *Ostpolitik*," 25.
26. "The Future Tasks of the Alliance ('The Harmel Report')," http://www.nato.int/docu/basictxt/b671213a.htm.
27. "Mutual And Balanced Force Reductions: Declaration adopted by Foreign Ministers and Representatives of Countries participating in the NATO Defence Program," http://www.nato.int/docu/comm/49-95/c680624b.htm.

28. Quoted in Niedhart, "U.S. Détente and West German *Ostpolitik*," 26.
29. Quoted ibid.
30. Quoted ibid., 30.
31. Quoted in Holger Klitzing, "To Grin and Bear It: The Nixon Administration and *Ostpolitik*," in *Ostpolitik, 1969–1974: European and Global Responses*, ed. Carole Fink and Bernd Schaefer (Cambridge and New York: Cambridge University Press, 2009), 85.
32. Schaefer, "The Nixon Administration and West German *Ostpolitik*," 50–51.
33. Quoted ibid., 55.
34. Niedhart, "U.S. Détente and West German *Ostpolitik*," 31.
35. Quoted in Jussi M. Hanhimäki, *The Flawed Architect: Henry Kissinger and American Foreign Policy* (New York: Oxford University Press, 2004), 86.
36. Ibid., 87.
37. Schaefer, "The Nixon Administration and West German *Ostpolitik*," 61.
38. Klitzing, "To Grin and Bear It," 80–86, 109–10.
39. Quoted in Link, "Ostpolitik," 37.
40. Georges-Henri Soutou, "President Pompidou, Ostpolitik, and the Strategy of Détente," in *The Strategic Triangle: France, Germany, and the United States in the Shaping of the New Europe*, ed. Helga Haftendorn et al. (Baltimore, MD: Johns Hopkins University Press and the Woodrow Wilson Center Press, 2007), 242.
41. Ibid., 236.
42. Ibid., 232, 236–37; Soutou, "The Linkage between European Integration and Détente," 28–29; Marie-Pierre Rey, "Chancellor Brandt's *Ostpolitik*, France, and the Soviet Union," in Fink and Schaefer, *Ostpolitik, 1969–1974*, 115–17.
43. Soutou, "President Pompidou, Ostpolitik, and the Strategy of Détente," 236–37; idem, "The Linkage between European Integration and Détente," 31; idem, "La problématique de la détente et le testament stratégique de Georges Pompidou," *Cahiers du Centre d'études d'histoire de la défense*, no. 22 (2004): 95.
44. Soutou, "President Pompidou, Ostpolitik, and the Strategy of Détente," 234–36, 240–42; Rey, "Chancellor Brandt's *Ostpolitik*, France, and the Soviet Union," 114–15.
45. Rey, "Chancellor Brandt's *Ostpolitik*, France, and the Soviet Union," 120–21.
46. Soutou, "President Pompidou, Ostpolitik, and the Strategy of Détente," 238, 252–53.
47. Angela Romano, *From Détente in Europe to European Détente: How the West Shaped the Helsinki CSCE* (Brussels: P.I.E. Peter Lang, 2009), 206–17; Daniel Möckli, *European Foreign Policy During the Cold War: Heath, Brandt, Pompidou and the Dream of Political Unity* (London: I.B. Tauris, 2009), 99–139.
48. On Western European–U.S. concerns, see Schulz and Schwartz, "The Superpower and the Union in the Making," 360. On British uneasiness over the agreement, see Alastair Noble, "Kissinger's Year of Europe, Britain's Year of Choice," in Schulz and Schwartz, *The Strained Alliance*, 224.
49. Soutou, "The Linkage between European Integration and Détente," 27; idem, "President Pompidou, Ostpolitik, and the Strategy of Détente," 243.
50. James, *International Monetary Cooperation since Bretton Woods*, 243–51.
51. Barry J. Eichengreen, *Globalizing Capital: A History of the International Monetary System* (Princeton, NJ: Princeton University Press, 1996), 140.
52. British Foreign and Commonwealth Office (FCO), minute, cable to Sir Thomas Brimelow, 18 July 1973, doc. 162, in Keith A. Hamilton, ed. *Documents on British Policy Overseas. The Year of Europe: America, Europe and the Energy Crisis, 1972–1974*, vol. III.4 (London: Whitehall History Publishing, 2006).
53. Mark Mazower, *Dark Continent: Europe's Twentieth Century* (New York: A.A. Knopf, 1999), 293.
54. Schulz and Schwartz, "The Superpower and the Union in the Making," 361.

55. U.S. President Dwight Eisenhower defended the 1957 Rome Treaty against opposition from Britain, Canada, Australia, and New Zealand (Lucia Coppolaro, "The United States and EEC Enlargement (1969–1973): Reaffirming the Atlantic Framework," in *Beyond the Customs Union: The European Community's Quest for Deepening, Widening and Completion, 1969–1975*, ed. Jan van der Harst [Brussels: Bruylant, 2007], 139). On customs unions under GATT, see Ronald Findlay and Kevin H. O'Rourke, *Power and Plenty: Trade, War, and the World Economy in the Second Millennium* (Princeton, NJ: Princeton University Press, 2007), 490.

56. European Commission, "COM(74) 1090 final, Report on the tariff negotiations which it conducted under Article XXIV(6) of the General Agreement on Tariffs and Trade (GATT), 11 July 1974," http://aei.pitt.edu/8897/01/31735055278927_1.pdf.

57. "Mémorandum de la Commission européenne sur la position de la CEE dans les prochaines négociations commerciales avec les Etats-Unis et les autres pays industrialisés (10 avril 1973)," *Europe Documents*, no. 732 (1973): 1–6; FCO, minute, cable to Brimelow, 18 July 1973.

58. GATT, *GATT Activities in 1973* (Geneva: GATT Secretariat, 1974).

59. James, *International Monetary Cooperation since Bretton Woods*, 251–55.

60. Barry J. Eichengreen, *The European Economy since 1945: Coordinated Capitalism and Beyond* (Princeton, NJ: Princeton University Press, 2007), 253–54, 263.

61. Ibid., 5–7, 246–56. For a comparative analysis of economic convergence, see Angus Maddison, *Dynamic Forces in Capitalist Development: A Long-Run Comparative View* (Oxford: Oxford University Press, 1991), 128–64.

62. James, *International Monetary Cooperation since Bretton Woods*, 254.

63. Giuliano Garavini, *Dopo gli imperi. L'integrazione europea nello scontro Nord-Sud* (Florence: Le Monnier Università, 2009), 205.

64. "Sommet européen de Paris : atlantisme, pétrole et pacte social," *Le Figaro*, 9 December 1973; "Copenhague," *L'Aurore*, 13 December 1973.

65. Lundestad, *The United States and Western Europe since 1945*.

66. FCO, Paris telegram 1122, 28 August 1973, doc. 210, in Hamilton, *Documents on British Policy Overseas*.

67. On French anti-Americanism, see Richard F. Kuisel, *Seducing the French: The Dilemma of Americanization* (Berkeley and Los Angeles: University of California Press, 1993); Denis Lacorne, Jacques Rupnik, and Marie-France Toinet, eds., *L'Amérique dans les têtes. Un siècle de fascinations et d'aversions* (Paris: Hachette, 1986); Philippe Roger, *L'ennemi américain. Généalogie de l'antiaméricanisme français* (Paris: Editions du Seuil, 2002). On European ambivalence toward Americanization, see Richard H. Pells, *Not Like Us: How Europeans Have Loved, Hated and Transformed American Culture since World War II* (New York: Basic Books, 1997); Rob Kroes, *If You've Seen One, You've Seen the Mall: Europeans and American Mass Culture* (Urbana: University of Illinois Press, 1996); Victoria De Grazia, *Irresistible Empire: America's Advance through Twentieth-Century Europe* (Cambridge, MA: Belknap Press of Harvard University Press, 2005).

68. Soutou, "La problématique de la détente et le testament stratégique de Georges Pompidou," 87–92.

69. Georges-Henri Soutou, "Georges Pompidou et Valéry Giscard d'Estaing : deux réconciliations et deux ruptures avec les Etats-Unis," *Relations internationales*, no. 119 (2004): 310–11. See also idem, "Le président Pompidou et les relations entre les Etats-Unis et l'Europe," *Journal of European Integration History* 6, no. 2 (2000): 111–46.

70. Eric Bussière, "Georges Pompidou, les Etats-Unis et la crise du système monétaire international," in *Georges Pompidou et les Etats-Unis, « une relation spéciale », 1969–1974*, ed. Eric Bussière and François Dubasque (Brussels: Peter Lang, forthcoming); idem,

"Georges Pompidou et la crise du système monétaire international : intérêt national, solidarité européenne et enjeux internationaux," in *Georges Pompidou face à la mutation économique de l'Occident, 1969–1974*, ed. Eric Bussière (Paris: Presses universitaires de France, 2003), 92–93.

71. Keith Hamilton, "Britain, France, and America's Year of Europe, 1973," *Diplomacy & Statecraft* 17, no. 4 (2006): 871–95; Pierre Mélandri, "Une relation très spéciale. La France, les Etats-Unis et l'année de l'Europe, 1973–1974," in *Georges Pompidou et l'Europe*, ed. Association Georges Pompidou (Brussels: Editions Complexe, 1995), 89–131; Möckli, *European Foreign Policy During the Cold War*, 354, 63; Fabian Hilfrich, "West Germany's Long Year of Europe: Bonn between Europe and the United States," in Schulz and Schwartz, *The Strained Alliance*, 237–56.

72. Noble, "Kissinger's Year of Europe, Britain's Year of Choice"; Catherine Hynes, *The Year That Never Was: Heath, the Nixon Administration and the Year of Europe* (Dublin: University College Dublin Press, 2009), chaps. 4–8; Jussi M. Hanhimäki, "Kissinger et l'Europe : entre intégration et autonomie," *Relations internationales*, no. 119 (2004): 319–32; Hamilton, "Britain, France, and America's Year of Europe, 1973"; Niklas H. Rossbach, *Heath, Nixon and the Rebirth of the Special Relationship: Britain, the US and the EC, 1969–74* (Basingstoke, UK: Palgrave Macmillan, 2009), 122–60.

73. See in particular the collection of essays in Schulz and Schwartz, *The Strained Alliance*.

74. Möckli, *European Foreign Policy During the Cold War*.

75. Ibid., 368.

76. See, for example, Serge Berstein and Jean-François Sirinelli, eds., *Les années Giscard. Valéry Giscard d'Estaing et l'Europe, 1974–1981* (Paris: Armand Colin, 2006); Association Georges Pompidou, *Georges Pompidou et l'Europe*; Soutou, "Georges Pompidou et Valéry Giscard d'Estaing"; idem, "President Pompidou, Ostpolitik, and the Strategy of Détente."

77. See in particular Association Georges Pompidou, ed., *Action et pensée sociales chez Georges Pompidou* (Paris: Presses universitaires de France, 2004); idem, ed., *Georges Pompidou face à la mutation économique de l'Occident, 1969–1974* (Paris: Presses universitaires de France, 2003); idem, ed., *Un politique : Georges Pompidou* (Paris: Presses universitaires de France, 2001); idem, ed., *Culture et action chez Georges Pompidou* (Paris: Presses universitaires de France, 2000); idem, *Georges Pompidou et l'Europe*; Bussière and Dubasque, *Georges Pompidou et les Etats-Unis*; Eric Bussière, ed. *Georges Pompidou et le monde des campagnes, 1962–1974* (Brussels: Peter Lang, 2007); idem, ed., *Georges Pompidou et la modernité, les tensions de l'innovation, 1962–1974* (Brussels: Peter Lang, 2006).

78. Frédéric Bozo, *La politique étrangère de la France depuis 1945* (Paris: Editions La Découverte, 1997), 4; Jean-Pierre Dubois, "La conception de la présidence de Valéry Giscard d'Estaing," in *Les années Giscard. Institutions et pratiques politiques, 1974–1978*, ed. Serge Berstein, Jean-François Sirinelli, and René Rémond (Paris: Fayard, 2003), 59–60; Pierre Mélandri, "La France et l'Alliance atlantique sous Georges Pompidou et Valéry Giscard d'Estaing," in *La France et l'OTAN, 1949–1996*, ed. Maurice Vaïsse, Pierre Mélandri, and Frédéric Bozo (Brussels: Editions Complexe, 1996), 519; Maurice Vaïsse, "Valéry Giscard d'Estaing de la défense de l'Europe à la défense européenne," in Berstein and Sirinelli, *Les années Giscard*, 207–29; idem, *La puissance ou l'influence? La France dans le monde depuis 1958* ([Paris]: Libraire Arthème Fayard, 2009), 9–10; idem, "Changement et continuité dans la politique européenne de la France," in Association Georges Pompidou, *Georges Pompidou et l'Europe*, 29–42. For a critical analysis of a de Gaulle–centered scholarship, see Laurent Warlouzet, "Charles de Gaulle's Idea of Europe: The Lasting Legacy," *Kontur*, no. 19 (2010): 21–31.

79. Vaïsse, *La puissance ou l'influence?* 18.

80. The only exception is Pascaline Winand, "Loaded Words and Disputed Meanings: The Year of Europe Speech and Its Genesis from an American Perspective," in van der Harst, *Beyond the Customs Union*, 297–315.

81. William I. Hitchcock, *The Struggle for Europe: The Turbulent History of a Divided Continent, 1945–2002* (New York: Doubleday, 2003), 243–46, 257–62; Tony Judt, *Postwar: A History of Europe since 1945* (London: William Heinemann, 2005), 453–83.

82. Mazower, *Dark Continent: Europe's Twentieth Century*, 328; Hitchcock, *The Struggle for Europe*, 244.

83. Marie-Thérèse Bitsch, *Histoire de la construction européenne de 1945 à nos jours*, 5th ed. (Brussels: Editions Complexe, 2008), 196–97; Desmond Dinan, *Europe Recast: A History of European Union* (Basingstoke, UK: Palgrave Macmillan, 2004), 125–66; Bino Olivi and Alessandro Giacone, *L'Europe difficile. La construction européenne* (Paris: Editions Gallimard, 2007), 130–52. Although Dinan's chapter on the 1970s is significantly entitled "Reversal" and argues that "developments ... proved disappointing," it reckons that the story was not "unremittingly gloomy."

84. Reappraisals of the traditional narrative include R.T. Griffiths, "A Dismal Decade? European Integration in the 1970s," in *Origins and Evolution of the European Union*, ed. Desmond Dinan (Oxford and New York: Oxford University Press, 2006); van der Harst, *Beyond the Customs Union*, 6–7; Antonio Varsori, "Introduzione—Alle origini del presente: l'Europa occidentale nella crisi degli anni '70," in *Alle origini del presente. L'Europa occidentale nella crisi degli anni Settanta* (Milan: Franco Angeli, 2008), 9–22; Johnny Laursen, ed. *From Crisis to New Dynamics: The European Community 1974–83* (Brussels: Bruylant, forthcoming).

85. On the European Monetary System, see Emmanuel Mourlon-Druol, "The Emergence of a European Bloc? A Trans-and Supranational History of European Monetary Cooperation, from the Failure of the Werner Plan to the Creation of the European Monetary System, 1974–1979" (Ph.D. thesis, European University Institute, 2010). On new common policies, see Antonio Varsori and Lorenzo Mechi, "At the Origins of the European Structural Policy: The Community's Social and Regional Policies from the Late 1960s to the Mid-1970s," in van der Harst, *Beyond the Customs Union*, 223–50; Simone Paoli, *Il sogno di Erasmo. La questione educativa nel processo di integrazione europea* (Milan: Franco Angeli, 2010); Laura Scichilone, *L'Europa e la sfida ecologica. Storia della politica ambientale europea, 1969–1998* (Bologna: Il Mulino, 2008).

86. Mirroring the 1970 Davignon Report, which uncoupled foreign policy from institutional reform, the two historiographies have tended to develop in parallel. A handful of articles on the institutional history of EPC discuss both topics: Davide Zampoli, "I primi passi della Cooperazione politica europea: problematiche ed evoluzione istituzionale," in *Alle origini del presente. L'Europa occidentale nella crisi degli anni Settanta*, ed. Antonio Varsori (Milan: Franco Angeli, 2008), 169–92; idem, "Verso una political estera comune: problemi di coordinamento tra i lavori della Cooperazione Politica e della Communità negli anni Settanta," in *La Comunità europea e le relazioni esterne, 1957–1992*, ed. Alessandra Bitumi, Gabriele D'Ottavio, and Giuliana Laschi (Bologna: Clueb, 2008), 41–63. The nascent historiography on EPC, however, tends to gloss over the institutional debate, except to the extent that it pertained to EPC: Möckli, *European Foreign Policy During the Cold War*; Romano, *From Détente in Europe to European Détente*. Conversely, recent work on the European Council does not link institutional reforms to EPC: Emmanuel Mourlon-Druol, "Filling the EEC Leadership Vacuum? The Creation of the European Council in 1974," *Cold War History* 10, no. 3 (2010): 315–339.

Chapter 1

MEETING THE AMERICAN CHALLENGE
France and the Year of Europe

An American initiative provided the original impetus for France's reassessment of the value of collective European action. The Year of Europe was officially designed to revitalize the Atlantic Alliance in a context of growing transatlantic economic rivalry and rising U.S. protectionism. It was also, and perhaps primarily, intended to adjust the set of economic, political, and security interrelations between Western Europe and the United States. The U.S. goal was to persuade its allies to be more accommodating in economic matters and to assume a greater share of the security load within a U.S.-led Western order. As such, the plan was likely to arouse suspicion in Western Europe, particularly in France. Contrary to Kissinger's later assertions, senior U.S. officials anticipated such resistance. What they did not expect, however, was that Kissinger's plea for a new "Atlantic charter" would spur EC states to assert their distinctiveness in the international arena. In September 1973, the nine EC countries presented a draft declaration of principles between the EC and the United States which proclaimed the "distinctiveness" of a united Europe and its rightful place in world affairs.[1] To French Foreign Minister Michel Jobert, this was a remarkable turnaround: "only a good loser could have accepted this outcome; Europe was now laying claims to existence!" ("Il eût fallu, certes, être très beau joueur pour voir sans frémir les cartes être ainsi retournées. Voilà que l'Europe, néant docile, prétendait exister!")[2] Kissinger

Notes for this section begin on page 46.

clearly did not accept this ending. In his memoirs, he accuses Jobert of having "ruthlessly used our effort to conciliate France as a device to isolate us" by putting together a "coalition of negation."[3]

The real story was more complex. French political actors and the press were mostly hostile to the proposed charter because they regarded it as a covert attempt to reassert U.S. leadership in Europe in the context of superpower détente. Despite their ambivalent feelings, their EC counterparts wished to respond positively to the U.S. overture and pressed for elaborating a draft declaration within the framework of EPC. French officials initially resorted to delay tactics, but under increased EC pressure they wound up accepting Britain's proposal for two declarations, an EC-U.S. statement and a NATO declaration.[4] While taking this step during the second half of August, they shifted the thrust of the British draft away from Atlantic unity and toward European distinctiveness. This move was broadly congruent with de Gaulle's early 1960s vision of a "European Europe" that would be independent from the United States. Nonetheless, this was a policy shift—one that went beyond acceptance or non-acceptance of a joint EC Nine response to Kissinger's overture. The French government had agreed to what it had always opposed: EPC discussions on U.S.-European relations. Because it fueled fears of a U.S.-Soviet condominium, the U.S.-Soviet Agreement on the Prevention of Nuclear War was an influential factor. But so too were the deterioration of Franco-American relations after 1971 and growing French concerns about U.S. unilateral impulses.

Linking Economics and Security: A New U.S. Initiative on Europe

Several factors coalesced at the end of Nixon's first term to persuade the White House of the need to reappraise U.S.-European relations.[5] The imminent end of the Vietnam War was expected to free up resources for new policy designs. It also called for moves that would restore American prestige. Strains in U.S.-European economic relations and a budding mood of isolationism in Congress encouraged a reassessment of U.S. policy toward Western Europe. Calls for troop redeployment had not subsided since the early 1970s. Détente with the Soviet Union, moreover, had not spared the necessity of a solid transatlantic alliance. Quite the opposite, U.S. officials felt that transatlantic cohesion was crucial to the success of this policy, and that it could not be taken for granted given Brandt's *Ostpolitik*.[6]

The story of the origins of the Year of Europe deserves to be told, as it is still partially clouded in mystery.[7] Some years later, Kissinger asserted that the Year of Europe was "born in the office of the President of the French Republic."[8] Largely untapped archives belie this claim. Planning began several weeks before Kissinger's December 1972 meeting with Pompidou. As head of the National Security Council (NSC), Kissinger played a critical role in this process. He set the stage for an initiative on Europe as early as September 1972. On 16 September, he declared that Nixon hoped soon to resume consultation with his allies.[9] Less than two weeks later, he told French Foreign Minister Maurice Schumann that the U.S. government planned to "create a little task force" on U.S. relations with Western Europe. The goal was to establish an overarching political framework in order to prevent future clashes on trade and monetary issues.[10] The NSC staff was immediately set to work, but progress was initially slow. After Nixon's November reelection, Kissinger complained about the approach of his trusted NSC adviser on Europe, Helmut Sonnenfeldt, who had like him emigrated from Nazi Germany to the United States:[11] "the one trouble I have with Sonnenfeldt is that son of a bitch turns everything into a Federal case. Now for the last two months I wanted a study on Europe and he's still negotiating it."[12] A week later, Kissinger commissioned a trans-departmental study of all current and future issues in transatlantic relations.[13] At the same time, U.S. officials began to refer to the "Year of Europe."[14]

The notion of linkage was central to the study the NSC issued in December 1972.[15] The gist of National Security Study Memorandum (NSSM) 164 was that "political, security, military, economic, scientific and technological issues" were interdependent. Its central claim was that the U.S.-European security and economic interrelationships must be "brought into a balance more satisfactory to the U.S." NSSM 164 outlined three possible strategies: seek more integrated relations with Western Europe through enhanced cooperation; attenuate these ties, allowing them to "deteriorate if necessary"; and maintain existing security arrangements while improving the U.S. economic position. The first option was meant to strengthen "transatlantic cohesion." NSSM 164, however, warned against restrictions on U.S. freedom of action and potential European opposition. The other two alternatives implied an explicit strategy of linkage—one that the Nixon administration had applied in its dealings with the Soviet Union, making progress in one area conditional upon progress in another.[16] The second option assumed a confrontational stance. The United States would "vigorously" pursue its own interests, taking advantage of its strategic and economic preeminence "to extract economic concessions from Europe." The third option was designed to square the circle: the United States should seek to reform the world economic system and the Western security structure, but without risking "ruptures ... or even a deterioration in the general climate of transatlantic relations." NSSM 164 portrayed this last option as "a balanced approach" that met "pressure in the U.S. and Western Europe for 'setting the transatlantic house in order.'"

In seeking to strike equilibrium between competing views, the NSC's memorandum inevitably aroused criticism. Acting Assistant Secretary of Commerce Lawrence Fox wrote that the study failed fully to address the trade and monetary objectives of the United States.[17] Fox encouraged the White House to pursue a more aggressive linkage approach. Another commentary stated that NSSM 164 gave insufficient weight to U.S. financial and economic interests, and urged the administration to reassert its claim for burden-sharing.[18]

NSSM 164 stopped short of advocating a hard bargaining strategy but implied a cross-issue linkage approach that was bound to arouse resistance in Western Europe. U.S. officials were fully aware of it. Vernon A. Walters, deputy director for central intelligence, cautioned that "European resistance to being engulfed by their American friends may be at an all-time high."[19] With incredible prescience, the NSC warned that France would play "a leading role in asserting a European identity."[20] A special assistant—presumably to the State Department—even anticipated the French line of argument. The two alternatives, he maintained, should be more clearly stated: a closer relationship with Europe involved "more Atlanticism"; looser ties implied "more European integration and independence."[21]

Convergent Ideas, Diverging Aims:
Monnet and the Nixon White House

While preparing for the Year of Europe, the U.S. government consulted with one of the prime promoters of a united Europe: the Frenchman Jean Monnet. Monnet's U.S. contacts from World War II to the 1960s have been studied extensively.[22] What scholars have yet to acknowledge is his influence in shaping the Year of Europe and the close relationship he built with Kissinger in the last decade of his life.[23] Monnet's and Kissinger's ultimate goals differed. The former was set upon building a strong united Europe; the latter wished to strengthen transatlantic cohesion under U.S. leadership. Yet in the early 1970s, both men felt the need to revitalize the transatlantic relationship. Such convergence bears testimony to the widening gulf between both sides of the Atlantic.

Two opposing dynamics shaped the dialogue between U.S. officials and Monnet: U.S. planning for the Year of Europe and the new drive toward European integration following the 1969 EC Hague summit. Monnet first met the U.S. ambassador to France in October 1972. Emboldened by the results of the 1972 EC Paris summit, he encouraged the United States to call for a new U.S.-European dialogue early in Nixon's second term.[24] Monnet recommended handling matters "at a political level." Top officials, he insisted, "had a vested interest in the nation-state and resisted both progress toward European unity and constructive international solutions." The Nixon administration, he went on to say, should push for a summit meeting including the U.S. president, the EC heads of state or government, and the president of the European Commission. In December 1972, Monnet's trusted aide Jacques van Helmont and Monnet himself met with two senior U.S. officials: Abraham Katz, head of the State Department's office of regional and political affairs, and Robert Hormats of the NSC. Van Helmont first reported Monnet's belief in the need to hold talks among U.S. and European decision makers in order to foster a "positive psychological and intellectual context."[25] This suggestion was reminiscent of a 1962 resolution by Monnet's Action Committee for the United States of Europe, which called for an institutionalized dialogue between the EC and the United States. Transatlantic strains, particularly EC-U.S. economic tensions, had made it timely again. Soon thereafter, Monnet suggested a procedure for such a dialogue: both sides should temporarily set aside security matters and institute a group of "wise men" responsible for reviewing economic issues.[26]

Monnet's suggestions received attention in high places. Secretary of State William Rogers summarized them in a memorandum for Nixon and thought the proposal warranted careful consideration.[27] Rogers's memorandum probably never reached the president's desk, as Sonnenfeldt advised Kissinger not to pass it along.[28] The NSC expert noted that European leaders were "now coming forth with various ideas on how to handle U.S.-Western European relations." Sonnenfeldt therefore questioned the desirability of giving Monnet's approach priority. Nonetheless, he kept Kissinger thoroughly apprised of Monnet's suggestions, as he had done three months earlier.[29]

Monnet's views possibly contributed to shaping the Year of Europe. In any case, the Nixon administration's new policy design gave the old Europeanist an opportunity to push forth his plan for an EC-U.S. dialogue. Monnet's hope was that such dialogue would help to further European integration. In fact, it was confrontation, rather than dialogue, that would foster European foreign policy cooperation, if not integration per se. Even so, Monnet's expectations eventually proved closer to the truth than those of the NSC. To be sure, the Year of Europe would not bring about the transatlantic partnership resting on two equal pillars that he was calling for.[30] Nonetheless, it ultimately gave new impetus to EPC, spurring the EC Nine to be more assertive rather than more sensitive to U.S. interests.

Setting the Stage: Constructive Competition
or Economic Competition

The talks with Monnet initiated a broad range of transatlantic conversations. From January to April 1973, Nixon, Kissinger and the NSC staff met with senior French, British, West German, Italian, and other Western European officials. With perhaps more clarity of purpose than he had at the time, Kissinger states in his memoirs that the U.S. process of consultation "was completed on April 19, 1973" when he gave British Cabinet Secretary Sir Burke Trend an advance text of his speech.[31] Records of this preliminary consultative process highlight both U.S. officials' awareness of potential resistance to their plan and their determination to overcome it. As such, they point to the quasi-belligerent stance of the Nixon White House. The U.S. government had definitely changed tone toward its European allies since the 1960s.

As is evident from the records of the February 1973 Nixon-Heath summit, the NSC staff was aware of the challenge at hand. Initially, Sonnenfeldt even doubted whether the meeting should initiate "the substantive dialogue" that the United States intended to carry out with Europe.[32] A week later he presented Kissinger with a more definite statement,[33] but the future secretary of state relied on Sonnenfeldt's earlier analysis while drafting his memorandum for the president.[34] Sonnenfeldt had warned that Western European leaders would not enter the proposed dialogue "with much clarity or unity of purpose," in part because of their concerns over cross-issue bargaining.[35] The NSC also stressed that France was likely to oppose "a more institutionalized dialogue" than the present semiannual consultations between the EC commissioner for foreign affairs and the under secretary of state for economic affairs. "The French and others," it stated, "would look upon this as an effort by the U.S. to intervene directly in Community decisions."[36]

Nixon's talks with Heath nevertheless prompted him to announce that, having achieved peace in Vietnam, he would begin to focus on Europe. Western European decision makers, he warned, would have to choose between constructive competition and economic confrontation.[37] Kissinger took a softer line when meeting with Luxembourger Premier Gaston Thorn a few weeks later. He stressed that the goal was not to achieve a "quid pro quo" between economic and strategic issues, but rather to take vexing issues out of the hands of technical experts. He promised to look after the matter himself as soon as he could take focus away from Vietnam.[38]

The mission of Peter Peterson, Nixon's former secretary of commerce, to Western Europe and Japan confirmed the administration's intention to rebalance the transatlantic relationship to the United States' benefit.

Peterson's tough talk targeted monetary and trade issues: the reform of the international monetary system; the CAP; the tariff implications of the EC enlargement; the EC's preferential trade agreements with Israel (1970), Spain (1970), and European Free Trade Association countries (1972); and finally, the reverse trade preferences granted by African countries to EC states. The U.S. government was asking for the elimination of such preferences in the enlarged agreement with former colonies that would replace the Yaoundé Convention.[39] Peterson chastised the EC for its "rigidity," particularly with respect to agriculture, and its tendency to be increasingly inward-looking. EC states, he stated, should devote more time to improving transatlantic relations and less to their own internal disputes.[40]

At the same time, the White House began planning for a presidential visit to Europe. The details of the trip were highly controversial.[41] In January 1973, Pompidou opposed Brandt's idea of a meeting between Nixon and the EC Council of Foreign Ministers.[42] He saw it as a step toward an institutionalized EC-U.S. dialogue and was only willing to endorse a meeting between Nixon, on the one hand, and the EC Council and European Commission presidents on the other.[43] In March, the White House proposed a bilateral Franco-American summit, hoping that it would be an initial step toward an Atlantic meeting.[44] Pompidou accepted the idea so long as it did not entail an official visit. France and the United States settled on the neutral site of Iceland.[45]

In preparing the ground for the Year of Europe, Kissinger used arguments that were partly tactical but also partly proceeded from genuine feelings. It would be helpful to "get an overall framework to discuss economics, defense and political issues" and hence avoid confrontation, he told France's Ambassador to the United States Jacques Kosciusko-Morizet.[46] Fading elite support for the Atlantic Alliance and the resulting risk of dwindling Western cohesion, he claimed, called for a new policy move:

> We are looking for something we can do, maybe later this year, that could have a dramatic impact on the American public…. With Brezhnev there will be a tremendous publicity thing. We have to avoid a situation where when everyone hears about Europe it is always unpleasant news. We have to reconstruct the situation where we can get the conscious elite support in this country.[47]

The "tremendous publicity thing" with Brezhnev referred to the planned Agreement on the Prevention of Nuclear War. Kissinger would repeat this argument ad nauseam. He warned Jobert, for instance, that if Western leaders failed to act, there would be "an enormous problem in Western countries." In all of them, foreign policy successes were increasingly "identified with relations with adversaries, while relations with friends seem to turn on technical issues and occasional recitation of formulas."[48]

Although his insistence on declining public support for Atlantic integration was strategically motivated, Kissinger harbored genuine concerns about the change in U.S. attitudes toward Europe. "We are dealing with the last generation of Americans who have an emotional relationship to Europe," he told his friend François de Rose, who served as France's permanent representative on the North Atlantic Council (NAC) from 1970 to 1975.[49] Kissinger certainly had a point when he stated that "the generation that supported Atlantic relations is fading from office."[50] Committed Europeanists like George Ball, McGeorge Bundy, and John Tuthill had all vanished from the political scene.[51]

Not only were senior U.S. officials aware of potential European opposition to a new transatlantic "dialogue," but they also anticipated that their French counterparts would be difficult. This did not undermine their determination to put transatlantic relations on a new footing. Instead, they resorted to a mix of strategies. While in Paris, Peterson used harsh language, in line with Nixon's stance, but Kissinger went to pains to cajole the French. Kissinger even persuaded Nixon to travel to Iceland to accommodate Pompidou's wishes. He would be particularly aggravated upon realizing that these efforts had been useless.

A "New Atlantic Charter" for a "New Era"

Kissinger launched the Year of Europe in a speech at the annual luncheon of the Associated Press on 23 April. The transcripts of his telephone conversations shed new light on the origins of this speech. It was not a hastily drafted piece of writing.[52] Kissinger consulted not only his immediate staff but also State Department officials.[53] On 17 April, he told John Andrews, speechwriter to the president, that he would give a speech on "Atlantic affairs" that would be "somewhat important." Bill Hyland and Peter Rodman of the NSC were in charge of drafting it.[54] Two days later, Kissinger informed Walter Stoessel, assistant secretary of state for European affairs, that he might be giving a speech "at the president's request to a publishers group about Europe." Although it would not be anything "world shaking," he wanted Stoessel to have a look at the draft. In keeping with his distrust of bureaucracy, he asked him to come to his office to avoid the document "bouncing around the Department."[55] Kissinger may have told Stoessel that the speech was Nixon's idea in order to buttress his stance vis-à-vis the State Department. It is doubtful, however, that he acted on his own initiative. To be sure, the Watergate scandal was gaining momentum. The resignation of Nixon's closest aides—Bob Haldemann, his chief of staff, and John Ehrlichmann, his aide in charge of domestic affairs—lay only a few days ahead.[56] But Kissinger had not yet gained the upper hand over foreign-policy making.

In his speech, Kissinger situated the U.S. move in the context of a rapidly changing world order. He pointed to U.S.-Soviet nuclear parity and to the shifting balance of economic power between the United States, on the one hand, and Western Europe and Japan on the other. "New realities," he proclaimed, called for "new approaches." He also used the arguments of generation change and U.S. isolationism. A new generation of European decision-makers, he stated, had begun to take peace and stability for granted and were reluctant to invest the resources required to maintain them. U.S. elites, moreover, were becoming increasingly disinclined to sustain the global commitments of the United States.[57] In urging Western Europe to join the United States in elaborating an "Atlantic charter," Kissinger borrowed the title of a June 1941 statement by U.S. President Franklin D. Roosevelt and British Premier Winston Churchill.[58] This declaration, he asserted, would define the basic goals of the Atlantic Alliance in an evolving world and thus usher in "a new era of creativity in the West."

Few might have taken issue with such lofty statements if Kissinger had not proceeded to give Western European governments something of an ultimatum: the new "charter" should be ready in time for Nixon's visit in the fall. Heedless of European sensitivities, he went on to contrast America's global responsibilities with Western Europe's regional interests:

> Diplomacy is the subject of frequent consultations but is essentially being conducted by traditional nation-states. The United States has global interests and responsibilities. Our European allies have regional interests. These are not necessarily in conflict, but in the new era neither are they automatically identical.

Kissinger also appeared to abandon the U.S. pledge to support European integration. Although the U.S. government was prepared to "make concessions to its further growth," he declared, European unity was not "an end in itself."

The timing of Kissinger's Year of Europe address—well into the first half of 1973—struck many commentators as odd. Some connected it to the accelerating momentum of Watergate. It is not altogether implausible that Nixon asked Kissinger to give a landmark speech on Europe to distract attention from his domestic trouble. The idea of a European initiative, however, had crystallized much earlier. Moreover, Kissinger's statements reflected his long-standing interest in the "troubled" transatlantic partnership[59]—as early as 1965, the Harvard professor had urged the Johnson administration to devise "new forms of Atlantic cooperation."[60] They also summed up the issues U.S. officials had discussed since Nixon's reelection, both internally and in meetings with Western European decision makers.

Creating a U.S.-Ruled "Global Alliance": The Views from the Quai d'Orsay and the Elysée Presidential Palace

Viewed from Paris, Kissinger's speech was untimely. French officials had watched the recent progress in U.S.-Soviet relations with concern, fearing that the May 1972 SALT 1 Agreement—an Anti-Ballistic Missile Treaty and an Interim Agreement on the Limitation of Strategic Offensive Arms—would undermine U.S. nuclear deterrence and spur the U.S. and the Soviet governments to look suspiciously upon third nuclear parties.[61] In his June 1972 talks with Soviet Foreign Minister Andrei Gromyko, Pompidou explicitly referred to his fears of a future U.S.-Soviet condominium. French officials were also opposed to the planned MBFR negotiations.[62] The main U.S. rationale for MBFR was to resist domestic pressure for unilateral troop withdrawals.[63] Gaullist France remained principally opposed to negotiations between the two Cold War blocs.[64] The MBFR talks, French officials noted, might encourage the United States and the Soviet Union to talk over the heads of Western European countries.[65] They also worried that an MBFR agreement would worsen the existing East-West imbalance in conventional forces and foster the neutralization of Central Europe.[66] The talks, Pompidou had warned Brezhnev in 1970, might lead to the withdrawal of foreign troops from the two halves of Germany and hence to the reunification of an uncontrollable Germany.[67] Pompidou was most likely playing on Brezhnev's fears about the resurgence of German power, but his concerns were genuine. Interestingly, French documents mentioned yet another argument against MBFR: a reduction in conventional armaments would impair the development of a European defense force. This claim was spelled out as early as 1971, rather than only in 1973, as Soutou argues.[68]

France and the United States, moreover, were at cross-purposes over the Conference on Security and Cooperation in Europe. During his October 1969 trip to the Soviet Union, Foreign Minister Schumann had expressed support for a European security conference. There were concerns within the Quai d'Orsay that the Soviet Union might achieve recognition of the 1945 settlement and strengthen its influence by dividing Western Europe from the United States.[69] Nevertheless, French officials saw multiple potential benefits from the proposed conference: they hoped to contain *Ostpolitik* within a wider framework, reduce the Soviet sway over Eastern Europe, and foster the free flow of ideas between East and West as well as the protection of human rights across the Iron Curtain.[70] The Nixon administration, by contrast, was deeply suspicious of the plan.[71] The Soviet Union, it warned, could use the conference to secure endorsement of the post-war settlement and create an illusory sense of security, leading to reduced American influence in Europe. Consequently, the U.S. government linked its participation to an agreement on Berlin and the start of MBFR talks. By the end of 1971, French officials seemed willing to soften their stance on human rights to hasten the start of the CSCE conference.[72] Nonetheless, they disapproved of the U.S. preference for a quickly concluded conference at the expense of civil liberties and human rights.[73] During the multilateral preparatory talks held from November 1972 to July 1973, the U.S. delegation was careful not to antagonize America's allies, but it nevertheless refrained from pushing for a strong human rights agenda.[74]

Monetary matters had their share in the deterioration of Franco-American relations in 1971 and 1972. Pressure on the dollar did not subside following the 1971 Smithsonian Agreement, and the Nixon administration was obviously unwilling to restore the dollar-gold convertibility. The gradual unraveling of Bretton Woods prompted Pompidou to place renewed emphasis on EC monetary cooperation.[75] In a March 1972 meeting with Heath, he spoke in favor of a "European monetary area" serving as a shield against "the vicissitude of the dollar."[76] Pompidou's hope was also that institutionalized European cooperation would contribute to a reform of the international monetary order based on fixed exchange rates.[77] The May 1972 establishment of the "snake" was a step in this direction. Pompidou hoped to combine this accord with a broader reform of the international monetary order based on fixed exchange rates. Speculative attacks against the dollar in February 1973 and West Germany's ensuing decision to let the mark float ended all hopes of rescuing Bretton Woods. Senior officials within the French finance ministry recommended a fixed exchange rate between the franc and the dollar. The central bank president, Bernard Clappier, and Pompidou's economic adviser, Jean-René Bernard, supported a joint float of the EC Nine's currencies instead. Pompidou opted for the second option despite his misgivings about a West German mark–dominated EC zone.

Some scholars have argued that "the increasingly poisonous atmosphere created by U.S.-European economic tensions" brought to a halt the "limited improvement in U.S.-French political relations" that had occurred after 1969.[78] Others have noted that Pompidou conceived of the "snake" as "a weapon … against the U.S. dollar and the monetary privilege of the United States."[79] Given the reserve currency status of the dollar, the United States did not have to balance its external accounts. However, in his recent reassessment Marc Trachtenberg claims that economic issues "were not enough to drive the two countries apart."[80] Pompidou's government was not "overly concerned about this set of issues." Nor was the French stance particularly problematic for the Nixon administration. The French insistence on some form of fixed exchange rate regime, Trachtenberg states, implied that an agreement would be harder to achieve, but the Nixon administration was happy to live indefinitely with the existing floating arrangements. This argument is plausible, but what it underestimates is the negative impact of U.S. monetary policy on French views of the Nixon administration.

Against this inauspicious background, official French appraisals of Kissinger's address were, predictably, largely negative. Jobert pointedly summarized Pompidou's and his own views: "What business is it of his!"[81] De Gaulle would not have disputed his analysis: "It was the same old view; the United States pressed for strengthening NATO beyond its present scope and structure, requesting its members to abide by the prevailing U.S. foreign policy consensus." With a few exceptions, senior officials shared Jobert's assessment of the Year of Europe as a U.S. attempt to reassert its leadership in the West in the context of a changed geopolitical order.

Kosciusko-Morizet was among the few French diplomats who cast a friendly eye on Kissinger's address.[82] He welcomed the U.S. government's overture and its seemingly conciliatory attitude. More specifically, he singled out four positive elements: Kissinger's recognition of Europe's status as a separate entity and partner of the United States, his emphasis on the need to restore equilibrium to the world financial system, his reassertion of the United States' commitment to both détente and troop maintenance, and his call to start talks on a higher political level. Kosciusko-Morizet's only qualm was that "Europe"—used, as was often the case, as shorthand for both Western European nations and the EC—had not taken the initiative. By striking first, he stated, the United States was in a position of strength ("supériorité de l'offensive").[83] This warlike vocabulary shows that even a U.S.-friendly ambassador thought of transatlantic relations in terms of competition, if not harsh antagonism.

Outside governmental circles, Monnet welcomed the U.S. move. In meetings with U.S. officials, he voiced doubts as to the likelihood of arriving at a new charter by the end of 1973.[84] Publicly, however, Monnet lent his support to the idea of a U.S.-European declaration of principles. In an op-ed piece published in *Le Monde,* he encouraged EC leaders to respond positively to the U.S. overture. In its May 1973 resolutions, Monnet's action committee declared itself confident that a joint examination of U.S. and European views would lay the basis for a "balanced and friendly dialogue."[85] It recommended appointing two independent experts in charge of determining which topics ought to be tabled for discussion.

Most French political actors, however, were hostile. De Rose focused his criticisms on the security dimension of the U.S. initiative. The situation described by Kissinger, he maintained, was hardly new, namely, East-West nuclear parity and European vulnerability to both conventional and nu-clear attack.[86] He found the speech deeply worrying, feeling that it implic-itly called for a reexamination of the "flexible response" strategy adopted in the 1960s, that is, a gradual response to aggression using first conven-tional and then nuclear arms. To him, any reduction of conventional and nuclear armaments would undermine Western Europeans' confidence in their future. De Rose also suspected the U.S. government of seeking to bargain its security assistance against economic concessions. He therefore urged his NAC colleagues to discuss solely defense matters.[87]

Other criticisms targeted more specifically the alleged hegemonic inten-tions of the United States. To future Foreign Minister Jean Sauvagnargues, Kissinger's rhetoric concealed the administration's intention to build a U.S.-ruled "global alliance [*groupement mondial*]" —one in which "Europe" would play a subservient role.[88] Sauvagnargues was upset by Kissinger's portrayal of Europe's interests as "regional." Thereafter, White House and State Department officials did their best to repair the damage done by this description, repeatedly stressing that it was not intended to be norma-tive.[89] Nonetheless, among French government officials, Pompidou alone declared that he was not overly shocked as long as its meaning was in-deed descriptive.[90] Echoing Sauvagnargues, Jean-Bernard Raimond, Pom-pidou's foreign policy adviser, maintained that the U.S. government had little else to offer besides an assertion of its ambitions of power. Its goal, he stated, was to get a blank check to negotiate with the Soviet Union on be-half of the West, which meant treating "Europe" as a negligible entity.[91]

The memorandum the Quai d'Orsay issued on 28 April summed up these criticisms.[92] It placed special emphasis on Kissinger's perceived faux pas: his reference to Europe's "regional interests" and his intimation that European integration was not an end in itself. Kissinger had mentioned that Japan "must be a principal partner in our common enterprise."[93] The Quai d'Orsay thus accused the U.S. government of seeking to create "an ideological or economic bloc" devoid of any unified geographical basis. It also voiced concerns about a potential linkage strategy.

U.S. officials were right in predicting that the Year of Europe would meet resistance in France. In reviving concerns over U.S. power, it reig-nited fears of national decline. The very topic of Kissinger's speech, how-ever, spurred French officials to articulate their concerns in a European, rather than a national, idiom. They reasserted the notion of a "European Europe," which de Gaulle had advanced in the early and mid 1960s before setting his hopes on a pan-European security order.[94] In language remi-niscent of de Gaulle's, they portrayed deeper Euro-Atlantic integration and an independent Europe as antagonistic concepts. Kosciusko-Morizet rejected this opposition. "A European Europe" with "an Atlantic face," he maintained, was not an oxymoron.[95] Quite the opposite, this was an accurate description of reality, as the United States was the "necessary partner" of "Europe" in all fields. The French ambassador, however, was a lone voice. Most of his colleagues argued that any U.S.-sponsored revitalization of transatlantic ties would "dissolve the European project into a larger, U.S.-dominated entity."[96]

A Power-Hungry Giant or an Idol with Feet of Clay? The French Press and the Year of Europe

The leading French press institutions offered a similarly critical analysis of Kissinger's speech. Their comments focused on the supposed hegemonic ambitions of the United States, setting them in the context of détente and a changing economic order. Such congruence is noteworthy, as journalists were not made privy to the texts drafted within the Quai d'Orsay and the Elysée Presidential Palace. It bears evidence to an enduring elite consensus on the threat posed by U.S. power despite a pervasive sense of U.S. decline in the United States.

The French press was very vocal against the U.S. initiative. *La Nation*, the mouthpiece of Pompidou's Gaullist party, denounced the new "Kissinger doctrine" as a rebuttal of Nixon's proclaimed vision of a five-power world including the United States, the Soviet Union, China, Japan, and Western Europe.[97] Kissinger's sole objective, the paper contended, was to strengthen U.S. supremacy. His characterization of Europe's interests fit in with these general aims.[98] Jean Kanapa—a member of the Central Committee of the French Communist Party (PCF)—viewed this phrase through the prism of ideology as a sign of the United States' quest for hegemony in the capitalist world.[99] Some journalists, in contrast, framed their criticisms in Cold War language. *Le Monde* analyzed the Year of Europe as a U.S. attempt to secure Western European and Japanese endorsement of the planned Agreement on the Prevention of Nuclear War. What the White House was implicitly requesting was a "reassertion of the U.S. leadership in defense matters."[100] Both Gaullist and communist voices condemned Kissinger's revival of the logic of Cold War blocs. According to *La Nation*, Kissinger had reasserted Washington's role as Moscow's most privileged discussion partner in a bloc-to-bloc relationship.[101] On the left, Kanapa censured the alleged U.S. plan to create a new political, economic and military bloc comprising all major capitalist countries. "NO TO NIXON'S PLAN TO DIVIDE THE WORLD," Kanapa forcefully concluded.[102]

Surprisingly, press commentaries made scant references to Watergate, perhaps because the resignation of a number of its key perpetrators was still to come. The newspaper *Combat*, the mouthpiece of the noncommunist left, was fairly cautious in discussing the scandal. An editorial column stressed the French concerns over a possible attempt by Nixon to counteract the negative impact of Watergate and Vietnam on public opinion through a "victory" abroad.[103] Yet the French daily did not go so far as to accuse the U.S. president of trying to create a diversion.

Kissinger's mention of Japan, by contrast, received much editorial attention. Although Japan was a Pacific rather than an Atlantic country, his statement was not fully out of place. The Year of Europe was rooted in concerns over the shifting economic balance between both sides of the Atlantic. U.S. political and economic actors were also worried about Japan's drastically improved position in the world economy.[104] The Nixon administration had brought a new, combative style to U.S.-Japanese relations, fighting for improved market access and a realignment of the yen. Clearly, the French communist left was not sympathetic to such concerns. It interpreted Kissinger's reference to Japan in terms of the U.S. assertion of hegemony.[105] *Le Monde,* more subtly, posed a question: why should the Atlantic Alliance not be extended to the Pacific Ocean, since it already encompassed the Mediterranean? The answer was obvious: "this gigantic oceanic construct" posed a threat to "Europe's distinctiveness."[106]

Kissinger's address compelled the French press to call for greater European political unity in both institutional and foreign policy terms. Asking if Nixon planned to "ignore" or, worse, "dissolve" the "personality" of the EC, *Le Figaro* stated that the EC Nine actually intended, on the contrary, to assert it. They would do so through institutional reform leading to the emergence of "a true political union."[107] *Combat* urged the EC Nine to forge common foreign policy positions that they could defend unanimously. Failing that, Europe would become a mere "'geographical expression,'" the superpowers speaking over the heads of the individual states.[108] In *Le Figaro,* Roger Massip, a close acquaintance of Monnet, wrote that Kissinger's speech would force Western European governments to face reality.[109] They could not successfully engage in a fruitful dialogue with the United States without speaking "with a single voice."[110] *Le Monde,* however, sounded a pessimistic note: "Europe" first had to "exist" in order to respond to the United States.[111]

More broadly, the French press's analyses reflected a long habit of positioning America as a mirror and a foil to European societies. A series of articles published in *Le Monde* made this connection explicit.[112] These texts rearticulated many themes of French anti-Americanism, with an emphasis on U.S. cultural imperialism as exemplified by such symbols as "ketchup," "jeans," and "t-shirts." Like Kissinger, their author, Alain Clément, established a link between generational shift and the deterioration of transatlantic ties. Unlike the U.S. national security advisor, however, Clément did not lament the changes to elite opinion on both sides of the Atlantic. "The architects and the supporters of an 'Atlantic community,'" he argued, had done nothing to remove the "contradiction inherent in transatlantic relations."[113] Nevertheless, he believed that strains in U.S.-European relations signaled the end of a tradition, best embodied by Alexis de Tocqueville, in which America had sparked intense fascination and curiosity among French and other European observers.[114]

The French sociologist Aron made a similar point in his *Figaro* column: "A continent rather than a nation, America … has always provided fertile ground for dreams and nightmares in Europe."[115] Aron, who saw the French elites as guilty of overreaction, reckoned that Kissinger's mention of a new "Atlantic charter" was unfortunate. The fate of the first charter, he ironized, should have been enough to deter him from recycling the term. Nevertheless, Kissinger's characterization of Europe's "regional interests" contained more than a kernel of truth to Aron. Europeans, he argued, had no way to bring their joint influence to weigh upon events in the Middle East, or in Southeast or Northeast Asia.[116] Aron also believed that underneath the rhetoric, the speech was designed to underscore continuity in U.S. policy. He considered the French reactions to be particularly unwarranted since U.S. power was on the wane. The United States, he wrote in colorful language, was "neither the benevolent giant (or the philanthropically inclined brute) … nor the blood- and oil-hungry monster" that "an ignorant left" made it out to be.[117]

Since the interwar years, America had typically served as a reference in discussions of modernity.[118] In France, such commentaries often included elements of anti-Americanism: Americanization was portrayed as a threat to French culture and values, that is, ultimately, a threat to the French sense of identity.[119] Such concerns—which remained alive and well in the 1970s, as the protracted debate over Americanization attests[120]—shaped the controversy triggered by the Year of Europe. Although these fears had national roots, officials and the press couched them in a distinctively European idiom. Journalists even went one step further than governmental actors. Like state officials, they warned that the U.S. plan posed a dangerous threat to the "personality" of "Europe," but they also advocated both institutional EC reform and European foreign-policy cohesiveness. In reasserting the metaphor of the "single voice" of the 1972 Paris summit statement, they anticipated the French government's reappraisal of EPC.[121]

The Key to Unlock the Year of Europe

Elsewhere in Europe, Kissinger's speech received mixed reviews. Within the British Foreign and Commonwealth Office (FCO), the U.S. initiative reignited the old debate between the Europeanists and the Atlanticists. It also revealed differences between European-minded Premier Heath and his more U.S.-friendly foreign secretary, Sir Alec Douglas-Home.[122] On 27 April, Douglas-Home made a noncommittal statement, welcoming Kissinger's language as "realistic and timely" but wishing the EC had had more time to "find its way to common positions with greater delibera- tion."[123] On a long-planned visit to Washington, Brandt offered little other than expressions of goodwill and successfully petitioned Nixon to drop the phrase "Atlantic charter." While harboring reservations about certain aspects of the U.S. plan—notably its treatment of economic and defense issues as "one ball of wax"[124]—West Germany and Britain were concerned about France's opposition. Therefore, Kissinger had no choice but to focus on Paris as "the key to unlock the Year of Europe."[125]

U.S. officials first tried to defeat the French on their own terms. John Irwin, the new U.S. ambassador to France, underscored the French fears of U.S. interference in EC matters. To address these anxieties, he sug- gested emphasizing the interrelations between European and transatlan- tic integration.[126] Peter Flanigan, the president's assistant for international economic affairs, put forth a formula that skillfully connected the French concerns to the U.S. notions of "partnership" and "interdependence." Nixon, he stated, should tell Pompidou that the Year of Europe was de- signed to "strengthen the independence, autonomy and identity of the emerging European Union, while at the same time paving the way for a constructive economic interdependence among equal partners."[127] Ironi- cally, Flanigan's mention of the EC's "identity" prefigured the surge of this concept to the forefront of French discourse. So did Kissinger's use of the term "European identity" in a June 1973 memorandum to Nixon.[128]

Initially, Pompidou appeared amenable to discussion. In mid May, he reckoned that the various issues marring transatlantic relations could only be resolved within an overall framework.[129] He thus told Kissinger that he was willing to consider an overarching U.S.-European agreement. Pom- pidou was even more forthcoming with Heath: "Willy nilly, we will have to find a transatlantic arrangement which brings all elements together."[130] But this accommodating stance proved misleading. French officials re- mained opposed to a declaration of principles between the United States and its European allies. The Quai d'Orsay argued that it would only add new obligations to existing ones.[131] At the Franco-American summit of Reykjavik, Pompidou asked skeptically: "Who declares what?"[132] A bilat- eral statement between the United States and a European country, he went on to say, was meaningful, but an EC-U.S. statement was not. It was not even feasible because the EC was "an economic and not a political entity," and that there was only "one true European" in Britain, namely, Heath.

Subsequent events would show that this assessment of the British political establishment was not far off the mark.

The Reykjavik summit yielded mixed results for the White House. U.S. officials went some way toward enticing French cooperation. They offered to extend their nuclear cooperation to the design of new technology—the new generation of missiles and multiple independently targetable reentry vehicle warheads.[133] Franco-U.S. talks so far had only focused on the technology of existing missiles and on the Soviet Union's anti-ballistic missile systems. At an ensuing press conference, Pompidou departed from his predecessors' stance by publicly declaring himself in favor of the maintenance of U.S. troops in Europe.[134] Nonetheless, the summit fell far short of U.S. objectives.[135] Pompidou refused to commit to any procedure for discussing the Year of Europe. Facetiously asking whether it was meant to "beatify" or "strangle" Europe, he resisted the U.S. plan to hold preliminary quadripartite talks with Britain and West Germany.[136] He recommended using traditional bilateral channels instead, allegedly to avoid upsetting the smaller EC states.[137] Nixon and Kissinger reluctantly agreed, hoping that bilateral discussions would be a stepping-stone toward a larger forum.[138]

The U.S.-Soviet Agreement on the Prevention of Nuclear War of 22 June heightened French suspicion about U.S. policy. The U.S. government had kept its allies regularly informed of the progress of the talks.[139] On 18 May, Kissinger had spoken at length with Pompidou. U.S. policy, he stated, "may be complex, but it is not stupid."[140] It was "a question of playing China against the Soviet Union." The Nixon administration had to ensure that its policy did not "serve as a pretext for a Soviet attack against China" and hence seem directed against the Soviet Union. The planned nuclear agreement was not a "capitulation" to the Soviets, but rather "an attempt to enmesh them." Kissinger had allegedly "never used such frankness" in discussing the matter with another government. Pompidou may well have understood Kissinger's rationale, as Trachtenberg argues.[141] Nonetheless, the nuclear agreement of 22 June made French officials and their EC counterparts uneasy.[142] Nixon and Kissinger insisted that the United States and the Soviet Union had solely pledged not to use nuclear weapons unless force was employed against another country.[143] This was to no avail, however; de Rose and the Quai d'Orsay's defense division maintained that the agreement, while asserting a U.S. right to universal intervention in case of a nuclear war, further undermined the credibility of U.S. nuclear deterrence.[144] Kosciusko-Morizet expressed similar criticisms.[145] All in all, the U.S.-Soviet accord exacerbated French fears of a U.S.-Soviet condominium.[146]

Despite this inauspicious beginning, Kissinger renewed his efforts to win over the French government. In early June, he presented Jobert with a suggested two-stage process: the United States, France, and other major

European countries would at first hold bilateral discussions while pursuing existing talks in NATO, GATT, and the IMF. Next, they would decide on the value of a joint meeting of their deputy foreign ministers.[147] He then gave Jobert, the FCO, and the West German foreign ministry two U.S.-European draft declarations—one drawn up by the NSC and the other by the State Department.[148] Kissinger recommended that Nixon, while meeting with Jobert in San Clemente, should point to the interconnections between the U.S.-Soviet and the transatlantic talks.[149] Jobert, however, was unswerving in his opposition. On 29 June, he urged the U.S. president not to present the European governments with set plans and formulas.[150] Two weeks later, he officially rejected the U.S. documents.[151] Jobert's characteristically sibylline words added to Kissinger's irritation: "It is a beautiful language—French—and he uses it well. Is he going to let me know what is acceptable? He told me what is not."[152]

Kissinger had not been oblivious to French ambiguities. He had even asked Jobert if the French planned to make a "serious effort" or whether they would only accept a joint meeting "in order to kill it."[153] But in his dealings with the allies, Kissinger demonstrated a degree of self-assurance that was unwarranted. Jobert would "go along but wants the credit," he stated overconfidently.[154] To be fair, the French strategy played its part in U.S. miscalculations. Rather than head-on opposition, Pompidou and the Quai d'Orsay resorted to dilatory tactics. EPC's existence would soon complicate this strategy. At this stage, however, Pompidou was unwilling to endorse a European response to the Year of Europe. His statement on the EC as a mere economic reality had a rhetorical function, but it also reflected deeper beliefs. Pompidou thought that European integration ought to proceed in stages, starting with economics and then moving to politics and defense. "I do not think that we can discuss political and eventually defense objectives when we have not been able to make one step forward with the economic and monetary union" decided at the 1972 Paris summit, Pompidou had told Heath in May 1973.[155]

Playing the Game of European Foreign Policy Cooperation

EPC brought an added layer of complexity to the transatlantic debate. West German and British officials believed that they could not ignore the U.S. overture, in part because of the security link. They also saw it as an opportunity to build up EPC and thus foster European political integration.[156] Brandt had been one of the main architects of EPC.[157] The scholarly prominence of *Ostpolitik* has tended to overshadow his emphasis on European integration,[158] which he set as his first priority in his 1969 and

1973 inaugural speeches.[159] At the same time, the smaller EC states were anxious not to be excluded from quadripartite talks, which had been frequent during the Berlin settlement negotiations. France's EC partners all used the EPC framework to pressure Pompidou's government into accepting a joint response to the U.S. initiative. Yet French officials feared that U.S.-EPC talks would divide and hence weaken the EC Nine. They first opposed any joint response to Kissinger's plea for an Atlantic declaration, a stance they shifted only in August 1973. But by then lending their support to an EC-U.S. draft declaration, they hoped to foster international recognition of a distinct European political personality. Jobert and Quai officials thus picked up a thread that had run through the early years of de Gaulle's presidency. Despite such lines of continuity, this was a significant step, given their prior opposition to EPC talks on transatlantic matters.

Earlier EPC attempts to discuss U.S.-European relations had stumbled upon French obstructionism.[160] The main arguments were already concerns over linkage bargaining and the impact of institutionalized EC-U.S. discussions on European independence. Deputy Political Director Claude Arnaud pointed to the risk of "globalization [*globalisation*]" — the French term coined for cross-issue bargaining — and "institutionalization." He believed that "one led automatically to the other."[161] During the first months of 1973, the Quai d'Orsay's only concession to its EC partners was on information sharing: foreign ministers might brief their EC counterparts on their discussions with U.S. officials. This procedure, Arnaud reckoned, might foster a better understanding of transatlantic issues and possibly a broad consensus among the EC Nine. "But it should not go any further," he forcefully asserted.[162] Arnaud therefore rejected Thorn's proposal that the rotating president of the EC Council of Ministers should travel to Washington at the beginning of his term.

The Year of Europe acted as a catalyst for EPC's involvement in transatlantic affairs. At the May meeting of the EPC Political Committee, EC states tried to persuade the Quai d'Orsay to endorse three proposals: a joint response to Kissinger's address, an appropriate preparation of the "constructive dialogue" proposed by the U.S. government, and a meeting between Nixon and the EC Council of Ministers during the U.S. president's trip to Europe.[163] Quai Political Director François Puaux stood his ground, securing a postponement of any decision, as did Jobert at the June ministerial meeting of EPC.[164] On 5 July, however, the Danish EC presidency presented the political directors with a draft of a U.S.-European declaration of principles. Arnaud questioned the desirability of such a text.[165] Pursuant to the decision taken by the British cabinet on 20 June, Sir Thomas Brimelow, permanent under-secretary of state at the FCO, sought to break the deadlock with a proposal to issue two statements: one pertaining to

NATO and the other to EC-U.S. relations.[166] Brimelow also suggested putting together an internal EC document defining the identity of the EC and its member states vis-à-vis the United States. Arnaud readily accepted the latter but rejected the former. Instead, he proposed drawing a list of discussion topics for a U.S.-European dialogue. The political directors finally settled on drawing a list of issues to be decided by the foreign ministers at their next EPC meeting. This was a first step toward a joint discussion of the transatlantic relationship.

Initially, Britain's public attitude toward the Year of Europe had been "benevolently neutral."[167] The security argument subsequently spurred it to take a more active stance.[168] To British officials, U.S. warnings against isolationists in Congress were not empty rhetoric. On 20 June, ministers concurred that Britain's "overriding concern" was to preserve U.S. involvement in the defense of Europe—both for its own sake and because it was deemed essential to West Germany's resolution as a member of NATO.[169] In endorsing the FCO's proposal for two declarations, cabinet members expected France to remain on the defensive. The French, they stated, felt that "Kissinger was blackmailing Europe."[170] The cabinet resolved that although times were not ripe for it, Britain should soon be ready to urge the EC Nine to get down to finding common ground.

While sharing British concerns about U.S. isolationism, West Germany had taken a more passive stance. The Franco-German entente remained a cornerstone of its foreign policy, which implied a cautious attitude.[171] The West German foreign ministry, however, saw cooperation with the United States as equally, and possibly more, important. It tried to square the circle by working behind the scenes. On 12 July, Foreign Minister Walter Scheel presented Kissinger with proposed guidelines for a declaration (*Gliederung und Inhalt der Atlantik-Erklärung*).[172] Kissinger was pleased and encouraged him to proceed with the drafting of the text.

Contrary to scholarly assertions, the EPC ministerial meeting of 23 July did not signal a French policy shift.[173] Jobert did not endorse the British-sponsored approach of two declarations. Rather, he continued to apply "delaying tactics" by "shifting" the thrust of EPC toward two tasks: drawing up a list of discussion topics for the prospective transatlantic dialogue, and defining European identity.[174] In appropriating the British idea of an "identity paper," Jobert gave it a new dimension.[175] He pleaded for characterizing European identity in and of itself, rather than in relation to the United States, as Brimelow had initially proposed. "Europe," he intimated, should "assert its identity everywhere, for all purposes and for its own benefit" ("tous azimuts, à tous usages, et pour elle-même").[176]

By July 1973, EPC had become fully involved in transatlantic matters, but the EC Nine had not yet agreed to respond to the Year of Europe through a joint statement. Pressure by EC states had done little to reduce French opposition. Instead, it had spurred the Quai d'Orsay to introduce diversions. By calling for a definition of European identity, Jobert took, however unwittingly, a groundbreaking step: the wording was new. Prior EC documents, particularly the statement of the 1972 Paris summit, had referred to Europe's "personality," if at all.[177] In political discourse, the word "identity" was still primarily associated with the nation-state. Unlike "European personality," the term "European identity" thus appealed to a European political entity and even to a European polity.

Multilevel Bargaining: A European Response to the Year of Europe

The Copenhagen meeting compelled the White House to step up the pressures on European decision-makers. Britain and West Germany announced that they would stop their bilateral exchange with the U.S. government due to "a strong ground-swell of opposition by the smaller countries to bilateralism between the larger European countries and the United States."[178] Nixon and Kissinger were furious. Their tough language would ultimately be counterproductive. It did prompt the FCO and the West German foreign ministry to try to overcome French resistance to a transatlantic declaration. When it finally agreed to an EPC draft declaration, however, Pompidou's government made sure to further its own interests. The statement that the EC Nine put forth in September 1973 consequently contained almost nothing that U.S. officials wanted. Its main emphasis was on European distinctiveness rather than the cohesion of the Atlantic Alliance.

The White House first attempted to use Nixon's planned trip to Europe as a bargaining chip. In mid July, Kissinger threatened Roberto Gaja, general secretary of the Italian foreign ministry at the Farnesina, with cancellation of the visit.[179] The U.S. president relayed this threat to Brandt in his letter of 30 July. Nixon would travel to Europe in the fall only on condition of the promise of a "result commensurate with the need for strengthening Atlantic relationships."[180] In a meeting with FCO officials the same day, Kissinger spoke harshly about European obstructionism.[181] To him, the Year of Europe was "over." He expressed doubts about the prospect of Nixon's trip to Europe, particularly since the details remained controversial. Just after the Reykjavik summit, Pompidou had ruled out any meeting of the U.S. president with the EC heads of state or government, saying: "It would be like Charlemagne convening his barons and laying down the law" ("Ce serait Charlemagne réunissant ses barons et leur dictant sa loi").[182] As an alternative, the West German foreign ministry suggested that Nixon might attend the NATO Council and then meet the EC Council and Commission presidents together with the EC foreign ministers. The White House, however, dismissed this plan as "preposterous."[183] There was more to this controversy than petty squabbling. The particulars of the visit stood as symbols of the transatlantic relationship and its underlying power dynamics. Pompidou was fully aware of this, as was Nixon, who warned that he would not sign a declaration at any level lower than heads of state or government.[184]

U.S. threats set in motion a flurry of diplomatic activity. On 3 August, Heath approached Brandt with a proposal for a tripartite meeting with Pompidou.[185] Judging the British offer "too dramatic," Brandt suggested holding separate, yet coordinated, meetings with Jobert at senior official level instead.[186] The FCO responded positively, but Bonn proceeded cautiously with its plan lest it look like collusion.[187] Brandt did not write to Pompidou until mid August.[188] Meanwhile, the West German foreign ministry had floated the idea of provisional statements to be issued during Nixon's fall visit while waiting until 1974 to publish a landmark transatlantic declaration.[189] The Quai d'Orsay said no, predictably, worried as it was that this might foster a "permanent dialogue" between the EC and the United States.[190] The FCO was desperately trying to achieve "the maximum compatibility" between its historically privileged relationship with the United States and its new European policy.[191] On 8 August, it moved to unveil its proposed Outline for a Declaration of Principles between the Community and the United States, along with a draft paper on the "Identity of the Nine vis-à-vis the U.S."[192] Senior British officials hoped that the September ministerial meeting of EPC would break the deadlock. As time went by, they became more on edge. By 17 August, they had concluded that they had "done too much in the way of stating points of view and not enough in the way of trying to persuade the French."[193] The British embassy in Paris was instructed to make active efforts to overcome French resistance. The British chargé, Christopher Ewart-Biggs, replied that the British outline might be perceived as "too much like what the Americans want"[194] and suggested the basis of a declaration that might be acceptable to the French, which would place greater emphasis on the development of a European personality and less on common Atlantic purposes.[195] Douglas-Home encouraged him to discuss his ideas with senior Quai officials.[196]

Facing pressures from all sides, Quai officials reappraised their strategy. Jobert may well state in his memoirs that, following their early July meeting, he realized Heath's views could "foster the birth of Europe and protect its identity against the American fatality."[197] But archival evidence attests only to French acceptance of the British approach at the very end of

August. Jobert, moreover, did not instigate the change all by himself. The claim that he "decided to take the bull by the horns" in July and use Kissinger's initiative to further European political unity is thus overstated and teleological.[198] Rather, during the month of August a consensus crystallized among French officials on the value of pursuing the British approach. On 27 August, Emmanuel de Margerie, Quai director for European affairs, reported concerns about the Italian stance. The Farnesina now wished to give priority to Nixon's visit and urged EC states to draft a "concluding declaration."[199] That same day, Ewart-Biggs met with Margerie and Puaux. Puaux hinted at a policy shift. If there was to be a declaration, he stated, the British draft—with the addition of a more European slant as Ewart-Biggs had suggested—could offer a basis for discussion.[200] Earlier in the month, Puaux had portrayed this text as "harmless": its wording was so vague that the United States could hardly use it as a political lever.[201] On 27 August, he recommended going along with the British approach. "We could usefully rely on the British to stiffen the Italians," he wrote to Jobert.[202] The French foreign minister had reached the same conclusion. In a secret meeting with Heath in South England on 26 August, Jobert said that the British draft was "a good one," meanwhile reserving Pompidou's final decision.[203] Brimelow was hopeful when he came to Paris on 29 August; he was not disappointed. Jobert indicated that France would accept the British document so long as the FCO was prepared to resist any substantial amendments.[204] Douglas-Home gave a cautious 'yes,'[205] which was enough to satisfy Jobert.[206]

The French policy reappraisal broke the impasse in EPC talks. The West Germans accepted the Anglo-French approach, but they publicly stated that they would have preferred stronger language on transatlantic ties in order to appease the U.S. government.[207] In early September, the EPC Political Committee amended the political paragraphs of the British draft.[208] Always mindful of preventing the formal institutionalization of EC-U.S. relations, Puaux refused to establish an ad hoc group to finalize its economic paragraphs.[209] Soon afterward, the West German government agreed to entrust the EC Committee of Permanent Representatives (COREPER) with this task.[210] At their ensuing Copenhagen meeting, the foreign ministers endorsed a revised British document, subject to governmental approval after finalization by COREPER.[211] Because Denmark held the EC's rotating presidency, they appointed Danish Foreign Minister Knud Børge Andersen to present it to, but not negotiate it with, Kissinger. They also asked the political committee to proceed with its work on European identity. Jobert insisted on the "psychological" importance of having a paper available for Nixon's visit.[212] Finally, they settled on a list of topics to be discussed with the United States.

The EC Nine's procedure caused anger in Washington. Newly appointed Secretary of State Kissinger and his staff had envisioned U.S.-led multilateral talks. Instead, they had to face a "fait accompli":[213]

> For the U.S. it is a new and extraordinary phenomenon in that Europe speaks with one voice, which we welcome, but that in the preparations of its position we were not consulted. Then a document is presented by a representative who is not empowered to negotiate but only to receive comments.... We seem to be talking to those who can't negotiate and those who can negotiate won't talk to us.[214]

The U.S. response threw into sharp relief the limits of the U.S. government's commitment to European integration. For all their talk of European political unity, U.S. officials were ultimately not prepared to deal with the EC as a single entity.[215] Kissinger even saw it as an "insult" not to be consulted by key allies like Britain, France, and West Germany before their discussions "with Norway, Luxembourg and even Ireland."[216] He was all the more upset since he had long warned against a "fait accompli."[217] After the Copenhagen meeting, Sonnenfeldt could only deplore that, by appointing a spokesman who was not empowered to negotiate, EC states had done what the United States had urged them not to do.[218]

The content of the draft proved just as infuriating to the U.S. government. Sonnenfeldt emphasized the "thinness" of the text.[219] NSC staff member Charles Cooper stated that there was nothing "new or of any substance" in its economic paragraphs.[220] The document did not hint at any new framework for solving transatlantic economic disputes. Instead, the EC Nine reasserted their stance on monetary reform—including "fixed but adjustable parities," the "general convertibility of currencies," and "the reduction in the role of national reserve currencies," that is, of the U.S. dollar.[221] It made no mention of specific trade issues. Paragraph 16 merely stated the signatories' readiness to play an active role in the upcoming GATT negotiations and recalled the agreement reached in Tokyo on the specificity of agricultural trade.[222] Worse, perhaps, the draft's political section placed greater emphasis on the EC's distinctiveness than on Atlantic unity. The FCO's draft of 8 August had struck a balance between both principles:

> The United States and the European Community
> At a time when world events are profoundly changing the international situation
> Aware that they have common values and common aspirations, and face similar problems and challenges
> ...
> Undertake to intensify their cooperation on an equal basis in accordance with the following principles and maintain a constructive dialogue.

General Principles
(I.) They will work in harmony to promote a better international equilibrium.
...
(II) The European Community, in establishing its position in world affairs as a distinct entity, will make a contribution commensurate to its human, intellectual and material resources. The United States, recognizing that the creation of the Community has enhanced the stability of Europe, will be glad to see the Community speaking with a single voice in international contexts.[223]

French misgivings about U.S. power produced a shift in emphasis. The final draft included a rather tepid reassertion of transatlantic ties. In line with the Quai d'Orsay's new insistence on defining a European identity, it gave greater prominence to the development of a distinct European entity. The preamble of the draft even implied that the proclaimed commitment of the EC heads of state or government to establishing a "European union" by 1980 was just as significant as recent Cold War developments:[224]

The United States of America on the one hand and the European Community and its member states on the other hand,
1. At a time when world events are profoundly changing the international situation, and when the Nine have affirmed their intention to transform, before the end of the present decade, the whole complex of their relations into a European union
...[225]

The General Principles section, moreover, began with a strong statement on the rise of a European world actor:

The United States, recognizing that the creation of the Community is an event of great international importance and has enhanced the stability of Europe, welcomes the intention of the Nine to ensure that the Community establishes its position in world affairs as a distinct entity.[226]

Kissinger thus bitterly asked if "a process that began as a renewal of Atlantic ties [was] to end by a recognition of Europe's unity—a unity that we have fostered and supported and could not have come into being without us."[227] The leaking of the EC draft to *The New York Times* was an aggravating factor, providing the American public with a benchmark against which to compare future texts.[228]

By September 1973, the Quai d'Orsay had acceded to its EC partners' demand to draft an EC-U.S. statement. Never before had EC states spoken with a single voice to the United States on such a broad range of topics, as Monnet had urged them to do since the 1960s. It is no small irony that a plan designed to produce a forceful reaffirmation of transatlantic unity should result in a powerful statement on European unity. Such irony

was clearly not to Kissinger's liking. The United States, he told FCO officials, had "never intended to use this initiative to build Europe: they had
wanted to build Atlantic unity."[229]

A European Response to National Anxieties

Almost despite themselves, the French had helped to put together a document in which EC states stated their aspirations to become an internationally influential actor. There is some truth to Kissinger's claim that "an
American initiative enabled Jobert to pursue the old Gaullist dream of
building Europe on an anti-American basis."[230] Government officials and
the press responded to what they perceived as a new "American challenge" — to quote the title of Jean-Jacques Servan-Schreiber's best-seller — by
reasserting de Gaulle's rhetoric.[231] Denouncing the U.S. threat to "Europe's
personality," they revived his dichotomy between a "European" and an
"Atlantic Europe." They only went along with the draft declaration called
for by their EC partners in order to assert claims to European influence
vis-à-vis the United States.

But there was more to the story than the pursuit of an old dream. Prior
to the summer of 1973, Pompidou's government had opposed any EPC
talks on transatlantic relations. By September 1973, French officials had
come to play by EPC's rules and helped to forge a coordinated European
response to the Year of Europe. This shift took place against the backdrop
of not only heightened concerns over a U.S.-Soviet condominium,[232] but
also more generally rising qualms about U.S. policy. The German factor
may have played its part too, as Heath argued at the time. The British premier had responded to Jobert's expressed concerns about West Germany's
inclination either to "move further to the East" or to become "purely Atlanticist" by stating that "this surely was a powerful reason for making
a success of the [transatlantic] work on which we were all engaged."[233]
Heath had felt that Jobert was responsive to this argument.

The French response to the Year of Europe hinted at change on yet another level. The U.S. initiative had exacerbated anxieties of national decline
and a loss of national identity. Not only were these concerns couched in a
European idiom, but the Quai d'Orsay also advanced the notion of a European identity. Jobert's call for a definition of European identity built on a
British proposal intended to "bring ... the French to cooperate on the two
transatlantic declarations."[234] Nonetheless, this was an important first step
toward popularizing a pioneering concept, that of a politically anchored
European identity. This term's rapid surge to prominence in French political discourse would make this move particularly significant.

The French show of strength would have implications for Franco-American relations. At the beginning of the summer, the U.S. government had seemed prepared to increase its nuclear assistance. Soutou states that Pompidou suspended nuclear cooperation in the fall of 1973. French officials, he claims, interpreted U.S. demands on French testing at the Nevada test site as a sign of the U.S. wish to control French nuclear developments. This, he states, prompted Pompidou to reembrace the orthodox Gaullist tenets of French security independence, as exemplified by his February 1974 "strategic will."[235] As Trachtenberg argues, it was U.S., not French, officials who first decided to put nuclear cooperation on hold.[236] Kissinger stated on 5 September that "the real quid pro quo [wa]s the basic orientation of French policy" and instructed Secretary of Defense James Schlesinger not to conclude anything with his French counterpart.[237] Kissinger possibly hoped that nuclear cooperation would work as an effective bargaining chip, but French officials would resist U.S. pressure, demonstrating their determination to assert a European personality vis-à-vis the United States.

Notes

1. *RM (73) 16 3ᵉ rev.: Outline for a Declaration of Principles between the United States of America and the European Community and its Member States,* Copenhagen, 17 September 1973, Ministère des affaires étrangères de la République française (MAE), EC files 1971–6, 3792.
2. Michel Jobert, *L'autre regard* (Paris: Grasset, 1976), 332.
3. Henry Kissinger, *Years of Upheaval* (Boston, MA: Little, Brown, 1982), 189.
4. Möckli argues that Jobert played a primary role in the change of position, which he traces largely to the U.S.-Soviet Agreement on the Prevention of Nuclear War. His argument is based on Jobert's memoirs. Clearly, Jobert was keen to cast a favorable light on his ministerial deeds. A closer examination of French archival records, however, shows that this change happened not in July but only during the second half of August in the context of increased EC pressure, and that Jobert was not alone in engineering it (Möckli, *European Foreign Policy During the Cold War,* 159–60).
5. Most accounts of Nixon's foreign policy treat U.S. relations with Western European allies as a peripheral topic: Tad Szulc, *The Illusion of Peace: Foreign Policy in the Nixon Years* (New York: Viking Press, 1978), 449, 690–92, 749; Richard C. Thornton, *Nixon-Kissinger Years: Reshaping America's Foreign Policy,* 2nd ed. (St. Paul, MN: Paragon House Publishers, 2001); William P. Bundy, *A Tangled Web: The Making of Foreign Policy in the Nixon Presidency* (New York: Hill and Wang, 1998), 413–19; Hanhimäki, *The Flawed Architect,* 274–77; Robert Dallek, *Nixon and Kissinger: Partners in Power* (New York: HarperCollins Publishers, 2007), 112–16, 473–76. For a historiographical review, see Luke A. Nichter, "Nixon and Europe: Transatlantic Policy in the Shadow of Other Priorities," in *A Companion to Richard M. Nixon,* ed. Melvin Small (Malden, MA: Blackwell Publishers, 2011), 444–59.

6. Hanhimäki, "Kissinger et l'Europe : entre intégration et autonomie," 325–26.
7. Recent studies fail to give a full account of the genesis of the Year of Europe, glossing over the preliminary work conducted by the National Security Council: ibid., 326; Winand, "Loaded Words and Disputed Meanings," 305–9; Hynes, *The Year That Never Was*, 76; Rossbach, *Heath, Nixon and the Rebirth of the Special Relationship*, 135–46.
8. Kissinger, *Years of Upheaval*, 130–31.
9. Memorandum of conversation (memcon) Pompidou/Kissinger, 15 September 1972, Centre historique des archives nationales (CHAN), 5AG2 1022.
10. Memcon Kissinger/Maurice Schumann, 28 September 1972, Nixon Presidential Materials (NPM), NSC, Country files, 679.
11. On Sonnenfeldt's profile and his ties to Kissinger, see Kenneth Weisbrode, *The Atlantic Century: Four Generations of Extraordinary Diplomats who Forged America's Vital Alliance with Europe* (Cambridge, MA: Da Capo Press, 2009), 205–7. In his 1969 performance appraisal, Kissinger portrayed Sonnenfeldt as "one of the best European experts in the country" (*Performance of Helmut Sonnenfeldt*, 25 September 1969, NPM, NSC, Name files, 834).
12. Telephone conversation (telcon) Kissinger/Peter Flanigan, 17 November 1972, 9:40 A.M., NPM, NSC, Kissinger files, Telcons, 17.
13. National Security Study Memorandums (NSSMs) were a series of policy papers produced by various departments. Kissinger secured the power to order them when joining the Nixon team in 1968 (Hanhimäki, *The Flawed Architect*, 24).
14. Acting Assistant Secretary of State George Springsteen asked the U.S. representative to the EC to suggest "how the 'year of Europe' might be celebrated" (Joseph Greenwald to Helmut Sonnenfeldt, 18 December 1972, U.S. National Archives and Records Administration [NARA], Records of the State Department [SD], Record Group [RG] 59, Lot files, Sonnenfeldt, 4).
15. Kissinger, *Memorandum for the Secretary of State, the Secretary of Defense, the Secretary of Commerce, the Secretary of the Treasury, the Secretary of Agriculture*, "NSSM 164: United States relations with Europe," 18 December 1972, NPM, NSC, Institutional files, 194.
16. Gaddis, *Strategies of Containment*, 308–14.
17. Lawrence Fox, *Memorandum to William Hyland, NSC Staff*, "Commerce Comments on NSSM 164: U.S. Relations with Europe," 4 January 1973, NPM, NSC, Institutional files, 194.
18. John Hart, *Memorandum for the Honorable Henry A. Kissinger*, "NSSM 164—U.S. Relations with Europe," 26 January 1973, NPM, NSC, Institutional files, 194.
19. Vernon Walters, *Memorandum for Henry A. Kissinger*, "NSSM 164—U.S. Relations with Europe," 3 January 1973, NPM, NSC, Institutional files, 194.
20. Kissinger, "NSSM 164: United States relations with Europe."
21. A.M. Christopher, *Memorandum for Mrs. Jeanne Davis, National Security Council Staff*, "Comments on NSSM 164 Study," 29 December 1972, NPM, NSC, Institutional files, 194.
22. Gérard Bossuat, "Jean Monnet, le Département d'Etat et l'intégration européenne (1952–1959)," in *Europe brisée, Europe retrouvée. Nouvelles réflexions sur l'unité européenne au XXe siècle*, ed. René Girault and Gérard Bossuat (Paris: Publications de la Sorbonne, 1994), 307–45; idem, "Jean Monnet et le partenariat atlantique des années soixante," *Relations internationales*, no. 119 (2004): 285–301; Clifford P. Hackett, ed. *Monnet and the Americans: The Father of a United Europe and His U.S. Supporters* (Washington, D.C.: Jean Monnet Council, 1995); Klaus Schwabe, "Jean Monnet, les Etats-Unis et le rôle de l'Europe au sein de la Communauté atlantique," in *Jean Monnet, l'Europe et les chemins de la paix*, ed. Gérard Bossuat and Andreas Wilkens (Paris: Publications de la Sorbonne,

1999), 275–93; Pascaline Winand, "De l'usage de l'Amérique par Jean Monnet pour la construction européenne," in Bossuat and Wilkens, *Jean Monnet*, 252–71.

23. See Monnet's correspondence with Kissinger, Fondation Jean Monnet pour l'Europe (FJM), AMK C 23/6/240-AMK C 23/6/280. Monnet sent his first letter to Kissinger on 23 January 1969 to wish him good luck in his new job (FJM, AMK C 23/6/240). The last piece in the series is a thank-you letter Monnet wrote to Kissinger for speaking highly of him in a television interview (FJM, AMK C 23/6/280).

24. Memcon John Irwin/Monnet, 25 October 1972, NPM, NSC, Subject files, 322. Theodore Elliot, *Memorandum for Mr. Henry A. Kissinger*, "Deputy Secretary Irwin's conversation with Jean Monnet on U.S.-European dialogue," 9 November 1972, NPM, NSC, Subject files, 322.

25. Jacques van Helmont, *Conversation V.H. et MM. Petrow, Katz, Hormats*, 5 December 1972, FJM, AMK 104/1/9. "Déclaration commune—Dixième session (Paris les 17 et 18 décembre 1962)," quoted in full in Pascaline Winand and Fondation Jean Monnet pour l'Europe, "20 ans d'action du Comité Jean Monnet (1955–1975)," *Problématiques européennes*, no. 8 (2001): 69–73.

26. Van Helmont, *Conversation : M. Katz, M. Hormats, M. Petrow, JM, VH, 9 décembre 1972*, FJM, AMK 104/1/11.

27. William Rogers, *Memorandum for the President*, "Monnet proposal on U.S.-Western European dialogue," 22 January 1973, NPM, NSC, Subject files, 322.

28. Sonnenfeldt, *Memorandum for Mr. Kissinger*, "Secretary Rogers on EC-U.S. dialogue," 26 January 1973, NPM, NSC, Subject files, 322.

29. Sonnenfeldt, *Memorandum for Mr. Kissinger*, "Monnet on U.S.-European dialogue," undated [on or after 25 October 1973], NPM, NSC, Subject files, 322.

30. Monnet, *Mémo*, 16 January 1973, FJM, AMK 104/1/12.

31. Kissinger, *Years of Upheaval*, 151. See also Hamilton, "Britain, France, and America's Year of Europe, 1973," 875.

32. Sonnenfeldt, *Memorandum for Mr. Kissinger*, "Your meeting with Sir Burke Trend, Tuesday, January 16," 15 January 1973, NPM, NSC, VIP files, 942.

33. Sonnenfeldt, *Memorandum for Mr. Kissinger*, "Memo to the President on Heath visit," 23 January 1973, NPM, NSC, VIP files, 942.

34. Kissinger, *Memorandum for the President*, "Your meetings with Prime Minister Heath," 31 January 1973, NPM, NSC, VIP files, 942.

35. Sonnenfeldt, *Memorandum for Mr. Kissinger*, "Memo to the President on Heath visit," 23 January 1973, NPM, NSC, VIP files, 942.

36. *Background Materials on Economic Issues—B1. U.S. Support for the EC* (attached to Kissinger's *Memorandum for the President*, 31 January 1973), NPM, NSC, VIP files, 942.

37. François de La Gorce, telegram 7092-6, 2 February 1973, MAE, U.S. files 1970–5, 1137. See also Szulc, *The Illusion of Peace*, 690.

38. Jacques Kosciusko-Morizet, telegram 1517-28, 24 February 1973, MAE, U.S. files 1970–5, 1137.

39. Guia Migani, "Gli Stati Uniti e le relazione eurafricane da Kennedy a Nixon," in *Dollari, petrolio e aiuti allo sviluppo. Il confronto Nord-Sud negli anni '60–70*, ed. Daniele Caviglia and Antonio Varsori (Milan: Franco Angeli, 2008), 48.

40. Memcon Michel Debré/Peterson, 18 February 1973, MAE, U.S. files 1970–5, 73; Memcon André Bettencourt/Peterson, 19 February 1973, CHAN, 5AG2 117; Memcon Schumann/Peterson, 20 February 1973, MAE, U.S. files 1970–5, 731.

41. Shortly after Nixon's reelection, a White House official confirmed in a meeting with a French official that Nixon intended to go to Europe in early 1973 (Kosciusko-Morizet, telegram 8318-26, 1 December 1973, MAE, U.S. files 1970–5, 1136).

42. Memcon Pompidou/Willy Brandt, second meeting, 22 January 1973, CHAN, 5AG2 1012. Sonnenfeldt portrayed Brandt's proposal as identical to Monnet's approach (*Memorandum for Mr. Kissinger,* "Secretary Rogers on EC-U.S. dialogue," 2 February 1973, NPM, NSC, Subject files, 322). In fact, Monnet had initially suggested a meeting with the EC heads of state or government—as opposed to the EC Council of Foreign Ministers (Memcon Irwin/Monnet, 25 October 1972, NPM, NSC, Subject files, 322). In further conversations with van Helmont, however, Abraham Katz referred to Monnet's idea of a delegation comprised of the presidents of the EC Council of Ministers and of the European Commission (van Helmont, *Conversation VH/M. Abraham Katz/M. Petrow,* 15 November 1972, FJM, AMK 104/1/7).

43. Rogers, *Memorandum for the President,* "Brandt-Pompidou discussion of Nixon's expected trip to Europe," 1 February 1973, NPM, NSC, Subject files, 322.

44. Kissinger, *Years of Upheaval,* 148–49. On 29 March 1973, Kosciusko-Morizet informed Kissinger that Pompidou had agreed to meet Nixon (Memcon Kissinger/Kosciusko-Morizet, 29 March 1973, NPM, NSC, Henry A. Kissinger [HAK] files, Office files: Europe, 56).

45. Kissinger initially suggested Martinique. Pompidou rejected the idea because of the hot weather—a consideration probably related to his declining health—and because meeting on the island would have implied an official visit (Memcon Kissinger/Kosciusko-Morizet, 13 April 1973, NPM, NSC, HAK files, Office files: Europe, 56).

46. Memcon Kissinger/Kosciusko-Morizet, 29 March 1973, NPM, NSC, HAK files, Office files: Europe, 56.

47. Memcon Kissinger/Kosciusko-Morizet, 13 April 1973, NPM, NSC, HAK files, Office files: Europe, 56.

48. Memcon Kissinger/Jobert, 17 May 1973, NPM, NSC, HAK files, Office files: Europe, 56.

49. François de Rose, interview with the author, 30 April 2007. De Rose listed Kissinger among the few Americans with whom he struck a lifelong friendship.

50. Memcon Kissinger/Knud Børge Andersen, 25 September 1973, NPM, NSC, Presidential memcons, 1027.

51. Pascaline Winand, *Eisenhower, Kennedy, and the United States of Europe* (New York: St. Martin's Press, 1993), 149–52, 365–66.

52. Winand mentions Kissinger's "confession" to Jobert that he only finished writing his speech two days before delivering it (idem, "Loaded Words and Disputed Meanings," 309).

53. On this interpretation, see Rossbach, *Heath, Nixon and the Rebirth of the Special Relationship,* 146.

54. Telcon Kissinger/John Andrews, 17 April 1973, 9:30 A.M., NPM, NSC, Kissinger files, Telcons, 19.

55. Telcon Kissinger/Walter Stoessel, 19 April 1973, 9:52 A.M., NPM, NSC, Kissinger files, Telcons, 19.

56. Dallek, *Nixon and Kissinger,* 473.

57. Henry A. Kissinger, "Address at Associated Press Luncheon," *USA documents,* no. 26 (1973).

58. On the first Atlantic Charter, see Douglas Brinkley and David R. Facey-Crowther, eds., *The Atlantic Charter* (New York: St. Martin's Press, 1994).

59. Henry Kissinger, *The Troubled Partnership: A Re-Appraisal of the Atlantic Alliance* (Garden City, NY: Doubleday, 1966). On the 1960s roots of the Year of Europe speech, see Winand, "Loaded Words and Disputed Meanings," 299–302.

60. Kissinger, *The Troubled Partnership,* 241.

61. Soutou, "President Pompidou, Ostpolitik, and the Strategy of Détente," 238.

62. Soutou, "The Linkage between European Integration and Détente," 27.
63. Stephan Kieninger, "Transformation or Status Quo: The Conflict of Stratagems in Washington over the Meaning and Purpose of the CSCE and MBFR, 1969–1973," in *Helsinki 1975 and the Transformation of Europe*, ed. Oliver Bange and Gottfried Niedhart (New York: Berghahn Books, 2008), 71–72; Michael Cotey Morgan, "The United States and the Making of the Helsinki Final Act," in *Nixon in the World: American Foreign Relations, 1969–1977*, ed. Fredrik Logevall and Andrew Preston (Oxford and New York: Oxford University Press, 2008), 168.
64. Mélandri, "La France et l'Alliance atlantique sous Georges Pompidou et Valéry Giscard d'Estaing," 530.
65. Soutou, "La problématique de la détente et le testament stratégique de Georges Pompidou," 100.
66. Soutou, "President Pompidou, Ostpolitik, and the Strategy of Détente," 238; Rey, "Chancellor Brandt's *Ostpolitik*, France, and the Soviet Union," 124.
67. Soutou, "President Pompidou, Ostpolitik, and the Strategy of Détente," 241.
68. See MAE, Service des pactes et du désarmement, *Note*, 30 September 1971 MAE, U.S. files 1970–5, 733. Soutou, "President Pompidou, Ostpolitik, and the Strategy of Détente," 246.
69. Soutou, "President Pompidou, Ostpolitik, and the Strategy of Détente," 234.
70. Ibid.; Marie-Pierre Rey, "France and the German Question in the Context of Ostpolitik and the CSCE, 1969–1974," in Bange and Niedhart, *Helsinki 1975 and the Transformation of Europe*, 59–60.
71. On the U.S. stance, including disagreements between Nixon and Kissinger on the one hand and the State Department on the other, see Morgan, "The United States and the Making of the Helsinki Final Act"; Kieninger, "Transformation or Status Quo," 71–78.
72. Soutou, "President Pompidou, Ostpolitik, and the Strategy of Détente," 241, 245.
73. Ibid., 246.
74. Morgan, "The United States and the Making of the Helsinki Final Act," 170–71.
75. Bussière, "Georges Pompidou, les Etats-Unis et la crise du système monétaire international"; idem, "Georges Pompidou et la crise du système monétaire international," 83, 89–90, 97. On Pompidou's monetary policy, see also Gérard Bossuat, "Le président Georges Pompidou et les tentatives d'Union économique et monétaire," in Association Georges Pompidou, *Georges Pompidou et l'Europe*, 405–46.
76. Quoted in Bossuat, "Le président Georges Pompidou et les tentatives d'Union économique et monétaire," 427.
77. Bussière, "Georges Pompidou et la crise du système monétaire international," 83.
78. Frank Costigliola, *France and the United States: The Cold Alliance since World War II* (New York and Toronto: Twayne Publishers and Maxwell Macmillan, 1992), 173. On the role of monetary disagreements in the deterioration of Franco-American relations, see also Soutou, "Le président Pompidou et les relations entre les Etats-Unis et l'Europe," 129.
79. Bossuat, "Le président Georges Pompidou et les tentatives d'Union économique et monétaire," 425.
80. Marc Trachtenberg, "The French Factor in U.S. Foreign Policy During the Nixon-Pompidou Period, 1969–1974," *Journal of Cold War Studies* 13, no. 1 (2011): 24.
81. Jobert, interview, 18 September 1990, MAE, Archives orales (AO), Jobert.
82. Kosciusko-Morizet, telegram 2849-55, 23 April 1973, MAE, U.S. files 1970–5, 1137.
83. Kosciusko-Morizet, telegram 2885-98, 25 April 1973, MAE, U.S. files 1970–5, 1137.
84. *Résumé d'un entretien entre Jean Monnet et Henry Kissinger, 18 mai 1973*, FJM, AMK C 23/6/259.
85. *Résolutions adoptées par le Comité. Dix-huitième session*, 3 May 1973, FJM, AMK 104/1/16.

86. De Rose, telegram 861-70, 26 April 1973, MAE, U.S. files 1970–5, 1137.
87. De Rose, telegram 956-9, 10 May 1973, MAE, U.S. files 1970–5, 1137.
88. Jean Sauvagnargues, telegram 1998-2006, 26 April 1973, MAE, U.S. files 1970–5, 1137.
89. Kosciusko-Morizet, telegram 2954, 27 April 1973, MAE, U.S. files 1970–5, 1137.
90. Memcon Pompidou/Kissinger, 18 May 1973, CHAN, 5AG2 1022. Memcon Pompidou/ Edward Heath, first meeting, 21 May 1973, CHAN, 5AG2 1015.
91. Jean-Bernard Raimond, *Note pour Monsieur le président de la République*, 3 May 1973, CHAN, 5AG2 1021.
92. MAE, Direction des Affaires politiques, circular telegram 260, 28 April 1973, MAE, U.S. files 1970–5, 1137.
93. Kissinger, "Address at Associated Press Luncheon."
94. General de Gaulle used this phrase on several occasions, notably in his 23 July 1964 press conference at the Elysée Palace (Charles de Gaulle, *Discours et messages*, 5 vols. [Paris: Plon, 1970], vol. 4, 228.)
95. Kosciusko-Morizet, telegram 2885-98, 25 April 1973, MAE, U.S. files 1970–5, 1137.
96. MAE, Direction d'Amérique, *Note : projet de nouvelle charte atlantique*, 14 May 1973, MAE, U.S. files 1970–5, 727.
97. "La nouvelle charte atlantique dans la presse parisienne," *Le Monde*, 26 April 1973.
98. Ibid.
99. Jean Kanapa, "Non au plan Nixon de partage du monde !" *L'Humanité*, 26 April 1973.
100. Maurice Delarue, "Les Neuf ont ébauché les grandes lignes d'une politique de l'Europe vis-à-vis des Etats-Unis," *Le Monde*, 12 September 1973.
101. "La nouvelle charte atlantique dans la presse parisienne," *Le Monde*, 26 April 1973.
102. Kanapa, "Non au plan Nixon de partage du monde !"
103. "Editorial," *Combat*, 24 April 1973.
104. Michael A. Barnhart, "From Hershey Bars to Motor Cars: America's Economic Policy toward Japan, 1945–1976," in *Partnership: The United States and Japan, 1951–2001*, ed. Akira Iriye and Robert A. Wampler (Tokyo and New York: Kodansha International, 2001), 201–22; Thomas W. Zeiler, "Nixon Shocks Japan, Inc.," in Logevall and Preston, *Nixon in the World*, 289–308.
105. Yves Moreau, "Le néo-atlantisme," *L'Humanité*, 25 April 1973.
106. Headline, *Le Monde*, 25 April 1973.
107. "Editorial," *Combat*, 24 April 1973; "La nouvelle charte atlantique proposée par Washington," *Le Figaro*, 26 April 1973.
108. Jean-Pierre-Cornet, "La nouvelle 'charte atlantique' sera accueillie à Paris avec circonspection et avec plus de faveur à Londres et à Bonn," *Combat*, 25 April 1973.
109. Eric Roussel, *Jean Monnet, 1888–1979* (Paris: Fayard, 1996), 704–5.
110. Roger Massip, "Editorial," *Le Figaro*, 23 April 1973.
111. "Editorial," *Le Monde*, 25 April 1973.
112. Alain Clément, "Le temps des récriminations. I—Le partage du fardeau," *Le Monde*, 25 April 1973; idem, "Le temps des récriminations. II—L'empire céleste," *Le Monde*, 26 April 1973; idem, "Le temps des récriminations. III—Des messianiques fatigués," *Le Monde*, 27 April 1973.
113. Clément, "Le temps des récriminations. I."
114. Alexis de Tocqueville, *De la démocratie en Amérique* (Paris: C. Gosselin, 1835–1840).
115. Raymond Aron, "II. Du défi au déclin (14 mai 1973)," in *Les articles de politique internationale dans Le Figaro de 1947 à 1977*, 1212.
116. Aron, "I. L'heure de vérité (12–13 mai 1973)," in *Les articles de politique internationale dans Le Figaro de 1947 à 1977*, 1210.
117. Aron, "II. Du défi au déclin (14 mai 1973)," 1212.

118. See, for example, Mary Nolan, *Visions of Modernity: American Business and the Moderniza-tion of Germany* (New York: Oxford University Press, 1994); Emilio Gentile, "Modernity: Fascism and the Ambivalent Image of the United States," *Journal of Contemporary History* 28, no. 1 (1993): 7–29; Ruth Ben-Ghiat, *Fascist Modernities: Italy, 1922–1945* (Berkeley: University of California Press, 2001); Marjorie A. Beale, *The Modernist Enterprise: French Elites and the Threat of Modernity, 1900–1940* (Stanford, CA: Stanford University Press, 1999).

119. Kuisel, *Seducing the French;* Lacorne, Rupnik, and Toinet, *L'Amérique dans les têtes;* Roger, *L'ennemi américain;* Nolan, *Visions of Modernity.*

120. Raymond Aron, *Plaidoyer pour l'Europe décadente* (Paris: Robert Laffont, 1977); Alain de Benoist, *Vu de droite. Anthologie critique des idées contemporaines* (Paris: Copernic, 1977); Jean-Marie Benoist, *Pavane pour une Europe défunte. L'adieu aux technocrates* (Paris: Denoël-Gonthier, 1978); Henri Gobard, *La guerre culturelle. Logique du désastre* (Paris: Copernic, 1979); Jean-François Revel, *Ni Marx, ni Jésus. De la seconde révolution américaine à la seconde révolution mondiale* (Paris: Robert Laffont, 1970); Jacques Thibau, *La France colonisée* (Paris: Flammarion, 1980).

121. "Statement from the Paris Summit (October 1972)," *Bulletin of the European Communities,* no. 10 (1972): 14–26.

122. Hynes, *The Year That Never Was,* 107, 110–12, 144–45. On mixed reactions by British of-ficials, see also Noble, "Kissinger's Year of Europe, Britain's Year of Choice," 225. For an interpretation of Heath's Europeanism as shaped by the vision of a partnership between two equal pillars, see Rossbach, *Heath, Nixon and the Rebirth of the Special Relationship,* 122–60.

123. Quoted in Hamilton, "Britain, France, and America's Year of Europe, 1973," 877.

124. FCO, Planning Staff draft paper, 20 August 1973, quoted ibid., 873. FCO officials fre-quently used this metaphor to designate cross-issue linkages. See, for instance, FCO, Paris telegram 1112, 24 August 1973, doc. 205, in Hamilton, *Documents on British Policy Overseas. The Year of Europe;* FCO, Copenhagen telegram 417, 19 October 1973, doc. 308, ibid.; FCO, telegram 1196 to UKREP, 3 October 1973, doc. 241, ibid.; FCO, Washington telegram 612, 16 February 1974, doc. 555, ibid. On the British stance, see also Rossbach, *Heath, Nixon and the Rebirth of the Special Relationship,* 144, 150.

125. Kissinger, *Years of Upheaval,* 163.

126. Irwin, telegram 3409 to Secretary of State, 16 May 1973, NPM, NSC, VIP files, 949.

127. Flanigan, *Memorandum for the President,* "Pompidou meeting," 24 May 1973, NPM, NSC, VIP files, 949.

128. Kissinger, *Memorandum for the President,* "Meeting with French Foreign Minister Michel Jobert (Jo-Barie) ("Mr. Minister")," 29 June 1973, NPM, NSC, Country files, 679.

129. Memcon Kissinger/Pompidou, 18 May 1973, NPM, NSC, HAK files, Office files: Europe, 56.

130. Memcon Pompidou/Heath, first meeting, 21 May 1973, CHAN, 5AG2 1015.

131. MAE, *Note de synthèse : entretiens de Reykjavik, 31 mai — 1er juin 1973,* 18 May 1973, CHAN, 5AG2 1023.

132. Memcon Pompidou/Nixon, first meeting (with the participation of Kissinger), 31 May 1973, CHAN, 5AG2 1023.

133. Soutou, "Georges Pompidou et Valéry Giscard."

134. Soutou, "Le président Pompidou et les relations entre les Etats-Unis et l'Europe," 137.

135. Kissinger, *Memorandum for the President,* "Meeting with President Pompidou, Iceland," undated, NPM, NSC, VIP files, 949.

136. Memcon Pompidou/Nixon, second meeting, 31 May 1973, CHAN, 5AG2 1023.

137. On 2 June, Kissinger briefed U.S. diplomats, saying that that there would be bilateral

consultations between the United States, France, Britain and West Germany, and then a meeting at a higher level. Soon thereafter, Jobert lamented that the U.S. ambassador at Luxembourg had made it "seem like a French proposal to exclude others." Kissinger readily apologized and blamed the State Department bureaucracy: "To the extent that our ambassadors did this, they were wrong. Because your president made it clear he did not want to give the impression of exclusivity" (Memcon Kissinger/Jobert, 8 June 1973, NPM, NSC, HAK files, Office files: Europe, 56).

138. Memcon Pompidou/Nixon, second meeting, 31 May 1973, CHAN, 5AG2 1023. Kissinger told Belgian Political Director Etienne Davignon that the U.S. was "only using the bilateral approach tactically" (Memcon Kissinger/Davignon, 20 June 1973, NPM, NSC, HAK files, Office files: Europe, 54).

139. Memcons Kissinger/Kosciusko-Morizet, 29 March and 18 May 1973, NPM, NSC, HAK files, Office files: Europe, 56. Kissinger stated in June 1973 that the French government had had knowledge of the U.S.-Soviet talks since September 1972 (Kissinger, *Memorandum for the President*, "Meeting with French Foreign Minister Michel Jobert," 29 June 1973, NPM, NSC, Country files, 679). On 3 May, Kosciusko-Morizet was even shown the draft agreement and allowed to take notes (Memcon Sonnenfeldt/Kosciusko-Morizet, 3 May 1973, NPM, NSC, HAK files, Office files: Europe, 56).

140. Memcon Pompidou/Kissinger, 18 May 1973, NPM, NSC, HAK files, Office files: Europe, 56 / CHAN, 5AG2 1022.

141. Trachtenberg, "The French Factor in U.S. Foreign Policy During the Nixon-Pompidou Period, 1969–1974," 36.

142. On West German concerns about the agreement, see Hilfrich, "West Germany's Long Year of Europe," 239, note 8.

143. Memcon Kissinger/Kosciusko-Morizet, 18 May 1973, NPM, NSC, HAK files, Office files: Europe, 56. Letters from Nixon to Pompidou, 20 and 24 June 1973, CHAN, 5AG2 115. Hanhimäki states that Kissinger viewed the inclusion of obligations to third countries as a major victory: a bilateral accord on nonuse would have given the Soviets a free hand to use nuclear weapons against China or NATO members (Hanhimäki, *The Flawed Architect*, 509).

144. MAE, Service des pactes et du désarmement, *Note : accord entre les Etats-Unis et l'URSS sur la prévention de la guerre nucléaire*, 25 June 1973, MAE, Soviet Union (SU) files 1971–6, 3724; de Rose, telegram 1364-71, 25 June 1973, MAE, SU files 1971–6, 3724.

145. Kosciusko-Morizet, diplomatic dispatch 2139-42, 5 July 1973, MAE, SU files 1971–6, 3693.

146. Mélandri, "La France et l'Alliance atlantique sous Georges Pompidou et Valéry Giscard d'Estaing," 526.

147. Memcon Jobert/Kissinger, 8 June 1973, MAE, Secrétariat général, 2.

148. On the submission of the texts to the FCO, see Hynes, *The Year That Never Was*, 148–49, 156.

149. Kissinger, *Memorandum for the President*, "Meeting with French Foreign Minister Michel Jobert," 29 June 1973, NPM, NSC, Country files, 679.

150. Memcon Jobert/Nixon, 29 June 1973, MAE, Secrétariat général, 2.

151. Jobert to Kissinger, 16 July 1973, NPM, NSC, HAK files, Office files: Europe, 56. Raimond was also critical of the U.S. drafts, and the NSC document in particular (Raimond, *Note pour Monsieur le président de la République : documents remis par M. Jobert à son retour des Etats-Unis*, 4 July 1973, CHAN, 5AG2 1021).

152. Memcon Kissinger/La Gorce, 16 July 1973, NPM, NSC, HAK files, Office files: Europe, 56.

153. Memcon Kissinger/Jobert, 8 June 1973, NPM, NSC, HAK files, Office files: Europe, 56.

154. Memcon Kissinger/Davignon, 20 June 1973, NPM, NSC, HAK files, Office files: Europe, 54.
155. "Je ne crois pas que l'on puisse parler politique, avec pour finalité la défense, alors que nous n'avons pas encore réussi à faire un pas en avant dans le domaine de l'union économique et monétaire" (Memcon Pompidou/Heath, first meeting, 21 May 1973, CHAN, 5AG2 1015).
156. Möckli, *European Foreign Policy During the Cold War*, 151–52, 154. On Brandt's desire to foster EPC, see also Hilfrich, "West Germany's Long Year of Europe," 132.
157. Hilfrich, "West Germany's Long Year of Europe," 243.
158. Ibid., 238.
159. Werner Link, "Aussen- und Deutschlandpolitik in der Ära Brandt, 1960–1974," in *Republik im Wandel, 1969–1974. Die Ära Brandt*, ed. Karl Dietrich Bracher, Wolfgang Jäger, and Werner Link (Stuttgart and Mannheim: Deutsche Verlags-Anstalt and F.A. Brockhaus, 1986–1987), 241, 243. On the importance of European integration in Brandt's foreign policy, see Helga Grebing, Gregor Schöllgen, and Heinrich August Winkler, eds., *Willy Brandt. Berliner Ausgabe*, 10 vols. (Bonn: Dietz, 2000–2009), vol. 6, 22–25.
160. MAE, political director [François Puaux], *Note : relations entre l'Europe et les Etats-Unis*, 18 January 1973, MAE, U.S. files 1970–5, 1137.
161. MAE, Direction d'Europe, circular telegram 254, 26 April 1973, MAE, U.S. files 1970–5, 1137.
162. MAE, Deputy Political Director [Claude Arnaud], *Note : l'Europe et les Etats-Unis, thème d'échange de vues dans le cadre de la coopération politique*, 28 March 1973, MAE, U.S. files 1970–5, 1137.
163. MAE, Direction d'Europe, circular telegram 320, 30 May 1973, MAE, EC files 1971–6, 3810.
164. *RM/RC (73): VIIe réunion ministérielle, Luxembourg, 5 juin 1973—relevé de conclusions*, MAE, EC files 1971–6, 3792.
165. MAE, Direction d'Europe, circular telegram 415, 10 July 1973, MAE, EC files 1971–6, 3792.
166. Hamilton, "Britain, France, and America's Year of Europe, 1973," 880.
167. FCO, minute, Crispin Tickell to Charles Wiggins, 18 June 1973, doc. 129, in Hamilton, *Documents on British Policy Overseas. The Year of Europe*.
168. FCO, minute, Douglas-Home to Heath, 18 June 1973, doc. 130, ibid.
169. FCO, Cabinet minutes, 20 June 1973, doc. 137, ibid.
170. FCO, Cabinet minutes, 20 June 1973, doc. 137, ibid.
171. Memcon Paul Frank/Brimelow, 17 August 1973, in Ilse Dorothee Pautsch, ed. *Akten zur Auswärtigen Politik der Bundesrepublik Deutschland 1973*, 3 vols. (Munich: Oldenbourg, 2004), vol. 2, 1270–73.
172. Memcon Walter Scheel/Kissinger, 12 July 1973, ibid., 1143–46.
173. Möckli, *European Foreign Policy During the Cold War*, 163; Claudia Hiepel, "Kissinger's 'Year of Europe'—a Challenge for the EC and the Franco-German Relationship," in van der Harst, *Beyond the Customs Union*, 277–96.
174. MAE, political director [Puaux], *Note pour le ministre : Europe-Etats-Unis*, 20 August 1973, MAE, EC files 1971–6, 3810. Jobert's delaying tactics did not escape the attention of FCO officials (FCO, telegram 1528 to Washington, 24 July 1973, doc. 167, in Hamilton, *Documents on British Policy Overseas. The Year of Europe: America, Europe and the Energy Crisis, 1972–1974*.
175. FCO, telegram 1528 to Washington, 24 July 1973, doc. 167, ibid.
176. MAE, Direction d'Europe, circular telegram 446, 24 July 1973, MAE, EC files 1971–6, 3810.

177. "Statement from the Paris Summit (October 1972)"; Raimond, *Note pour Monsieur le président de la République*, 4 July 1973, CHAN, 5AG2 1021.
178. Quoted in Hynes, *The Year That Never Was*, 158–59.
179. La Gorce, telegram 4549-59, 21 July 1973, MAE, U.S. files 1970–5, 1137; François Lucet, telegram 2057-66, 25 July 1973, MAE, U.S. files 1970–5, 1137.
180. Quoted in Kissinger, *Years of Upheaval*, 191.
181. Record of meeting Kissinger/Sir Burke Trend, 30 July 1973, doc. 179, in Hamilton, *Documents on British Policy Overseas. The Year of Europe*.
182. Quoted in Jacques Jacquet-Francillon, "Signature demain à Bruxelles de la nouvelle 'charte atlantique': Nixon se fait consacrer leader de l'Occident avant de rencontrer Brejnev à Moscou," *Le Figaro*, 26 June 1974.
183. Kissinger, *Years of Upheaval*, 186.
184. Record of meeting Kissinger/Trend, 30 July 1973, doc. 179, in Hamilton, *Documents on British Policy Overseas. The Year of Europe*.
185. Memcon Frank/Sir Nicholas Henderson, 6 August 1973, in Pautsch, *Akten zur Auswärtigen Politik der Bundesrepublik Deutschland 1973*, vol.2, 1211–14.
186. Letter from Brandt to Heath, 7 August 1973, ibid., 1214–16.
187. FCO, Bonn telegram 876, 9 August 1973, doc. 197, in Hamilton, *Documents on British Policy Overseas. The Year of Europe*.
188. Letter from Brandt to Pompidou, 7 August 1973, in Pautsch, *Akten zur Auswärtigen Politik der Bundesrepublik Deutschland 1973*, vol. 2, 1251–52.
189. MAE, political director [Puaux], *Note : rapports Europe-Etats-Unis*, 11 August 1973, MAE, EC files 1971–6, 3810.
190. MAE, Direction des Affaires politiques, circular telegram 504, 31 August 1973, MAE, U.S. files 1970–5, 1137.
191. Quoted in Hynes, *The Year That Never Was*, 192.
192. MAE, political director [Puaux], *Note : entretien avec M. Ewart-Biggs—relations Europe-Etats-Unis*, 9 August 1973, MAE, U.S. files 1970–5, 1137; FCO, telegram 189 to Copenhagen, 8 August 1973, doc. 192, in Hamilton, *Documents on British Policy Overseas. The Year of Europe*; FCO paper, undated, doc. 193, in Hamilton, *Documents on British Policy Overseas. The Year of Europe*.
193. FCO, Bonn telegram 895, 17 August 1973, doc. 200, in Hamilton, *Documents on British Policy Overseas. The Year of Europe*.
194. FCO, Paris telegram 1092, 20 August 1973, doc. 201, ibid.
195. FCO, Paris telegram 1093, 20 August 1973, doc. 202, ibid.
196. FCO, telegram 637 to Paris, 24 August 1973, doc. 206, ibid.
197. Michel Jobert, *Mémoires d'avenir* (Paris: Grasset, 1974), 245.
198. Möckli, *European Foreign Policy During the Cold War*, 160.
199. MAE, director for European affairs [Emmanuel de Margerie], *Note : rapports Europe-Etats-Unis. Vues italiennes*, 27 August 1973, MAE, U.S. files 1970–5, 1137.
200. MAE, director for European affairs [Margerie], *Note : relations Europe Etats-Unis : réflexions du Foreign Office et document britannique*, 27 August 1973, MAE, U.S. files 1970–5, 1137; FCO, Paris telegram 1122, 28 August 1973, doc. 210, in Hamilton, *Documents on British Policy Overseas. The Year of Europe*.
201. MAE, political director [Puaux], *Note : entretien avec M. Ewart-Biggs—relations Europe-Etats-Unis*, 9 August 1973, MAE, U.S. files 1970–5, 1137.
202. MAE, political director [Puaux], *Note : rapports Europe Etats-Unis. Remarques sur les vues anglaises et italiennes*, 27 August 1973, MAE, U.S. files 1970–5, 1137.
203. FCO, telegram 640 to Paris, 27 August 1973, doc. 209, in Hamilton, *Documents on British Policy Overseas. The Year of Europe*.

204. Memcon Jobert/Brimelow, 29 August 1973, MAE, EC files 1971–6, 3810; FCO, Paris telegram 1126, 29 August 1973, doc. 212, in Hamilton, *Documents on British Policy Overseas. The Year of Europe.*
205. FCO, telegram 649 to Paris, 1 September 1973, doc. 215, in Hamilton, *Documents on British Policy Overseas. The Year of Europe.*
206. FCO, Paris telegram 1146, 3 September 1973, doc. 216, ibid.
207. Frank, record of conversation with Jobert, 31 August 1973, in Pautsch, *Akten zur Auswärtigen Politik der Bundesrepublik Deutschland 1973*, vol.2, 1325–29.
208. MAE, Direction des Affaires politiques to French embassy (Ambafrance) in Copenhagen, telegram 210, 6 September 1973, MAE, EC files 1971–6, 3810.
209. MAE, Direction des Affaires politiques, circular telegram 511, 6 September 1973, MAE, U.S. files 1970–5, 1137.
210. Jacques Morizet, telegram 2139-42, 7 September 1973, MAE, U.S. files 1970–5, 1137.
211. MAE, Direction des Affaires politiques, circular telegram 523, 12 September 1973, MAE, EC files 1971–6, 3792.
212. MAE, Direction des Affaires politiques, circular telegram 520, 12 September 1973, MAE, EC files 1971–6, 3792.
213. Irwin, telegram to Kissinger, 7 September 1973, NPM, NSC, HAK files, Office files: Europe, 56.
214. Memcon Kissinger/Andersen, 25 September 1973, NPM, NSC, Presidential memcons, 1027; *RM (73) 16 3ᵉ rev.: Outline for a Declaration of Principles between the United States of America and the European Community and its Member States*, Copenhagen, 17 September 1973, MAE, EC files 1971–6, 3792.
215. Record of meeting Kissinger/Trend, 30 July 1973, doc. 179, in Hamilton, *Documents on British Policy Overseas. The Year of Europe.*
216. Ibid.
217. Ibid.; Kissinger, *Memorandum for the President*, "Talk with French chargé," 31 July 1973, NPM, NSC, HAK files, Office files: Europe, 56; Irwin, telegram to Kissinger, 7 September 1973, NPM, NSC, HAK files, Office files: Europe, 56.
218. Sonnenfeldt, *Memorandum for Mr. Kissinger*, "Copenhagen meeting on the Year of Europe," 11 September 1973, NPM, NSC, Subject files, 409.
219. Sonnenfeldt, *Memorandum for Mr. Kissinger*, "Year of Europe," 20 September 1973, NPM, NSC, Country files, 679.
220. Charles A. Cooper, *Memorandum for Mr. Kissinger*, "Draft declaration of principles," 21 September 1973, NPM, NSC, Subject files, 322.
221. *RM [73] 16 3ᵉ rev.: Outline for a Declaration of Principles between the United States of America and the European Community and its Member States*, Copenhagen, 17 September 1973, MAE, EC files 1971–6, 3810.
222. GATT, *GATT Activities in 1973.*
223. FCO, telegram 189 to Copenhagen, 8 August 1973, doc. 192, in Hamilton, *Documents on British Policy Overseas. The Year of Europe.*
224. "Statement from the Paris Summit (October 1972)."
225. *RM [73] 16 3ᵉ rev.: Outline for a Declaration of Principles between the United States of America and the European Community and its Member States.*
226. Ibid.
227. Memcon Kissinger/Andersen, 25 September 1973, NPM, NSC, Presidential memcons, 1027.
228. Memcon Kissinger/Jobert, 26 September 1973, NPM, NSC, Country files, 679.
229. Record of meeting Kissinger/Trend, 30 July 1973, doc. 179, in Hamilton, *Documents on British Policy Overseas. The Year of Europe.*

230. Kissinger, *Years of Upheaval*, 165.
231. Jean-Jacques Servan-Schreiber, *Le défi américain* (Paris: Denoël, 1967).
232. Möckli, *European Foreign Policy During the Cold War*, 160.
233. FCO, telegram 640 to Paris, 27 August 1973, doc. 209, in Hamilton, *Documents on British Policy Overseas. The Year of Europe.*
234. FCO, telegram 2409 to Washington, 3 December 1973, doc. 433, ibid.
235. Soutou, "Le président Pompidou et les relations entre les Etats-Unis et l'Europe," 138–39; idem, "La problématique de la détente et le testament stratégique de Georges Pompidou," 105–7.
236. Trachtenberg, "The French Factor in U.S. Foreign Policy During the Nixon-Pompidou Period, 1969–1974," 40.
237. Ibid., 39.

Chapter 2

CONSTRUCTING A EUROPEAN IDENTITY

Kissinger had envisioned a single overarching charter, but the Year of Europe provoked the drafting of three documents: a declaration pertaining to EC-U.S. relations, another to the identity of the EC and its member states, and a third to NATO. The draft EC-U.S. statement instigated bitter rifts between the United States and the EC Nine, especially France. The painstaking negotiation process that took place in the fall of 1973 speaks to the potency of words. These talks may have begun to "look surreal" against the background of the transatlantic strife caused by the Yom Kippur War.[1] The fact that in this context neither side seemed willing to let go of the declarations demonstrates the importance of language as a tool for legitimation in international politics.

Competing visions of European unity lay at the root of this controversy. Since the 1950s, the U.S. government had welcomed political union among its allies. Ultimately, however, senior U.S. officials were not prepared to accept the consequences of a political Europe. Kissinger and Nixon could not tolerate a united Europe that might differ from, and even contradict, U.S. views.[2] This was not lost on French decision-makers, who interpreted the Americans' amendments to the EC draft as proof of their intentions to strengthen U.S. leadership in Western Europe. Intra-EC and U.S.-EC talks prompted French officials to articulate and assert more forcefully their vision of Europe as a world actor. They did so using ideas both old and new: de Gaulle's notion of a European Europe and the new concept of a European identity. Although the Year of Europe acted as a catalyst for the popularization of this latter concept, governmental actors and press commentators went beyond a defensive use of the term, imbuing it with broader meaning. The task of defining European identity in a common EC document underwent a similar transformative process. French officials, who played a leading role in drafting this text, originally thought of it in defensive terms. The Declaration on European Identity, published in December 1973, broke new ground in affirming the building blocks of the emerging European polity.

Restructuring the West: Bilateral and Trilateral Statements

Despite his qualms about the EC draft, Kissinger proved willing to build upon it. The delicate diplomatic dance between the EC Nine and the United States entered a new phase on 29 September, when the Nixon administration submitted its proposed amendments. The ensuing talks demonstrated that officials on both sides of the Atlantic, particularly in Paris and Washington, were acutely aware of the symbolic value of this declaration exercise. Each party brought various resources to bear upon the bargaining game in order to impose not only its preferred phrasing in the EC-U.S. statement but also its favored set of related declarations: bilateral statements with the other two major industrialized countries, Japan and Canada, or a trilateral U.S.-Europe-Japan declaration. They invested time in this project because they knew that different wordings could help to legitimize competing geopolitical visions. U.S. officials were anxious to underscore not only transatlantic cohesion and interdependencies, but also "the essentially trilateral nature of maintaining an orderly world economy."[3] Their French counterparts opposed what they perceived as a discourse of domination. What the Nixon administration wished to impose, they argued, was a geopolitical order in which Western European states would play second fiddle. Consequently, they pushed for the international assertion of the European entity vis-à-vis not only the United States but also the rest of the industrialized world.

The EC-U.S. talks reflected three main negotiation positions. The Nixon administration sought to reintroduce the key tenets of the Year of Europe. The Quai d'Orsay opposed the proposed U.S. modifications straight out, while the FCO did its best to act as mediator. The U.S. amendments re-established Atlantic unity as a central theme of the declaration, with an emphasis on an Atlantic "partnership." They also underscored the notion of "interdependence." A new paragraph asserted the signatories' conviction that "their relationships in all spheres [we]re mutually interdependent, and that the challenges and opportunities of the future can be most effectively met jointly by policies and actions based on a spirit of partner-ship."[4] There were also several references to defense matters. Pompidou, however, was loath to compromise: "We must be very firm: in short, these amendments are unacceptable, and we will not accept them."[5] French officials made it clear that they would reject the U.S. changes because they implied a European "allegiance" to the United States.[6] They justified their stance by equating their opposition with the defense of Europe's genuine interests. "I hardly needed to join this resolutely European chorus," Puaux stated while reporting that his EC colleagues had backed him.[7] In striking a middle ground, the FCO hoped to reconcile its traditional commitment to the Anglo-American relationship with its new dedication to European unity. FCO officials analyzed the proposed U.S. modifications as "not unreasonable," even if "one or two" went "rather too far."[8] They recommended accepting as many as possible, so long as they were consistent with British views and with achieving an agreement among the EC Nine.[9]

Expecting "the French" to be "the main problem," the FCO proved willing to go a long way toward meeting their concerns.[10] So did other EC states. Therefore, the revised EC draft made no use of such key U.S. concepts as "partnership," "interdependence" and "Atlantic community."[11] It did not mention the MBFR talks, in which France still refused to participate, and merely alluded to strategic matters based on the formula enshrined in the 1972 Paris statement.[12] Furthermore, the brief for the acting Danish president of the Political Committee stated that EC states' bilateral contacts with the United States would increasingly rest on "common positions they have reached à Neuf."[13] In line with French misgivings about institutionalized EC-U.S. ties, it asserted the EC Nine's opposition to any new "procedure" or "machinery." The Quai d'Orsay had insisted that the word "machinery" be added. Clearly, it wanted to leave nothing to chance. Mirroring shared concerns over the "globalization" of transatlantic negotiations, the brief also rejected any language that implied a negotiating link between economic and military issues. The EC Nine, it added, preferred leaving security matters out of the EC-U.S. statement—still a more cautious phrasing than the Quai d'Orsay would have liked.

On the surface, the ensuing EPC-U.S. talks proceeded smoothly. U.S. officials assumed a cooperative stance. British and West German officials commented on the friendly atmosphere of the political directors' meeting with Stoessel and Sonnenfeldt in mid October.[14] The FCO gave much of the credit to the U.S. envoys. They had accepted "with regret but without recrimination and ad referendum" the rejection of their linkage approach and of their proposed institutionalization of EC-U.S. relations. They had refrained from "press[ing] too hard for words like 'partnership' and 'interdependence.'"[15] But this friendly appearance hid a less cheerful reality. In late October, Kissinger bluntly told the West German ambassador that he was "bored" with the declaration. He was even unsure that it was worth further consideration.[16] Shortly thereafter, Britain's U.S. Ambassador Lord Roger Cromer warned against underestimating the U.S. determination to put "more substance" and "some more inspired wording" into the draft.[17] He suggested injecting new thoughts into it. His advice, however, went unheeded. After an EPC-U.S. meeting in mid November, Puaux satisfactorily reported that his EC colleagues had done little to accommodate the United States.[18] By the end of the month, Kissinger had openly stated his dissatisfaction with both procedure and content. EC states, he complained, let France set the tone.[19] The declaration had been drained of both substance and "emotional content."[20]

Hoping to have the French stance fully represented, Jobert thought of putting together an accommodating NATO document. The goal was to have the Nixon administration "swallow" the EC-U.S. draft, which "essentially conveyed the message," namely, the unity of the EC Nine vis-à-vis the United States.[21] In early September, Jobert secretly instructed de Rose to draft a text that would meet and possibly outdo U.S. expectations.[22] With help from aide Pierre Caraud, de Rose promptly put pen to paper. Jobert endorsed his draft after securing Pompidou's approval during their China trip in September 1973. While translating it, de Rose borrowed wording from the June 1973 NSC draft declaration in order to make it more appealing to the U.S. government.

Kissinger suggested that the U.S. government was very pleased with France's NATO draft in his meeting with Jobert on 26 September.[23] U.S. records, however, tell a more nuanced story.[24] The text went some way toward meeting U.S. concerns.[25] It proclaimed the indivisibility of allied security and committed the European members of NATO to maintaining an adequate defense capability. Nonetheless, it also reasserted the cardinal principles of the French security policy, some of which the U.S. government had yet to endorse—notably, the "specificity" of European defense and the French and British nuclear forces' contribution to Allied deterrence. The draft further contained a veiled allusion to the risk of a U.S.-Soviet condominium. The United States, it stated, was determined to oppose any situation that would expose its allies to "external political or military pressures likely to deprive them of their freedom." More problematically, as Kissinger wrote to Jobert, the draft failed to address such central issues as the MBFR, burden-sharing, and inter-allied consultation.[26] The NSC staff nonetheless recommended using it as a basis for discussion because it had "the great advantage of coming from the leading NATO dissident."[27] Sonnenfeldt believed that in due time other NATO members would raise all the issues that mattered to the United States. Initially, Kissinger reserved the right to submit a separate draft, but he did not follow suit.[28] NATO members therefore decided to work from the French draft.[29] On 11 October, Kissinger went so far as to praise Jobert for a text that "really was better than anything we could produce."[30] Kissinger's rhetoric should not be taken at face value. Given his misgivings about the text, it is questionable that "the French maneuver had its share in persuading the U.S. to let the [EC] Nine have their own declaration."[31] If the French move had any influence, it was minor.

Talk of associating Japan with the Year of Europe proved more divisive. The French and the U.S. governments found themselves once more at cross-purposes. Mindful of Japan's economic rise, the Nixon administration wanted to rebalance its set of economic and security interrelationships with its Eastern ally. A trilateral approach could serve this purpose by enabling the United States to draw links between security and economic matters in concurrent negotiations.[32] Given strained U.S.-Japanese relations, U.S. officials were also keen to meet Japanese expectations. Their French counterparts, however, disapproved of trilateralism in all its forms, seeing it as yet another way for the United States to strengthen its leadership in, and even to assert its hegemony over, the West.[33] Pompidou made it clear in a conversation with Brandt: "We are categorically opposed to the Kissinger doctrine of a triangle or a circle including Japan."[34]

Significantly, the Quai d'Orsay turned to EPC to defeat such trilateral designs. On the whole, EC states were reluctant to involve the United States in their relationship with Japan.[35] Many, however, wished to associate the Japanese to the Year of Europe.[36] In mid September, the FCO floated a proposal for a bilateral declaration between the EC Nine and Japan.[37] The Quai d'Orsay actively supported it. The Political Committee soon put together a draft, which the Danish EC presidency submitted to the Japanese government in November 1973.[38] The EC Nine's démarche prompted U.S. criticisms of lack of consultation.[39] Kissinger censured "a deliberate Franco-British attempt to forge European unity by distancing Europe from the U.S."[40] Japanese reactions were mixed.[41] The Japanese government clearly preferred a trilateral approach. As early as September, it had presented a draft for a trilateral statement.[42] In an attempt to win it over, Margerie suggested making a parallel offer to Canada. The EC Nine, he argued, could leverage on the Japanese fears of being overtaken by the Canadians.[43] Margerie's arguments struck a chord with Quai officials. In subsequent months, Jobert and Puaux lobbied for an EC-Canada declaration.[44] They would relax their efforts only after the shelving of the EC-U.S. statement.[45]

The French NATO draft and its push for EC-Japan/Canada statements demonstrated France's new commitment to EPC. Jobert and his staff were now determined to push through the EC-U.S. statement. Their hope was that "with a good document on defense, the rest would go through."[46] Instead of straight-out excluding Japan from the declaration exercise, they went for a bilateral EPC approach to Japan, thus further asserting the status of the European entity as a world actor. This shift was not lost on the FCO. "During the summer meetings of political directors," an FCO official reported, "he [Puaux] had to be heavily sedated at night to get any sleep at all. He is now an enthusiast for political cooperation and an advocate of it in Paris."[47] Jobert hardly needed any convincing. Many years later, de Rose portrayed him as both an ego-sensitive individual ("un coq dressé sur ses ergots") who was painfully aware of France's diminishing world role and an astute politician ("un fin politique").[48] The French strategy in the fall of 1973, and particularly the NATO draft, demonstrated Jobert's ability to temper his dogmatic rigidity with a dose of pragmatism, but it stumbled upon external opposition. The Japanese remained supportive of a trilateral approach. The French NATO draft did not go far enough to mollify the Nixon administration. Kissinger remained determined to have a "substantial" EC-U.S. statement,[49] as opposed to the "pallid" draft as it now stood.[50] On 11 December, he would request a shorter, more "punchy" and more "eloquent" statement.[51]

A War of Words and Ideas

The talks over the proposed EC-U.S. statement were painstaking, but there was more to the debate than "legalistic" squabbling.[52] The U.S. amendments prompted French officials and press commentators to articulate more cogently their concept of a European world actor. They also compelled Pompidou's government to reaffirm its opposition to a potential linkage strategy. In so doing, French officials disseminated a neologism, "globalization [*globalisation*]"—one that had a different, although related, meaning from its present-day use.

Franco-U.S. disagreements centered around a series of words, notably "partnership" and "interdependence." "Partnership" had long been a contentious word in Franco-U.S. relations. John F. Kennedy's call of 4 July 1962 for an "Atlantic partnership"—reiterated in his 1963 address in the Frankfurt Assembly Hall—had aroused suspicions in Paris.[53] Kennedy had prefaced his proposal by reaffirming the U.S. support for European integration.[54] He had taken great care to stress that such partnership would rest on a basis of "full equality." De Gaulle, however, was unconvinced.[55] Monnet's advance backing of the plan did nothing to help. In June 1962, his Action Committee had called for "a partnership among equals between the United States and Europe." Such partnership, it stated, was a prerequisite for peaceful relations between East and West.[56] Because of his integrationist bent, however, Monnet did not have de Gaulle's ear. A decade later, Pompidou's government was still reluctant to enter into an alliance "between wolf and sheep."[57] Pompidou disliked the word "partnership." "I certainly do not want it," he wrote in the margins of a report.[58] "Partnership" had no equivalent in French, but the FCO proved overoptimistic when it suggested using it in English while translating it in French as "close cooperation [*coopération étroite*]".[59] The Quai d'Orsay petitioned its EC partners to expunge all lexical variants of the term from the U.S. amendments in both English and French.[60]

French opposition to this concept was rooted in an awareness of power asymmetries. To Quai officials, there could only be a meaningful partnership between two equal partners, and in the context of U.S.-European relations, the equality of the two partners remained elusive.[61] They agreed with Monnet that European integration would make it possible, but this still was a long-term prospect. Meanwhile, "Europe" would "tag along behind its powerful American 'partner.'"[62] Etienne Burin des Roziers, the French permanent representative to the EC, took this reasoning one step further. The terms "partnership" and "Atlantic community," he claimed, implied a way of thinking that contradicted the French policy line: use of the terms presupposed a U.S. desire to reduce the EC to a docile ally.[63]

"Interdependence," an increasingly popular construct in U.S. political circles and academia, proved just as divisive. The ascendancy of this concept in the 1970s reflected concerns over waning U.S. power. NSSM 164 used the term to describe a situation in which industrialized countries were increasingly dependent upon one another and contacts between them reached "far beyond intergovernmental cooperation."[64] Harvard Professors Robert Keohane and Joseph Nye subsequently defined "complex interdependence" as an ideal type characterized by numerous channels of communication, including informal ties among governmental elites, lack of hierarchy between negotiation topics, and reduced usability of force.[65] Keohane and Nye recognized that asymmetries conferred initial bargaining advantages on the less dependent actor. Nevertheless, their argument implied that interdependence reduced the ability of the superpowers to influence outcomes based on their military superiority.[66]

French officials, by contrast, interpreted "interdependence" as denoting European subordination. Puaux considered it an "ambiguous" term.[67] Connecting the two concepts of interdependence and partnership, Burin des Roziers maintained that they laid the basis for strengthened U.S. dominance in Western Europe. At stake was nothing less than the EC's "independence."[68] "For the United States," he stated, "this year is the 'year of Europe': we had no reason to make it the 'year of America.'" Burin des

Roziers was certainly among those who thought that the adjective "interdependent" could be interpreted as "I depend, you rule."[69] French dailies were similarly suspicious of the term. *Le Figaro* praised the government's efforts to resist growing U.S.-European "interdependence" and thereby assert "Europe's personality."[70] Likewise, the communist left cast transatlantic interdependence and European independence as antagonistic concepts.[71]

Governing officials coined the word "globalization [*globalisation*]" to designate a related concern: cross-issue linkage bargaining, particularly between economic and defense topics. For some time they had criticized the U.S. intent to pursue multi-topic transatlantic negotiations, but they did not use the term "globalization" until after Kissinger's Year of Europe speech. I found its first occurrence in a Quai circular telegram dated 26 April 1973. Chastising the United States for its "globalization intentions," this telegram stated—as the Quai d'Orsay would in numerous other instances—that trade, currency, and defense issues were best discussed within separate, specialized institutions: GATT, the IMF, and NATO.[72] French misgivings were not wholly unfounded.[73] The Nixon-Kissinger team disapproved of the tough stance advocated by officials in the Department of Commerce and the Department of the Treasury. Nevertheless, recalibration of the U.S.-European interrelationships was one of the main objectives of the Year of Europe.[74]

The September 1973 agreement on a new GATT round hardly modified this agenda, even if the devaluation-induced improvement in the U.S. balance of payments soon reduced the urgency of new trade and monetary agreements.[75] Discussing the U.S. amendments, Quai officials repelled any language that could imply a negotiating link between economic and defense issues. They also insisted that any reference to security belonged to the NATO declaration: the EC-U.S. statement should deal solely with economic and political matters.[76] French officials were not alone in criticizing the linkage intention of the Nixon administration.[77] Their British counterparts often criticized its "one ball of wax" approach[78] and, on occasion, used a lexical variant of the new French word: "globalize," "globalization."[79] The English word "globalization" was first used in 1961, but it would not gain wider currency until the mid 1980s. It is an interesting finding that its 1980s popularization had roots reaching back to Paris in the 1970s, even though the term was then ascribed a different, albeit connected, meaning: the linkage of multiple policy fields, as opposed to the process of growing worldwide ties in the economic, cultural, social, technological, and political fields. The French would later introduce a different term to designate this process of increasing world interconnectedness: *mondialisation*.[80]

The institutionalization of EC-U.S. relations was another contentious issue. Since the early 1970s, the Nixon administration had called for a more formalized consultation framework. The two-stage process by which the EC Nine had agreed on a draft prior to submitting it to Kissinger had given the matter added urgency. One of the proposed U.S. amendments was designed to prevent this scenario from occurring again. It provided for "consultative and cooperative arrangements" between the United States and the EC/EPC.[81] In a December 1973 speech, Kissinger reiterated the U.S. wish to have "frank consultations" on issues affecting U.S. interests "*before*[82] final decisions are taken by the Community."[83] He prefaced his demand by saying that the United States had "no intention of becoming a tenth member of the Community," but to no avail. Any institutionalized EC-U.S. ties, Pompidou told Brandt, meant granting the United States the status of a "censor" and even that of an "additional [EC] commissioner."[84] In a similar vein, Burin des Roziers maintained that any institutionalized cooperation would place the EC under U.S. "tutelage."[85] To Kosciusko-Morizet, the two-stage procedure used by the EC Nine to put together the draft declaration was essential for the self-assertion of "Europe."[86]

Competing visions of Euro-American relations shaped and, in turn, fueled this battle of words. French officials dreamed of an equal power relation between Western Europe and the United States. Their U.S. counterparts thought of the Atlantic Alliance as ultimately U.S.-led. In crystallizing such disagreements, this verbal feud encouraged dichotomous thinking in both Paris and Washington. U.S. officials endeavored to buttress their stance through mutually exclusive categories: Atlantic cohesion versus Atlantic disunity. In September 1973, Kissinger urged EC leaders to decide whether they wished to build "Europe" at the expense of Atlantic relations or wanted instead to strengthen the transatlantic relationship.[87] Richard T. Kennedy from the NSC staff argued against such stark binary thinking. France's EC partners, he stated, favored a third way, namely, an "autonomous" Europe within the framework of the Atlantic Alliance.[88] In his December report to the president, Kissinger, however, was even blunter: "Clearly our recent tough talk has had its impact and we can expect the Europeans to curb their impulse to show their 'identity' by kicking us."[89] Future National Security Advisor Brent Scowcroft, who was then serving as Kissinger's deputy in the State Department, advocated an accommodating gesture, namely, recognizing that European unity would "manifest itself by a growing distinctness from the U.S."[90] But he added this telling caveat: "[we] think it in the long run destructive both of genuine European unity and, obviously, Atlantic cohesion if European distinctness is made synonymous with a pattern of opposition to the U.S."[91] French officials and the press made use of their own set of binary categories: an Atlantic and a European Europe. Puaux used them to analyze his EC counterparts' stance on the U.S. amendments.[92] *Le Monde* reckoned that setting a "European Europe" against an "American Europe" was an oversimplification. "[But] just as a good caricature reduces the human physiognomy to its essentials," it stated, "this [formula] brought into sharp focus the terms of the debate."[93]

Words are potent political tools. They mobilize, legitimize, and lay the basis for change. The multifarious functions of language explain why a seemingly innocuous declaration of intent became so conflict-ridden. Some of the proposed U.S. modifications had practical implications, representing the possible institutionalization of an EC/EPC-U.S. dialogue. Others did not, but the FCO was mistaken in hoping to convince the French to "lean in the direction of accepting U.S. amendments unless undesirable practical results would flow from doing so."[94] Words gave meaning to and legitimized entrenched or changing power relations and economic interdependencies. French officials fought against such words as "partnership" and "interdependence" because they saw them as fostering U.S. domination over Western Europe and hence France. They would in turn use language to try to impose a competing vision. This endeavor brought the term "European identity" to the forefront of French political vocabulary.

Forging a Common Political Identity: The Declaration on European Identity

While U.S.-EC talks stalled, the EC Nine moved swiftly with their planned definition of European identity. On 14 December, the foreign ministers of the EC Nine issued a Declaration on European Identity. Once dismissed as a mere "footnote in EU history,"[95] the text has recently been reappraised as a "pioneering document."[96] What is missed in this appraisal, however positive, is that the declaration not only proclaimed the distinctiveness of the European entity on the global stage but also laid the basic values of a European political community.

Jobert was not acting on an impulse on 23 July, when he urged the EC foreign minister to define European identity. Three days before, his staff had issued a memorandum with a proposed definition of European identity.[97] This document struck a defensive note. Its basic principle was differentiation: any definition of European identity, it stated, meant distinguishing the EC from other political entities. Several of its definitional provisions referred to the colonial past of EC states and their efforts to retain sway in the developing world. The text, moreover, equated the term "identity" with the Gaullist category of "independence." A European identity necessitated safeguarding European independence, a task requiring "a European defense force." It also involved active efforts to preserve European cultural diversity. This cultural element both alluded to the threat of Americanization and reflected the long-standing role of the French state in promoting cultural influence ("rayonnement").[98] To Quai officials, "Europe" ought to "foster the various cultures that had made its civilization influential" ("assurer à chacune des cultures qui ont fait son rayonnement un développement satisfaisant").[99] The document ended on a Gaullist note: Europe should not be reduced to "a geopolitical stake [*un enjeu*]," "a bargaining tool [*un objet de marchandage*]," or "a subservient group of states [*un conglomérat d'Etats tenus en tutelle*]."

France, Britain, and Ireland all submitted draft papers on European identity in September 1973. The French text pointed to the same desire to preserve European—that is, ultimately, French—influence and cultural distinctiveness as the July memorandum did, but it was less defensive in nature.[100] The notion of independence stood less prominently in the text. The document still objected to the institutionalization of "globalized" talks between the EC and the United States. Nonetheless, the section entitled "European identity vis-à-vis the rest of the world" discussed a broader range of topics, including the United States and former EC states' colonies as well as India, China, Canada, and Eastern Europe. The drafts submitted by Britain and Ireland differed in focus. The British document was entitled "The Identity of the Nine vis-à-vis the United States."[101] Though starting with a general definition of European identity, it explicitly sought to lay the basis for a transatlantic dialogue, with an emphasis on both procedure and content. The Irish draft, by contrast, was more "conceptual" in nature.[102] It put forward a definition that emphasized the institutional underpinnings of the EC and the intention of the EC heads of state or government to achieve a "European union" by 1980.[103]

Ensuing EPC talks highlighted tensions between France's reappraisal of EPC and the enduring influence of the Gaullist legacy. Despite their conversion to EPC, Quai officials criticized the FCO's suggestion to refer to a "common foreign policy" and to stipulate that the bilateral contacts of EC states with third countries would rest on jointly pre-agreed positions. They feared that these provisions would lay the ground for a binding EPC.[104] Clearly, French officials wanted to retain their full ability to make independent decisions, even if they were now willing to play the game of foreign policy cooperation. As a compromise, Pompidou proposed the vague wording of his September 1973 press conference, namely, "a European policy."[105] The EC Nine reached a somewhat ambiguous agreement.[106] The final document referred to "a truly European policy [*une politique proprement européenne]*" in French, but to a "genuinely European *foreign* policy" in English.[107]

It should come as no surprise that France and Ireland, a non-NATO member, opposed the FCO's proposed references to NATO.[108] French officials feared that the mention of "an adequate and autonomous defense within the Atlantic Alliance" might provide a basis for enhancing NATO's Eurogroup and possibly pressuring France to join it. Pompidou had made it clear that "we will not let ourselves be led into NATO through the Eurogroup."[109] In his November 1973 talks with Scheel, Jobert reasserted the French misgivings about this NATO-based grouping.[110]

The French stance on a European defense was more complex.[111] The Quai d'Orsay dismissed as "premature" Britain's suggestion to refer to a "European defense policy."[112] Its July memorandum on European identity, however, had specifically referred to "a European defense."[113] The origin of this step back most likely lay in Pompidou's reservations. He had repeatedly stressed that the EC Nine should first move forward with their planned currency and economic union before thinking of political and, even more so, defense unity.[114] Pompidou even thought the final EPC compromise went too far: "The Nine … agree that in the light of the relative military vulnerability of Europe, the Europeans should, if they wish to preserve their independence, hold to their commitments and make constant efforts to ensure that they have adequate means of defense at their disposal."[115] He had suggested instead: "the Europeans should be aware of the problem raised by their own defense effort."[116] Pompidou's instructions, however, did not reach Puaux until after the Political Committee meeting.[117]

Mention of "a European defense" in the July memorandum reflected Jobert's forays into this field. In his speech of 19 June to the French National Assembly, Jobert had alluded to possible talks on defense among EC states. The EC Nine, he deplored, were "defenseless." The "defense of Europe," he thus announced, would be an important topic in the negotiations to take place within and outside Europe in 1973.[118] The NSC understood Jobert's position as a "slight shift in French defense policy."[119] During the summer, Jobert authorized the staff of the Quai d'Orsay's new planning section to initiate secret talks with Britain on European defense. He himself agreed to discuss the matter with his West German counterpart. Contrary to Soutou's assertions, we do know how Jobert responded to Scheel on 9 November.[120] The French foreign minister showed himself to be quite forthcoming. He recognized that the EC states should proceed in stages toward a common defense and even suggested that talks could begin within the EPC framework before 1980.[121] True, Jobert's statement of 21 November to the Western European Union (WEU) Assembly was less bold, disappointing the British and West German foreign ministries.

Jobert encouraged Western European countries to engage in discussions ("effort de dialogue et de réflexion") on defense matters within the WEU, rather than the EPC, framework.[122] This more cautious view most likely reflected Pompidou's stance.

Hard-headed pragmatism shaped Pompidou's skepticism. There was much to be said for the EC Nine's lack of readiness to move into this field, but concerns about *Ostpolitik* probably influenced his attitude too. Brandt had been the first to broach the topic in his meeting with Pompidou on 21 June.[123] The West German chancellor and foreign ministry made further overtures at the end of November.[124] Pompidou had the habit of annotating the papers that were sent to him. These handwritten comments are a valuable source of information for historians. His comment on the West German proposal to discuss a common security policy among the EC Nine was laconically eloquent: "careful!! [*prudence!!*]."[125] The adjective was even underlined four times. It is perhaps an exaggeration to claim, as Soutou does, that Pompidou viewed these proposals as a step toward a Soviet-German condominium.[126] Nonetheless, his uneasiness about *Ostpolitik* most likely prompted him to prioritize U.S. troop maintenance, as opposed to European defense, in order to prevent West Germany's drift toward the East.[127]

The EC Nine's text on a European identity had not been intended as a public statement, but the foreign ministers chose to publish it during the EC summit of Copenhagen.[128] The Declaration on European Identity issued on 14 December was largely based upon the French draft, even if a certain amount of revision had occurred to incorporate elements from the British and Irish texts. Parts I and II still described the internal characteristics of the EC ("The Unity of the Nine Member Countries of the Community") and its identity vis-à-vis the rest of the world ("The European Identity in Relation to the World"). Part III, by contrast, was new. In line with the Irish emphasis on institutions, it outlined the future of European unification ("The Dynamic Nature of the Construction of a United Europe"), reasserting the proposed goal of transforming "the whole complex of ... [intra-EC] relations into a European Union."[129] Part I also included a new paragraph on the institutional underpinnings of the emerging European entity, namely, the EC and EPC. Disagreements as to how to refer to EC/EPC-U.S. relations had a peculiar result: the EC Nine glossed them over. Consequently, the United States was a more tangential topic in the final text than in the French draft—not to mention the British one.

The Copenhagen Declaration broke new ground in affirming the sociocultural underpinnings of a united Europe. Neither the EC's founding documents (the 1957 Rome Treaty and the 1965 merger treaties) nor contemporaneous reports and statements (the 1970 and 1973 EPC reports, the

1969 Hague and 1972 Paris summit statements) had used words such as "culture," "value," and "civilization" in connection to a united Europe.[130] Culture had been one of the pillars of de Gaulle's 1960 proposal for intergovernmental cooperation, along with foreign policy, economics, and defense.[131] The committee in charge of discussing this proposal had even created a group responsible for drafting proposals for cultural cooperation.[132] The words "culture" and "civilization" were mentioned in both versions of the Fouchet Plan.[133] The Fouchet plans, however, referred exclusively to a "union of states." As evident from its title, the declaration, by contrast, encompassed both the EC as such and its member states. In underscoring a shared cultural legacy and common political values, this text provided the nascent European entity with a broad civilizational and ideological basis:

> 1. The Nine European States might have been pushed towards disunity by their history and by selfishly defending misjudged interests. But they have overcome their past enmities and have decided that unity is a basic European necessity to ensure the survival of the civilization which they have in common.
> The Nine wish to ensure that the cherished values of their legal, political and moral order are respected, and to preserve the rich variety of their national cultures. Sharing as they do the same attitudes to life, based on a determination to build a society which measures up to the needs of the individual, they are determined to defend the principles of representative democracy, of the rule of law, of social justice—which is the ultimate goal of economic progress—and of respect for human rights.
> ...
> 3. The diversity of cultures within the framework of a common European civilization, the attachment to common values and principles, the increasing convergence of attitudes to life, the awareness of having specific interests in common and the determination to take part in the construction of a United Europe, all give the European Identity its originality and its own dynamism.[134]

Such statements may seem innocuous. Unlike recent efforts to issue a European constitution, the EC Nine made no attempt to specify the nature of the EC's civilizational heritage through references to Christianity, the Greco-Roman tradition, and the Enlightenment.[135] Some of the political values listed in Paragraph 1—representative democracy and respect for human rights, the rule of law, and social justice—had already acquired international recognition, in words if not in deeds, notably through their enshrinement in the 1948 United Nations Universal Declaration of Human Rights.[136] Nevertheless, it was the first joint attempt by EC governing elites to define the European project in broader political and cultural terms. The concept of representative democracy also mentioned in Paragraph 1, moreover, had not yet gained the degree of general acceptance that it has achieved today within the EU. Only a decade earlier, there had been those who, like de Gaulle and Adenauer, had been inclined to think that Spain's dictatorial regime did not automatically debar it from EC membership. This issue would gain new prominence in 1974 with the fall of the Regime of the Colonels in Greece. Should Greece be allowed to join the EC despite its authoritarian past? This would be a controversial question.[137] In stressing the notion of democracy in the declaration, the foreign ministers of the EC Nine took a clear stand on the future of the European polity.

The Copenhagen Declaration marked an important milestone in the construction of a politically circumscribed European identity. In acting as a catalyst, the "American challenge" gave it a defensive twist.[138] But the text went far beyond U.S.-European relations. Instead of paving the ground for a transatlantic dialogue, it was a statement on European identity in and of itself. Two wider trends, moreover, were influential in shaping this definitional exercise: the tradition of viewing America as an object of both fascination and contempt; and, more broadly, a model of comparative self-identification dating to the middle Ages, wherein the awareness of a common European cultural heritage had crystallized through encounters with an "other" — Moor, Ottoman, or Native American.[139] These three factors shaped the efforts of French officials and their EC counterparts to forge consensus on a broad characterization of the emerging European entity — including culture, politics, and such sensitive matters as defense and foreign policy. Before long, this endeavor had struck a chord with wider segments of French elite opinion.

A New Legitimizing Category of French Political Life

The French discussion of "European identity" did not remain confined to a small circle of bureaucrats. Through the early 1970s, the use of the term as a geographically circumscribed cultural heritage had prevailed. A shift occurred in 1973. When the phrase "European identity" surged to the forefront of French political discourse in the fall of 1973, commentators mainly used it to refer to the nascent European entity,[140] very often seizing upon this word to assert Europe's claims to world influence. On occasion, they also stressed the internal characteristics of European identity. In so doing, they paved the way for a broader understanding of this concept in the French public sphere.

To be fair, French officials had already used the term "European identity" in connection to the EC in the early 1970s, but they had done so only sporadically. A 1972 Quai memorandum had discussed one of the topics selected for the Paris summit — namely, the EC's external relations — under the heading "The Future of the European Project: The Assertion of a

Genuine European Identity." The text itself, however, mentioned the "personality" rather than the "identity" of Europe."[141] In a 1972 speech, Pompidou had referred to "European identity" while discussing U.S. and Soviet concerns about European integration.[142] These statements, however, were exceptions.

In 1973, in contrast, the concept of a politically anchored European identity suddenly gained wider currency in governmental talk. The Year of Europe was an important factor behind its dissemination. Government officials found it an effective rhetorical tool to try to defeat the Nixon administration's imputed quest for strengthened leadership. Burin des Roziers used it to justify the French rejection of the U.S. amendments. The U.S. government had asked that the phrases "on the one hand" and "on the other" be removed from the opening sentence of the EC Nine's draft ("The United States of America on the one hand and the European Community and its member states on the other hand...") to avoid conveying an impression of separateness.[143] Burin des Roziers analyzed this request as a sign of the U.S. intention to treat "European identity" as not "an end in itself."[144] On a more general level, he warned that the proposed U.S. changes would deprive "Europe" of its "autonomy" and even of a "genuine identity."[145] Pompidou endorsed this analysis.[146] In a similar vein, Quai Secretary-General Geoffroy de Courcel restated French opposition to institutionalized EC-U.S. talks, arguing that the EC states had merely begun to forge a common "identity."[147] French officials also summoned up the notion of a European identity to counter the U.S. and Japanese plan for a trilateral declaration. Quai Asia Director Henri Froment-Meurice told Japan's ambassador to France that any triangular designs would undermine the EC's efforts to define a "separate identity."[148]

The concept of European identity also became central to wider discussions of world affairs. French officials used it during and after the Yom Kippur War as they watched, with consternation, France's (and Britain's) de facto exclusion from the cease-fire and peace negotiations. More broadly, they came to subsume under this notion their ideal of an internationally influential Europe. Speaking to the Rotary Club of Toledo, Ohio, Kosciusko-Morizet urged the U.S. government to accept "Europe's" claim to world influence and its attendant "duty" to assert its "identity."[149] As newly appointed foreign minister, Sauvagnargues would similarly equate European identity with European self-assertion in the international arena.[150]

This line of argument resonated with journalists. *Le Figaro* warned that the proposed U.S. amendments implied an unwanted interference in the EC's internal affairs and hence sounded the death knell for European identity.[151] It also linked the concept of European identity to the forging of joint European positions in international affairs. The EC Nine's decision to try to define their common identity, he stressed, would finally compel them to speak "with a single voice."[152] This was wishful thinking. Massip was probably aware of it. He would often restate his plea for collective European action, framing it in terms of European identity.[153] Likewise, *Le Monde* journalists implied that a European identity presupposed a European foreign policy.[154] Aron made the same point in his newspaper column: a European identity entailed a common diplomacy.[155]

Some commentaries—though mostly from outside governmental circles—were already hinting at a more widely conceived, politically defined European identity. In a speech in Washington, D.C., French European Commission President François-Xavier Ortoli drew an analogy between European and U.S. identity:

> Just as Californians and Texans travelling to Europe are viewed as "Americans," I have come here as a "European." I can sense that a European identity is emerging in our nine EC member states, and I believe that the European people must live in ever closer union.[156]

Ortoli used the term on other occasions during his 1973 U.S. trip, but he remained vague as to what it meant.[157] Pierre Drouin was more specific in *Le Monde*. Making a normative argument, he cautioned that a united Europe would only find its identity if it fostered a distinct societal model that eschewed the trappings of dogmatic Marxism and the "Promethean frenzy" of American consumerism.[158] In the aftermath of the Yom Kippur War, Massip merged the older, cultural meaning of the term with its new, politically circumscribed usage. European nations, he stated, should act jointly to regain their influence in Middle East and world affairs. Only then could they safeguard their distinct "civilization" and "identity."[159] In another instance, Massip implicitly defined European identity in institutional terms. Being close to Monnet, he argued that its assertion required reforms that would enhance the EC's institutions.[160]

By 1974, European identity had become a key category of French political discourse. America logically acted as a defining "other." In 1972, Pompidou had warned against using "European identity" as a "polemical" catchword while discussing U.S.- and Soviet-European relations.[161] He restated this point during a 1973 trip to Italy, presumably to reassure his hosts: transatlantic ties made it more "urgent" to define a "European identity," but this exercise should not challenge (Western) Europe's "alliances," that is, the Atlantic Alliance.[162] In practice, the term "European identity" proved convenient as a discursive weapon against U.S. policy, but its use was not purely instrumental. The term also came to encapsulate the vision of a European world actor. In line with the Copenhagen Declaration's emphasis on a shared culture and common values, the press even began to give it a sociocultural substance. This was a first important step toward the popularization of the term "European identity" as designating the identity of the emerging European polity.

An Important Political Concept

The Year of Europe spurred the French to play a leading role in defining and asserting a politically circumscribed European identity. The FCO had provided the initial idea, but the December 1973 Declaration on European Identity was markedly different from what British officials had envisioned. It was not "a confidential note" dealing with U.S.-European relations."[163] Rather, it proclaimed the distinct identity of the nascent European entity. This statement was the result of joint decision-making within EPC. Jobert had suggested defining European identity in and of itself; the Quai d'Orsay, the FCO, and the Irish foreign ministry had all provided drafts; and the Farnesina had lobbied for the publication of the text.[164]

The Declaration on European Identity was a landmark statement. No prior EC text had referred to a "European identity." Never before had EC states endeavored to draw the shape and contours of a united Europe. Subsequent documents would build on its three-pronged approach: internal cohesion, relations with the world, and European unification as a dynamic process.[165] The declaration also helped foster consensus on a founding political ideal. Further statements and treaties would elaborate on the political principles enshrined in it.[166] Last but not least, its twin notions of civilizational unity and cultural diversity would become a central theme of European political discourse that would be encapsulated in the phrase "unity in diversity" in the 2004 draft Constitutional Treaty.[167]

The surge of the term "European identity" to the forefront of the French political vocabulary did not entail a switch of allegiance from the French nation to a united Europe among the elites. Government officials, in particular, remained prickly about sovereignty issues. While negotiating the second report on EPC during the first half of 1973, they had insisted on maintaining a clear distinction between the intergovernmental EPC mechanisms and the partly supranational EC institutions.[168] To reassert this distinction, they even requested that the meetings of the EPC and EC Council of Foreign Ministers of 23 July be held in different cities: Copenhagen, the capital of the EC presidency, and Brussels, the headquarters of the EC institutions. The Quai d'Orsay was just as sensitive about sovereignty issues while discussing the Declaration on European Identity.

Nonetheless, the new prominence of this phrase in French political talk was highly significant. The concept of a politically defined European identity had farther-reaching implications than de Gaulle's phrase "a European Europe." It conjured up the notion of a European polity, and it could potentially refer to a locus of allegiance other than the nation-state. As such, it could compete with, and possibly supersede, French identity as a meaningful category of French political life. Its popularization was particularly important as the governing elites simultaneously endeavored to translate into reality the idea of a distinct European identity on the global stage. They had begun to tread that path in the summer of 1973 by helping to forge a joint European response to the Year of Europe. They would do so more forcefully in the wake of the Yom Kippur War. The fourth Arab-Israeli war and its aftermath would indeed prompt them to consider anew the value of collective action in a strategically sensitive region.

Notes

1. Möckli, *European Foreign Policy During the Cold War*, 230.
2. Winand, "Loaded Words and Disputed Meanings," 315.
3. Robert Hormats, *Memorandum for the Secretary*, "Issues for your meeting with Jobert," 27 June 1973, NPM, NSC, Country files, 679.
4. *Outline for a Declaration of Principles between the United States of America and the European Community and its Member States*, quoted in full in MAE, Direction des Affaires politiques, circular telegram 563, 1 October 1973, MAE, U.S. files 1970–5, 1137.
5. Pompidou, margin comment on summary document dated 8 October 1973, CHAN, 5AG2 1035.
6. MAE, political director [Puaux], *Note pour le ministre*, 13 October 1973, MAE, EC files 1971–6, 3795.
7. Pierre Pélen, Copenhagen telegram 911-8, 19 October 1973, MAE, U.S. files 1970–5, 1137.
8. FCO, letter from Cromer to Brimelow, 3 October 1973, doc. 239, in Hamilton, *Documents on British Policy Overseas. The Year of Europe*.
9. FCO, telegram 1195 to UKREP Brussels, 3 October 1973, doc. 240, ibid.
10. FCO, telegram 1196 to UKREP Brussels, 3 October 1973, doc. 241, ibid.
11. *European Second Draft for a Declaration of Principles between the United States of America and the European Community and its Member States*, 18 October 1973, Historical Archives of the European Union (HAEU), Fonds Emile Noël (EN), 1909.
12. Paragraph 7 of the 1972 Paris statement read: "The construction of Europe will allow it, in conformity with its ultimate political objectives, to affirm its personality while remaining faithful to its traditional friendships and to the alliances of the Member States" ("Statement from the Paris Summit [October 1972]").
13. *Draft Brief for the President of the Political Committee on 18 October*, MAE, EC files 1971–6, 3810.
14. Günther van Well, circular telegram 3745, 22 October 1973, in Pautsch, *Akten zur Auswärtigen Politik der Bundesrepublik Deutschland 1973*, vol. 3, 1629–33.
15. FCO, Copenhagen telegram 417, 19 October 1973, doc. 308, in Hamilton, *Documents on British Policy Overseas. The Year of Europe*.

16. FCO, Bonn telegram 1165, 1 November 1973, doc. 355, ibid. British diplomats were shown an account of the conversation "in the strictest confidence and without authorization."

17. FCO, letter from Cromer to Brimelow, 6 November 1973, doc. 374, ibid.

18. MAE, Secrétariat général, circular telegram 780, 13 December 1973, MAE, U.S. files 1970–5, 1137. Responsibilities were split between the Political Committee (political paragraphs) and COREPER (economic paragraphs). The European Commission's staff informed the Political Committee of the outcome of COREPER's discussions (Secretariat General of the European Commission, *Les relations avec les Etats-Unis,* 12 December 1973, HAEU, EN, 1909).

19. FCO, Washington telegram 3674, 24 November 1973, doc. 412, in Hamilton, *Documents on British Policy Overseas. The Year of Europe.*

20. Stoessel communicated Kissinger's viewpoint to Kosciusko-Morizet for Jobert's information (Secretary of State, telegram 2357704 to American Embassy Paris, undated [on or after 27 November 1973], NPM, NSC, Country files, 679).

21. De Rose, interview, 23 September 1988, MAE, AO, de Rose.

22. De Rose, interview, 23 September 1988. Soutou argues that Jobert drafted the text on instructions from Pompidou, but he substantiates his claim only by referring to a box number, as opposed to a specific document in Pompidou's archives (Soutou, "President Pompidou, Ostpolitik, and the Strategy of Détente," 250–51, 257, note 85).

23. Memcon Jobert/Kissinger, 26 September 1973, MAE, Secrétariat général, 2 / NPM, NSC, Country files, 679. For this interpretation, see also Möckli, *European Foreign Policy During the Cold War,* 178–79; Mélandri, "Une relation très spéciale," 534. For a more balanced and accurate interpretation, see Soutou, "Le président Pompidou et les relations entre les Etats-Unis et l'Europe," 142.

24. Letter from Kissinger to Jobert, 28 September 1973, NPM, NSC, Country files, 679; Sonnenfelt, *Memorandum for the Secretary,* "Jobert's NATO declaration: how to proceed," 2 October 1973, NPM, NSC, Country files, 679.

25. Soutou, "Le président Pompidou et les relations entre les Etats-Unis et l'Europe," 140. For the French draft, see CHAN, 5AG2 1021.

26. Letter from Kissinger to Jobert, 28 September 1973, NPM, NSC, Country files, 679.

27. Sonnenfelt, *Memorandum for the Secretary,* "Jobert's NATO declaration: how to proceed," 2 October 1973, NPM, NSC, Country files, 679.

28. Memcon Jobert/Kissinger, 26 September 1973, MAE, Secrétariat général, 2 / NPM, NSC, Country files, 679.

29. FCO, UKDEL NATO telegram 653, 10 October 1973, doc. 257, in Hamilton, *Documents on British Policy Overseas. The Year of Europe.* Britain, the Netherlands, NATO Secretary-General Joseph Luns, West Germany, and Canada had all tabled a draft (van Well, memorandum, 13 August 1973, in Pautsch, *Akten zur Auswärtigen Politik der Bundesrepublik Deutschland 1973,* vol. 2, 1225–31; van Well, telegram 3229 to German delegation to NATO, 21 September 1973, ibid., 1418–22).

30. Memcon Jobert/Kissinger, 11 October 1973, NPM, NSC, Country files, 679.

31. Möckli, *European Foreign Policy During the Cold War,* 179.

32. Hormats, *Memorandum for the Secretary,* "Issues for your meeting with Jobert," 27 June 1973, NPM, NSC, Country files, 679.

33. MAE, Direction d'Asie-Océanie, *Note : relations Europe—Japon,* 14 November 1973, CHAN, 5AG2 1012.

34. Memcon Pompidou/Brandt, 27 November 1973, CHAN, 5AG2 1012. Jobert conveyed the same message to Kissinger (Memcon Kissinger/Jobert, 11 October 1973, NPM, NSC, Country files, 679).

35. Guiringaud, New York telegram 4717-21, 27 September 1973, MAE, U.S. files 1970–5, 1137.
36. Van Well, Washington telegram 1309, 2 May 1973, in Pautsch, *Akten zur Auswärtigen Politik der Bundesrepublik Deutschland 1973*, vol. 2, 625–31; van Well, New York telegram 1139, 26 September 1973, ibid., 1445–48.
37. Jacques de Beaumarchais, London telegram 2715-19, 18 September 1973, MAE, U.S. files 1970–5, 1137.
38. *CP(73)80 déf.: Brief for the Ambassador of the Presidency of the Nine in Tokyo*, 12 November 1973, HAEU, EN, 1909.
39. Stoessel carried this message to Denmark's U.S. ambassador soon after the EC initiative (Kosciusko-Morizet, Washington telegram 7665-7, 23 November 1973, MAE, U.S. files 1970–5, 1137). The U.S. chargé spoke in terms similar to Puaux's a few days later (Secretary of State, telegram 2357704 to American Embassy Paris, undated [on or after 27 November 1973], NPM, NSC, Country files, 679).
40. FCO, Washington telegram 3674, 24 November 1973, doc. 412, in Hamilton, *Documents on British Policy Overseas. The Year of Europe*.
41. Margerie, *Note : relations Europe-Japon et déclaration "triangulaire,"* 22 November 1973, MAE, U.S. files 1970–5, 1137. During his 20 November meeting with Margerie, Japan's ambassador to France dismissed the EC draft as a "piece of paper [*bout de papier*]."
42. Louis de Guiringaud, New York telegram 4717-21, 27 September 1973, MAE, U.S. files 1970–5, 1137. The Quai d'Orsay did not receive a copy of the Japanese draft until after the Europe trip of Japanese Foreign Minister Makiko Tanaka (Henri Froment-Meurice, *Note : entretien avec l'ambassadeur du Japon*, 24 October 1973, MAE, U.S. files 1970–5, 1137).
43. Margerie, *Note : relations Europe-Japon et déclaration"triangulaire,"* 22 November 1973, MAE, U.S. files 1970–5, 1137.
44. The EC Presidency approached the Canadian government on 14 December. At the 4 March 1974 ministerial meeting of EPC, Jobert forcefully pleaded for an EC-Canada statement. As a result, EC foreign ministers instructed the Political Committee to prepare a document based on a draft to be submitted by the Quai d'Orsay (*Compte-rendu de la réunion ministérielle du 4 mars 1974 au titre de la coopération politique européenne à Bruxelles*, MAE, EC files 1971–6, 3792).
45. MAE, Direction d'Europe, *Note : réunion du Comité politique (11 juillet) — Europe/Canada*, 5 July 1974, MAE, EC files 1971–6, 3792.
46. De Rose, interview, 23 September 1988, MAE, AO, de Rose.
47. FCO, Copenhagen telegram 417, 19 October 1973, doc. 308, in Hamilton, *Documents on British Policy Overseas. The Year of Europe*.
48. De Rose, interview with the author, Paris, 30 April 2007. De Rose also portrayed Jobert as someone who was "very intelligent but struggled with self-doubt" ("très intelligent, mais horriblement complexé").
49. Pickering, *Secretary's Staff Meeting: Summary of Decisions*, undated [on or after 30 November 1973], NARA, SD, RG 59, Lot files, Kissinger, 1.
50. FCO, Washington telegram 3674, 24 November 1973, doc. 412, in Hamilton, *Documents on British Policy Overseas. The Year of Europe*.
51. [Kissinger], *Talking Points for the President on European Aspects of the Trip*, 22 December 1973, NPM, NSC, HAK files, Trip files, 43; Brent Scowcroft, *Memorandum for the President*, "Additional report of the secretary of his final day in Brussels," 11 December 1973, NPM, NSC, HAK files, Trip files, 43.
52. Scowcroft, *Memorandum for the President*, "Additional report of the secretary of his final day in Brussels," 11 December 1973, NPM, NSC, HAK files, Trip files, 43.

53. On Kennedy's policy toward Western Europe, see Oliver Bange, *The EEC Crisis of 1963: Kennedy, Macmillan, De Gaulle and Adenauer in Conflict* (New York: St. Martin's Press, 2000); Erin R. Mahan, *Kennedy, de Gaulle and Western Europe* (Houndmills, UK, and New York: Palgrave Macmillan, 2002); Winand, *Eisenhower, Kennedy, and the United States of Europe.*

54. John F. Kennedy, "Address at Independence Hall, Philadelphia, 4 July 1962," http://www.jfklibrary.org/Historical+Resources/Archives/Reference+Desk/Speeches/JFK/003POF03IndependenceHall07041962.htm.

55. Frédéric Bozo, *Deux stratégies pour l'Europe. De Gaulle, les Etats-Unis et l'Alliance atlantique, 1958–1969* (Paris: Plon, 1996). On Kennedy's vision of a transatlantic partnership, see Winand, *Eisenhower, Kennedy, and the United States of Europe,* 126–27.

56. Action Committee for the United States of Europe (ACUSE), *Déclaration commune du 26 juin 1962,* quoted in full in Winand and Fondation Jean Monnet pour l'Europe, "20 ans d'action du Comité Jean Monnet (1955–1975)," 66, 68. Subsequent resolutions reiterated this plea for a partnership among equals (ACUSE, *Dixième session [Paris, les 17 et 18 décembre 1962],* ibid., 69, 71; *Onzième session [Bonn, 1er juin 1963], Déclaration commune,* ibid., 75, 78–79; *Douzième session [Berlin, les 8 et 9 juin 1965],* ibid., 87–88).

57. Roger Massip, "Editorial : de Copenhague à Tokyo," *Le Figaro,* 24 April 1973.

58. Pompidou, margin comment on summary document dated 12 December 1973, CHAN, 5AG2 1054/2.

59. FCO, telegram 1196 to UKREP, 3 October 1973, in Hamilton, *Documents on British Policy Overseas. The Year of Europe.*

60. MAE, political director [Puaux], *Note pour le ministre,* 13 October 1973, MAE, EC files 1971–6, 3795.; Pélen, Copenhagen telegram 906-10, 18 October 1973, MAE, U.S. files 1970–5, 1137.

61. MAE, Direction des Affaires politiques, circular telegram 260, 28 April 1973, MAE, U.S. files 1970–5, 1137.

62. Jacques Jacquet-Francillon, "Etats-Unis : une mauvaise humeur tactique," *Le Figaro,* 9–10 March 1974.

63. Etienne Burin des Roziers, Brussels telegram, 4 October 1973, CHAN, 5AG2 1021.

64. Kissinger, *Memorandum for the Secretary of State, the Secretary of Defense, the Secretary of Commerce, the Secretary of the Treasury, the Secretary of Agriculture,* "NSSM 164: United States relations with Europe," 18 December 1972, NPM, NSC, Institutional files, 194.

65. Robert O. Keohane and Joseph S. Nye, *Power and Interdependence: World Politics in Transition,* 3rd ed. (New York: Longman, 2001); Joseph S. Nye, "Independence and Interdependence," *Foreign Policy,* no. 22 (1976): 130–61.

66. Keohane and Nye, *Power and Interdependence,* 16.

67. MAE, political director [Puaux], *Note pour le ministre,* 20 August 1973, MAE, EC files 1971–6, 3810.

68. Burin des Roziers, Brussels telegram 3365-90, 6 October 1973, MAE, U.S. files 1970–5, 1137.

69. Nye, "Independence and Interdependence," 132.

70. Jacques Ogliastro, "'C'est la fin de la dispute la plus inutile du monde,' dit Jean Sauvagnargues," *Le Figaro,* 20 June 1974.

71. Yves Moreau, "Editorial : Graves abandons," *L'Humanité,* 11 December 1974.

72. MAE, Direction des Affaires politiques, circular telegram 254, 26 April 1973, MAE, U.S. files 1970–5, 1137.

73. On French criticisms of the United States' "globalization" intents, see Beaumarchais, London telegram 2864-70, 4 October 1973, MAE, U.S. files 1970–5, 1137; MAE, Direction d'Europe, circular telegram 603, 15 October 1973, MAE, U.S. files 1970–5, 1137.

74. Kissinger, *Memorandum for the Secretary of State...*, "NSSM 164: United States relations with Europe," 18 December 1972, NPM, NSC, Institutional files, 194.
75. FCO, Washington telegram 3752, 2 December 1973, doc. 432, in Hamilton, *Documents on British Policy Overseas. The Year of Europe.*
76. Beaumarchais, London telegram 2864-70, 4 October 1973, MAE, U.S. files 1970–5, 1137.
77. Hamilton, "Britain, France, and America's Year of Europe, 1973," 873; Möckli, *European Foreign Policy During the Cold War,* 148–49.
78. FCO, Planning Staff draft paper, 20 August 1973, quoted in Hamilton, "Britain, France, and America's Year of Europe, 1973," 873; FCO, telegram 1196 to UKREP Brussels, 3 October 1973, doc. 241, and FCO, Copenhagen telegram 417, 19 October 1973, doc. 308, both in Hamilton, *Documents on British Policy Overseas. The Year of Europe.*
79. FCO, telegram 562 to Paris, 18 July 1973, doc. 164, and FCO, minute, Michael D. Butler to Antony Acland, 8 October 1973, doc. 254, both in Hamilton, *Documents on British Policy Overseas. The Year of Europe.*
80. Alain Rey and Tristan Hordé, eds., *Dictionnaire historique de la langue française* (Paris: Dictionnaires Le Robert, 2006), 2273.
81. *Outline for a Declaration of Principles between the United States of America and the European Community and its Member States,* quoted in full in MAE, Direction d'Europe, circular telegram 563, 1 October 1973, MAE, U.S. files 1970–5, 1137.
82. Original emphasis.
83. [Kissinger], *Talking Points for the President on European Aspects of the Trip,* 22 December 1973, NPM, NSC, HAK files, Trip files, 43.
84. Memcon Pompidou/Brandt, 27 November 1973, CHAN, 5AG2 1012.
85. Burin des Roziers, Brussels telegram 3365-90, 6 October 1973, MAE, U.S. files 1970–5, 1137.
86. Kosciusko-Morizet, Washington telegram 5928, 27 September 1973, MAE, U.S. files 1970–5, 1137.
87. Memcon Kissinger/Andersen, 25 September 1973, NPM, NSC, Presidential memcons, 1027.
88. Richard T. Kennedy, *Memorandum to Bill Hyland,* "State's talking points for Jobert meeting," 27 June 1973, NPM, NSC, Country files, 679.
89. Scowcroft, *Memorandum for the President,* "Additional report of the secretary of his final day in Brussels," 11 December 1973, NPM, NSC, HAK files, Trip files, 43.
90. Hanhimäki, *The Flawed Architect,* 299.
91. Scowcroft, *[Memorandum] to Kissinger,* "Points for your possible meeting with Giscard," undated [December 1973], NPM, NSC, HAK files, Trip files, 42.
92. Pélen, Copenhagen telegram 911-8, 19 October 1973, MAE, U.S. files 1970–5, 1137.
93. Maurice Duverger, "Europe européenne ou Europe américaine," *Le Monde,* 1 June 1973. See also Henri de Kergorlay, "Entre Paris et ses partenaires: une vieille querelle qui rebondit avec chaque crise," *Le Figaro,* 15 February 1974; Yves Moreau, "L'Europe atlantique," *L'Humanité,* 14 February 1974.
94. FCO, telegram 1195 to UKREP Brussels, 3 October 1973, doc. 240, in Hamilton, *Documents on British Policy Overseas. The Year of Europe.*
95. Ine Megens, "The December 1973 Declaration on European Identity as the Result of Team Spirit among European Diplomats," in van der Harst, *Beyond the Customs Union,* 338.
96. Möckli, *European Foreign Policy During the Cold War,* 220.
97. MAE, Direction d'Europe, *Note : réunion ministérielle (Copenhague — 23 juillet) — relations Europe/Etats-Unis — contenu possible d'un document à élaborer sur l'identité européenne par rapport aux Etats-Unis,* 20 July 1973, MAE, EC files 1971–6, 3810.

98. Alain Dubosclard et al., *Entre rayonnement et réciprocité. Contributions à l'histoire de la diplomatie culturelle* (Paris: Publications de la Sorbonne, 2002); François Roche and Bernard Piniau, *Histoires de diplomatie culturelle des origines à 1995* (Paris: La documentation française, 1995).

99. MAE, Direction d'Europe, *Note : réunion ministérielle (Copenhague—23 juillet)—relations Europe/Etats-Unis—contenu possible d'un document à élaborer sur l'identité européenne par rapport aux Etats-Unis,* 20 July 1973, MAE, EC files 1971–6, 3810.

100. *Coopération politique européenne CSCE (73) 65F. De l'identité européenne,* 4 September 1973, CHAN, 5AG2 1021.

101. *European Political Cooperation GC (73) 37 UK. The Identity of the Nine vis-à-vis the United States,* 4 September 1973, MAE, EC files 1971–6, 3810.

102. *RM (73)17P: Rapport du Comité politique sur les délibérations du Comité concernant l'identité européenne,* Copenhagen, 7 September 1973, MAE, EC files 1971–6, 3792.

103. "Statement from the Paris Summit (October 1972)."

104. MAE, Direction d'Europe, *Note : Comité politique des 12/13 novembre—identité européenne,* 9 November 1973, MAE, EC files 1971–6, 3795.

105. Pompidou, margin comment on Raimond, *Note pour Monsieur Balladur,* 13 November 1973, CHAN, 5AG2 1035.

106. "Déclaration sur l'identité européenne (Copenhague, 14 décembre 1973)," *Bulletin des Communautés européennes, Supplément,* no. 12 (1973): 127–30.

107. My emphasis. "Declaration on European Identity (Copenhagen, 14 December 1973)," *Bulletin of the European Communities,* no. 12 (1973): 118–22; "Déclaration sur l'identité européenne (Copenhague, 14 décembre 1973)."

108. MAE, Direction d'Europe, *Note : Comité politique des 12/13 novembre—identité européenne,* 9 November 1973, MAE, EC files 1971–6, 3795.

109. Pompidou, margin comment on summary document *Grande-Bretagne* dated 18 August 1972, CHAN, 5AG2 1014.

110. Memcon Scheel/Jobert, 9 November 1973, in Pautsch, *Akten zur Auswärtigen Politik der Bundesrepublik Deutschland 1973,* vol. 3, 1797–98; Memcon Scheel/Jobert, 26 November 1973, ibid., 1901–8.

111. For a similar interpretation on the difference between Pompidou's and Jobert's views, see Möckli, *European Foreign Policy During the Cold War,* 218.

112. MAE, Direction d'Europe, *Note : Comité politique des 12/13 novembre—identité européenne,* 9 November 1973, MAE, EC files 1971–6, 3795.

113. MAE, Direction d'Europe, *Note : contenu possible d'un document à élaborer sur l'identité européenne par rapport aux Etats-Unis,* 20 July 1973, MAE, EC files 1971–6, 3810.

114. Memcon Pompidou/Heath, first meeting, 21 May 1973, CHAN, 5AG2 1015; Memcon Pompidou/Heath, second meeting (secret section), 16 November 1973, CHAN, 5AG2 1015.

115. "Declaration on European Identity (Copenhagen, 14 December 1973)."

116. "l'Europe doit prendre conscience du fait que se trouve posé dans la fidélité etc., le problème de son propre effort de défense" (Pompidou, margin comment on Raimond, *Note pour Monsieur Balladur,* 13 November 1973, CHAN, 5AG2 1035).

117. Raimond, *Note pour Monsieur Balladur,* 13 November 1973, CHAN, 5AG2 1035. Puaux thought that he had Jobert's final instructions (ibid.).

118. Jobert, *Mémoires d'avenir,* 266–67.

119. Richard T. Kennedy, *Memorandum to Bill Hyland,* "Department of State's talking point for the Jobert meeting," 27 June 1973, NPM, NSC, Country files, 679.

120. Soutou, "La problématique de la détente et le testament stratégique de Georges Pompidou," 101. For a detailed account of the meeting, see memcon Scheel/Jobert, 9 Novem-

ber 1973, in Pautsch, *Akten zur Auswärtigen Politik der Bundesrepublik Deutschland 1973*, vol. 3, 1791–96.

121. Memcon Scheel/Jobert, 9 November 1973, in Pautsch, *Akten zur Auswärtigen Politik der Bundesrepublik Deutschland 1973*, vol. 3, 1791–96.

122. Soutou, "La problématique de la détente et le testament stratégique de Georges Pompidou," 101.

123. For an analysis of the 21 June discussion on defense, see Hans-Peter Schwartz, "Willy Brandt, Georges Pompidou und die Ostpolitik," in *Willy Brandt und Frankreich*, ed. Horst Möller and Maurice Vaïsse (Munich: Oldenburg, 2005), 156, 163.

124. Memcon Pompidou/Brandt, second meeting, 26 November 1973, CHAN, 5AG2 1012.

125. Pompidou, margin comment on summary document dated 4 December 1973, CHAN, 5AG2 1054.

126. Soutou, "President Pompidou, Ostpolitik, and the Strategy of Détente," 249; idem, "La problématique de la détente et le testament stratégique de Georges Pompidou," 102.

127. Wilfried Loth, "Willy Brandt, Georges Pompidou und die Entspannungspolitik," in Möller and Vaïsse, *Willy Brandt und Frankreich*, 178.

128. MAE, Direction d'Europe, circular telegram 722, 22 November 1973, MAE, EC files 1971–6, 3792.

129. "Declaration on European Identity (Copenhagen, 14 December 1973)."

130. "Davignon Report (Luxembourg, 27 October 1970)," *Bulletin of the European Communities*, no. 11 (1970): 9–14; "Second Report on European Political Cooperation in Foreign Policy Matters (Copenhagen, 23 July 1973)," *Bulletin of the European Communities*, no. 9 (1973): 14–21; "Statement from the Paris Summit (October 1972)"; "Treaty Establishing a Single Council and a Single Commission of the European Communities," *Official Journal of the European Communities*, no. 152 (1967): 2–12; "Treaty Establishing the European Economic Community," http://eur-lex.europa.eu/en/treaties/index.htm#founding. The Hague communiqué was the only exception, but it referred to culture in a broader sense: "The Heads of State or Government … have a common conviction that a Europe composed of States which, in spite of their different national characteristics, are united in their essential interests … is indispensable if a mainspring of development, progress and culture, world equilibrium and peace is to be preserved" ([Irish government], *Membership of the European Communities: Implications for Ireland, Laid by the Government before Each House of the Oireachtas* [Dublin: The Stationery Office, 1970], 109–12).

131. On the Fouchet Plan, see the special issue of *Revue d'Allemagne et des pays de langue allemande* 29, no. 2 (1997); Maurice Vaïsse, *La grandeur. Politique étrangère du général de Gaulle, 1958–1969* (Paris: Fayard, 1998), 175–90.

132. Corinne Defrance, "La culture dans les projets d'union politique de l'Europe (1961–1962)," *Revue d'Allemagne et des pays de langue allemande* 29, no. 2 (1997): 289–302.

133. "Draft Treaty — Fouchet Plan II (18 January 1962)," in *Selection of Texts Concerning Institutional Matters of the Community from 1950 to 1982* (Luxembourg: European Parliament, 1982): 119–21.

134. "Declaration on European Identity (Copenhagen, 14 December 1973)."

135. The 28 May 2004 draft of the Constitutional Treaty mentioned the legacy of Hellenist and Roman traditions and of the Enlightenment (Gérard Bossuat, "Histoire d'une controverse. La référence aux héritages spirituels dans la Constitution européenne," *Matériaux pour l'histoire de notre temps*, no. 78 (2005): 68–82. The Catholic Church and Christian leaders requested the inclusion of a reference to Christianity. The resulting controversy prompted the Presidium of the European Convention to draft a shorter, more general statement: "DRAWING INSPIRATION from the cultural, religious and humanist inheritance of Europe, from which have developed the universal values of the

inviolable and inalienable rights of the human person, freedom, democracy, equality and the rule of law" ("Treaty Establishing a Constitution for Europe," *Official Journal of the European Union* 47, no. C310 [2004]: 1–474).

136. General Assembly United Nations, "The Universal Declaration of Human Rights," http://www.un.org/en/documents/udhr/index.shtml.

137. On Greece and the EC, see Eirini Karamouzi, "Telling the Whole Story: America, the EEC and Greece, 1972–1974," in *Europe in the International Arena During the 1970s: Entering a Different World*, ed. Antonio Varsori and Guia Migani (Brussels: Peter Lang, 2011), 355–374; Mario Del Pero et al., *Democrazie. L'Europa meridionale e la fine delle dittature* (Florence: Le Monnier, 2010).

138. Servan-Schreiber, *Le défi américain.*

139. Frank Pfetsch, "La problématique de l'identité européenne," *The Tocqueville Review*, no. 2 (1998): 87–103; Antonio Varsori, "Les mers, frontières de l'Europe et leur rôle dans la formation de l'identité européenne," in *Identité et conscience européennes au XXe siècle*, ed. René Girault (Paris: Hachette, 1994), 157–67.

140. Mirroring the polysemy of the word "Europe," "European identity" has various meanings. French historians tend to define it in cultural terms. Robert Frank distinguishes between "European identity," "European consciousness," and "European sentiment." "European identity" is defined as an awareness of shared cultural traditions. "European consciousness" is characterized as the perceived necessity of building a united Europe. "European sentiment" is used to describe an emotional commitment to the European project (*le degré d'adhésion affective à la nécessité de faire l'Europe*) (Robert Frank, "Introduction," in *Les identités européennes au XXe siècle. Diversités, convergences et solidarités*, ed. Robert Frank and Gérard Bossuat [Paris: Publications de la Sorbonne, 2004], 9). Wilfried Loth accepts Frank's proposed distinction between the terms "European identity" and "European consciousness" (Wilfried Loth, "Europäische Identität und europäisches Bewusstsein," in *Nationale Identität und transnationale Einflüsse. Amerikanisierung, Europäisierung und Globalisierung in Frankreich nach dem Zweiten Weltkrieg* [Munich: Oldenburg, 2007], 35–52). Gérard Bossuat offers roughly the same definition: "European identity" is taken to designate the values shared by all European societies, while "European consciousness" implies a recognition of European unity (Gérard Bossuat, "La quête d'une identité européenne," in *La culture et l'Europe. Du rêve européen aux réalités*, ed. Antoine Mares (Paris: Institut d'études slaves, 2005), 19–43). Some historians and most political scientists, however, use "European identity" to refer specifically to the EC/European Union. For an introduction to the political science literature, see Jeffrey T. Checkel and Peter J. Katzenstein, *European Identity* (Cambridge, UK, and New York: Cambridge University Press, 2009); Jeffrey T. Checkel, "International Institutions and Socialization in Europe: Introduction and Framework," *International Organization* 59, no. 4 (2005): 801–26.

141. MAE, Direction d'Europe, *Note : préparation de la conférence au sommet. Aspects politiques et institutionnels*, 4 September 1972, MAE, EC files 1971–6, 3791; MAE, Direction d'Europe, *Note : préparation du sommet (notes de la présidence),* 20 June 1972, MAE, EC files 1971–6, 3791.

142. Quoted in *Note rédigée par Ruggiero à la demande de M. Mansholt*, Brussels, 19 June 1972, MAE, EC files 1971–6, 3795. During his July 1972 talks with Brandt, Pompidou used the term "European identity" in a similar context (Memcon Pompidou/Brandt, 4 July 1972, CHAN, 5AG2 1011).

143. Froment-Meurice, *Note : entretien avec l'ambassadeur du Japon*, 24 October 1973, MAE, U.S. files 1970–5, 1137.

144. Burin des Roziers, Brussels telegram, 4 October 1973, CHAN, 5AG2 1021.

145. Pompidou to Brandt, 16 October 1973, CHAN, 5AG2 1009.

146. Pompidou wrote in the margins: "good telegram" (Pompidou, margin comment on Burin des Roziers, Brussels telegram, 4 October 1973, CHAN, 5AG2 1021).

147. Geoffroy de Courcel to Ambafrance Washington, telegram 749, 11 December 1973, MAE, U.S. files 1970–5, 721. See also MAE, Direction des Affaires politiques, circular telegram 504, 31 August 1973, MAE, U.S. files 1970–5, 1137.

148. Froment-Meurice, *Note: entretien avec l'ambassadeur du Japon*, 24 October 1973, MAE, U.S. files 1970–5, 1137.

149. Kosciusko-Morizet, *Etats-Unis, Europe, France. Convergences et obstacles*, 12 November 1973, MAE, U.S. files 1970–5, 725.

150. [Sauvagnargues], *Organisation de l'Europe [Mémorandum sur le Conseil européen remis au président à mon retour de Corse]*, September 1974, MAE, Archives privées (AP), 373.

151. Yann de l'Ecotais, "La Communauté n'est pas un club anti-américain," *Le Figaro*, 18 March 1974.

152. Headline, *Le Figaro*, 7 September 1973.

153. Roger Massip, "Les Européens au pied du mur," *Le Figaro*, 15–16 December 1973; Roger Massip, "Bilan positif," *Le Figaro*, 17 December 1973.

154. Maurice Delarue, "La réunion de Copenhague," *Le Monde*, 11 September 1973; Paul Fabra, "La crise de l'énergie: une politique commune reste à inventer," *Le Monde*, 10 December 1974.

155. Aron, "II. L'identité perdue (15 février 1974)," in Georges-Henri Soutou, *Les articles de politique internationale dans Le Figaro de 1947 à 1977*, vol. 3, 1350.

156. *SEC(73)3412-F: Déclaration faite par M. François-Xavier Ortoli, président de la Commission des Communautés européennes, lors de son arrivée en visite officielle à Washington (D.C.)*, 30 September 1973, HAEU, EN, 1566.

157. *Déclaration du président Ortoli à Blair House, le 1er octobre 1973, à l'issue de ses entretiens avec le président Nixon*, HAEU, EN, 1567.

158. Pierre Drouin, "Une Communauté sans prophète," *Le Monde*, 15 December 1973.

159. Roger Massip, "Sauver la Communauté," *Le Figaro*, 1 November 1973.

160. Roger Massip, "Editorial : Décider," *Le Figaro*, 9 December 1973.

161. Quoted in *Note rédigée par Ruggiero à la demande de M. Mansholt*, Brussels, 19 June 1972, MAE, EC files 1971–6, 3795.

162. Letter from Pompidou to Brandt, 8 August 1973, CHAN, 5AG2 1009.

163. FCO, letter from Michael Alexander to Lord Bridges, 15 November 1973, doc. 392, in Hamilton, *Documents on British Policy Overseas. The Year of Europe.*

164. MAE, Rome telegram 3051-66, 10 November 1973, CHAN, 5AG2 1035.

165. Vlad Constantinesco, "Le rôle du Conseil européen dans la formation d'une identité européenne," in *Institutions européennes et identités européennes*, ed. Marie-Thérèse Bitsch, Wilfried Loth, and Raymond Poidevin (Brussels: Bruylant, 1998), 439.

166. Ibid.

167. Marie-Thérèse Bitsch, Wilfried Loth, and Raymond Poidevin, "Institutions européennes et identités européennes," in *Les identités européennes au XXe siècle. Diversités, convergences et solidarités*, ed. Robert Frank and Gérard Bossuat (Paris: Publications de la Sorbonne, 2004), 131–32; Luisa Passerini and Hartmut Kaelble, "European Identity, the European Public Sphere, and the Future of 'Europe,'" in Frank and Bossuat, *Les identités européennes au XXe siècle*, 91–100.

168. "Second Report on European Political Cooperation in Foreign Policy Matters (Copenhagen, 23 July 1973)."

Chapter 3

WAR IN THE MIDDLE EAST

The Europeanization of France's Arab Policy

Six months after the launch of the Year of Europe, the Yom Kippur War compelled French officials to go further in their reappraisal of EPC. It is my contention that the Europeanization of Arab and Middle East policy under Pompidou's government was intentional. "Arab policy" is a hazy concept. It can refer either to France's take on the Middle East conflict or to its relations with Arab states, which are interrelated but not fully overlapping issues. This term, moreover, has both a descriptive and a normative, that is, pro-Arab meaning. I use it here in a value-neutral way to designate France's approach toward Arab states, and I refer to its stance on the Arab-Israeli conflict as its Middle East policy.

The French government began to Europeanize its Middle East policy in 1971 and 1972 while pressing for a common, Arab-friendly stance on the conflict. These attempts were, however, half-hearted at best. The real shift occurred in the aftermath of the Yom Kippur War. The Quai d'Orsay played an active role in drafting a joint EPC declaration on the Arab-Israeli conflict. It also presented a blueprint for a Euro-Arab partnership.

The exclusion of France and other European countries from the Middle East peace process was an important factor behind these moves.[1] But there was more to the story. Faced with the increasing influence of the United States in the Middle East, French officials suddenly became more acutely aware of France's geopolitical decline. Since the nineteenth century, and

---

Notes for this section begin on page 105.

except for a brief interlude during the period of decolonization, successive French governments have made consistent and successful efforts to assert their influence in the Arab world. The Yom Kippur War did not deter the French from pursuing this path, but Pompidou and the Quai d'Orsay took a conscious step in favor of a European, rather than a strictly national, approach. In so doing, they gave a European dimension to France's long-standing Arab policy.

The Revival of French Arab Policy

Attempts by the French state to assert its influence in the Arab world date back to the Napoleonic era. Colonization and, subsequently, the League of Nations' mandate system, allowed it to impose its authority in the region. Decolonization dealt a blow to Franco-Arab relations. The 1962 Evian peace accords with Algeria, however, laid the basis for their revival.[2] As early as 1962, the French government restored diplomatic relations with Jordan, Saudi Arabia, and Syria. It reestablished diplomatic ties with Iraq and Egypt in 1963. During the mid to late 1960s, it strengthened its political and economic relations with Arab states. There were concerns about access to raw materials. Algeria's 1965 dismissal of the economic provisions of the Evian accords prompted the (partly state-owned) French oil companies to diversify their supply sources. The French armaments industry was pleased to find new clients in the Arab world.[3] This policy was also driven by foreign policy concerns. De Gaulle was anxious to reassert France's influence on the Southern rim of the Mediterranean and to speak in a different voice from the United States.[4]

The 1960s revival of Franco-Arab ties implied a rebalancing of France's relationship with Israel. The Fourth Republic had built an alliance with the new Jewish state, based on the experience of World War II and a shared ideological mindset—a socialist ideal, a commitment to Republican values, and a refusal to compromise with totalitarianism.[5] In 1960, de Gaulle, who had returned to power two years earlier, ended nuclear cooperation with Israel, even though he subsequently authorized French firms with existing contracts to continue their work on the Dimona reactor.[6] In 1963, he rejected the Israeli proposal for a treaty of alliance. Despite this rebalancing, France and Israel maintained friendly ties during the early to mid 1960s, pursuing economic, technical and cultural cooperation talks.[7]

The 1967 Six-Day War, by contrast, marked a "turning point" in Franco-Israeli relations.[8] De Gaulle had not purposely planned this shift. His stance on the conflict was essentially shaped by broader geopolitical concerns. He feared that an Israeli attack in response to the Egyptian closure of the Straits of Tiran would lead to a global conflict involving the United

States and the Soviet Union.[9] He thus banned all arms deliveries to front-line states—an embargo which was clearly directed against Israel.[10]

Though unintended, the Franco-Israeli "divorce" paved the way for a pro-Arab French Middle East policy.[11] De Gaulle refused to acknowledge Israel's territorial gains. On 23 November 1967, the United Nations Security Council (UNSC) voted a resolution on "The situation in the Middle East." UNSC Resolution 242 requested "withdrawal of Israeli armed forces from territories occupied in the recent conflict."[12] The Soviet and the Arab delegations had wanted the word "all" to precede the word "territories." The FCO had suggested "the" instead. Israel won the case. Both were omitted from the English text, but the definite article was reintroduced in the French translation.[13] On 27 November, de Gaulle caused further consternation in Tel Aviv, censuring Israel's conquest ambitions and calling the Jews "an elite people, sure of themselves and domineering."[14]

Despite this, the end of France's special relationship with Israel did not constitute a complete break with the past. De Gaulle remained adamant about Israel's right to "live in peace within secure and recognized boundaries."[15] From 1969 onwards, President Pompidou trod in his footsteps. He insisted on the need for a comprehensive settlement based on UNSC Resolution 242, meaning full Israeli withdrawal, but also the recognition of Israel by Arab states.[16] In line with de Gaulle's 1967 proposal, Pompidou also supported four-power talks on the Middle East—including Britain, France, the Soviet Union, and the United States—to reduce the risk of bipolar confrontation.[17] The U.S. government remained skeptical: the three other states might have the opportunity to apply joint pressure on the United States to force Israel to make more far-reaching concessions than it had been willing to make.[18] Four-power talks nonetheless took place from 1969 to 1971.

Predictably, France's Arab-friendly Middle East policy enhanced its standing in the Arab world. Building upon this momentum, Pompidou went further than de Gaulle in strengthening ties with Arab states. Iraq and Libya became the top clients of France's armaments industry.[19] Pompidou even supported a major arms deal with the new Libyan ruler, Muammar al-Gaddafi, in the face of strong U.S. opposition.[20] Angry pro-Israeli supporters mobbed Pompidou and his wife during a long-planned visit to the United States. The French ambassador to the United States, who received much of the blame, reported that this incident had dealt "a severe blow [*un coup de froid*]" to Franco-U.S. relations.[21]

At Cross Purposes: EC States and the Middle East, 1970–1973

EPC provided Pompidou's government with an opportunity to push for its Middle East agenda within a European framework. Foreign Minister

Maurice Schumann, a European-leaning Gaullist,[22] suggested the Middle East be one of the first two topics to be discussed within EPC, along with the CSCE. Schumann's receptiveness was in sharp contrast to Pompidou's skepticism. The French president had been opposed to the creation of EPC and remained doubtful of its value. With time, even Schumann's enthusiasm waned, as the gap between France and its pro-Israeli EC partners proved unbridgeable.[23]

Pompidou's initial opposition to EPC seems puzzling. His election in 1969 had opened the way for a European *relance*. Setting forth his triptych "completion, deepening, widening," he had softened the edges of de Gaulle's doctrine on European integration.[24] Any such adjustment was hardly needed in EPC's case: Pompidou's government was able to ensure that EPC remained strictly intergovernmental. The president's handwritten comments point to two main concerns. He feared that EPC would strengthen the influence of middle-ranking diplomats and hence weaken his control over foreign policy-making. Commenting on an EPC report, he asked ironically whether the political directors would now give instructions to the foreign ministers. "It is the everlasting Brussels trend," he added, namely, "as soon as six officials get together, they think of themselves as the [European] Commission."[25] Pompidou also worried about the implications of EC enlargement. So long as there were questions about future EC membership, he claimed, "there [was ...] no point in putting provocative sign-posts in an empty store."[26] According to Schumann, Pompidou only agreed to the enshrinement of a provision for political unification in The Hague communiqué to prevent his EC counterparts from asking for cooperation within a broader framework including the four applicant countries.[27] Pompidou probably felt that a broader forum would restrict his room for maneuver. His opposition hardly subsided with time. After The Hague summit, he repeatedly instructed Schumann to slow down progress toward the establishment of EPC.[28] He later had harsh words for the first EPC report on the Middle East: "it's cat food" ("c'est de la bouillie pour chats").[29]

Unlike Pompidou, Schumann saw EPC as an opportunity to give more clout to France's Middle East policy. He was fully aware of the challenge at hand given the pro-Israeli outlook of West Germany and the Netherlands. Brandt was intent on balancing the West German commitment to Israel with friendlier relations with Arab states. Nonetheless, his government's stance still reflected a strong sense of responsibility toward the Jewish people.[30] The West German government was also anxious to avoid conflict with the United States, which had developed a close friendship with Israel since the mid-1960s.[31] Likewise, the Netherlands had developed a special alliance with Israel since the 1950s, supplying it with armaments during the wars of 1956 and 1967.[32] Publicly, Schumann stated that intra-EC differences were a very good reason to discuss the Middle East within EPC and thereby test the willingness of the six EC states (the Six) to achieve foreign policy unity.[33] In truth, the Quai d'Orsay hoped to bring its EC partners closer to its views.[34]

The Quai d'Orsay initially scored points. The report adopted by EC foreign ministers in May 1970—also known as the Schumann Paper—implicitly endorsed the French interpretation of UNSC Resolution, quoting the incriminating sentence of the French text: "withdrawal of Israeli forces from *the* territories occupied in the recent conflict."[35] The only gesture of goodwill toward Israel was a provision for minor and mutually agreeable boundary adjustments. But the Quai's hopes soon proved ill-founded. Schumann failed to convince his EC counterparts to publicize the report.[36] The result was confusion and disagreement, pointing to insuperable divisions among EC states. Kosciusko-Morizet, then serving as ambassador to the United Nations (UN), reported that his EC counterparts in New York had received conflicting instructions—report formally, versus informally, to UN Secretary-General U Thant—or no instructions at all.[37] Scheel even publicly dismissed the report as a working paper devoid of practical implications.[38] The matter was not settled until July 1971 when the Political Committee decided that the Six's ambassadors would draw upon the Schumann Paper in their talks with relevant parties.[39]

Subsequent EPC talks on the Middle East were also marked by confusion and disagreements. In July 1971, the Political Committee painstakingly agreed to draft a report on the "commitments to, and guarantees of, peace [*engagements de paix et garanties juridiques d'un règlement*]."[40] The Quai d'Orsay speedily set its staff to work. The French drafts, however, went further than what the Dutch were prepared to accept. At the September 1972 Political Committee meeting, the Dutch refused to use them as a basis for a joint report.[41] In February 1971, the Political Committee endorsed a watered-down version of the French texts, but even these documents proved controversial. The political directors recommended that the Six refer to them while talking to high-level mediators—the new UN secretary-general, Kurt Waldheim, and the special UN representative for the Middle East, Gunnar Jarring.[42] West Germany, however, warned against hampering U.S. peace efforts.[43] As a result, the Six scaled down their ambitions. They concurred that the text offered a basis for discussion but decided to keep it secret.[44]

The 1973 enlargement of the EC did little to foster consensus. Mindful of its dependency on Arab oil, the FCO had "adjusted its sails to the Arab wind" since the early 1970s.[45] Denmark, by contrast, was quite pro-Israeli. Quai and FCO officials, moreover, had become increasingly convinced that only the United States could pressure Israel into making the concessions required to break the deadlock.[46] Jarring's efforts to bring the parties to the negotiating table had been unsuccessful. With his 1972 expulsion of 20,000 Soviet advisers, Egyptian President Anwar el-Sadat had signaled his willingness to work with the U.S. government toward a settlement. The Israeli leadership, however, had refused to meet his request for a commitment to withdrawal from the Sinai Desert prior to the negotiations. The Israelis had little incentive to do so because their positions on the Golan Heights and the Suez Canal gave them the security they wanted.

This set of factors paralyzed EPC. During the months leading up to the Yom Kippur War, only Italy pushed for a European initiative on the Middle East.[47] Quai officials rejected the Italian proposal as pointless.[48] Douglas-Home concurred: "our experience suggests that we would be unable to secure firm agreement on anything worthwhile amongst the Nine."[49] Consequently, even a modest Italian proposal for a $5 billion assistance plan to Egypt received the cold shoulder.[50] There was no lack of awareness of the dangers at hand. At Reykjavik, Pompidou expressed concerns about a possible Arab radicalization and the use of oil as a political weapon.[51] FCO officials thought it increasingly likely that Egypt would resort to military action.[52] In June 1973, Heath warned Nixon that unless the West could "do something about the Arab-Israeli problem" its "whole industrial power and progress" would be at risk. But it would take a war and an oil crisis to spur the EC Nine into action.[53]

Giving a New Impulse to a Political Europe: Pompidou and the Yom Kippur War

During the summer and fall of 1973, Pompidou amended his stance on a political Europe. As late as May 1973, he had expressed doubts as to the EC states' readiness to move beyond economic integration.[54] Concerns about U.S. power in the context of the Year of Europe and the Agreement on the Prevention of Nuclear War had prompted an initial reappraisal. Pompidou announced the shift in his press conference of 27 September, declaring that France was ready to participate in regular EC summits within the EPC framework.[55] He took another significant step in the aftermath of the Yom Kippur War. In his statement to the French Council of Ministers of 31 October, Pompidou announced his intention to take the lead on EC political reform. The time had come, he argued, to demonstrate that European integration rested on a solid basis and could "contribute to the resolution of world problems" ("faire la preuve et l'épreuve de la solidité de la construction européenne, comme de sa capacité de contribuer au règlement des problèmes mondiaux").[56] Translating his words into action, he immediately put this suggestion in a letter to his EC counterparts.[57]

The institutionalization of EC summits had been the idea of Monnet.[58] By 1973, Monnet and his aides had become convinced that progress on European integration, particularly on the planned regional development fund and economic and monetary union, required "a European [political] authority."[59] Monnet had also come to recognize that in the short run only the heads of state or government could constitute this authority.[60] In September 1973, Monnet unveiled his plan to Jobert, Heath and Brandt.[61] His proposal struck a chord in Paris. Jobert passed on his blueprint for a "temporary European government" to Pompidou during an airplane flight over Tibet. He subsequently reported: "I believe he [Pompidou] liked it" ("mon impression, c'est que ça a accroché").[62] Monnet's idea would indeed inspire Pompidou's initiative for institutionalized summitry.

Pompidou's move was not directly connected to the West German overtures on European defense and his concerns over *Ostpolitik,* as Soutou argues.[63] The decisive factors were the U.S.-Soviet "*tête-à-tête*" over the Middle East and the exclusion of Western European countries from the cease-fire and peace talks.[64] The Yom Kippur War turned the Middle East into a Cold War hot spot. Both the United States and the Soviet Union set up airlifts to resupply their allies with military equipment.[65] The Soviet Union initiated its airlift to Egypt and Syria on 9 October. Initially, the Nixon administration withheld full-scale assistance to Israel in order to pressure it into accepting a cease-fire.[66] Sadat, however, opposed a cease-fire that did not request Israeli withdrawal to the 1967 pre-war lines, prompting Nixon to order a full-scale airlift. Nonetheless, senior U.S. officials remained anxious to prevent an escalation into an all-out confrontation. Responding to Brezhnev's request for urgent consultations, Kissinger flew to Moscow on 20 October. The two men rapidly agreed on a simple cease-fire. The UNSC merely endorsed the U.S.-Soviet text on 22 October.[67] UNSC Resolution 338 called for an immediate cease-fire and the start of "negotiations between the parties concerned under appropriate auspices." The phrase "appropriate auspices" was intentionally left vague. Kissinger clearly had no intention of involving the former mandatory powers—France and Britain—in the peace discussions. The strategy which he would implement in subsequent weeks and months was designed to put the United States in a position of unilateral advantage in the Middle East. It had three main components: win Sadat's trust; convince the Israeli government that it had to compromise with its Arab neighbors; and minimize the Soviet role while letting the Soviet leaders believe that they remained involved.[68]

The war strained France's bilateral ties with Washington. In Paris, the U.S. airlift to Israel came in for harsh criticism. On 11 October, Jobert urged

Kissinger to "press the Israelis" and "put heavy pressure on your friend Brezhnev to stop the supply of equipment."[69] U.S. officials subsequently tried to assuage the French by arguing that the United States had not initiated its own resupply effort until "the Soviets had been engaged in massive resupply for five days," but to no avail.[70] The French government also criticized the alleged U.S. attempt to use the Middle East crisis to strengthen its relative power position. The Nixon administration had tabled several proposals in the North Atlantic Council for using NATO resources in the Middle East, reviving the old quarrel of whether "out-of-area issues" were the proper concerns of the alliance.[71] It also used its bases on West German territory to resupply Israel. French officials therefore condemned the U.S. use of "NATO and détente to gain support for its position in the Middle East."[72] They also disapproved of West Germany's permissivism. Scheel authorized the shipments, provided the U.S. government assumed full responsibility for them.[73] Publicly, West German officials hid behind the argument that they did not know the destination of U.S. planes. News of the loading of military equipment onto Israeli ships in Bremerhaven put them in an awkward position. Only then did the West German government lodge a complaint of a "breach of German neutrality."[74]

Pompidou was mostly concerned about the implications of the U.S.-Soviet "*tête-à-tête*" for French influence, but he had a point when he criticized such polarization as potentially explosive.[75] The immediate aftermath of the Yom Kippur War witnessed the most serious Cold War crisis since the 1962 Cuban missile confrontation. In his meeting with Israeli Prime Minister Golda Meir on 22 October, Kissinger implicitly encouraged the Israelis to continue their military advances for a few hours after the cease-fire became effective.[76] Israel did just that, hoping to encircle the Egyptian Third Army. On 23 October, the UNSC passed another cease-fire resolution, but fighting went on. Sadat soon pleaded for a joint U.S.-Soviet peace-keeping force. The Soviet leadership seized the opportunity. On 24 October, Brezhnev sent a letter warning that the Soviet Union would take "appropriate steps unilaterally" if the United States failed to accept this proposal.[77] Brezhnev was probably bluffing. Kissinger's reading of his message as an ultimatum was an alarmist interpretation.[78] It prompted him to call for an emergency night session of the National Security Council which resolved to place U.S. forces throughout the world on the highest peacetime alert level (Def Con 3).

The U.S. nuclear alert caused friction within the Atlantic Alliance. Only Britain received an advance warning. In meetings with French officials, Kissinger alleged that the urgency of Brezhnev's warning had left the U.S. government but little time for consultation.[79] He admitted that "in all candor, perhaps we should have told you," but went on to say that "our experience in this crisis with the Europeans is they have behaved not as friends but as hostile powers." Kissinger was particularly aggravated by the refusal of America's NATO allies, except for the Netherlands, to authorize U.S. transport planes to fly over their territory.[80] The Dutch government had even decided to supply Israel directly with arms, although the two countries had somewhat grown apart in the early 1970s.[81] Kosciusko-Morizet was correct in judging Kissinger's view of consultation a one-way process designed to ensure Western European support for U.S. policy.[82] "Let's be honest," Kissinger bluntly told Cromer, "we could have consulted to the devil and back with the Europeans and they would not have changed one iota."[83]

Pompidou's attempt to rebalance power relations in the West resonated with elite opinion in France and the French press. In politics, Pompidou told Heath, you have to "take the plunge [*se lancer*]." Europe had been missing from the international arena. It was time for the EC Nine to try and repair this "humiliation" by giving a new impulse to what was "essential, namely, political cooperation."[84] French journalists expressed similar ideas. The Middle East, *Le Monde* argued, had highlighted Western Europe's weakness. Pompidou's call for regular EC summits was "a salutary reaction [*un sursaut salutaire*]."[85] In *Le Figaro*, Massip portrayed Pompidou's initiative as a commendable attempt to shake the EC out of its "apathy." But strengthened cooperation, as opposed to genuine integration, he warned, might not suffice to halt the decline of "European nations."[86] In hinting at the need for institutional reform, Massip prefigured the rationale of Foreign Minister Sauvagnargues for an institutional *relance* in the summer of 1974.

Pompidou's plan for enhanced European political leadership was both reminiscent of, and different from, the Fouchet Plan. Like de Gaulle, Pompidou's objective was to challenge the ascendancy of the superpowers and to counter the trend toward bipolarity.[87] Unlike de Gaulle, his aim was not to establish a parallel set of institutions to weaken and even torpedo the EC. Pompidou's proposal also had a different meaning because EPC was already in place. French officials would instantly attempt to translate the president's words into deeds in the Middle East and the Arab world. U.S. Ambassador Irwin worried that France might now be poised to achieve its goal of "a strong, prosperous and independent EC, in which France plays the leading role and through which France can pursue national objectives."[88] Irwin's analysis of the French motives was perceptive: French officials still pursued national goals. Nonetheless, in applying EPC to Middle East and Arab matters, they were to demonstrate a new commitment to collective European action.

Leaning on Europe: The Declaration on the Middle East

In March 1973, Jobert, a Morocco-born pied-noir, replaced Schumann as foreign minister.[89] As secretary-general of the Elysée, Jobert had been among those advising Pompidou to strengthen France's ties to the Arab world.[90] His appointment, however, did not shift the Quai d'Orsay's position on EPC in the Middle East, nor did the outbreak of the Yom Kippur War on 6 October. The critical factor behind the French reassessment was the war itself and its handling by the superpowers.

When war began, the prospects for common European action were bleak. The EC Nine remained sharply divided. The Quai d'Orsay and the FCO maintained their pro-Arab posture. During a parliamentary hearing, Jobert asked whether "an attempt to go home really qualif[ied] as an unexpected attack" ("Est-ce que tenter de remettre les pieds chez soi constitue vraiment une agression imprévue ?").[91] More discreetly, the FCO recommended prioritizing Britain's oil supplies and hence "taking care not to identify ourselves in any way with the Israeli war effort [...] and to express as much sympathy as possible with the Arab side."[92] The Dutch and the Danish governments, in contrast, remained supportive of Israel, holding Egypt and Syria responsible for the war.[93] The Danish prime minister even created a stir by publicly stating that he would be "willing to defend the aggressiveness of Israel to a large extent."[94] The EC Nine thus agreed to nothing beyond a simple cease-fire appeal on 13 October.[95]

The Arab use of oil as a political weapon soon gave new impetus to EPC. On 17 October, nine Arab countries—Abu Dhabi, Algeria, Bahrain, Egypt, Kuwait, Libya, Qatar, Saudi Arabia, and Syria—jointly agreed to cut their monthly oil production by 5 percent.[96] On 19 October, Nixon's request of a \$2.2 billion appropriation for Israel triggered further restrictions on oil supplies. The following day, King Faisal of Saudi Arabia decreed a total embargo on oil deliveries to the United States. Fellow Arab oil producers soon followed suit, extending the embargo to the Netherlands.[97] Pressure increased further after the end of hostilities. On 5 November, the Organization of Arab Petroleum Exporting Countries (OAPEC) resolved to reduce production to 25 percent below its September level.[98] These measures caused acute shortage concerns in the West. Western European countries relied on imported oil to meet over 50 percent of their energy needs.[99] Even France's pro-Israeli EC partners now became willing to make a gesture of goodwill toward the Arabs. West Germany, in particular, supported an Italian-Belgian proposal on 17 October for an EPC initiative. Its foreign ministry steered a difficult course between West Germany's pro-Israeli public opinion on the one hand, and domestic oil supply concerns on the other. Only through a joint position did it consider it possible to square the circle.[100] On 22 October, the EPC expert committee in charge of the Middle East drafted a proposed statement.[101]

This pro-Arab shift of EC states would not by itself have prompted the Quai d'Orsay to see EPC in a new light. Instead, the key factor was the prospect of being excluded from the Middle East peace process. On 17 October, Puaux dismissed the proposed EPC initiative as pointless and potentially harmful.[102] If anything, the EPC draft statement strengthened the French misgivings. The Quai d'Orsay rejected it as offering little else than a rephrasing of UNSC Resolution 338.[103] Quai officials were well aware that the phrase "under appropriate auspices" was designed as a way to bypass the UN.[104] Both Kissinger, who was determined to gain the upper hand in the Middle East, and the Israelis, who viewed the UNSC as a "a fourteen to one majority against them," were opposed to a UN-sponsored peace conference.[105] Not long thereafter, the Quai d'Orsay changed its strategy. The particular rationale behind this shift has been overlooked. French officials certainly shared their EC partners' dissatisfaction with Kissinger's Cold War approach to the conflict and their prospective exclusion from the peace negotiations.[106] Yet they more specifically decided to use EPC in order to strengthen their case for UN primacy. Puaux recommended supporting a joint statement if and only if it asserted the rightful role of the UN in the future peace process.[107] This rationale was not lost on the FCO. The French, it argued, were trying to use their status of permanent UNSC member to "keep in the act."[108] Only in this way could the Quai d'Orsay hope to get "a seat at the peacemaking table."

Oil restrictions, by contrast, were not a factor behind this reassessment. The French political and economic establishment counted on its ties with Arab decision-makers in order not to bear the brunt of their oil policy. By late November, several Arab governments had indeed pledged to keep French oil deliveries at their September level.[109] Meeting in Algiers on 26–28 November, the Arab League summit resolved to draw up a list of "friendly," "neutral," and "enemy-supporting" countries.[110] Within the EC, only France and Britain would qualify as "friendly."[111] In 1974, the French government would conclude bilateral deals—providing set quantities of oil in exchange for industrial investment—with Saudi Arabia, Iran, and Iraq.[112] Britain and other EC states would also follow this bilateral path, albeit with varying degrees of success.[113]

Seizing the initiative, the Quai d'Orsay submitted a draft for a European declaration. In line with Puaux's recommendations, Pierre Pélen, the French ambassador in Copenhagen, drafted a text emphasizing the special responsibilities of the UN and of the UNSC.[114] Initially, many of his EC colleagues refused to agree to anything more than preliminary talks.[115] But they finally went ahead with the French proposal, worried as they were

about further oil restrictions. On 31 October in Copenhagen, the ambassadors of the EC Nine presented their governments with a revised version
of the French text for approval.[116]

EC states quickly endorsed the draft, but British support concealed
misgivings. FCO officials felt that "Europe [was] [...] too large and its vital interests too closely involved for it to sit silent while great events take
place over their [sic] heads."[117] They were in favor of peace talks taking
place under a UN umbrella. Nonetheless, they considered a peace settlement to be so crucial to British interests that they were unwilling to hold
it up "by insisting on any particular procedure."[118] The text's emphasis
on the UN, they argued, could only "exasperate" the Nixon administration. In an attempt to reconcile Britain's conflicting commitments to EPC
and to the Anglo-American relationship, the FCO's Middle East unit suggested a two-pronged approach: British officials should work to convince
the French to accept a more limited UN involvement. Meanwhile, Britain
should publicly support the EPC document while privately explaining its
position to the U.S. government.[119] This proposed double game hinted at
future contradictions between EPC and transatlantic cooperation.

The Declaration on the Middle East published on 6 November, however, had an even stronger pro-Arab leaning than the Copenhagen draft.
Even more surprisingly, the last-minute changes to the text were Britain's
rather than France's doing.[120] The French draft had been intended as a consensus document. Douglas-Home thought up eleventh-hour changes to
answer the Dutch plea for EC assistance without undermining Britain's
privileged position in the Arab world. Like the Quai d'Orsay, the FCO was
loath to challenge the Arab embargo, as "it seem[ed] very likely that [...]
if we were to divert oil supplies to them, we should join the Dutch in the
dog-house, which would further decrease Arab oil production."[121] With
transatlantic and Anglo-American relations under strain, however, FCO
officials were anxious not to let "the European alternative" fall apart.[122]
Douglas-Home's hope was that an Arab-friendly statement would solve
this conundrum: the EC Nine would have "a firm [...] position" on which
to base their efforts to convince the Arabs to moderate the embargo, while
Britain would not bypass it.[123] The initial draft had called for negotiations
based on UNSC Resolutions 242 and 338. It had also stated that any settlement should provide for international guarantees, including a peace-
keeping force and demilitarized zones.[124] Dispelling all ambiguities, the
Declaration of 6 November backed the French interpretation of Resolution
242, urging Israel "to end the territorial occupation which it ha[d] maintained since the conflict of 1967."[125] It also supported the Arab stance on
occupied Palestine, casting the Palestinian issue as a political, rather than

a refugee, problem.[126] The French government had endorsed this view since 1970.[127]

The Declaration was a historical novelty. Never before had EC states spoken with a single voice on a major international issue. Critics ascribed its pro-Arab tilt to the blackmail of the Arab oil embargo. In his communiqué of 9 November, Israeli Foreign Minister Abba Eban summed up its content as "oil for Europe rather than peace for the Middle East."[128] The pro-Israeli French daily *L'Aurore* deplored that the EC Nine had "happily sacrificed" the Jews in order to keep their own gas stations open.[129] A "political Europe [*l'Europe politique*]," it noted ironically, had been born "on an oriental rug." There was some truth to this claim, but it did not hold for France. The French, as the FCO argued, were unwilling to accept "the realities of the situation," namely, the new leading role of the United States in the Middle East.[130] Nonetheless, they partly came to terms with reality in acknowledging the need for collective action in order to retain influence over the Middle East. This move was congruent with the new French emphasis on a European identity. Jobert's proposed Euro-Arab partnership would further substantiate this concept.

Jobert Takes the Lead: Toward a Euro-Arab Partnership

Through his last-minute amendments to the Declaration, Douglas-Home had fostered the Europeanization of France's Middle East policy. The Europeanization of its Arab policy was the result of a more preconceived plan in Paris, albeit one that materialized over time. It also targeted rising U.S. influence in the region: on 11 November, Kissinger had brokered a disengagement agreement between Egypt and Israel at the kilometer 101 checkpoint. The Declaration was specifically designed to assert a European voice vis-à-vis the United States and, to a lesser extent, the Soviet Union on the Middle East conflict. The Quai d'Orsay's proposed Euro-Arab dialogue was aimed at counterbalancing such influence through strengthened ties with Arab states.[131]

Jobert first floated the idea of a Euro-Arab partnership in his Tunis address of 15 November 1973. His speech drew on the long pre-existing notion of a Euro-African partnership ("Eurafrique").[132] The 1975 Lomé Convention would deal a serious blow to its underlying neo-colonial paradigm.[133] But Jobert still found this notion relevant or at least useful in appealing to his audience. "Europe," he declared, should be linked to "Africa." The "Northern fringe of Africa," which was also the "Southern rim of the Mediterranean," was the best place to start.[134] Jobert clearly intended this plan to serve a broader geopolitical purpose. Closer ties between Europe and the Maghrib, he maintained, would create "a new form of solidarity" and thus contribute to détente.

Tunis was not an accidental choice. Jobert's visit had long been planned, but he knew that his hosts had warmly approved the Declaration on the Middle East. The Tunisian leaders signaled their support by inviting the EC Nine's ambassadors to listen to Jobert's speech. During his meeting with Jobert, Foreign Minister Mohammad Masmoudi deplored U.S. meddling in Egyptian affairs, calling upon EC states to become involved in the Middle East negotiations.[135]

For all his talk on U.S. single-handedness, Jobert probably reckoned that a European peace initiative was unlikely to be successful. He erred on the side of caution while talking to Masmoudi.[136] His goal was rather to counteract the ascendancy of the United States and the Soviet Union through strengthened Euro-Arab ties. He spelled out the principles of an alternative strategy in his speech of 21 November to the WEU Assembly. Reiterating Pompidou's qualms about the U.S.-Soviet *"tête-à-tête"* in the Middle East, he spoke at length about détente. In a Gaullist vein, he argued that détente should rest on two principles: the equality of states and the freedom of nations. He then urged the EC Nine to foster détente through a closer relationship with the Mediterranean world and the Middle East. "Europe" and Mediterranean countries, he stated, had a shared destiny. Likewise, the "political, cultural and human" ties binding "Europe" and the Middle East were firmly anchored in history and geography.

The Quai d'Orsay counted on Jobert's request—reiterated in his 30 November address to the French Senate—to gain leverage in the Arab world and eagerly followed its reception in Arab capitals. Initially, news from Syria was disappointing. André Nègre, the French ambassador in Damascus, wrote that the Syrian press had given it little attention. Nègre blamed it on the use of the oil weapon, which fueled a "mostly superficial, anti-European sentiment."[137] Ensuing reports were more encouraging: the Syrian leadership had welcomed Jobert's overture.[138] Jobert's gesture also struck a chord in all Maghrib countries, particularly Tunisia.[139] Echoing Jobert's words in his December speech at the Italian-African Institute, Masmoudi argued for a Euro-Arab rapprochement.[140]

The Quai d'Orsay matched Jobert's new Euro-Arab rhetoric with an unprecedented commitment to European unity. When the FCO recommended an EPC démarche to get the oil embargo lifted, Jobert and his staff warned against playing the solidarity card "the wrong way" and objected to linking the Declaration to oil.[141] Nevertheless, Quai officials knew that EPC required sacrifices, and they eventually accepted the proposed EPC démarche. Much to the FCO's satisfaction, the French ambassadors in the

Arab world duly carried out their mission without seeking to sabotage it or doing their job half-heartedly.[142]

Jobert's initiative had given a European dimension to a long-standing national policy—one that was designed to assert French influence in the Arab world. As such, it went beyond the need to "compensate for Europe's exclusion from the Middle East peace process."[143] A Euro-Arab partnership served essentially the same purpose as France's Arab policy, whether in its colonial or in its Gaullist guise,[144] but the means were different. They involved leaning on Europe, as opposed to following a strictly national route. By accepting the EPC démarche against their perceived interests, French officials had passed a first test of European solidarity.

The Arab Magi in Copenhagen

Arab countries played a critical role in translating Jobert's ideas into policy. There was a weak consensus among the EC Nine despite the Declaration on the Middle East. Due to enduring divisions between pro-Israeli and pro-Arab states, they disagreed as to what to do next. The governments of Arab states provided Jobert and the Quai d'Orsay with essential support. The EC Nine would find themselves hard-pressed to turn them down when they sent a mission to the December 1973 EC summit to plead for strengthened Euro-Arab ties. It is my contention that the League of Arab States purposely responded to Jobert's overture even though it acted on its own initiative.[145]

It did not take long for Arab leaders to endorse Jobert's vision. In spite of the EPC démarche, OAPEC did not lift the embargo. At its mid November Algiers summit, the League of Arab states officialized OAPEC's discriminative policy, pressing the EC to take an even clearer stand against Israeli occupation.[146] In language reminiscent of Jobert's speeches, its communiqué also pointed to the shared interests and the civilizational ties binding "Europe" and "Arab countries" and pleaded for "mutually beneficial cooperation." Secretly, the League decided to send envoys to the EC summit which was slated for mid December in Copenhagen.[147]

Pursuing a two-pronged approach, Arab states refused to relax their oil pressure on the West but moved speedily to promote a Euro-Arab rapprochement. Syrian leaders made it clear: OAPEC would not lift its oil restrictions so long as pro-Israeli EC states had not demonstrated through actions their commitment to an Arab-friendly peace settlement in the Middle East.[148] The Algerian and Saudi oil ministers came to Europe in late November with an even starker message. Oil production would only return to normal after a satisfactory settlement of the Arab-Israeli conflict.

It was now up to Western European governments, they argued, to exert pressure on the United States.[149] This harsh language, however, was tempered by the League's plans for the EC summit. By 3 December, Arab officials had informed the French embassies in Algeria, Morocco, and Tunisia of the intention to send delegates to Copenhagen.[150]

In moving swiftly, Arab countries caught the French government off guard. Initial French reactions pointed to conflicting agendas between the Elysée and the Quai d'Orsay. Initially, Pompidou reacted suspiciously. The Copenhagen meeting, he wrote, is not meant to address Arab matters. "Our [EC] partners should not fall into the trap even if they are struggling with oil restrictions," he added. There was some irony in this statement. After all, the French foreign minister had first floated the idea of a Euro-Arab rapprochement.[151] Yet Pompidou had conceived of the summit as a "fireside chat." His proposed objective was to foster consensus on broad political and economic issues pertaining to the "future of Europe," notably institutionalized summitry.[152] The Arab mission clearly thwarted such plans.

News of the planned mission did not remain secret for long. The Moroccan ambassador to Denmark informed both the Danish EC Presidency and his French counterpart of the plan on 12 December.[153] Pélen relayed the information to Paris, where the news reached the Quai d'Orsay around midday.[154] Probably because they were unsure how to react, Quai officials did not immediately contact their embassies. Jean-Marie Soutou, the French ambassador in Algiers, heard the news through the Agence France Presse, France's news agency.[155] Soutou therefore had to wait until his conversation with Quai Levant and North Africa Director Guy de Commines the next day to voice cautious support for the League's initiative.[156]

The League's announcement prompted a flurry of diplomatic activity. Algeria's lobbying for a meeting with the EC heads of state or government proved unsuccessful. Nonetheless, the EC Nine agreed to organize a meeting at ministerial level, as initially requested by the Moroccan ambassador.[157] The meeting was scheduled for 10:30 A.M. on 14 December but was delayed until the evening due to the late arrival of the four Arab envoys: Masmoudi (Egypt), Abdelaziz Bouteflika (Algeria), Mansour Khaled (Sudan), and Adnane Pachachi (United Arab Emirates).[158] The talks took place in an unheated room of Christiansborg Castle, the Danish government building. This small gesture of inhospitality was designed to highlight the hardships suffered by Western Europeans as a result of the Arab oil policy. The four Arab foreign ministers, however, remained impervious to the cold. They hinted at possible adjustments for Arab-friendly states, but they reasserted OAPEC's policy line. Building on the Algiers communiqué, however, they also called for closer Euro-Arab ties in the economic, cultural, and technical fields.[159]

The Copenhagen summit highlighted lasting disagreements on the Middle East among the EC Nine. On the morning of 15 December, Pompidou pressed his EC counterparts to issue a joint statement which would plainly request Israel to withdraw to the 1967 pre-war lines.[160] Failure to do so would be a setback for the EC and its nascent "European policy," he warned, equating French and European interests. To Brandt, however, the Declaration on the Middle East of 6 November sufficed for the time being. Heath was no more successful when he called in the afternoon for a statement that would beg Israel to match the commitment of Arab states to peace with a pledge of withdrawal.[161] Pompidou did his part to try and convince the participants. This text, he argued, would specify the obligations of both parties, that is, the implementation of UNSC Resolution 242 in all its parts and the recognition of Israel's right to "existence" and "security." This was to no avail, Brandt and his Danish, Dutch, and Luxembourger counterparts rejected the proposal. Consequently, the summit communiqué merely reasserted the EC Nine's commitment to the November Declaration and their willingness "to assist in the search for peace and in the guaranteeing of a settlement."[162]

Despite such hesitation, the Arab mission put Jobert's emerging Euro-Arab strategy on a more solid footing. It made it difficult for France's EC partners to reject the French concept. In the FCO's words, "since the dialogue was suggested by the Arabs, it would be at best churlish and at worst dangerous to resist it."[163] FCO officials and their EC counterparts feared that the Arabs might then retaliate through further oil restrictions. Speaking on behalf of the EC Nine, the Danish prime minister insisted on the harmful effects of the Arab oil policy, but he also expressed interest in Euro-Arab cooperation.[164] The League's mission also showed that the Declaration on European Identity, which was published the same day, was not empty rhetoric. Arab leaders clearly viewed the EC Nine as a valid discussion partner. Comparing the Arab emissaries to the biblical magi, *L'Aurore* ironized that they had confirmed the existence of a new European identity.[165] In positive language, *Le Monde* and *Le Figaro* stated that this surprise visit spoke of the rightful role of a united Europe in the international arena.[166]

EPC Taken to Task: The French Plan for a Euro-Arab Dialogue

The oil weapon had provided an auspicious background for France's Arab and Middle East policies, but it was also conducive to OPEC's assertiveness. By January 1974, OPEC had quadrupled the posted price of crude oil. The first oil shock would complicate France's policy designs by entangling EPC in the transatlantic relationship.

The Quai d'Orsay was quick to respond to the Arab overture at Copenhagen. By 29 December, its Middle East unit had produced a blueprint for a Euro-Arab dialogue. The plan provided for cooperation across a wide range of fields, particularly oil, technology, and economics.[167] It also set forth a five-stage procedure: initial EPC discussions; talks between the presidents of the EC and the Arab League; the establishment of expert committees; a Euro-Arab ministerial meeting; and, finally, a summit of the EC and Arab heads of states or government.

Due to U.S. opposition, the proposed Euro-Arab dialogue received a mixed reception when it was unveiled at the EPC Political Committee meeting on 10 January 1974.[168] The British, Italian, and Belgian delegates supported it, but their West German and Dutch counterparts proved harder to convince. The FCO was mindful of U.S. hostility. Meanwhile, the Nixon administration had advanced its plan for institutionalized cooperation among oil-importing advanced countries. Cromer warned that the U.S. government would view a Euro-Arab conference as running counter to its own energy policy.[169] To FCO officials, however, there was also one positive aspect to the French proposal. It might help to "let the Dutch off the hook" and to convince Arab leaders to stop using the oil weapon against Western Europe.[170] Their hope was that U.S. officials would swallow the plan because it encompassed all—rather than only oil-producing—Arab countries.[171] The Italian political director, Roberto Ducci, endorsed it because it was congruent with Italy's Mediterranean designs: to strengthen Italian influence based on its position as a "bridge [*paese ponte*]" between the Northern and the Southern rims of the Mediterranean.[172] Ducci's hope was to reconcile the proposed dialogue with U.S. policy. The Dutch and West German political directors, however, were uneasy about the plan.[173] The Hague even presented a rival proposal offering financial help to the Palestinians.[174] Puaux interjected that the Arab emissaries had pleaded for cooperation, not aid. He won the case. The political directors resolved to draft a report based on the French blueprint.

The Quai d'Orsay still faced an uphill battle. The three expert committee meetings held from 18 January to 1 February 1974 witnessed heated debate. Denmark, the Netherlands and West Germany took a hostile stance out of concern for the U.S. government. The West German delegate warned that as acting head of EPC, Scheel would have to notify Kissinger of the plan. Quai officials suspected their Dutch counterparts—probably correctly—of trying to postpone any decision until after the U.S.-sponsored energy conference planned for mid February.[175] Even the European Commission expressed reservations. The proposed dialogue encompassed political and economic issues. As such, it impinged on the EC's and hence on its own prerogatives.[176]

On 7 February, the Political Committee endorsed a watered-down version of the French plan, subject to ministerial approval.[177] A significant amount of redrafting had occurred without undermining the core of the French strategy. Oil was excluded, though somewhat ambiguously, from the Euro-Arab dialogue. The Political Committee's report stated that the proposed dialogue "went far beyond oil," and that oil matters should not be its "starting point."[178] Political issues were also explicitly left out. Kissinger had engaged in his step-by-step diplomacy, persuading Sadat and Syrian President Hafiz al-Assad to participate in separate, U.S.-mediated negotiations with Israel.[179] A Euro-Arab dialogue, he warned, would lump together topics which he wished to keep separate—particularly Egyptian- and Syrian-Israeli relations and the Palestinian issue.[180] Above all, he did not want any third party to interfere with his peace efforts. Nonetheless, the Euro-Arab dialogue could still fulfill its original purpose, that is, strengthen European influence in the Arab world through an institutionalized partnership.

The meeting of 7 February took place against the background of heightened Franco-U.S. tensions over the Middle East peace negotiations. The Quai d'Orsay had failed to get its second-best option accepted: Waldheim's active participation in the talks with a clear mandate from the UNSC.[181] Although the U.S. government had agreed to Waldheim's participation, Nixon had ensured Meir that his role would be purely symbolic.[182] The conference opened in Geneva on 21 December under joint U.S. and Soviet chairmanship. Waldheim was present, but Kissinger was clearly leading the game. "Your strategy is working well," he cabled Nixon, "we are the only participant who is in close touch with all the parties, the only power that can produce progress, and the only one that each is coming to in order to make that progress."[183] Syria's refusal to attend in the absence of a Palestinian delegation did not disturb him. Quite the opposite, it was "a blessing in disguise," making it easier for the Israelis to participate on the eve of a domestic election. The conference was adjourned after a day and a half, clearing the way for Kissinger's unilateral shuttle diplomacy. During his January 1974 trip to Saudi Arabia, Kuwait, and Syria, Jobert once again spoke out against Europe's exclusion from the Middle East peace talks. Assuming an almost antagonistic stance, he insisted that the EC Nine and Arab states had a shared interest in breaking free from their dependency upon the superpowers.[184]

Progress in the Middle East peace negotiations clearly strengthened Jobert's resolve to proceed with his plan for a Euro-Arab partnership. He even alluded to it in his conversation with Syrian Foreign Minister Abdul Halim Khaddam.[185] The Quai d'Orsay's willingness to compromise on oil and political issues testified to its commitment to the plan. So did its conciliatory position vis-à-vis the European Commission. Quai officials had always been adamant about keeping a clear distinction between the EC and EPC. Nonetheless, they agreed to assign joint responsibility for the dialogue to both sets of institutions, which somewhat blurred this divide. On 7 February, the EC Nine were thus poised to engage in an unprecedented endeavor. The Mediterranean policy adopted by the EC Council of Ministers in November 1972 had been designed to provide a framework for bilateral—trade, financial, and technical—agreements with Mediterranean countries.[186] The Euro-Arab dialogue, by contrast, entailed wide-ranging cooperation between the EC Nine as a single entity and the Arab world as a whole.

A New Commitment to Collective Action

The onset of the first oil crisis facilitated the Europeanization of France's Middle East and Arab policies. But oil per se was not the only, or even the major factor driving French policy. French officials relied on their bilateral ties with Arab states to secure their supplies, and they were slow to take stock of the implications of the price increase. Their prime motivations lay elsewhere. They were related to concerns about shifting power relations in a changing geo-political context. Losing ground in the Middle East caused particular concern since the region fell within what French officials had traditionally viewed as their sphere of influence. Leaning on Europe to reverse a trend toward decline was congruent with the underlying principles of de Gaulle's Fouchet plans. Yet it is noteworthy that Pompidou had initially been opposed to foreign policy cooperation, and that prior to the Yom Kippur War the Quai d'Orsay had only feebly supported EPC's work on the Middle East. This Europeanization process, moreover, went beyond de Gaulle's designs. Their participation in the EPC démarche marked a new dedication to collective action—a shift which has gone unnoticed in the literature.[187] U.S. opposition to the Euro-Arab dialogue would give the French an opportunity to demonstrate this commitment more forcefully.

In publishing their Declaration on the Middle East, EC states established an important milestone. For the first time in the EC's history, they had spoken to the world jointly on a major international issue. Their text laid the basis for the Middle East diplomacy of the nascent European entity. Its key principles—the right of every state in the region "to live in peace within secure and recognized boundaries" and the need to account for "the legitimate rights of the Palestinians"—would shape subsequent statements on the Arab-Israeli conflict.[188]

Oil acted as a catalyst for European foreign policy unity. Without the Arab oil restrictions, Israeli-friendly countries would not have been willing to publish a statement which then qualified as pro-Arab. With concerns shifting from supplies to prices in 1974, oil would ironically put this newly found cohesion to the test, reasserting the significance of the transatlantic relationship. The disagreements which marred the preliminary talks on the Euro-Arab dialogue were a warning sign of future difficulties.

Notes

1. Möckli, *European Foreign Policy During the Cold War*, 201–02, 241–42.
2. David Styan, *France & Iraq: Oil, Arms and French Policy Making in the Middle East* (London and New York: I.B. Tauris, 2006), 50.
3. André Nouschi, *La France et le monde arabe. Depuis 1962, mythes et réalités d'une ambition* (Paris: Vuibert, 1994), 122; Vaïsse, *La grandeur*, 644–45.
4. Vaïsse, *La puissance ou l'influence?* 370.
5. Schillo, *France-Israël, 1948–1959*.
6. Avner Cohen, *Israel and the Bomb* (New York: Columbia University Press, 1998), 73–75.
7. Vaïsse, *La puissance ou l'influence?* 357.
8. Bozo, *La politique étrangère de la France depuis 1945*, 53.
9. Ibid.; Vaïsse, *La puissance ou l'influence?* 365.
10. Vaïsse, *La grandeur*, 636.
11. Ibid., 365.
12. United Nations Security Council, "Resolution 242 of 22 November 1967: The Situation in the Middle East," http://daccessdds.un.org/doc/RESOLUTION/GEN/NR0/240/94/IMG/NR024094.pdf?OpenElement.
13. Ibid.
14. Charles de Gaulle, *Discours et messages*, 5 vols. (Paris: Plon, 1970), vol. 5, 532.
15. United Nations Security Council, *Resolution 242 of 22 November 1967*.
16. Vaïsse, *La puissance ou l'influence?* 368.
17. Antoine Coppolani, "La France et les Etats-Unis dans les négociations quadripartites sur le Moyen-Orient (1969–1971)," in *Les relations franco-américaines au XXe siècle*, ed. Pierre Mélandri and Serge Ricard (Paris: L'Harmattan, 2004), 193–207; Yves-Henri Nouailhat, "Les divergences entre la France et les Etats-Unis face au conflit israélo-arabe de 1967 à 1973," *Relations internationales*, no. 119 (2004): 334–44; Vaïsse, *La grandeur*, 635.
18. For a brief analysis of the four-power talks, see Peter Hahn, "Conflict and Cooperation: Pompidou, Nixon and the Arab-Israeli Conflict, 1969–1974," in *Georges Pompidou et les Etats-Unis, « une relation spéciale », 1969–1974* ed. Eric Bussière and François Dubasque (Brussels: Peter Lang, forthcoming).
19. Bozo, *La politique étrangère de la France depuis 1945*, 62–3; Vaïsse, *La puissance ou l'influence?* 371.
20. Pompidou tried his best to defend the deal against U.S. criticisms (letter from Pompidou to Nixon, 11 March 1970, CHAN, 5AG2 115). Kissinger, however, remained skeptical, saying to Lucet: "You like to live dangerously" (letter from Lucet to son Jean-Louis, junior diplomatic adviser to the president, 13 March 1970, CHAN, 5AG2 115). On U.S.

reactions to the arms deal, see also Hahn, "Conflict and Cooperation: Pompidou, Nixon and the Arab-Israeli Conflict, 1969–1974."

21. Lucet, interview, 27 June 1986, MAE, AO, Lucet. Georges-Henri Soutou maintains that the trip had little impact on France's U.S. policy (Soutou, "Le président Pompidou et les relations entre les Etats-Unis et l'Europe"). Maurice Vaïsse, by contrast, argues that it poisoned (*envenimer*) Franco-American relations (Maurice Vaïsse, "Les 'relations spéciales' franco-américaines au temps de Richard Nixon et Georges Pompidou," *Relations internationales*, no. 119 (2004): 351).

22. Vaïsse, *La puissance ou l'influence?* 35.

23. The only archival-based study of these preliminary talks is Möckli, *European Foreign Policy During the Cold War*, 68–78.

24. Vaïsse, "Changement et continuité dans la politique européenne de la France."

25. Pompidou, margin comment on MAE, telegram 120-35 dated 29 January 1971, CHAN, 5AG2 1035.

26. Pompidou, margin comment on Direction d'Europe, *Note*, 1 June 1970, CHAN, 5AG2 1035.

27. Raimond, *Note pour Monsieur le président de la République*, 6 January 1970, CHAN, 5AG2 1035.

28. Pompidou, margin comment on Raimond, *Note pour Monsieur le président de la République*, 6 January 1970, CHAN, 5AG2 1035; Pompidou, margin comment on MAE, circular telegram 209, 3 June 1970, CHAN, 5AG2 1049; "Davignon Report (Luxembourg, 27 October 1970)."

29. Pompidou, margin comment on MAE, telegram 120-35 dated 29 January 1971, CHAN, 5AG2 1035.

30. On West Germany and the Middle East, see Haim Goren, *Germany and the Middle East: Past, Present, and Future* (Jerusalem: Hebrew University Magnes Press, 2003); Helmut Hubel, "Germany and the Middle East Conflict," in *Germany and the Middle East: Patterns and Prospects*, ed. Shahram Chubin (London: Pinter, 1992), 41–54; Josef Joffe, "Reflections on German Policy in the Middle East," in *Germany and the Middle East: Patterns and Prospects*, ed. Shahram Chubin (London: Pinter, 1992), 195–209; Markus A. Weingardt, *Deutsche Israel- und Nahostpolitik. Die Geschichte einer Gratwanderung seit 1949* (Frankfurt and New York: Campus, 2002).

31. On the U.S.-Israeli rapprochement, see Warren Bass, *Support Any Friend: Kennedy's Middle East and the Making of the U.S.-Israel Alliance* (Oxford and New York: Oxford University Press, 2003); Abraham Ben-Zvi, *Decade of Transition: Eisenhower, Kennedy, and the Origins of the American-Israeli Alliance* (New York: Columbia University Press, 1998); Zachary K. Goldman, "The Cold War and Israel. Ties That Bind: John F. Kennedy and the Foundations of the American–Israeli Alliance," *Cold War History* 9, no. 1 (2009): 23–58; Vaughn P. Shannon, *Balancing Act: US Foreign Policy and the Arab-Israeli Conflict* (Aldershot, UK, and Burlington, VT: Ashgate, 2003), 54–60.

32. Duco Hellema, Cees Wiebes, and Toby White, *The Netherlands and the Oil Crisis: Business as Usual* (Chicago: University of Chicago Press, 2004), 17.

33. *Intervention de M. Maurice Schumann, ministre des affaires étrangères [au colloque européen des jeunes parlementaires]*, 16 December 1970, FJM, AMK 114/4/44.

34. MAE, Sous-direction du Levant, *Note : consultation à Six sur le Proche-Orient*, 23 April 1971, MAE, Middle East files 1971–2, 2021.

35. *Session ministérielle sur la coopération politique, 13–14 mai 1971. Relevé de conclusions*, MAE, EC files 1971–6, 3795. My emphasis.

36. MAE, Sous-direction du Levant, circular telegram 255, 6 July 1971, MAE, Middle East files 1971–2, 2021.

37. Kosciusko-Morizet, New York telegram 2254-7, 2 June 1971, MAE, Middle East files 1971–2, 2021.
38. Alain Greilsammer and Joseph Weiler, *Europe's Middle East Dilemma: The Quest for a Unified Stance* (Boulder, CO: Westview Press, 1987), 28; Weingardt, *Deutsche Israel- und Nahostpolitik. Die Geschichte einer Gratwanderung seit 1949*, 210.
39. MAE, Sous-direction du Levant, circular telegram 255, 6 July 1971, MAE, Middle East files 1971–2, 2021.
40. MAE, Direction d'Europe, circular telegram 260, 7 July 1971, MAE, EC files 1971–6, 3794.
41. MAE, Direction d'Europe, circular telegram 346, 23 September 1971, MAE, EC files 1971–6, 3794.
42. *CPE/RC(72)1: 11ᵉ réunion du Comité politique, Luxembourg, 15–16 février 1972. Relevé de conclusions*, MAE, EC files 1971–6, 3795.
43. MAE, Direction d'Europe, circular telegram 181, 14 April 1971, MAE, EC files 1971–6, 3795.
44. MAE, Direction d'Europe, circular telegram 181; MAE, Sous-direction du Levant, *Note : consultations des pays de la C.E.E. sur le Proche-Orient*, 15 May 1972, MAE, Middle East files 1971–2, 2022.
45. FCO, minute, Douglas-Home to Heath, 7 June 1973, doc. 112, in Hamilton, *Documents on British Policy Overseas. The Year of Europe.*
46. MAE, Sous-direction du Levant, *Note : les Etats-Unis et la crise du Proche-Orient*, 15 May 1973, MAE, U.S. files 1970–5, 727; FCO, minute, Anthony Parsons to Antony Acland, 7 June 1973, doc. 111, in Hamilton, *Documents on British Policy Overseas. The Year of Europe*; FCO, minute, Douglas-Home to Heath, 7 June 1973, doc. 112, ibid.; FCO, telegram 1268 to Washington, 15 June 1973, doc. 126, ibid.; FCO, telegram 1269 to Washington, 15 June 1973, doc. 127, ibid.
47. MAE, Direction d'Europe, circular telegram 542, 23 November 1972, MAE, EC files 1971–6, 3791. On Italy and the Middle East, see Daniele Caviglia and Massimiliano Cricco, eds., *La diplomazia italiana e gli equilibri mediterranei. La politica mediorientale dell'Italia dalla guerra dei Sei Giorni al conflitto dello Yom Kippur* (Soveria Mannelli: Rubbettino Editore, 2006); Luca Riccardi, *Il problema Israele. Diplomazia italiana e PCI di fronte allo stato ebraico (1948–1973)* (Milan: Guerini studio, 2006).
48. MAE, Sous-direction du Levant, circular telegram 36, 19 January 1973, MAE, EC files 1971–6, 3804; MAE, Sous-direction du Levant, *Note : réunion des experts du Proche-Orient*, 14 March 1973, MAE, EC files 1971–6, 3792.
49. FCO, minute, Douglas-Home to Heath, 7 June 1973, doc. 112, in Hamilton, *Documents on British Policy Overseas. The Year of Europe.*
50. Möckli, *European Foreign Policy During the Cold War*, 195.
51. Memcon Pompidou/Nixon, third meeting, 1 June 1973, CHAN, 5AG2 1023.
52. FCO, minute, Douglas-Home to Heath, 7 June 1973, doc. 112, in Hamilton, *Documents on British Policy Overseas. The Year of Europe.*
53. On the EC nine's wait-and-see stand in the run-up to the war: *CP/RC (73)5: 18ᵉ session du Comité politique, Bruxelles, 16/17 janvier 1973. Relevé de conclusions*, MAE, EC files 1971–6, 3804. MAE, Sous-direction du Levant, *Note : réunion des experts du Proche-Orient*, 14 March 1973, MAE, EC files 1971–6, 3792; *RM/0C(73)1: VIe réunion ministérielle, Bruxelles, 16 mars 1973. Relevé de conclusions*, MAE, EC files 1971–6, 3792; MAE, Sous-direction du Levant, circular telegram 342, 8 June 1973, MAE, EC files 1971–6, 3804; MAE, Direction d'Europe, *Note : réunion du groupe de travail Moyen-Orient, Copenhague, le 3 septembre 1973*, undated, MAE, EC files 1971–6, 3804.
54. Memcon Pompidou/Heath, first meeting, 21 May 1973, CHAN, 5AG2 1015.

55. Pompidou, press conference, 27 September 1973, CHAN, 5AG2 633.
56. President's statement at the French Council of Ministers, 31 October 1973, CHAN, 5AG2 1036.
57. See, for example, letter from Pompidou to Brandt, 31 October 1973, CHAN, 5AG2 1009.
58. On Monnet's role in the creation of the European Council, see Marie-Thérèse Bitsch, "Jean Monnet et la création du Conseil européen," in *Jean Monnet, l'Europe et les chemins de la paix*, ed. Gérard Bossuat and Andreas Wilkens (Paris: Publications de la Sorbonne, 1999), 399–410; Pascal Fontaine, "Le rôle de Jean Monnet dans la genèse du Conseil européen," *Revue du marché commun*, no. 229 (1979): 357–65.
59. van Helmont, *Note de réflexion*, FJM, AMK 116/1/26.
60. Monnet, handwritten notes, "Londres," 16 September 1973, FJM, AMK 116/1/38.
61. *Entretien avec Michel Jobert aux Affaires étrangères à 11h30*, 8 September 1973, FJM, AMK 116/1/28; Monnet, handwritten notes, "Londres," 16 September 1973, FJM, AMK 116/1/38; Monnet, handwritten notes, "Voyage à Bonn 18–20 septembre 1973," FJM, AMK 116/2/46.
62. *Note de Jean Monnet,* 21 September 1973, FJM, AMK 116/1/44.
63. Soutou, "President Pompidou, Ostpolitik, and the Strategy of Détente," 249.
64. President's statement at the French Council of Ministers, 31 October 1973.
65. William B. Quandt, *Peace Process: American Diplomacy and the Arab-Israeli Conflict since 1967,* 3rd ed. (Washington, D.C., and Berkeley: Brookings Institution Press and University of California Press, 2005), 114. On the Cold War and the Middle East, see Rashid Khalidi, *Sowing Crisis: The Cold War and American Dominance in the Middle East* (Boston: Beacon Press, 2009); E. M. Primakov, *Russia and the Arabs: Behind the Scenes in the Middle East From the Cold War to the Present* (New York: Basic Books, 2009).
66. Quandt, *Peace Process: American Diplomacy and the Arab-Israeli Conflict since 1967,* 110.
67. United Nations Security Council, "Resolution 338: Cease-Fire in the Middle East (22 Oct)," http://daccess-dds-ny.un.org/doc/RESOLUTION/GEN/NR0/288/65/IMGNR028 865.pdf?OpenElement.
68. Quandt, *Peace Process: American Diplomacy and the Arab-Israeli Conflict since 1967,* 132–33.
69. Memcon Kissinger/Jobert, 11 October 1973, NPM, NSC, Country files, 679.
70. George Springsteen, deputy assistant secretary for European affairs, and Joseph Sisco, assistant secretary of state for Near Eastern and South Asian affairs, both impressed this argument upon Kosciusko-Morizet (Secretary of State, telegram 206601 to American Embassy Paris, 18 October 1973, NPM, NSC, Country files, 679; Secretary of State, telegram 206998 to American Embassy Paris, 19 October 1973, NSC, Country files, 679).
71. On the debate on out-of-area issues, see Gianni Bonvicini, "Out-of-Area Issues: A New Challenge to the Atlantic Alliance," in *The Atlantic Alliance and the Middle East,* ed. Joseph I. Coffey and Gianni Bonvicini (Pittsburgh, PA: University of Pittsburgh Press, 1989), 1–16.
72. American Embassy Paris, telegram 27488 to Secretary of State, 23 October 1973, NPM, NSC, Country files, 679.
73. Hilfrich, "West Germany's Long Year of Europe: Bonn between Europe and the United States," 245.
74. Department of State, telegram 212618 to American Embassy Bonn, 27 October 1973, ibid., 2009.
75. Pompidou, statement at the French Council of Ministers, 31 October 1973, CHAN, 5AG2 1036.
76. Hanhimäki, *The Flawed Architect: Henry Kissinger and American Foreign Policy,* 313–14.

77. Quoted in Quandt, *Peace Process: American Diplomacy and the Arab-Israeli Conflict since 1967*, 121.
78. Hanhimäki, *The Flawed Architect: Henry Kissinger and American Foreign Policy*, 315.
79. Secretary of State, telegram 211737 to American Embassy Paris, 27 October 1973, NPM, NSC, Country files, 679.
80. Hynes, *The Year That Never Was: Heath, the Nixon Administration and the Year of Europe*, 194, 197.
81. Hellema, Wiebes, and White, *The Netherlands and the Oil Crisis: Business as Usual*, 27–39.
82. Secretary of State, telegram 2357704 to American Embassy Paris, undated [on or after 27 November 1973], NPM, NSC, Country files, 679.
83. Telcon Kissinger/Cromer, 26 October 1973, 9:25 P.M., NPM, NSC, Kissinger files, Telcons, 23.
84. Memcon Pompidou/Heath, second meeting, 16 November 1973, CHAN, 5AG2 1015.
85. "Le Sursaut," in *Le Monde*, 1 November 1973.
86. Roger Massip, "Sauver la Communauté," in *Le Figaro*, 1 November 1973.
87. On de Gaulle, see Vaïsse, *La puissance ou l'influence?* 100.
88. American Embassy Paris, telegram 28311 to Secretary of State, 1 November 1973, NPM, NSC, Country files, 679.
89. Vaïsse, *La puissance ou l'influence?* 35.
90. Bozo, *La politique étrangère de la France depuis 1945*, 62–63.
91. Quoted in Mary Kathleen Weed, *Michel Jobert et la diplomatie française. L'image publique d'un homme secret* (Paris: Editions F. Lanore, 1988), 132.
92. FCO, minute, Parsons to Alexander, 11 October 1973, doc. 259, in Hamilton, *Documents on British Policy Overseas. The Year of Europe.*
93. H. A. Jawad, *Euro-Arab Relations: A Study in Collective Diplomacy* (Reading, UK: Ithaca Press, 1992), 72.
94. Quoted in Christian Thune, "Denmark," in *European Foreign Policy-Making and the Arab-Israeli Conflict*, ed. David Allen and Alfred Pijpers (The Hague and Hingham, MA: Martinus Nijhoff Publishers, 1984), 80.
95. "Appeal of the Nine Foreign Ministers of 13 October for a Suspension of Hostilities in the Middle East," in *Texts Relating to the European Political Cooperation* (Bonn: Press and Information Office of the Government of the Federal Republic of Germany, 1974).
96. Jawad, *Euro-Arab Relations: A Study in Collective Diplomacy*, 65–66.
97. Hellema, Wiebes, and White, *The Netherlands and the Oil Crisis: Business as Usual*, 53–55.
98. Fiona Venn, *The Oil Crisis* (London and New York: Longman, 2002), 18f.
99. Wilfrid L. Kohl, "Energy Policy in the Communities," *Annals of the American Academy of Political and Social Science* 440 (1978), 111–21.
100. German foreign ministry, circular telegram 114, 19 October 1973, in Pautsch, *Akten zur Auswärtigen Politik der Bundesrepublik Deutschland 1973*, vol. 3, 1608–12.
101. Pélen, Copenhagen telegram 924-32, 23 October 1973, MAE, EC files 1971–6, 3804.
102. Pélen, Copenhagen telegram 898-905, 18 October 1973, MAE, EC files 1971–6, 3804.
103. Pélen, Copenhagen telegram 924-32, 23 October 1973, MAE, EC files 1971–6, 3804.
104. Council, "Resolution 338: Cease-Fire in the Middle East (22 Oct)".
105. FCO, Brief by Middle East unit, 3 November 1973, doc. 365, in Hamilton, *Documents on British Policy Overseas. The Year of Europe.* Quandt, *Peace Process: American Diplomacy and the Arab-Israeli Conflict since 1967*, 132–33.
106. Möckli, *European Foreign Policy During the Cold War*, 202. Möckli discusses the motivations of the EC nine as a group.
107. MAE, political director [Puaux], *Note pour le ministre*, 30 October 1973, MAE, EC files 1971–6, 3804.

108. FCO, brief by Middle East unit, 3 November 1973.

109. MAE, Direction des Affaires économiques et financières, *Note : attitude des divers pays de l'OPAEP vis-à-vis de la France*, 13 December 1973, MAE, Economic affairs files, 412.

110. MAE, Sous-direction du Levant, *Note : évolution de la crise du Proche-Orient depuis le 25 octobre 1973*, 5 December 1973, MAE, Tunisia files 1973–82, 573.

111. Daniel Yergin, *The Prize: The Epic Quest for Oil, Money, and Power* (New York: Simon & Schuster, 1991), 605.

112. Robert J. Lieber, *The Oil Decade: Conflict and Cooperation in the West* (New York: Praeger, 1983), 85; Fiona Venn, *Oil Diplomacy in the Twentieth Century* (Basingstoke: Macmillan, 1986), 150; Armelle Demagny-Van Eyseren, "Les réactions de la présidence française face au choc pétrolier," in *Milieux économiques et intégration européenne au XXe siècle. La crise des années 1970 — De la conférence de La Haye à la veille de la relance des années 1980*, ed. Eric Bussière, Michel Dumoulin, and Sylvain Schirmann (Brussels: P.I.E. Peter Lang, 2006), 105–17.

113. On bilateral agreements with producers, see Francesco Petrini, "L'arma del petrolio: lo 'shock' petrolifero e il confronto Nord-Sud. Parte prima. L'Europa alla ricerca di un' alternativa: la Communità tra dipendenza energetica ed egemonia statunitense," in *Dollari, petrolio e aiuti allo sviluppo. Il confronto Nord-Sud negli anni '60–70*, ed. Daniele Caviglia and Antonio Varsori (Milan: Franco Angeli, 2008), 79–107.

114. Pélen, Copenhagen telegram 1009-15, 31 October 1973, MAE, EC files 1971–6, 3804.

115. MAE, Sous-direction du Levant, *Note : la crise du Proche-Orient (entretiens entre M. le président de la République et M. Heath)*, 14 November 1973, MAE, EC files 1971–6, 3804.

116. Statement quoted in full in COREU CPE/MUL 57, Copenhagen, 31 October 1973, MAE, EC files 1971–6, 3798.

117. FCO, telegram 2207 to Washington, 2 November 1973, doc. 362, in Hamilton, *Documents on British Policy Overseas. The Year of Europe*.

118. FCO, brief by Middle East unit, 3 November 1973, doc. 365, ibid.

119. FCO, brief by Middle East unit, 3 November 1973, doc. 365, ibid.

120. FCO, brief by Middle East unit, 3 November 1973, doc. 365, ibid.

121. FCO, telegram 196 to The Hague, 1 November 1973, doc. 357, in Hamilton, *Documents on British Policy Overseas. The Year of Europe*.

122. FCO, telegram to J.O. Wright, 2 November 1973, doc. 360, ibid.

123. FCO, Cabinet minutes, 8 November 1973, doc. 383, ibid.

124. Text quoted in full in Pélen, Copenhagen telegram 1016-8, 31 October 1973, MAE, EC files 1971–6, 3804.

125. "Declaration of the Nine Foreign Ministers of 6 November 1973, in Brussels, on the Situation in the Middle East," in *Texts Relating to the European Political Cooperation* (Bonn: Press and Information Office of the Government of the Federal Republic of Germany, 1977), 63–64.

126. For Arab-sponsored UN resolutions casting the Palestinian issue in political terms, see United Nations General Assembly, "Resolution 2628 of 4 November 1970: The Situation in the Middle East," http://unispal.un.org/UNISPAL.NSF/0/8A68B2315AF81A ED82560DE006E2BEB; idem, "Resolution 2949 of 8 December 1972: The Situation in the Middle East," http://daccess-dds-ny.un.org/doc/RESOLUTION/GEN/NR0/269/79/IMG/ NR026979.pdf?OpenElement.

127. Nouailhat, "Les divergences entre la France et les Etats-Unis face au conflit israélo-arabe de 1967 à 1973," 338.

128. "Statement by Foreign Affairs Minister Eban," in *Israel's Foreign Relations: Selected Documents 1947–1974*, ed. Meron Medzini (Jerusalem: Ministry for Foreign Affairs, 1976), 1065–66.

129. Roland Faure, "Editorial : L'union sacrée," in *L'Aurore*, 7 November 1973.
130. FCO, telegram 2207 to Washington, 2 November 1973, doc. 362, in Hamilton, *Documents on British Policy Overseas. The Year of Europe.*
131. *Texte du discours prononcé le 21 novembre par le ministre*, MAE, International organization (IO) files 1971–1976, 2909
132. Marie-Thérèse Bitsch and Gérard Bossuat, eds., *L'Europe unie et l'Afrique : de l'idée d'Eurafrique à la convention de Lomé I* (Brussels, Paris, and Baden-Baden: Bruylant, L.G.D.J., and Nomos, 2005).
133. Jean-Marie Palayret, "Mondialisme contre régionalisme : CEE et ACP dans les négociations de la convention de Lomé, 1970–75," in *Inside the European Community: Actors and Policies in the European Integration*, ed. Antonio Varsori (Baden-Baden and Brussels: Nomos and Bruylant, 2006), 369–97.
134. *Allocution de M. Michel Jobert (Hôtel Hilton, 15 novembre 1973)*, MAE, Tunisia files 1973–82, 572.
135. On Tunisia's foreign policy, see Kenneth J. Perkins, *Tunisia: Crossroads of the Islamic and European Worlds* (Boulder, CO, and London: Westview Press and C. Helm, 1986); Michael M. Laskier, "Israeli-Tunisian Relations between Bourguibism and Nasserism," in *Israel and the Maghreb: From Statehood to Oslo* (Gainesville: University Press of Florida, 2004), 187–217; Michel Brondino, "Bourguiba, *Policy Maker* entre mondialisation et tunisianité : une approche systémique et interculturelle," in *Habib Bourguiba. La trace et l'héritage*, ed. Michel Camau and Vincent Geisser (Paris: Éditions Karthala, 2004), 463–73.
136. Memcon Jobert/Masmoudi, 15 November 1973, MAE, Tunisia files 1973–82, 572.
137. Nègre, Damascus telegram 1182-4, 30 November 1973, MAE, Syria files 1973–82, 51.
138. MAE, Sous-direction du Levant, *Note de synthèse : voyage officiel de M. Jobert en Syrie (28–29 janvier)*, 18 January 1974, MAE, Syria files 1973–82, 44.
139. MAE, Sous-direction du Levant, *Note de synthèse : Tunisie*, 7 December 1973, MAE, Tunisia files 1973–82, 573.
140. MAE, Sous-direction du Levant, *Note de synthèse : Tunisie*, 7 December 1973.
141. FCO, brief by Middle East unit, 3 November 1973, doc. 365, in Hamilton, *Documents on British Policy Overseas. The Year of Europe;* FCO, Paris telegram 1543, 11 November 1973, doc. 386, ibid.
142. FCO, letter from Albert Craig to Richard Faber, 28 November 1973, doc. 424, ibid.
143. Möckli, *European Foreign Policy During the Cold War*, 280, 242.
144. On continuity between the colonial and the Gaullist era, see Henry Laurens, *Le royaume impossible. La France et la genèse du monde arabe* (Paris: Armand Colin, 1990), 179.
145. Möckli overlooks this connection (Möckli, *European Foreign Policy During the Cold War*, 242; Hiepel, "Kissinger's 'Year of Europe'—a Challenge for the EC and the Franco-German Relationship," 293).
146. Yergin, *The Prize: The Epic Quest for Oil, Money, and Power*, 605; Summary of the Algiers communiqué in MAE, Sous-direction du Levant, *Note : évolution de la crise du Proche-Orient depuis le 25 octobre 1973*, 5 December 1973, MAE, Tunisia files 1973–82, 573.
147. Jean-Marie Soutou, Algiers telegram 3537-41, 12 December 1973, MAE, EC files 1971–6, 3804.
148. Nègre, Damascus telegram 1170-4, 26 November 1973, MAE, Syria files 1973–82, 51.
149. MAE, Sous-direction du Levant, *Note de synthèse : évolution de la crise du Proche-Orient depuis le 25 octobre 1973*, 5 December 1973, MAE, Tunisia files 1973–82, 573.
150. Elysée diplomatic advisers, *Les Neuf, le Moyen-Orient et le pétrole*, 3 December 1973, CHAN, 5AG2 1054.
151. Pompidou, margin comment on Elysée diplomatic advisers, *Les Neuf, le Moyen-Orient et le pétrole*, 3 December 1973, CHAN, 5AG2 1054.

152. Raimond, *Note pour Monsieur le président de la République : partie politique du dossier pour les entretiens franco-allemands (26–27 novembre 1973)*, CHAN, 5AG2 1012; Memcon Jobert/ Scheel, Paris, 26 November 1973, MAE, EC files 1971–6, 3789.

153. COREU CPE/MUL ETR 109, Copenhagen, 12 December 1973, MAE, EC files 1971–6, 3789.

154. The Quai d'Orsay received Pélen's telegram at 1:49 P.M. (Pélen, Copenhagen telegram 1225-6, 12 December 1973, MAE, EC files 1971–6, 3789). COREU CPE/MUL ETR 109 only reached Paris at 9:03 P.M.

155. Soutou, Algiers telegram 3537-41, 12 December 1973, MAE, EC files 1971–6, 3804.

156. Soutou, Algiers telegram 3545-8, 13 December 1973, MAE, EC files 1971–6, 3804.

157. Soutou, Algiers telegram 3545-8, 13 December 1973.

158. Jean Lecerf, "En attendant les représentants des Etats arabes," in *Le Figaro*, 15–16 December 1973.

159. CPE/MUL ETR 116A, Copenhagen, 17 December 1973, MAE, EC files 1971–6, 3804.

160. MAE, Direction des Affaires politiques, circular telegram 784, 18 December 1972, MAE, EC files 1971–6, 3789.

161. MAE, Direction des Affaires politiques, circular telegram 783, 18 December 1972, MAE, EC files 1971–6, 3789.

162. "Final Communiqué issued by Anker Jørgensen following the Copenhagen European Summit (Copenhagen, 14 and 15 December 1973)," *Bulletin of the European Communities*, no. 12 (1973): 9–11.

163. FCO, telegram 110 to Washington, 16 January 1974, doc. 507, in Hamilton, *Documents on British Policy Overseas. The Year of Europe.*

164. MAE, Direction des Affaires politiques, circular telegram 784, 18 December 1972, MAE, EC files 1971–6, 3789.

165. Yves Benoît, "Face aux émissaires arabes, le dur apprentissage de la personnalité," in *L'Aurore*, 17 December 1973.

166. "Le sommet de Copenhague risque de se transformer en une conférence européo-arabe," in *Le Monde*, 15 December 1973; Jean Lecerf, "En attendant les représentants des Etats arabes," in *Le Figaro*, 15–16 December 1973.

167. MAE, Sous-direction du Levant, *Note : coopération Europe des Neuf—pays arabes*, 29 December 1973, MAE, EC files 1971–6, 3804.

168. MAE, Sous-direction du Levant, *Note : Comité (10–11 janvier)—Proche-Orient*, 12 January 1974, MAE, EC files 1971–6, 3796.

169. FCO, Washington telegram 126, 10 January 1974, doc. 500, in Hamilton, *Documents on British Policy Overseas. The Year of Europe.*

170. FCO, minute, M.D. Butler to Parsons, 20 December 1974, doc. 478, ibid.

171. FCO, telegram 110 to Washington, 16 January 1974, doc. 507, ibid.

172. Quoted in Silvio Labbate, "L'Italia e lo shock petrolifero del '73 tra interesse nazionale e vincoli europei" (paper presented at the Seminario di Storia Internazionale dell'Età Contemporanea (SSIEC—SISSCO), Università degli Studi di Padova, 28–29 January 2010). On Italy and the Middle East, see Caviglia and Cricco, *La diplomazia italiana e gli equilibri mediterranei. La politica mediorientale dell'Italia dalla guerra dei Sei Giorni al conflitto dello Yom Kippur*; Riccardi, *Il problema Israele. Diplomazia italiana e PCI di fronte allo stato ebraico (1948–1973).*

173. MAE, Sous-direction du Levant, *Coopération européo-arabe (groupe d'experts Proche-Orient) le 18 janvier 1974*, 21 January 1974, MAE, EC files 1971–6, 3807.

174. MAE, Sous-direction du Levant, *Note : Comité (10–11 janvier)—Proche-Orient*, 12 January 1974, MAE, EC files 1971–6, 3796.

175. MAE, Sous-direction du Levant, *Coopération européo-arabe (groupe d'experts Proche-Orient) le 18 janvier 1974*, 21 January 1974, MAE, EC files 1971–6, 3807.

176. MAE, Sous-direction du Levant, circular telegram 81, 29 January 1974, MAE, EC files 1971–6, 3807.

177. *RM (74) 1 CP Proche-Orient : Rapport du Comité politique aux ministres des Affaires étrangères en vue de la réunion du 14 février*, 7 February 1974, MAE, EC files 1971–6, 3792.

178. *RM (74) 1 CP Proche-Orient : Rapport du Comité politique aux ministres des Affaires étrangères en vue de la réunion du 14 février.*

179. On Kissinger's shuttle diplomacy, see Hanhimäki, *The Flawed Architect: Henry Kissinger and American Foreign Policy*, 324–31.

180. Memcon Kissinger/Douglas-Home, 10 February 1974, NARA, SD, RG 59, Lot files, Kissinger, 4.

181. Kosciusko-Morizet, New York telegram 7883-90, 3 December 1973, MAE, U.S. files 1970–5, 721.

182. Quandt, *Peace Process: American Diplomacy and the Arab-Israeli Conflict since 1967*, 139.

183. Quoted in Hanhimäki, *The Flawed Architect: Henry Kissinger and American Foreign Policy*, 321.

184. MAE, Sous-direction du Levant, circular telegram 91, 31 January 1974, MAE, Syria files 1973–82, 44.

185. MAE, Sous-direction du Levant, *Note : visite du ministre*, 30 January 1974, MAE, Syria files 1973–82, 44.

186. Jawad, *Euro-Arab Relations: A Study in Collective Diplomacy*, 31–35.

187. Möckli notes France's initial opposition to the démarche, but he does not highlight the meaning of its eventual agreement to participate (Möckli, *European Foreign Policy During the Cold War*, 206–07).

188. "Declaration of the Nine Foreign Ministers of 6 November 1973, in Brussels, on the Situation in the Middle East."

Chapter 4

Kissinger, Jobert, and the Oil Shock

The Arab use of oil as a political weapon had helped foster a single European voice in Arab and Middle East matters, but at the same time it put intra-EC relations under strain. When war in the Middle East broke out, EC states had failed to make headway with their planned common energy policy. In discriminating among them, the Arab producers made this an even more remote prospect. The embargo against the Netherlands and the supply cuts encouraged the pursuit of national interest. As a result, each EC state took the bilateral route to try and secure its oil supplies from the Arabs.

The oil shock sowed further discord. The Arab oil restrictions encouraged OPEC to assert its market power. By January 1974, it had quadrupled the posted price of crude petroleum. In the face of spiraling energy bills with momentous economic implications, Western European decision-makers increasingly felt that "Europe's best interests now require[d] greater priority to be given on the European side to the content of the transatlantic relationship than was given during the Year of Europe."[1] U.S. international energy policy, however, exacerbated Franco-American differences. The proposed U.S. blueprint for cooperation between advanced consumer countries came across in the Arab world as an attempt at intimidation. As such, it contradicted the basic tenets of France's Arab policy. French officials also saw the U.S. plan as yet another scheme to reassert U.S. control over Western Europe. They attempted to defeat it, pleading for the use of the existing Organization for Economic Cooperation and Development (OECD) instead and for initiating a consumer-producer dialogue.

Notes for this section begin on page 134.

In setting France and the United States on a collision course, the oil crisis prompted both French and U.S. officials to reassert their vision of transatlantic relations. The Nixon administration turned European endorsement of the U.S. plan into a test of Atlantic cohesion. French officials cast any new mechanism for institutionalized cooperation as a threat to the independence of the nascent European entity. Facing radicalized positions, EC states were de facto forced to choose between Paris and Washington. Hard-headed economic realities made France's European option appear ever less appealing than the prospect of transatlantic cooperation. Jobert found himself isolated at the energy conference staged in Washington in February 1974. Nonetheless, it is an exaggeration to state that the French, and Pompidou and Jobert in particular, "were the great losers of the Washington meeting."[2] When push came to shove, France's EC partners did choose to support U.S. international energy policy, but they subsequently did their best to mend fences with France and reassert European unity. They endorsed the Euro-Arab dialogue, although it was much decried in Washington. French press records, on the other hand, point to increasing French skepticism toward the government's policy. Jobert's doggedness did not receive "a good deal of domestic backing."[3] Quite the opposite, many politicians and commentators had begun to question it, arguing that the very objective of building an influential European entity required compromise at times.

The Achilles' Heel of Western Economies

By 1973, the industrialized West was playing a dangerous game. Imported oil had become crucial to its prosperity, and this dependency was a serious cause of economic vulnerability. Western leaders, however, had failed to formulate, let alone adopt, comprehensive solutions to reduce their dependency. So long as cheap fossil fuels contributed to high growth rates, there was no economic pressure to act. Oil alarmists were vocal on both sides of the Atlantic, including those who predicted that world oil production was reaching its limits. Their warnings did not go unheeded, but disagreements on the appropriate course of action meant that industrialized countries failed to join forces to address the challenge. By 1973, the stage was set for a shift in the power balance between oil producers and consumers—one that would have momentous economic implications.

Certainly, oil producers did not wait for Arab output cuts to start modifying the terms of trade with their Western clients. Market forces were moving in their favor. By the early 1970s, the oil industry had turned from a buyers' to a sellers' market. OPEC had expanded its membership from its five founding members to eleven. The seven main oil companies, the so-called "seven sisters," had lost ground to newcomers in the industry that were willing to offer better terms for access to highly prized resources. Rapidly rising demand had strengthened the bargaining power of suppliers. In 1971, oil companies agreed to requests from producer states for higher crude prices. On 14 February and 20 March, they signed two agreements with the Persian Gulf states and Libya, respectively, which provided for an immediate price increase and a 2.5 percent inflation-adjusted yearly rise. In June, OPEC successfully demanded a 20 percent share—to be gradually increased to 51 percent—in the oil companies operating within its members' territory.

Meanwhile, the West had become increasingly dependent on oil imports. In all Western European countries with the exception of Britain, oil had replaced coal as the main source of energy supply.[4] This shift entailed high vulnerability to external shocks. By 1972, 99 percent of oil was imported and met more than 50 percent of Western Europe's energy requirements.[5] The level of vulnerability varied across countries, being particularly high in France and much lower in the United States. French oil imports as a share of total energy consumption rose from 69 percent in 1971 to 75 percent in 1973.[6] Since it was itself an oil producer, the United States relied on foreign oil to meet only 35 percent of its energy needs. West Germany stood somewhere in the middle, with crude oil imports accounting for 42 percent of domestic energy consumption.

Western policy-makers were slow to take stock of this changing geo-economic environment. In 1970, the U.S. Task Force on Oil Import Control sounded the alarm bell. Ironically, its forecasts were overoptimistic. The report predicted that U.S. oil imports would reach 5 million barrels per day (mbd) in 1980. They had already exceeded six mbds by 1973.[7] This acceleration notwithstanding, the Nixon administration took a wait-and-see attitude. Nixon and his aides did not act upon the State Department's 1972 plea to establish a policy framework—including Canada, Japan, Britain, and the EC—to reduce the risks of an energy-induced economic crisis.[8] Not until April 1973 did Nixon make a plea to Congress over enhanced cooperation between developed oil-importing countries. The Six had not made much more progress. Energy made it onto the agenda of the 1972 EC Paris summit, albeit low on the list of priorities, after monetary union and regional policy. The summit communiqué merely stipulated that member states ought to stockpile ninety days' worth of oil. The European Commission subsequently suggested raising this figure to 120 days. Energy was a central topic of the EC Council of Foreign Ministers in May 1973, but the talks ended in disarray. The Council only settled on a broad framework for national emergency plans: member states had until June 1974 to pass legislation on oil rationing and price control in case of crisis.

There was more to this failure to act than complacency. Energy was a divisive topic among EC countries. Paradoxically, energy had been a key pillar of European integration with the 1951 creation of the European Coal and Steel Community (ECSC). In 1957, the signatories of the Treaty of Rome had pledged to make proposals for a common energy policy.[9] The Six, however, failed to translate words into action despite the 1967 merging of the executives of the ECSC, the European Atomic Energy Community, and the European Economic Community.[10] Diverging policy traditions were a major impediment. The French government pursued a "dirigiste" approach involving tight market regulation.[11] French oil companies enjoyed guaranteed market shares, while price control held imports down.[12] The Netherlands and Britain, by contrast, favored a laissez-faire, free-market system. These two countries were home to two of the "seven sisters," BP and Royal Dutch Shell. Their governments opposed any policy with a French flavor lest it should upset the "well-established organization" of the two companies.[13] Britain, moreover, was poised to become a producer in its own right after the discovery of oil and gas fields in the North Sea during the 1960s.[14] It was weary of EC regulation, which might impinge on its ability to exploit these resources as a national asset.[15] Such differences on the respective roles of markets and state contributed to the meager results of the EC Council in May 1973. All participants except Jobert supported a Commission proposal for energy talks with the United States and Japan.[16] The French aversion to trilateralism had its share in this outcome, but Jobert also wanted to ensure that the EC first had a (French-inspired) common energy policy before initiating discussions with third parties.[17] This divide prefigured future Franco-EC clashes over energy.

The Arab Use of Oil as a Weapon: Panic and Division

Following the outbreak of the Yom Kippur War, the Arab use of oil as a political weapon caused acute shortage concerns in Western Europe. These fears were overblown. One Arab producer, Iraq, refused to cut back production. Iran and oil-rich Latin American countries did not reduce their output, nor did they apply the export embargo. Consequently, the world's supply shortfall approximated only 9 percent.[18] Between October 1973 and March 1974, Western European reserves remained above eighty days' worth of consumption,[19] but this only became known ex post facto.

By mid November, OAPEC countries had cut production twice, on 17 October and 5 November, respectively.[20] Would they go on reducing output each month until the West, particularly the United States, forced Israel to compromise? Would the embargo be extended? Such questions loomed large in capitals across the Western world. In encouraging self-serving behavior, they would exacerbate existing EC differences.

The oil embargo against the Netherlands produced tension among EC states. The Dutch government repeatedly pleaded for EC solidarity, pointing to the centrality of the Port of Rotterdam in the oil trade. It found a sympathetic ear only in Bonn and Copenhagen.[21] In fact, the EC did not have an emergency oil-sharing plan, but the OECD did. France and Britain argued against activating this plan, anxious as they were to maintain their standing in the Arab world. Bluntly put, the FCO's strategy was to "put Britain first." Britain's "tenacious policy" during the Yom Kippur War had won it "a privileged position" with Arab producers. It did not want to let this position be "erode[d]" by putting itself "in the same boat as the Dutch."[22] The Quai d'Orsay's line was essentially the same, although Quai officials used more convoluted language, even internally. Nevertheless, the apparent solidarity of the Danish and West German positions only concealed concerns about a possible extension of the embargo to their countries, which would be first in line if OAPEC decided to take that course of action.[23]

The Dutch were not the only ones to worry about shortages. In all Western consumer states, such anxieties fostered narrow national policies. The French government was chastised for its bilateral agreements with producers, but it was not alone[24]—its EC partners followed the same route, with varying degrees of success.[25] Given its pro-Arab posture, Britain fared quite well. Before long, the FCO had received assurances that the producers would minimize the impact of the cutback on British supplies.[26] Britain went on to make approaches in Abu Dhabi, Saudi Arabia, Qatar, and Kuwait,[27] and in January 1974 it concluded a bilateral deal with Iran.[28] From the outset, Italian Foreign Minister Aldo Moro had maintained that bilateral deals could set an example for the EC: they were mutually beneficial as they involved both oil sales and the transfer of knowledge and technology.[29] This was the rhetoric of delusion or wishful thinking, for bilateralism encouraged competition, rather than cooperation, among EC states.

Arab oil policy was not alone to blame for European disunity. The old divide between state intervention and laissez-faire persisted. At the December 1973 Copenhagen summit, the Dutch, Danish, and West German heads of government pressed for an oil-sharing mechanism. Predictably, their French and British counterparts said no. British foreign policy had

"made it difficult for the Arabs to carry out severe cuts of our supplies ...
but given half a chance I believe that they would do so," Douglas-Home
warned.[30] This was not the whole story, however. Britain remained wary
of EC oil and gas regulation. In Copenhagen, Douglas-Home appeared
willing to compromise. Pledging urgent action toward a common energy
policy, the EC heads of state or government settled on a two-pronged approach.[31] They instructed the EC Council of Foreign Ministers to establish
an Energy Committee composed of senior officials and to create instru-
ments for information sharing and coordinated consumption reduction.[32]
They also asked the Commission to present proposals for ensuring "the
orderly functioning of the common market for energy." But this consensus
proved short-lived. The FCO was determined to protect Britain's ability
to "exploit the North sea as a national asset."[33] Initially, it recommended
taking a cautious line. New legislation proposed for the purpose of information sharing should be "as uncontentious as possible," and any new
powers should be "of short duration."[34] At the EC Council meeting of 17–
18 December, Douglas-Home went back on Heath's Copenhagen pledge.
Resorting to a quid pro quo strategy, he tied British endorsement of an
energy plan to an agreement on a "substantial" regional development
fund[35]—one that would correct "structural and regional imbalances" in
the enlarged EC, as had been decided at the 1972 Paris summit.[36] West
Germany was expected to be the largest net payer, but its government was
not prepared to pay as much as Heath's cabinet wanted it to.[37]

By December 1973, OAPEC's policy had pushed oil to the top of the EC
Nine's agenda. Rather than act as a catalyst for a common energy policy,
however, it fueled division. In the short run, this self-seeking behavior
made little difference. Pompidou's rationale was basically sound: "if someone cries for help on a beach, we should ... do everything to save him from
drowning, but there is no point in everyone's drowning with him."[38] An
EC oil-sharing mechanism might have prompted the Arab producers to
extend the geographic scope of the embargo. Oil companies took it upon
themselves to distribute supplies fairly evenly across Western Europe in
a more discreet way than governments could have done.[39] Non-Arab oil
was directed to countries that were embargoed or on the "neutral" list.
Arab oil was channeled to the countries labeled as "friendly."[40] The U.S.
Federal Energy Administration retrospectively analyzed this allocation
system as "equitable."[41] Admittedly, Belgium, the Netherlands, Britain,
Italy, and Spain introduced export controls, but prohibitions were limited
to refined goods.[42] In the medium term, however, these narrow national
agendas would become increasingly untenable. Supply was only one side
of the story. The fourfold increase in the price of oil would soon spur a
new sense of urgency throughout the Western world.

The United States Steps In: Kissinger's Pilgrims' Speech

OPEC's move to raise the posted price of oil forced the U.S. government to take an international initiative. Its proposal not only targeted oil but was also linked to its broader European agenda, including the Year of Europe. As such, it magnified disagreements between Paris and Washington. In connecting oil matters to the transatlantic relationship, U.S. officials caused the oil shock to produce further tension among EC states.

The Arab oil supply restrictions prompted an initial strategy reappraisal on the part of the United States, albeit one with only a national dimension. On 7 November 1973, Nixon warned that the United States was "heading toward the most acute shortages of energy since World War II."[43] The shortage, he predicted, would average 10–17 percent during the winter. To meet the challenge, he proclaimed a wide range of measures. Some, such as the lowering of home thermostats, required self-regulation by citizens. Others entailed government regulation: reduced speed limits, energy saving in governmental buildings, and the prohibition of plant conversion from coal to oil. Nixon also announced plans to create a Federal Energy Administration to provide his government with the means to pursue a coherent policy. Meanwhile, he created a provisional institution, the Federal Energy Office.[44]

Before long, however, price, rather than supply, had emerged as the crux of the problem. Until 1971, the price of oil had been almost stable in nominal terms. A barrel of Saudi Arabian light crude had cost $1.93 in 1955, as against $2.18 in 1971.[45] In real terms the price of oil had even decreased. The twin devaluations of the U.S. dollar in 1971 and in 1973 caused further unease among the producers. In January 1973, Saudi light crude sold for $2.59 a barrel, which implied a much slower rise than that of the commodity index.[46] Over time, spot—as opposed to pre-agreed—prices came to reflect world inflationary pressure and the tightening of the oil market, reaching over $5 a barrel. The Arab oil restrictions further encouraged producers to assert their market power. On 16 October 1973, the Gulf States raised the posted price of oil by 70 percent to $5.11 a barrel, bringing it in line with the spot market.[47] Through this powerful gesture, the producers demonstrated that they had become "masters of [their] ... commodity."[48] The days when oil companies set prices unilaterally were a thing of the past.

The new assertiveness of producers combined with a jittery spot market—with bids as high as $16 a barrel—spurred the U.S. government to go international.[49] On 12 December, the Nixon administration reintroduced its pre-crisis proposal for organized cooperation among industrialized countries. In a speech delivered to the Pilgrims of Great Britain—a British-American association fostering ties among British and U.S. elites—Kissinger called for "an Energy Action Group ... with a mandate to develop within three months an initial action program for collaboration in all areas of the energy problem."[50] The energy challenge, he declared, was one that "the United States could solve alone with great difficulty, and that Europe cannot solve in isolation at all." The goal was to prevent a "ruinous" competition for oil and hence to secure the required energy supplies at reasonable prices. Kissinger's proposed measures included energy conservation, new sources of energy, incentives for producers to increase output, and an international research program on energy-efficient technologies and alternative energies.

The U.S. government proposed the creation of the Energy Action Group (EAG) as a response to the energy crisis, but the plan was also designed to reassert the United States' leadership over its European allies. In a preparatory study, NSC staff members Sonnenfeldt and Jan Lodal had recommended pursuing "quiet, high level consultations on the conditions under which joint countermeasures of all types might be taken." Such talks, they stated, would demonstrate the U.S. "leverage in the oil situation."[51] Kissinger was sufficiently astute politically not to refer to U.S. influence in his speech. Nevertheless, he did reassert several of the topics that lay at the heart of the Year of Europe. European unity, he declared, should not "be at the expense of the Atlantic community," and "as an old ally" the United States should be consulted "before final decisions are taken."[52] He also presented Western European decision-makers with a stark choice: "creativity together or irrelevance apart."

Broad foreign policy considerations shaped French opposition to the U.S. plan. French officials saw the EAG as another device to strengthen U.S. power in Western Europe. Kissinger, they argued, had not eased "the pressure" he had applied on "Europe" since April to make it think of its future "within the framework of a U.S.-ruled Atlantic community."[53] They were also mindful of Arab opposition to institutionalized consumer cooperation. In an attempt to reduce such concerns, Kissinger stated that the EAG would "not be an exclusive organization of consumers": "The producing nations should be invited to join it from the very beginning with respect to any matters of common interest."[54] This assurance did not suffice. Quai Director for Economic and Financial Affairs Jean-Pierre Brunet warned that France's participation would impair its standing in the Arab world.[55] More forcefully, Pompidou ruled out any "consumer cartel [*syndicat de consommateurs*]."[56] "We cannot afford ourselves the luxury of three or four years of trouble and misery until the Arabs understand," he told Kissinger on 20 December.

Elsewhere in Western Europe, however, the rise in oil prices reasserted the value of the transatlantic relationship. From Washington, Ambassador

Berndt von Staden urged the West German government to "react positively" to the U.S. plan for both "political-psychological" and "substantive" reasons.[57] A negative reaction would upset senior U.S. officials. It would also, von Staden argued, quoting Kissinger, strengthen the position of the U.S. economic lobbies that pressed for "unilateral action [*Alleingang*]" in order to strengthen America's world economic position. Overall, officials in Bonn appraised the U.S. proposal positively. So did their British counterparts. With transatlantic relations under strain, this "major American initiative" could help to "mend fences with Europe."[58] Moreover, the FCO considered joint U.S.-European action necessary to address "the extravagant increase in the price of oil."[59] Recent developments had clearly altered British priorities. British interests in the Arab world were no longer uppermost in shaping the FCO's stance, even if it insisted that the EAG should avoid any semblance of confrontation.[60]

In this context, French officials tried to outmaneuver the U.S. government rather than oppose it head-on. A Quai d'Orsay memorandum laid out a two-pronged counterproposal: recommending a search for short-term solutions within a Euro-Arab framework, and pleading for long-term Western cooperation within the OECD.[61] Pompidou took the same line at the Copenhagen summit,[62] rejecting a British suggestion to welcome Kissinger's initiative in the summit communiqué and pointing to the role of the OECD. His EC counterparts agreed to declare it "useful to study with other oil-consuming countries within the framework of the OECD ways of dealing with the common short-term and long-term energy problems of consumer countries."[63] But the French victory proved short-lived, as a further increase in the price of oil soon boosted the appeal of transatlantic cooperation.

Paris and Washington at Cross-Purposes

In the last days of 1973, the oil challenge turned into a full-blown crisis. On Christmas Eve, OAPEC chose to maintain the export embargo but cancelled the 5 percent production cutback planned for January 1974.[64] The softening of the Arab stance brought little comfort to Western decision-makers. The day before, in Tehran, OPEC had raised the posted price of oil by another 130 percent from $5.12 to $11.65.[65] This decision was not politically motivated. The Shah of Iran was one of the staunchest advocates of a sharp increase; Iran, a non-Arab country, was the main supplier of crude oil to Israel. An Arab country, by contrast, provided a voice of moderation: the Saudi oil minister argued against setting official crude prices close to the highest spot market levels.[66] Rather than political motives, this move reflected the new assertiveness of producers in a favorable market environment. By renewing the sense of urgency, it prompted the French and the U.S. governments to come up with competing plans. OPEC's policy thus widened the Franco-U.S. rift.

OPEC's Tehran meeting strengthened the U.S. government's resolve to press ahead with its plan for consumer cooperation. On 9 January, Nixon issued an invitation for an energy conference in Washington on 11–12 February. The participants were to include Britain, Canada, France, Italy, Japan, the Netherlands, Norway, the United States, and West Germany.[67] Nixon urged the creation of a task force in charge of forging "a concerted consumer position for a new era of petroleum consumer-producer relations." The main objective, Kissinger told his staff, was to establish an agreement among oil-importing countries.[68] "If that can't be achieved," he warned, "you have no prayer of rolling back prices." To make its proposal more palatable to the French and British governments, the Nixon administration "doctor[ed] [it] up" with the promise of a consumer-producer meeting to be convened within ninety days of the conference.

Predictably, French officials reacted negatively. The planned conference confirmed their suspicions about U.S. ulterior motives. In practice, they argued, the proposal came down to "creating under U.S. control the United States/Europe/Japan community that Mr. Kissinger has pressured us all year to accept through his proposed Atlantic Declaration."[69] To support his claim, Gabriel Robin, Pompidou's diplomatic adviser, needed only to mention the location of the conference—Washington, as opposed to Paris, which hosted the OECD—and the status of its participants—foreign ministers, rather than ministers of industrial affairs. Probably because of his frequent discussions with U.S. officials, Kosciusko-Morizet offered a kinder appraisal, reckoning that the Nixon administration genuinely believed in the need for international cooperation.[70] Nonetheless, he emphasized the administration's consciousness of its newfound leverage. Beyond transatlantic relations, French officials remained concerned about Arab opposition.[71] Reactions from radical Arab states vindicated their fears: Algeria's Ambassador to the UN Abdellatif Rahal, among others, had referred to U.S. plans as "harmful."[72]

French officials opted for a competing counterproposal. Their initial brainstorming generated several ideas. Robin recommended restricting the scope of the conference to preliminary talks and technical matters.[73] Brunet suggested linking the U.S. initiative to ongoing OECD work and requesting the producers' participation from the outset.[74] These suggestions, particularly the second, challenged the very premise of U.S. policy, namely, a drive to achieve enhanced cooperation among advanced countries. They were unlikely to find a favorable ear in Washington. The Quai d'Orsay finally opted for a counterproposal that was independent of the U.S. initiative. On 18 January, Jobert asked UN Secretary-General Waldheim to convene a world energy conference under UN auspices.[75] The meeting's objectives were projected to be twofold: to assess the economic impact of recent developments in energy matters, and to establish basic principles of cooperation between producers and consumers.

Jobert's proposal caused a diplomatic row between Paris and Washington. The U.S. Ambassador to the UN Clyde Ferguson publicly censured it. Assuming an antagonistic stance, he even accused the French of deliberately seeking to thwart U.S. plans. Ferguson's criticisms were so derogatory that Kosciusko-Morizet lodged an official protest.[76] In insisting that the Quai d'Orsay had formulated its plan prior to Nixon's invitation, the French ambassador had a point.[77] A Quai memorandum issued one day before Nixon's letter had already mentioned the idea of a world energy conference.[78]

Ferguson's tirade was much ado about nothing. Waldheim welcomed Jobert's proposal, bringing it to the attention of the UN Economic and Social Council.[79] But the French concept failed to get unanimous support among producers. Radical Arab states, particularly Algeria, wanted to extend the scope of the proposed meeting beyond petroleum to all raw materials.[80] Anxious to prevent a split between the oil producers and other developing countries, the Algerian leadership was determined to use the energy crisis to shift the terms of trade between raw materials importers and exporters.[81] On 31 January, Algeria tabled a proposal of its own: to convene an extraordinary session of the UN General Assembly to lead a global discussion of development issues and international economic relations.[82] France's EC partners were even less receptive to the French proposal. Even the comparatively Arab-friendly FCO was critical. UN procedures, it stated, were "cumbersome," and a UN conference was unlikely to operate on a timescale commensurate with the urgency of the situation.[83] Most importantly, the FCO did not want to support any step that might hamper U.S. policy.[84] It would soon become obvious that the French efforts to outmaneuver the United States had come to nothing.

An Impossible Compromise?

Overall, Nixon's invitation elicited positive responses from EC states. Initially, the FCO distinguished "three schools of thought."[85] Britain, Italy, the Netherlands, and West Germany took "a positive line."[86] Belgium, Denmark, Ireland, and presumably Luxembourg (although it was not mentioned) insisted on the need for a joint EC approach because they had not been invited. France "fell into a category of [its] own." Once the Nixon administration extended its invitation to all EC states and to the European Commission, this triad gave way to a binary opposition between France and its EC partners. The EC Nine worked to forge a unified position but managed only to reach an ambiguous compromise on the eve of the conference.

To be fair, even the representatives of the first "school of thought" were not unreservedly pleased with Nixon's initiative. They continued to harbor concerns about Arab reactions. FCO officials in particular insisted that the conference should immediately be followed by a dialogue with the producers.[87] The West German foreign ministry criticized U.S. official statements for vindicating the Arab interpretation of the conference as "confrontation[al]."[88] Other criticisms touched on the implications of the meeting for transatlantic relations. West German Secretary of State Paul Frank censured the U.S. government for turning every issue into a "test for Alliance cohesion."[89] Kissinger's handling of the initiative, he stated, suggested that the U.S. goal was to align the European and the Japanese positions with U.S. policy.

In the end, the arguments in favor of the U.S. plan prevailed. The perennial issue of strategic interdependence was a factor: the West German foreign ministry, for one, was not willing to risk another clash with the United States that could undermine U.S. security assistance.[90] More importantly, perhaps, the quadrupling of oil prices not only strained the balance of payments of consumer countries but also "cast in doubt the capacity of the world economic system to sustain it."[91] To the FCO, the proposed U.S. response could have "a crucial role" in meeting this challenge.[92] Transatlantic cooperation and the prospect of oil-sharing in the case of shortage was an attractive option, since the United States was more self-sufficient in energy than either Western Europe or Japan.[93] It was also better positioned to weather the storm and hence stood to attract the surplus oil revenues that could fund future balance-of-payments deficits.[94]

French opposition, however, did not subside with time. In COREPER talks, Burin des Roziers insisted that by addressing issues of substance, the conference would impinge on the EC's ability to make independent decisions. The meeting, he added, might be upgraded into a steering group, which would then control international cooperation on energy.[95] If anything, the preparatory documents distributed by the U.S. government on 31 January heightened French suspicions. The United States' insistence on forging a unified consumer front as a prerequisite for talks with the producers came in for pointed criticism.[96] The proposed creation of an energy task force—renamed Energy Coordinating Group (ECG)—triggered unanimous opposition within French government circles.[97] On 4 February, COREPER adopted a report based on the position paper issued by the Commission.[98] The French delegation, however, circulated a separate draft mandate and endorsed the COREPER report only to the extent that it did not contradict its own paper.

Would the EC Nine succeed in speaking with one voice at the conference? The task looked momentous. On 5 February, the EC foreign ministers settled on a common mandate.[99] At first glance, the text went a long way toward meeting French concerns.[100] The objectives assigned to Commission President Ortoli and acting Council President Scheel in Paragraph III were derived from the French draft mandate: oppose talks on substance, plead for an association of producers, and reject the institutionalization of the conference as well as the creation of a new cooperation framework.[101] However, the claim that "the French had their way" is overstated.[102] There was a fair amount of ambiguity in the text. Paragraph V alluded to possible follow-up work: "The Washington Conference should ... examine the possibility of setting up working parties of suitable composition on certain concrete questions in the near future." This provision did not contradict the French line sensu stricto. A French interministerial committee had ruled that "under exceptional circumstances, and if there is no suitable framework" the EC could endorse the creation of working groups in charge of specific topics—as opposed to an all-inclusive institutional mechanism.[103] Nonetheless, this wording left much room for interpretation.

In truth, there was no genuine agreement. The EC Nine did not truly bridge their differences to endorse "a joint policy for the Washington Energy Conference."[104] Internal FCO documents stated that Britain could not oppose the proposed ECG from the outset, as it would be "a very serious matter for Anglo-American relations."[105] FCO officials drew comfort from the wording of the draft mandate. Paragraph V, they argued, was getting "pretty close to the concept of a task force or task forces," while Paragraph III could be read as merely excluding another foreign ministerial conference.[106] In meetings with U.S. officials, British Deputy Secretary of Energy Sir Jack Rampton and West German Deputy Finance Minister Otto Pöhl expressed support for the U.S. approach. They "freely admitted" that they only had to be cautious "because of the French."[107]

Such ambiguities were not lost on French officials. At the EC Council meeting of 5 February, Scheel declared that the conference could not avoid making decisions on substance. Jobert replied that this claim contradicted the proposed mandate, but to no avail. Burin des Roziers reported that the final talks were brief because everyone knew full well what the others' views—"avowed or unavowed"—were.[108] Nonetheless, on 6 February, the French government decided to send a delegation to Washington, which the EC mandate did not require it to do. Its communiqué sought to avoid any semblance of concession.[109] Rehearsing French opposition to a follow-up machinery, it listed "courtesy" considerations, along with concerns about European unity, as its prime motivations.

The EC Council's endorsement of a joint mandate was not "a tactical success" for EC states.[110] Conflicting agendas marred this apparent consensus. As was evident from internal U.S. documents, the Nixon administration was determined to take advantage of such differences. Kissinger's meeting with Scheel and Finance Minister Helmut Schmidt on 11 February shaped up "as real power plays to get the Germans moving."[111] Sonnenfeldt even urged Kissinger to overcome his "quiet infatuation with Jobert ... and really read him the riot act." Other European governments, he stressed, were "willing to move more than they ... [were]" but were hampered by their desire to avoid an open clash with France.[112] Reconciling the French, the U.S., and the intermediary EC positions began to look like a Herculean task.

Divide and Rule: The Washington Energy Conference

The Washington Conference opened on 11 February and lasted for three, rather than two days, as initially planned. The press portrayed it as a "Titanic confrontation" between Jobert and Kissinger.[113] Although the media placed perhaps too much emphasis on personalities, the French foreign minister and the U.S. secretary of state were in fact the main contenders. The records of Kissinger's telephone conversations confirm claims that his patience with the French had "come to a definite end."[114] Yet they also show that there was more to the story than a Franco-American feud. Kissinger was certainly exasperated with Jobert, but what was truly at stake was the power relationship between the United States and its allies. Nixon and Kissinger deemed it essential to reassert U.S. authority over Western European countries, and they would succeed at that.

Kissinger was in combative mode, but initially he tried accommodating tactics. On the eve of the conference, he had harsh words for his EC counterparts: "[Treasury Secretary George] Shultz and [Federal Energy Director William] Simon should talk—the foreign ministers are idiots, except for Home. Moro, Scheel, Jobert—they're all bad."[115] "I am an Atlanticist. But if we don't take tough action," he told Nixon, "we will lose the pro-American people in Europe because they can't point out the bad consequences of anti-American actions."[116] Kissinger's Washington opening speech, by contrast, eschewed threatening language.[117] Mindful of

Western European concerns, he stressed that the proposed ECG would prepare another conference, which would include "representatives of the less-developed countries."

Disagreements between the EC Nine soon came out into the open. During a late-night meeting on 10 February, Jobert did his best to persuade Scheel, acting president of the EC Council, to stick to the letter of the EC mandate.[118] The next day, Scheel nevertheless engaged in a delicate balancing act, suggesting that there was some room for negotiation on the U.S. proposal.[119] Speaking as West Germany's representative, Schmidt did not feel bound by the same constraints as Scheel. He openly supported the U.S. line and even censured the EC states that had struck bilateral deals with the producers—that is, essentially France and Britain—for pursuing beggar-my-neighbor policies.[120] Jobert immediately took his revenge, publicly criticizing Schmidt:

> And I will end by referring to Mr. Schmidt's words when he said that we should not all try and save our skin. Of course, when all is well, methods are friendly and perfectly courteous. But when everything goes awry, everyone tries to save their skin. I have nothing against it. But we do not all have the same skin. Some have it tight and gleaming. Others have it lean, and they worry about what they will eat tomorrow. Let us bear this in mind before passing moral judgments which are out of place here.[121]

Jobert also quoted extensively from a speech by U.S. Democratic Senator Edmund Muskie that condemned the administration's energy policy.

Jobert's tirade only hardened the U.S. position. Kissinger was furious.[122] "All my team is mad at me because Jobert gave a really vicious speech," he told Scowcroft,[123] and he even referred to him as a "bastard" in front of Nixon.[124] Kosciusko-Morizet was probably right in asserting some years later that Jobert's style was what most aggravated U.S. officials:

> Jobert could be sarcastic, acid, with the Americans, the Europeans ... we can say everything to the Americans, we can even be very blunt and firm with them, but we must do it with a smile and let them feel that even if we have different opinions, deep down feelings are unaffected. This is what Jobert had not understood.[125]

By its second day, the Washington Conference had turned into a power struggle. On 12 February, several delegations—British, Italian, and French—proposed compromise solutions, but senior U.S. officials assumed an unaccommodating stance.[126] Building upon prior proposals, Jobert suggested convening another meeting the next month at the Paris-based OECD. Only then would the participants set up a new framework for cooperation. Meanwhile, France was willing to establish, and participate in, a number of temporary mechanisms. "Actually, what they proposed would be quite tolerable if I trusted the sons of bitches," Kissinger told Scowcroft that night.[127] He expressed concerns that if the U.S. government bent, "the next time nobody will be with us." He used the same argument to discourage Nixon from amending the U.S. position.[128] The French, he stated, might promise their vote at the conference and "then drag us into guerrilla warfare on oil instrumentation." Kissinger was also concerned about a possible shift due to Pompidou's state of health. Although information that he had been suffering from a serious cancer was released only after his death, many government officials on both sides of the Atlantic knew about his illness. The future new French government, Kissinger warned, could very well go back on Jobert's word.[129]

Kissinger's stubbornness paid off, smashing the EC states' fragile unity to pieces. On the afternoon of the second day, the EC Nine chose to go each their own way. "We have broken the Community, just as I always thought I wanted to," Kissinger happily said that night.[130] Jobert failed to impose his standpoint during the subsequent evening session. On 13 February, all the participants except him endorsed a revised version of the U.S. draft communiqué. The French foreign minister abstained from its "most operational" paragraphs.[131] Paragraph 9 stated the signatories' willingness to develop "a comprehensive action program to deal with all facets of the current energy situation."[132] Jobert wanted this program to be set within the framework of the OECD, but his thirteen counterparts proved content with a less binding provision: "In so doing, they will build on the work of the OECD."[133] He also expressed dissent with the paragraph referring to the economic implications of the energy crisis because it gave an economic dimension to the conference. This argument spoke to French concerns about the "globalization" of U.S.-European relations. Most importantly, Jobert dissented with Paragraphs XVI and XVII, which established the ECG.

It is unclear whether Jobert had Pompidou's backing in dissociating himself from his EC colleagues. Years later, Jobert stated that he had called the Elysée Palace on 12 February to make sure that Pompidou was willing to face the consequences of a "stir [*scandale*]."[134] Secretary-General Edouard Balladur purportedly checked with Pompidou and reported the president's saying: "He [Jobert] has instructions, he should stick to them." Kosciusko-Morizet, however, told a different story. At this point in the conference it was nighttime in Paris, and Pompidou was not to be woken.[135] Historians will probably never know the truth, but Pompidou's declining health likely gave Jobert more room to maneuver.[136]

French officials were largely right in stating that their EC partners had reneged on the joint mandate.[137] During a meeting of the National

Assembly's Foreign Affairs Committee, Jobert warned that he would call his EC counterparts "traitors" on the next occasion.[138] The FCO defended its case by arguing that "this was not an occasion for taking the narrow legalistic view."[139] An FCO deputy undersecretary of state maintained that "in a negotiating situation one did not expect to achieve 100 percent of one's objectives." EC states could be pleased with the "90 percent" they had achieved.[140] This argument bordered on sophism. But what it all came down to was that other EC states had never intended to treat the agreed mandate as rigid guidelines, since it could hardly be reconciled with U.S. policy.

French worries about the Nixon administration's ulterior motives were not unfounded.[141] Such concerns possibly reflected "the same inferiority complex" that had shaped the French response to the Year of Europe, namely, the fear of "the American Leviathan" taking control of the emerging European entity.[142] But they also matched reality. "After the orgasm of our press for three days about that Titanic confrontation with Jobert he winds up having no votes and we have all of them," Nixon exclaimed after the conference.[143] Kissinger was of the same mind: "In addition to the communiqué, the fact of the matter is that it taught an important lesson to the European Community."[144] Nixon agreed: "The point is the European Community, instead of having a silly unanimity rule, learned they can't gang up against us and we can use it now, we can use it on trade, security, with everything else."[145]

Officials in other EC capitals were critical of Jobert's "obduracy."[146] In the last instance, however, each member state based its decision on what it perceived to be in its best interests. In the context of the energy crisis, the transatlantic link had gained renewed importance in all EC capitals except Paris. Senior U.S. officials repeatedly impressed the security argument upon their European interlocutors, which probably carried more weight in Bonn than in London or elsewhere.[147] The decisive factor was the oil shock and its implications for growth and international payments.[148] In this context, most Western European officials believed they could no longer resist U.S. plans. The new assertiveness of oil producers made it increasingly difficult for French governing elites to translate into reality their ideal of a European world entity speaking in a voice that differed from that of the United States.

Europe Implodes: A Surge of Pessimism in French Public Opinion

Jobert's obstinacy also came in for criticism from the French press. For the first time since the Year of Europe speech, transatlantic squabbling divided French elite opinion. Press and political commentators shared the government's suspicions toward the covert political agenda of the United States. Nonetheless, in the aftermath of the Washington Conference, voices from the left and the center judged Jobert's hard-line policy quite harshly, arguing that the goal of European unity called for a different course of action.

Initially, the French press largely echoed official criticisms of U.S. international energy policy. In *Le Figaro,* Jean Lecerf warned that the proposed ECG would give the United States a say in European affairs.[149] The center-left weekly *Nouvel observateur* stated that U.S. plans would lay the basis for a U.S.-ruled Atlantic community.[150] *Libération* presented a Marxist iteration of this argument: namely, that the U.S. government wanted to suppress opposition from "the European and Japanese bourgeoisies" in ongoing trade and monetary talks.[151] Further to the left, *L'Humanité* accused the United States of wanting to create a "Holy Alliance of capitalism" under its aegis.[152] The leftist daily *Combat* was one of the few newspapers to offer a more moderate appraisal, when it maintained that the Nixon administration was genuinely keen to address the challenge of the rise in oil prices.[153]

The Washington Conference broke this consensus. Jobert won unqualified approval from Gaullist and Gaullist-leaning commentators. *Le Figaro* criticized France's EC partners for surrendering to the United States and hence betraying the EC mandate.[154] Pompidou's Union des démocrates pour la République (UDR) portrayed France as a martyr.[155] Centrist and leftist voices, in contrast, chastised Jobert for his obstinacy. Centrist leader Jean Lecanuet maintained that Pompidou's government erred in trying to force EC states into taking a hostile stance toward their main guarantor of security.[156] France could not build a united Europe by itself, Lecanuet reminded *L'Aurore*'s readers. Former Prime Minister Pierre Mendès-France noted that wisdom would have counseled compromise.[157] *Le Monde* editorialist Paul Fabra even questioned the government's European commitment, pointing to its decision of 19 January to leave the EC currency snake.[158] *Combat* leveled a similar criticism, albeit focusing on Gaullist opposition to supranational governance. Gaullist France, it claimed, had never ended the "contradiction" marring its European policy. It cast itself as "the champion of a united Europe," but ever since de Gaulle it had blocked the institutional reforms that would have allowed the EC to "make its voice heard."[159]

Whether they blamed Paris or Washington for the wreckage of European unity, press commentators sounded the alarm. Predicting gloom and doom, *Le Figaro* stated that unless the EC Nine quickly bridged the gap among them, "Europe" would cease to exist. "Kissinger," it warned, "will have conducted a brilliant 'requiem for Europe.'"[160] On the left, *Combat* expressed deep concern over the Franco-German rift. "The European myth," it cautioned, "may no longer be enough to patch things together between France and Germany."[161] Likewise, *L'Aurore* editorialist Dominique Prado called up memories of World War II: "The conflict between France and Germany must end, or else Europe will fall to pieces, throwing today's history back into chaos."[162]

Aron was one of the very few French public voices not to join the chorus of fatalists. The French sociologist broadly shared the government's assessment of U.S. policy. Wider political concerns shaped U.S. international energy strategy:

> In his December speech and during the Washington Conference, Kissinger clearly offered a political response to an economic threat.... He surely wished to help restore the Atlantic community.[163]

But unlike government officials, Aron believed that the U.S. response did not threaten French or European independence. Jobert, he maintained, should have chosen between two competing interpretations: namely, that the Washington Conference was useless, or that it was part of an imperialistic plot. Nonetheless, he did not worry about Jobert's show of force. In parting company with its EC partners, Aron wrote, Pompidou's government had not broken with a Gaullist doctrine designed to earn France a special status. The French, he ironized, had got it all: they would avoid ECG membership while reaping the benefits of institutionalized Western cooperation. "Jobert," he concluded wryly, "is alone, and as everyone knows, 'glory is not easily shared.'"

The Washington Conference caused somewhat of a stir in French elite opinion. Jobert argued his case before the press, quoting from Paul Valéry's *Regards sur le monde*:

> The point is to know whether Valéry's statement was true: "Does Europe simply wish to be governed by an American commission?" I am not the one saying this. Paul Valéry did — a great poet who was not much involved in politics.[164]

Jobert's statement was an example of what the FCO described as "French conventional wisdom, which makes distrust of the Americans the measure of European cohesion."[165] Cracks, however, had appeared in the French consensus over his European crusade. Criticisms from the left and the center focused not only on his personal traits, but also on the underpinnings of Gaullist European policy. They pointed to an alternative European model — one that entailed a greater degree of supranational governance and a less combative stance toward the United States. As such, they anticipated the course of action that Giscard would take when coming to power two months later.

A Setback for European Political Cooperation?

To U.S. government staff based in Paris, "disagreement in evidence at the Washington Conference merely echoed, perhaps in higher decibels than usual the already existing disunity between members of the European Community."[166] Antagonistic policy traditions and Britain's determination to keep full control over its North Sea resources had hampered EC efforts to develop a common energy policy. The use of oil as a political weapon created further division among EC states, pushing each of them to act in a "spirit of apparent sauve-qui-peut."[167] It demonstrated the degree to which France, Britain, and in some degree Italy were in a different situation vis-à-vis Arab oil producers, pitting them against West Germany and the smaller EC countries. U.S. policy, however, also had its share in this display of disunity. The price surge may have reasserted the importance of the transatlantic relationship, but by presenting its ECG plan as a symbol of newly restored Atlantic cohesion, the U.S. government nevertheless widened the gap between France and its EC partners.[168]

In his concluding speech, Jobert declared that "tomorrow, elsewhere, my country will not feel so isolated."[169] Back in Paris, he cast himself "in the image of innocence violated."[170] Logically, officials in other EC capitals disagreed with his portrayal of France as the true supporter of "Europe." The British mission in Brussels remarked critically that the French goal was to ensure that the conference "[did] not interfere with their independence of action."[171] The reality lay somewhere in between. National interests certainly ranked high on the French government's agenda. But while French priorities encompassed French interests in the Arab world and petty competition with the United States, they also meant campaigning for a European entity that would have its own independent voice. The FCO recognized that French officials considered French and EC interests as inextricably linked: "the French ... want to minimize the role of international consumer cooperation and jealously to guard their own and the Community's freedom of action."[172]

Rather than a single voice, what the Washington Energy Conference heard was a Babel-like cacophony. The catastrophist undertone of many press articles, however, was unwarranted. To be sure, the prospects for a common energy policy were worse than ever, and the measures enshrined in the Copenhagen communiqué were destined to remain a dead letter.[173] So was Jobert's March 1974 proposal for a European Energy Agency.[174]

But the Washington meeting did not sound the death knell for the EC, as some observers noted at the time. In no-nonsense manner, the FCO recommended "warm sweet tea and a rest."[175] U.S. officials based in Paris predicted that "respective protagonists within the EC, well accustomed to such outbursts of varying intensity, are not likely to be inhibited for long and [the] EC likely [will] regain normal working atmosphere fairly soon."[176] Though not altogether ruling out a "deep crisis of confidence," the West German foreign ministry forecast that France would not use the conference to trigger "a serious EC crisis."[177]

What were the implications of the Washington Conference for European unity? The conference was not, strictly speaking, "a setback for EPC."[178] The EC Nine had not applied the EPC mechanisms to international energy matters, though they had discussed them within the EC framework. More importantly, Kissinger's hope that the conference had dealt a fatal blow to Euro-Arab cooperation was misguided.[179] The FCO still considered the Euro-Arab dialogue useful to placate Arab leaders.[180] The West German foreign ministry was anxious to repair ties with France and worried about a possible Arab backlash should the initiative be called off.[181] From the outset, Italy had been in favor of pursuing both institutionalized consumer cooperation—leading to a broader consumer-producer dialogue—and a narrower Euro-Arab partnership.[182] Senior U.S. officials had thus won "the first round" at the Washington Conference, but they had not heard the last of their French counterparts.[183]

Notes

1. FCO, Washington telegram 612, 16 February 1974, doc 555, in Hamilton, *Documents on British Policy Overseas. The Year of Europe.*
2. Möckli, *European Foreign Policy During the Cold War,* 278.
3. Ibid.
4. Fiona Venn, "International Cooperation Versus National Self-Interest: The United States and Europe During the 1973–1974 Oil Crisis," in *The United States and the European Alliance since 1945,* ed. Kathleen Burk and Melvyn Stokes (Oxford and New York: Berg Publishers, 1999), 75.
5. Kohl, "Energy Policy in the Communities."
6. International Energy Agency and Organisation for Economic Cooperation and Development, *Energy Balances of OECD Countries, 1971–1981* (Paris: International Energy Agency and Organisation for Economic Cooperation and Development, 1983), 156, 158. For 1973, Robert J. Lieber gives a lower figure of 67.6 percent (Lieber, *The Oil Decade: Conflict and Cooperation in the West,* 79).
7. Venn, "International Cooperation Versus National Self-Interest," 75.

8. Labbate, "L'Italia e lo shock petrolifero del '73 tra interesse nazionale e vincoli europei."
9. Barbara Curli, "Le origini della politica energetica comunitaria, 1958–1964," in *Diplomazia delle risorse. Le materie prime e il sistema internazionale nel Novecento,* ed. Massimiliano Guderzo and Matteo Luigi Napolitano (Florence: Polistampa, 2004), 95–118.
10. Kohl, "Energy Policy in the Communities," 112; Romano Prodi and Alberto Clô, "Europe," in *The Oil Crisis,* ed. Raymond Vernon (New York: Norton, 1976), 91–112.
11. Louis Turner, "The Politics of the Energy Crisis," *International Affairs* 50, no. 3 (1974): 407–8.
12. G. John Ikenberry, "The Irony of State Strength: Comparative Responses to the Oil Shocks in the 1970s," *International Organization* 40, no. 1 (1986): 105–37. French "dirigisme" went back to the 1924 creation of the Compagnie française des pétroles, which was later renamed TOTAL. The French government tightened its control of the oil industry in the postwar era by sponsoring the creation of the state-owned Entreprise de recherches et d'activités pétrolières (Styan, *France & Iraq,* 103–7).
13. FCO, Ronald Custis, Note, 31 January 1974, doc. 526, in Hamilton, *Documents on British Policy Overseas. The Year of Europe.*
14. Venn, *The Oil Crisis,* 50, 121.
15. FCO, telegram 1551 to UKREP, 17 December 1973, doc. 467, in Hamilton, *Documents on British Policy Overseas. The Year of Europe.*
16. Venn, "International Cooperation Versus National Self-Interest," 76.
17. Turner, "The Politics of the Energy Crisis," 406.
18. Yergin, *The Prize,* 596.
19. Venn, *The Oil Crisis,* 135; Prodi and Clô, "Europe," 101.
20. Yergin, *The Prize,* 588–89, 596.
21. Declaration of the Dutch government to the European Commission, 30 October 1973, quoted in full in *Aide-mémoire sur la réunion restreinte du Comité des représentants permanents tenue le 31 octobre,* HAEU, EN, 1909.
22. FCO, minute, cable to Wright, 2 November 1973, doc. 360, in Hamilton, *Documents on British Policy Overseas. The Year of Europe.*
23. For an analysis of the West German stance, see FCO, ibid.
24. Lieber, *The Oil Decade,* 85; Venn, *Oil Diplomacy in the Twentieth Century,* 150; Demagny-Van Eyseren, "Les réactions de la présidence française face au choc pétrolier."
25. On bilateral agreements with producers, see Petrini, "L'arma del petrolio."
26. FCO, memcon officials and oil company representatives, 7 November 1973, doc. 378, in Hamilton, *Documents on British Policy Overseas. The Year of Europe.*
27. FCO, minute, Egerton to John Taylor, 6 December 1973, doc. 440, ibid.
28. FCO, guidance telegram 18, 5 February 1974, doc. 536, ibid.
29. Labbate, "L'Italia e lo shock petrolifero del '73 tra interesse nazionale e vincoli europei."
30. FCO, minute, Acland to Marrack Goulding, 10 December 1973, doc. 443, in Hamilton, *Documents on British Policy Overseas. The Year of Europe.*
31. Turner, "The Politics of the Energy Crisis," 411.
32. "Annex to the Summit Conference Final Communiqué," *Bulletin of the European Communities,* no. 12 (1973): 11–12.
33. FCO, telegram 1551 to UKREP, 17 December 1973, doc. 467, in Hamilton, *Documents on British Policy Overseas. The Year of Europe.*
34. FCO, telegram 1551 to UKREP, 17 December 1973, doc. 467, ibid.
35. FCO, UKREP Brussels telegram 6420, 19 December 1973, doc. 472, ibid.
36. "Statement from the Paris Summit (October 1972)."
37. Möckli, *European Foreign Policy During the Cold War,* 239–40, 243–44.

38. Memcon Pompidou/Brandt, second meeting, 26 November 1973, CHAN, 5AG2 1012.
39. Turner, "The Politics of the Energy Crisis," 411.
40. Yergin, *The Prize*, 606.
41. Quoted ibid.
42. Ibid.; Prodi and Clô, "Europe," 100.
43. "'The Energy Emergency': Radio-Television Address by President Nixon, 7 November 1973," in Council on Foreign Relations, ed., *American Foreign Relations* (New York: New York University Press, 1976), 520–28.
44. Noel Koch, *Memorandum for Roy Ash et al.*, 3 December 1973, NPM, White House Central Files (WHCF), FG 6-26.
45. James, *International Monetary Cooperation since Bretton Woods*, 253.
46. Ibid.
47. Yergin, *The Prize*, 587.
48. Quoted from Saudi Oil Minister Ahmed Zaki Yamani, ibid., 588.
49. Ibid., 597.
50. "Address by Secretary of State Kissinger before the Pilgrims of Great Britain, London, December 12, 1973," in Council on Foreign Relations, *American Foreign Relations*, 566–75.
51. Jan Lodal and Sonnenfeldt, *Memorandum for Secretary Kissinger*: "Next steps in the European oil situation," 4 December 1973, NPM, NSC, Subject files, 322.
52. "Address by Secretary of State Kissinger before the Pilgrims of Great Britain, London, December 12, 1973," 567.
53. Gabriel Robin, *Note pour Monsieur le président de la République : entretien avec M. Kissinger, jeudi 20 décembre 1973*, 19 December 1973, CHAN, 5AG2 1023.
54. "Address by Secretary of State Kissinger before the Pilgrims of Great Britain, London, December 12, 1973," 567.
55. Jean-Pierre Brunet, *Note : propositions de M. Henry Kissinger dans le domaine de l'énergie*, 13 December 1973, MAE, Economic affairs files, 448; Brunet, *Pour le ministre*, 13 December 1973, MAE, Economic affairs files, 448.
56. Memcon Pompidou/Kissinger, 20 December 1973, CHAN, 5AG2 1023.
57. Von Staden, Washington telegram 46, 5 January 1974, in Ilse Dorothee Pautsch, ed. *Akten zur Auswärtigen Politik der Bundesrepublik Deutschland 1974*, 2 vols. (Munich: Oldenbourg, 2005), vol. 1, 16–18.
58. FCO, telegram 1535 to UKREP, 13 December 1973, doc. 458, in Hamilton, *Documents on British Policy Overseas. The Year of Europe.*
59. FCO, minute, Douglas-Home to Heath, 13 December 1973, doc. 461, ibid.
60. FCO, telegram 1535 to UKREP, 13 December 1973, doc. 458, ibid.
61. MAE, Direction des Affaires économiques et financières, *Note: propositions de M. Kissinger au sujet de l'énergie*, 19 December 1973, MAE, Economic affairs files, 448.
62. *Energy*, draft British communiqué, undated [12–15 December 1973], HAEU, EN, 1910; MAE, Direction des Affaires politiques, circular telegram 785, 28 April 1973, MAE, EC files 1971–6, 3789; "Annex to the Summit Conference Final Communiqué."
63. "Annex to the Summit Conference Final Communiqué."
64. Möckli, *European Foreign Policy During the Cold War*, 258.
65. James, *International Monetary Cooperation since Bretton Woods*, 254; Yergin, *The Prize*, 607.
66. Venn, *The Oil Crisis*, 21.
67. Nixon, letter to heads of government of major oil-consuming nations, 9 January 1974, MAE, Economic affairs files, 264.
68. Secretary's staff meeting, 8 January 1974, NARA, SD, RG 59, Lot files, Kissinger, 3.

69. Robin, *Note pour Monsieur Balladur,* 10 January 1974, CHAN, 5AG2 1023.
70. Kosciusko-Morizet, Washington circular telegram 143-50, 11 January 1974, MAE, Economic affairs files, 448.
71. MAE, Direction des Affaires économiques et financières, *Fiche : proposition de la Commission pour la conférence de Washington,* 30 January 1974, MAE, Economic affairs files, 448.
72. Jacques Lecompt (French permanent mission to the UN), New York telegram 546-52, 31 January 1974, MAE, Economic affairs files, 448.
73. Robin, *Note pour Monsieur Balladur,* 10 January 1974, CHAN, 5AG2 1023.
74. Brunet, *Pour le secrétaire général,* 10 January 1974, MAE, Economic affairs files, 448; Brunet, *Note pour le ministre : message de M. Nixon sur l'énergie,* 10 January 1974, MAE, Economic affairs files, 448.
75. MAE, Secrétariat général, telegram 52-4, 18 January 1974, MAE, Economic affairs files, 448.
76. Kosciusko-Morizet, Washington telegram 636-8, 26 January 1974, MAE, Economic affairs files, 448.
77. Kosciusko-Morizet, Washington telegram 711-24, 29 January 1974, MAE, Economic affairs files, 448.
78. Jean-Pierre Souviron (deputy director of the foreign minister's office), *Note : programme d'action en matière d'énergie,* 8 January 1974, MAE, Economic affairs files, 448.
79. Guiringaud, New York telegram 204-9, 18 January 1974, MAE, Economic affairs files, 448; Lecompt, New York telegram 349-55, 24 January 1974, MAE, Economic affairs files, 448.
80. Lecompt, New York telegram 546-52, 31 January 1974, MAE, Economic affairs files, 448. Algerian officials took the same line in their meetings with the French ambassador in Algiers (Soutou, Algiers telegram 264-7, 29 January 1974, MAE, Economic affairs files, 448).
81. Garavini, *Dopo gli imperi,* 210–12.
82. FCO, steering brief, 7 February 1974, doc. 539, in Hamilton, *Documents on British Policy Overseas. The Year of Europe.*
83. FCO, telegram 96 to UKREP Brussels, 24 January 1974, doc. 516, ibid.
84. FCO, steering brief, 7 February 1974, doc. 539, ibid.
85. FCO, UKREP Brussels telegram 168, 11 January 1974, doc. 504, ibid.; FCO, UKREP Brussels telegram 571, 31 January 1974, doc. 524, ibid.
86. FCO, UKREP Brussels telegram 168, 11 January 1974, doc. 504, ibid.
87. FCO, steering brief, 7 February 1974, doc. 539, ibid.
88. Frank, telegram 140 to von Staden, 31 January 1974, in Pautsch, *Akten zur Auswärtigen Politik der Bundesrepublik Deutschland 1974,* vol. 1, 124.
89. Ibid.
90. Möckli, *European Foreign Policy During the Cold War,* 265.
91. FCO, telegram 2 to Washington, 2 January 1974, doc. 487, in Hamilton, *Documents on British Policy Overseas. The Year of Europe.*
92. On Britain's stance, see also Noble, "Kissinger's Year of Europe, Britain's Year of Choice," 224–25.
93. FCO, steering brief, 7 February 1974, doc. 539, in Hamilton, *Documents on British Policy Overseas. The Year of Europe.* The communiqué of the Washington Conference subsequently stated that the action program "would include, as appropriate, the sharing of means and efforts, while concerting national policies in such areas as:—the conservation of energy and restraint of demand[;]—a system of allocating oil supplies in times of emergency and severe shortages..." (*Communiqué,* 13 February 1974, NPM, NSC, Subject files, 321).

94. Möckli, *European Foreign Policy During the Cold War*, 252.
95. FCO, UKREP Brussels telegram 571, 31 January 1974, doc. 524, in Hamilton, *Documents on British Policy Overseas. The Year of Europe.*
96. Jean-Pierre Cabouat (head of the foreign ministry's economic department), *Note : conférence de Washington*, 1 February 1974, MAE, Economic affairs files, 449.
97. Comité interministériel pour les questions de coopération économique européenne, *Note : préparation de la conférence de Washington*, 1 February 1974, MAE, Economic affairs files, 449.
98. *Rapport du Comité des représentants permanents au Conseil*, Brussels, 4 February 1974, MAE, Economic affairs files, 449.
99. FCO, UKREP Brussels telegram 690, 5 February 1974, doc. 534, in Hamilton, *Documents on British Policy Overseas. The Year of Europe.*
100. Burin des Roziers, Brussels telegram 543-56, 5 February 1974, MAE, Economic affairs files, 449.
101. The text of the draft mandate was in French. An English translation of the most salient paragraphs can be found in FCO, minute, Overton to Fenn, 7 February 1974, doc. 543, in Hamilton, *Documents on British Policy Overseas. The Year of Europe.*
102. Möckli, *European Foreign Policy During the Cold War*, 267.
103. Comité interministériel pour les questions de coopération économique européenne, *Note : préparation de la conférence de Washington*, 1 February 1974, MAE, Economic affairs files, 449.
104. Möckli, *European Foreign Policy During the Cold War*, 267.
105. FCO, minute, Overton to Fenn, 7 February 1974, doc. 543, in Hamilton, *Documents on British Policy Overseas. The Year of Europe.*
106. Ibid.
107. Scowcroft, telegram to Kissinger, 8 February 1974, NARA, SD, RG 59, Lot files, Sonnenfeldt, 4.
108. Burin des Roziers, Brussels telegram 624-39, 7 February 1974, MAE, Economic affairs files, 449.
109. *Communication du gouvernement sur la participation de la France à la conférence de Washington, lue à l'issue du Conseil des ministres le 6 février 1974*, CHAN, 5AG2 115.
110. Möckli, *European Foreign Policy During the Cold War*, 268.
111. Scowcroft, telegram to Kissinger, 8 February 1974, NARA, SD, RG 59, Lot files, Sonnenfeldt, 4.
112. Telcon Kissinger/Sonnenfeldt, 8 February 1974, 10:08 P.M., NPM, NSC, Kissinger files, Telcons, 24.
113. Telcon Kissinger/Nixon, 13 February 1974, 11:55 A.M., NPM, NSC, Kissinger files, Telcons, 24.
114. Möckli, *European Foreign Policy During the Cold War*, 269.
115. President's staff meeting, 9 February 1974, NPM, NSC, Presidential memcons, 1028.
116. Ibid.
117. "Opening Remark of the Honorable Henry A. Kissinger, Secretary of State, Washington Energy Conference, Washington, D.C., 11 February 1974," in *Department of State*, MAE, Economic affairs files, 449.
118. Philippe Simonnot and Henri Pierre, "Un ordre du jour très général," *Le Monde*, 12 February 1974.
119. Möckli, *European Foreign Policy During the Cold War*, 273.
120. Ibid.
121. "Discours prononcé par M. Michel Jobert, ministre des Affaires étrangères (Washington, 11 février 1974)," *Documents d'actualité internationale*, no. 12–13 (1974).

122. Telcon Kissinger/Alexander Haig, 11 February 1974, 3:40 P.M., NPM, NSC, Kissinger files, Telcons, 24.
123. Telcon Kissinger/Scowcroft, 11 February 1974, 5:35 P.M., NPM, NSC, Kissinger files, Telcons, 24.
124. Telcon Kissinger/Nixon, 11 February 1974, 6:30 P.M., NPM, NSC, Kissinger files, Telcons, 24.
125. Kosciusko-Morizet, interview, 20 January 1994, MAE, AO, Kosciusko-Morizet. See also Weed, *Michel Jobert et la diplomatie française*, 60–62. The adjective "sarcastic," however, better sums up Jobert's language than the word used by Weed, "humor."
126. Philippe Simonnot, "Une journée pénible," *Le Monde*, 14 February 1974.
127. Telcon Kissinger/Scowcroft, 12 February 1974, 7:45 P.M., NPM, NSC, Kissinger files, Telcons, 24. Jobert's compromise formula did not fall through due to Pompidou's rejection of a requested U.S. proviso, as Möckli argues based on Kissinger's memoirs (Möckli, *European Foreign Policy During the Cold War*, 275).
128. Telcon Kissinger/Nixon, 12 February 1974, unrecorded time, NPM, NSC, Kissinger files, Telcons, 24.
129. Telcon Kissinger/Scowcroft, 12 February 1974, 7:45 P.M., NPM, NSC, Kissinger files, Telcons, 24.
130. Telcon Kissinger/Scowcroft, 12 February 1974, 5:45 P.M., NPM, NSC, Kissinger files, Telcons, 24.
131. Telcon Kissinger/Nixon, 13 February 1974, 11:55 A.M., NPM, NSC, Kissinger files, Telcons, 24.
132. *Communiqué*, 13 February 1974, NPM, NSC, Subject files, 321.
133. *Compte-rendu de la séance du 13 février*, MAE, Economic affairs files, 450.
134. Jobert, interview, 29 October 1990, MAE, AO, Jobert.
135. Kosciusko-Morizet, interview, 20 January 1994, MAE, AO, Kosciusko-Morizet.
136. On this interpretation, see Vaïsse, *La puissance ou l'influence?* 37; Telcon Kissinger/Nixon, 11 February 1974, 6:30 P.M., NPM, NSC, Kissinger files, Telcons, 24.
137. MAE, Direction des Affaires économiques et financières, circular telegram 118, 14 February 1974, MAE, Economic affairs files, 450; FCO, memcon Wright/Philippe Cuvillier (French embassy in London), 15 February 1974, doc. 554, in Hamilton, *Documents on British Policy Overseas. The Year of Europe.*
138. Jobert, *L'autre regard*, 383.
139. FCO, guidance telegram 24, 14 February 1974, doc. 553, in Hamilton, *Documents on British Policy Overseas. The Year of Europe.*
140. FCO, memcon Wright/Cuvillier, 15 February 1974, doc. 554, ibid.
141. Although he does not rely on the records of Kissinger's phone conversations, Francesco Petrini makes a similar argument (Petrini, "L'arma del petrolio," 107).
142. FCO, Paris telegram 185, 9 February 1974, doc. 547, in Hamilton, *Documents on British Policy Overseas. The Year of Europe.*
143. Telcon Kissinger/Nixon, 13 February 1974, 11:55 A.M., NPM, NSC, Kissinger files, Telcons, 24.
144. Telcon Kissinger/Nixon, 14 February 1974, 6:15 P.M., NPM, NSC, Kissinger files, Telcons, 24.
145. Möckli is mistaken in suggesting that Nixon did not quite approve of the way in which Kissinger challenged the Europeans (Möckli, *European Foreign Policy During the Cold War*, 262–63).
146. FCO, Washington telegram 612, 16 February 1974, doc. 555, in Hamilton, *Documents on British Policy Overseas. The Year of Europe.* See also FCO, Washington telegram 540, 12 February 1974, doc. 548, ibid.

147. Memcon Scheel/Kissinger, 10 February 1974, in Pautsch, *Akten zur Auswärtigen Politik der Bundesrepublik Deutschland 1974*, vol. 1, 167.
148. FCO, Washington telegram 612, 16 February 1974, doc. 555, in Hamilton, *Documents on British Policy Overseas. The Year of Europe.*
149. Jean Lecerf, "Le pétrole et la puissance," *Le Figaro*, 4 February 1974.
150. Jacques Mornand, "Énergie : les verrous de Michel Jobert—à Washington, les 'Neuf' présenteront un front uni…, en paroles," *Le Nouvel observateur*, 11 February 1974.
151. "La conférence de Washington : une machine de guerre contre les pays producteurs de matières premières," *Libération*, 13 February 1974.
152. René Andrieu, "La Sainte Alliance," *L'Humanité*, 10 January 1974.
153. "Editorial," *Combat*, 1 February 1974.
154. Alain Vernay, "Conférence de Washington : travaux prolongés aujourd'hui pour dégager un compromis. Fossé élargi entre la France et ses partenaires européens," *Le Figaro*, 13 February 1974; Alain Vernay, "Editorial : La faille," *Le Figaro*, 14 February 1974.
155. Paul Fabra, "M. Sanguinetti : la France moins que jamais seule," *Le Monde*, 15 February 1974.
156. "Le Centre démocrate : un triste résultat," *Le Monde*, 15 February 1974.
157. "La France peut-elle s'en sortir : Pierre Mendès France et Jacques Delors répondent," *Le Nouvel observateur*, 18 February 1974.
158. Paul Fabra, "Les mobiles de l'isolement," *Le Monde*, 15 February 1974.
159. "Editorial," *Combat*, 14 February 1974.
160. Jacques Jacquet-Francillon, "Editorial : L'Europe en morceaux," *Le Figaro*, 13 February 1974.
161. François Schlosser, "Bonn—Paris : l'heure des quatre vérités," *Le Nouvel observateur*, 18 February 1974.
162. Dominique Prado, "Editorial," *L'Aurore*, 13 February 1974.
163. Aron, "Tout le monde est content (18 février 1974)," in Georges-Henri Soutou, *Les articles de politique internationale dans Le Figaro de 1947 à 1977*, vol. 3, 1355.
164. *Déclarations devant la presse audiovisuelle de Monsieur Michel Jobert à Paris, le 14 février 1974*, MAE, Economic affairs files, 450. Poet Paul Valéry had originally phrased it as a statement rather than a question: "Europe obviously wishes to be governed by a European commission. Its whole policy tends toward it. / Since we are unable to part with our history, happy people who do not have any, or hardly any, history will release U.S. from it." ("L'Europe aspire visiblement à être gouvernée par une commission américaine. Toute sa politique s'y dirige. / Ne sachant nous défaire de notre histoire, nous en serons déchargés par des peuples heureux qui n'en ont point ou presque point") (Paul Valéry, "Notes sur la grandeur et la décadence de l'Europe," in *Regards sur le monde actuel* [Paris: Stock, 1931]).
165. FCO, Paris telegram 185, 9 February 1974, doc. 547, in Hamilton, *Documents on British Policy Overseas. The Year of Europe.*
166. U.S. mission to OECD, telegram to Secretary of State, 22 February 1974, NPM, NSC, Country files, 680.
167. FCO, UKREP Brussels diplomatic report 149-74, 25 January 1974, doc. 517, in Hamilton, *Documents on British Policy Overseas. The Year of Europe.*
168. Memcon Kissinger/Douglas-Home, 10 February 1974, NARA, SD, RG 59, Lot files, Kissinger, 4.
169. Kosciusko-Morizet, Washington telegram 1118-94, 13 February 1974, MAE, Economic affairs files, 450.
170. Irwin, telegram 4642 to Secretary of State, 22 February 1974, NPM, NSC, Country files, 680.

171. FCO, UKREP Brussels telegram 571, 31 January 1974, doc. 524, in Hamilton, *Documents on British Policy Overseas. The Year of Europe.*
172. FCO, steering brief, 7 February 1974, doc. 539, ibid.
173. Möckli, *European Foreign Policy During the Cold War,* 250.
174. MAE, Centre d'analyse et de prévision, *Note : Agence européenne de l'énergie,* 18 July 1974, MAE, Economic affairs files, 406.
175. FCO, memcon Wright/Cuvillier, 15 February 1974, doc. 554, in Hamilton, *Documents on British Policy Overseas. The Year of Europe.*
176. U.S. mission to OECD, telegram to Secretary of State, 22 February 1974, NPM, NSC, Country files, 680.
177. Fredo Dannenbring, memorandum, 15 February 1974, in Pautsch, *Akten zur Auswärtigen Politik der Bundesrepublik Deutschland 1974,* vol. 1, 196–200.
178. Möckli, *European Foreign Policy During the Cold War,* 278–79.
179. Telcon Kissinger/Arthur Burns, 13 February 1974, 3:22 P.M., NPM, NSC, Kissinger files, Telcons, 24.
180. FCO, guidance telegram 24, 14 February 1974, doc. 553, in Hamilton, *Documents on British Policy Overseas. The Year of Europe.*
181. Van Well, memorandum, 15 February 1974, in Pautsch, *Akten zur Auswärtigen Politik der Bundesrepublik Deutschland 1974,* vol. 1, 200–02.
182. Labbate, "L'Italia e lo shock petrolifero del '73 tra interesse nazionale e vincoli europei."
183. Philippe Simonnot, "Le ministre veut bloquer la machine diplomatique mise en place par M. Kissinger," *Le Monde,* 13 February 1974.

Chapter 5

FROM A EUROPEAN COMMON VOICE TOWARD ATLANTICISM?

The Washington Conference had demonstrated that the French concept of an independent European entity—French-led—was losing ground among Western European policy-makers. For a while, however, it looked as though the French government had only suffered a temporary setback. The Franco-EC split merely meant postponing the next EPC ministerial meeting. The EC Nine's foreign ministers endorsed the Euro-Arab dialogue at their meeting on 4 March, triggering another round of confrontation with the United States. The Nixon administration had made it abundantly clear that it disapproved of the plan. The U.S. president and secretary of state retaliated by embarking on a verbal crusade against Western European decision-makers and their failure to do proper justice to the United States' security assistance. Throwing caution to the wind, an exasperated Nixon went as far as to raise the specter of a troop withdrawal. This verbal escalation only encouraged French officials to harden their stance. They rejected outright all U.S. requests for a formalized consultation procedure between EPC and the United States.

The theatrical dimension of this feud should not obscure its deeper meaning. The controversy brought into sharp focus the Franco-U.S. divide over transatlantic relations and the status of a united Europe within the Western world. Final endorsement of the Euro-Arab dialogue compelled the Nixon administration to remove the mask. It had been willing to pay lip service to a European identity so long as this concept had seemed a purely discursive construct. The decision taken by the EC Nine on 4 March showed that they were ready to translate words into action, even if it meant going against U.S. policy preferences. The Nixon administration could not tolerate this. It made no attempt to hide its opposition to a political Europe that would challenge it in foreign policy matters. The French critics of U.S. hegemonic intentions felt vindicated. The U.S. rhetoric only prompted them to reassert their vision of an independent European voice on the global stage, which they cast as incompatible with any U.S. interference in EPC and thus with ongoing EPC-U.S. consultation.

This dispute also demonstrated that any attempt to build a political Europe against the United States was doomed to failure, at least in the context of a crisis-ridden world. France's EC partners proved responsive to the U.S. government's qualms. They refused to forge ahead with the Euro-Arab dialogue, or even with EPC, unless they satisfied the United States on consultation. By June 1974, the French government had thrown in the towel, endorsing not only a "non-paper" laying out an informal consultation procedure, but also a NATO statement that included stronger language on consultation than it had long deemed acceptable. Meanwhile, Giscard had succeeded Pompidou as French president. Giscard was a centrist leader with a comparatively pro-American outlook, and change had been a key topic of his electoral campaign. But historians should not rush to conclude that this outcome reflected Giscard's Atlanticist creed. The Quai d'Orsay began compromising before the first round of the presidential elections. It did so to rescue the Euro-Arab dialogue, that is, a European, rather than a strictly national, project. Pompidou and perhaps even Jobert may have considered "abandoning EPC altogether" rather than "making concessions on consultation."[1] When it came to the breaking point, however, Jobert chose to compromise. Other senior Quai officials, moreover, played a key role in hammering out the final compromise on consultation in April and May 1974. Even under a strong presidential regime such as the French Fifth Republic, a number of individuals—rather than only one or two—shape policy-making, and this is even more the case during a phase of transition. Pompidou's death triggered political uncertainty in France, but it also created a window of opportunity for senior bureaucrats to bring their influence to bear upon policy decisions.

Kissinger Goes Awry: The Euro-Arab Dialogue

The foreign ministers of the EC Nine adopted the Euro-Arab dialogue project at their ministerial meeting in Brussels on 4 March. Prompted by tactical considerations, the Quai d'Orsay had requested that they meet without any preparatory session.[2] "We are best off … treating the Washington Conference as an interlude … leaving it up to our partners to signal, if need be, that they have changed their mind," Robin had admonished Pompidou.[3] This was a sound piece of advice. Heath and the FCO had largely stood on France's side on Euro-Arab matters. An FCO guidance telegram of 14 February stated that "our support for political cooperation between the Nine and the Arabs and for the development of economic relations between the Community and oil producers has not been diminished by the conference."[4] The FCO even instructed Cromer to assuage Kissinger by stressing the congruence between the Euro-Arab dialogue and U.S. Middle East policy as well as the risk of an Arab backlash should the dialogue be canceled.[5]

On 28 February, however, Heath lost the British general election. Wilson's Labour cabinet was not formed until 4 March, and Britain abstained from taking an official position at the EPC meeting. Nevertheless, the new Labour government was expected to reorient the course of British policy along pro-U.S. lines. The West German foreign ministry, concerned over both Franco-German relations and Arab expectations, still favored Euro-Arab cooperation,[6] yet it joined the Dutch in late February to suggest avoiding mention of a Euro-Arab ministerial summit.[7] On 4 March, Scheel took great care to stress that the proposed dialogue would not address political and oil-related matters and hence would not impinge on U.S. energy and Middle East policy designs. Nonetheless, on 4 March, the foreign ministers of the EC Nine adopted the report without amending it.

In essence, the Euro-Arab dialogue contradicted the tenets of the United States' Middle East policy. Since the end of the Yom Kippur War, Kissinger had pursued a step-by-step approach.[8] He saw the representatives of different Arab countries separately to prevent their talking themselves into "romantic frenzies."[9] The goal was to avoid an escalation of demands. An overall Euro-Arab dialogue contradicted this approach. Kissinger was especially worried about the proposed Euro-Arab ministerial summit. Such meetings, he repeatedly stated, would encourage Arab extremists to make radical statements that moderates might not be able to withstand. Consequently, the foreign ministers of the EC Nine would face pressure to endorse "every point on the Arab radicals' program."[10] Kissinger also feared the dialogue would act against U.S. efforts to keep certain topics separate—notably, Israeli-Syrian disengagement on the one hand, and the Palestinian issue and Jerusalem on the other. Such contradictions explain Kissinger's forceful reaction when he first learned about the plan. "I cannot tell you on the phone but they [the Europeans] are pursuing a more active anti-U.S. policy in the Middle East than the Russians," he said to

General John McCloy.[11] He sounded just as upset at the president's staff meeting: "Today I got a copy of this agenda and it's scary. This means the Europeans will add their weight to the Arabs in negotiations we have to carry."[12]

After the 4 March meeting, the U.S. officials' worries focused on the implications of the EC Nine's initiative for transatlantic relations. What was unacceptable was the launch of a major foreign policy initiative without prior consultation: "It is not a question of whether the decision in itself can harm us, it is when the secretary of state is in Brussels to brief NATO to be summoned to the EC and then to be informed of a decision that they have already taken, and that it is already in the newspapers."[13] Kissinger did not mince his words when he met with Scheel at the West German embassy on 4 March: "I have been summoned to be informed of something which we are known to be against. It is hardly a good procedure."[14]

Kissinger's surprise was more feigned than real. Not only had the Nixon administration long been aware of the plan, but several European diplomats—British, West German, and Italian in particular—had also kept their U.S. counterparts informed on the progress of the talks.[15] By 22 February, the State Department had even obtained a copy of the Political Committee's report from a Belgian diplomat.[16] Kissinger, however, drew a sharp distinction between information and consultation. Despite repeated U.S. requests, the EC had not officially consulted with the United States.[17] The Quai d'Orsay had adamantly opposed such consultations.[18] Bilateral information, Sonnenfeldt insisted, was not the same as consultation since "the positions which emerged from the process tended to be immutable."[19] Consultation, by contrast, was meant to give the United States an opportunity to feed its views into the EPC decision-making process. Bluntly put, it was designed to give the U.S. government a say in the formulation of EPC. Kissinger's reaction to EPC's decision of 4 March made this clear.[20] In weeks to come, he would no longer feel the need to hide behind a cloak of rhetoric. If Europe was to "float" its policy as a fait accompli, he warned, U.S. security assistance should no longer be taken for granted.[21]

Kissinger's understanding of consultation as a tool of persuasion explains why he felt that Scheel had "lied" to him about the Euro-Arab ministerial meeting.[22] During his four-hour conversation with Kissinger on 3 March, Scheel did not sound as "reassuring" as has been argued.[23] He downplayed the prospect of a ministerial summit, but he did not exclude it:

We will approach them [Arab leaders] and move very slowly when they are ready to talk with us.... We will say that we wish to discuss long-term cooperation.... Presumably we will reach some conclusion, perhaps to form mixed commissions of experts.... I will not stress a new foreign ministers' meeting because we don't want to get into the political questions.[24]

Likewise, the next morning Brandt told Kissinger that West Germany wanted to "approach the dialogue very carefully [*sehr vorsichtig angehen*]."[25] Neither Brandt nor Scheel, however, explicitly stated that there would be "no mention ... of a foreign ministers meeting with the Arabs."[26] Kissinger probably expected this feature to be removed from the plan because he had disapproved of it in front of both West German leaders and the British foreign secretary.[27]

Emotions ran high. Kissinger openly expressed his frustration on his return journey to Washington, speaking harshly about the EC Nine.[28] The journalists on the plane reported his words, quoting, as they usually did, "a senior State Department official." Kissinger was temperamental—so much so that Nixon had once thought aloud that "Henry needed psychiatric care."[29] He also had a big ego, possibly the greatest in U.S. government circles at the time,[30] and he cared deeply about his public image.[31] His reaction was consistent with these character traits. As the main architect of U.S. foreign policy, he took the EC Nine's "undignified" procedure as a personal offense.[32] To make it worse, the decision was "taken in public," which added humiliation to diplomatic frustration.[33]

But there was more to the story than a Kissingerian outburst of anger. Kissinger was adept at using the press to serve his own ends,[34] and probably spoke intentionally the way he did. As he told Sonnenfeldt, he wanted to use this event "as an excuse to show that this procedure will never be accepted again."[35] The notion of an independent European voice did not fit in with his foreign policy vision. On 7 March, he reiterated that "[Western] cohesion was essential," by which he meant Western cohesion under U.S. leadership.[36] The announcement of the Euro-Arab dialogue stretched his nerves to breaking point. He removed any lingering ambiguity: a politically unified Europe ought to remain within the U.S. shadow. His eruption of anger was designed to put this point across.

A Trial of Strength: Transatlantic Consultation

In March 1974, the Nixon administration opted for its policy of linkage with aggressive rhetoric. Public statements by senior U.S. officials vindicated the French critics of U.S. hegemonic intentions. U.S. records reveal that these criticisms were in fact valid. In the last instance, top U.S. officials—including Kissinger, Nixon, and senior advisers—proved unwilling to accept a politically independent Europe.[37]

In his 15 March speech to the Chicago Executive Club, Nixon warned of a troop withdrawal if the EC Nine did not factor U.S. foreign policy preferences into EPC. This threat was essentially rhetorical, for the U.S. government remained determined to keep the troops in Europe.[38] As some observers correctly analyzed, the tirade pointed to Nixon's irritation.[39] Although Kissinger duly praised him—as he did after every major presidential address—he was not thrilled about this gesture of bravado.[40] "He was a little rough[er] on the Europeans than I would have liked him to be," Kissinger cautiously told Scowcroft.[41] He spoke more freely in front of Sonnenfeldt: "I didn't want him to go this far."[42] The transcript of Kissinger's telephone conversation with Nixon on 15 March substantiates this claim.[43] They did not mention a possible troop withdrawal but signaled their intention to increase pressure on Western Europe by linking security and economic as well as political matters. Kissinger specifically encouraged Nixon to focus on the "general framework," that is, the interconnections between the strategic, the political, and the economic facets of the transatlantic relationship. Nixon fully agreed:

> Nixon: And I am going to say too that this is all part of the same situation. The Europeans cannot expect cooperation on the security front where the American role is indispensable to their survival and confrontation and at times even hostility on the economic front.
> Kissinger: And political front. That I think would be excellent.[44]

The Euro-Arab dialogue brought consultation to the forefront of transatlantic relations. This issue had been looming large in U.S.-European talks since the launch of the Year of Europe. The EPC decision of 4 March was the straw that broke the camel's back. Kissinger rattled off a list of complaints about inadequate consultation, particularly with respect to the "purely European" EC-U.S. draft declaration, the Declaration on the Middle East, and the EC Nine's démarche in Tokyo.[45] Senior U.S. officials were determined to end this procedure. The U.S. government put the Year of Europe declaration exercise on hold just as talks were about to resume. The decision was based on a new EC draft that was designed to answer Kissinger's plea for a more powerful statement.[46] Nixon also sent a letter to Brandt, reasserting the U.S. qualms about the lack of "intimate prior consultations" and deploring the increasingly "adversarial" character of inter-allied relations.[47] During his staff meeting on 11 March, Kissinger went as far as to suggest discarding the entire initiative.

> Who the hell wants it? ... the NATO declaration, as it now stands ... is really an instrument of French policy. It gets a U.S. security commitment, but the political and economic elements which we have always said are tied to the military commitment are scrubbed altogether.[48]

Arthur Hartman, the deputy secretary of state for European affairs, recommended "beef[ing] up" the NATO declaration instead. Preaching moderation, Sonnenfeldt similarly advised introducing in the NATO statement language that highlighted the indivisibility of the United States' security, political, and economic concerns. Their views prevailed. Sonnenfeldt was instructed to draft another letter to Brandt calling for stronger language on political consultation in the NATO declaration. Nixon's letter of 15 March stressed the need for "more organic consultative arrangements" as a prerequisite for further talks on the EC-U.S. statement.[49] The wording of the NATO declaration was more open-ended than Kissinger had originally implied. The United States, Nixon stated in his letter, would "have further views to convey to the allies ... at an early date." The State Department subsequently resolved that it would be up to the Europeans to decide if they wished to proceed with both declarations or with the NATO statement only.[50] Whichever option they chose, they would have to accept more potent language on consultation.

The hardening of the U.S. stance translated into a verbal escalation. In semiprivate settings, Kissinger gave free rein to his feelings. Like Nixon, albeit in a different vein, he made controversial statements. *The New York Times* quoted the secretary of state as saying to a group of Congressional wives that "there have been, very rarely, fully legitimate governments in any European country since World War I."[51] *Le Monde* told the same story: "if one is to believe 'dear Henry,' Europe has had few 'fully legitimate' governments since World War I."[52] *Le Figaro* also reported him as ironizing over European statesmen's penchant for summer vacations, reminding his audience that only a few days before the war broke out none of them were at their desks.[53] Existing scholarship tells the same tale.[54] Privately, however, Kissinger denied the reports. "I said that nobody ever—will ever recover from that [initiating a nuclear war] just as no European government that ended World War I ever recovered its legitimacy."[55] He gave a slightly different explanation to Scheel, one that was tinged with misogyny: "I saw the Congressional wives, on the theory that with so many ladies no three of them would agree with what I said."[56] Kissinger may not have known that the press were in the room, blaming the "vicious incompetence" of "those morons in the State Department" for not telling him.[57] Nonetheless, this was not a strictly official, closed-door meeting. His words spoke of a lack of caution and of his utter exasperation. In a rare gesture, he subsequently tried to make up for this "disaster" with a public apology.[58]

Transatlantic relations had acquired a theatrical dimension. Beyond the communication blunders and the rhetorical excesses of U.S. leaders, this drama confirmed what had been obvious from Kissinger's initial reaction to Scheel's briefing of 4 March on the Euro-Arab dialogue. The Nixon administration could not tolerate the emancipatory strivings of the EC Nine. Kissinger was especially infuriated about "the French," speaking "with considerable bitterness" about them.[59] French policy, he declared, was now "the greatest global opposition to U.S. foreign policy."[60] U.S. officials even blamed their EC partners for pursuing anti-American policies in seeking to maintain a united front: "the guiding principle of the Community appeared to be hostility to the U.S."[61] Moreover, they took a harder line on the notion of a European identity. "What really has to happen is for the Nine to scrap their famous identity paper," Sonnenfeldt wrote in unusually harsh language.[62] The times where U.S. officials declared themselves ready to welcome a European identity so long as it was not defined against the United States were now gone. Meeting with Scheel on his way to Moscow, Kissinger even called for a reorientation of European policy.[63]

The Nixon administration had clearly engaged in a trial of strength. Kissinger was convinced that the EC Nine would "cave."[64] He thought that U.S. diplomats were all too sympathetic to their concerns:

> I want our embassies to understand that they are to stop holding hands with the Europeans ... that we are winning .... I want to get it into the system so that our God damned embassies understand that ... they are not running a psychiatric social service for distraught Europeans.[65]

The West German embassy in Washington was probably correct in predicting that the U.S. government would try to "blow up [*sprengen*]" EPC unless its consultation request was met.[66] The ball now lay in the EC Nine's camp. The oil shock was hardly an auspicious background for France's European policy designs. The Quai d'Orsay would be hard pressed to keep the support of its EC partners.

France Stands Its Ground

The U.S. government's reaction magnified the contradictions underpinning the Euro-Arab dialogue. Most EC states, like West Germany, were of two minds about it due to U.S. opposition. By throwing a tantrum, the Nixon administration made their position almost untenable. Moreover, Britain, one of the dialogue's relatively keen supporters, reduced its level of support after the formation of the new Labour cabinet. French officials, by contrast, were more determined than ever to stand their ground. Jobert was resolved to resist, to the bitter end, any measures that might curtail European independence, and he was not alone: French diplomats, including the more U.S.-friendly among them, largely shared his views. Pompidou's handwritten comments, moreover, suggest that he supported his foreign minister and would not have exerted "a moderating influence" had he not been terminally ill.[67] That said, enduring disagreements between France and its EC partners would block progress on the Euro-Arab dialogue and even jeopardize EPC.

In hardening its stance, the Nixon administration only strengthened French apprehension about U.S. policy. The FCO called it an "escalation of mistrust through exaggeration."[68] Even those who had tried to act as mediators had harsh words for it. Kosciusko-Morizet's assessment of Kissinger's reaction combined irony and sympathy. For one year, he stated, the secretary of state had treated France like a privileged partner but was now behaving "a little like 'a scorned lover' [*une part de "dépit amoureux"*]."[69] This analysis was quite perceptive. Venting his emotions to Scheel, Kissinger said:

> I don't understand the French approach. What they have done is very short-sighted. We have tried to give priority to France in our relations and avoid some of the mistakes I saw during my service in the Kennedy administration. We saw Pompidou twice and I saw Jobert four times before we saw any German leaders.[70]

Despite Kosciusko-Morizet's mildly sympathetic outlook, he too censured the U.S. quest for power.[71] News of the Euro-Arab dialogue, he claimed, had spurred Kissinger to give concrete expression to his Year of Europe vision, namely, "a system based on unequal obligations." He even referred to Nixon's speech as "blackmail [*chantage à la sécurité*]."[72] Many of his French colleagues were even more critical and forcefully denounced America's muscle-flexing.[73] Pompidou himself reasserted his opposition to U.S. demands. "We need to be firm," he wrote only two weeks before his death. "We may inform the United States of EPC's work, but not consult with them," he added, "and we must resist their globalization intentions" ("Je suis tout à fait pour la fermeté, pour l'information soit, pour la consultation non, contre la globalisation").[74]

The U.S. rhetoric had the opposite effect in Bonn, prompting Brandt's government to move closer to U.S. views. Initially, Kissinger's reaction was deemed "unjustified":[75] Scheel had left him in no doubt about the Euro-Arab ministerial conference. He had even met Kissinger "70 percent of the way" by ensuring that oil and political issues would be excluded from the dialogue. Kissinger's "insistence on getting his way 100 percent" did not go down well in Bonn.[76] Despite this, West German officials were sensitive to the U.S. use of the security argument. The West German government had always resisted having to choose between France and the United States.[77] Its mediation efforts were nevertheless tilted toward Washington. In British eyes, "Bonn now seemed rather braver in relation to Paris."[78] Brandt's reply to Nixon's first letter stated his support for a suitable EC-U.S. "coordination" procedure.[79] The Quai d'Orsay criticized this as unduly forthcoming. Nixon had implicitly addressed Brandt as head of the rotating EC presidency. Brandt, French officials argued, should therefore have consulted with his EC partners before sending his reply.[80] Ironically, Nixon's second letter only compelled the West German foreign ministry to try harder to soften French opposition. On 21 March, West German Political Director Günther van Well presented Puaux with a proposed codification of EPC-U.S. consultation. The procedure clearly reflected U.S. views:

> If a member state government believes that an issue discussed within EPC bears on important American interests, the U.S. government should be informed. This should happen once consensus is reached on the matter, but before the decision is formulated in order to give the U.S. government an opportunity to lay out its views, which the EC Nine could take into account during their final discussion round.[81]

The acting president of the EC, Scheel, presented his colleagues with essentially the same proposal at the EPC ministerial meeting held on 1–2 April.[82]

In Britain, political change rather than U.S. pressure restored the preeminence of the transatlantic connection. Heath's government had endeavored to balance its potentially contradictory commitments to EPC and to close Anglo-U.S. ties. The new Labour cabinet, which was less Euro-friendly and more Atlanticist, put an end to this contradiction. Labour had taken a Euro-skeptic line in order to placate the rank-and-file and challenge the Tory Party.[83] Its 1974 manifesto contained a pledge to renegotiate terms for Britain's EC membership. Newly appointed Foreign Secretary James Callaghan, moreover, made it clear that he was an "Atlanticist."[84] He immediately placed renewed emphasis on Britain's relationship with the United States,[85] expressing support for the U.S. stance on consultation. The United States, he told Sonnenfeldt, should "be brought in at the earliest opportunity" in the EPC decision-making process.[86] During the same meeting, Brimelow, by contrast, almost supported the French position: "If the U.S. were present [in EPC] there would be ten not nine."[87] Callaghan knew that Heath's European credo would remain influential among FCO officials for a while. But he was nonetheless determined to reorient the course of British foreign policy along more pro-American lines.

France and its EC partners were now clearly at cross-purposes. West Germany's attempt at mediation ended up in endless nitpicking. Puaux criticized Brandt's use of the word "coordination," which, he argued, was even more binding than "consultation."[88] Pompidou substantially agreed, even if he recommended playing for time rather than confronting Bonn head-on.[89] At the ministerial meeting of EPC held on 1–2 April, Jobert nevertheless struck an uncompromising note:

> Beyond its skilful wording, it [the West German text] implies that consultation with the United States would take place at the level of the Political Committee. I cannot support this. I am against the idea that consultation could take place within our machinery.[90]

Belgian Political Director Etienne Davignon interjected that the proposed formula was intended strictly for internal use and hence would not feature in the EC-U.S. declaration—but to no avail. Jobert was willing to endorse a written procedure only if it provided for consultation once EPC had reached its final decision.[91] From a U.S. standpoint, however, such a provision amounted to information, not consultation.

By the spring of 1974, the transatlantic relationship had turned out to be the Achilles' heel of EPC. FCO officials had insisted that the new cabinet should lift its reserve on the Euro-Arab dialogue. Britain, they argued, needed "a reinsurance policy against further use of the oil weapon."[92] Callaghan heeded this plea, lifting the British reserve at the April meeting. Nonetheless, he requested "extensive and timely consultation" with the United States at every stage of the dialogue.[93] So did his West German, Danish, Dutch, Irish, and Luxembourger counterparts. Jobert, predictably, was opposed to this. The U.S. government, he warned, would attempt to shape its content and hence undermine its purpose. Moro and Belgian Foreign Minister Renaat van Elslande attempted to strike a compromise. They suggested starting with the exploratory phase of the dialogue and keeping the United States informed while deciding at a later stage on consultation with third parties. Their six other colleagues, however, said no because it meant endorsing the French view. They were clearly unwilling to risk another feud with the U.S. government.

As West German officials speculated, the issue of consultation raised a broader question, namely, the place of "the emerging European foreign policy ... in the existing network of international relations."[94] There was more to French opposition than stubbornness. French officials saw ongoing consultation as a challenge to the emerging European identity. In Puaux's words, if the EC Nine yielded, "Europe as such would no longer be listened to."[95] British Ambassador Cromer had initially recommended that both sides "moderate their attitude." The battle, however, was unequal.[96] World economic upheavals and political change in Britain had left France isolated. The time of reckoning had come. On 2 April—that is, on the second day of the EPC ministerial meeting—Pompidou succumbed to cancer. Despite widespread knowledge of his illness, his death came as a shock.[97] It would clear the way for an adjustment of French policy and hence for a new EPC consensus.

Rescuing the Euro-Arab Dialogue: The Gymnich Compromise

Giscard's election to the presidency on 19 May ended a brief period of uncertainty in French political life. The centrist leader was elected on the promise of change. He reiterated this commitment in his inaugural address: "I will lead change, but I will not do it alone."[98] His speech to the French parliament was couched in the same language: "You will take an active part in this process of change" ("C'est avec vous que ce changement doit se faire").[99] Giscard also had a more Atlantic profile than his predecessor.[100] Pompidou had not sent him to the Washington Conference because he seemed too inclined to compromise.[101] At the age of twenty-five, Giscard had spent six months touring the United States, where he acquired a good command of English. On the evening of his election, he made a gesture of goodwill toward the Anglo-American public by speaking in both French and English.[102] In U.S. policy circles, hopes were high for a reorientation of French policy toward a more U.S.-friendly course of action.

In May and June 1974, the Quai d'Orsay went a long way toward accommodating the United States on consultation. Oddly enough, this move had little to do with Giscard's election. The Quai d'Orsay made its first compromise in mid April, that is, prior to the first round of presidential elections. At the dinner of the Political Committee on 18 April, Deputy Political Director Arnaud suggested a gentlemen's agreement on consultation.[103] Initially, his West German colleague reacted negatively, pointing to domestic political constraints: the West German parliament wanted a written text. Bonn nevertheless went along with the French proposal. The foreign ministers of the EC Nine settled on the idea during an informal meeting at the German castle of Gymnich on 20–21 April. The Quai d'Orsay bent further at the end of May, endorsing a written record of the Gymnich accord, which the Nixon administration had requested.[104] In meeting this demand, senior Quai officials most likely acted on their own initiative rather than upon instruction from Giscard or Sauvagnargues. The Political Committee convened on 27 and 28 May. Sauvagnargues was not appointed foreign minister until 28 May and presumably did little beyond endorsing the fait accompli.

How can one explain the Quai d'Orsay's willingness to compromise? The weakening of Jobert's position possibly played a role. After all, Jobert owed his ministerial appointment to his long-standing ties with Pompidou.[105] After Pompidou's death, he may have been less inclined to assume a controversially uncompromising position. But the decisive factor was the Quai d'Orsay's keenness to proceed with the Euro-Arab dialogue. To the FCO, shelving the dialogue would not have "hurt the French" although it might have undermined "Europe's future relations with the Arabs." The French, it stated, could simply have said "that they had tried and failed."[106] In fact, French officials cared enough about the plan to bend on U.S.-EPC consultation. Admittedly, Arnaud did not explain the rationale for his proposed gentlemen's agreement.[107] On 8 May, however, Puaux urged Jobert to yield further if his EC counterparts made it a prerequisite for the launch of the Euro-Arab dialogue.[108] For all the French qualms about a written procedure, Puaux thought it best to accept the U.S. request rather than see the plan fail.

The Europeanization of France's Arab policy had been part of an effort to assert a distinct European identity on the global stage. It is significant that the Quai d'Orsay proved ready to pay a price for it. As newly appointed foreign minister, Sauvagnargues took care to emphasize that the consultation "non-paper" entailed no binding obligations and hence did not impair the EC Nine's ability to make independent decisions.[109] For months, however, French officials had been arguing the opposite. This document, moreover, did not fully address their concerns. After the Gymnich meeting, French and West German diplomats had discovered that they had different understandings of the agreement. Based on information from his British and Italian counterparts, van Well had reported that the Gymnich talks pointed to a "non-written" agreement on a "pragmatic … procedure" — one in which the EC Nine would decide in every single case whether they wished to consult with the United States.[110] Quai officials, by contrast, maintained that the foreign ministers of the EC Nine had merely agreed to decide on consultation on an ad hoc basis.[111] The non-paper did not provide for automatic consultation.[112] However, it did not require "a fair degree of consensus [*consensus minimum*]" on substance as a prerequisite for consultation either, as the French had wanted.[113]

EPC had become closely entangled in transatlantic relations. Delays in the start of the Euro-Arab dialogue demonstrated the importance of these interconnections. Only after the EC Nine and the U.S. government came to an agreement on consultation could the Euro-Arab dialogue begin. In June 1974, the Nixon administration still hoped to achieve "arrangements for consultations that are less ad hoc." For the time being, however, it was happy to live with the Gymnich non-paper and hailed "the EC's interest in improving the practice of consultation" as "a positive development."[114] There was "one last little drama" at the beginning of June. The West German presidency of the EC consulted more extensively with the U.S. government than the Quai d'Orsay would have liked.[115] Nonetheless, transatlantic and EC-U.S. tensions had by and large subsided, and on 10–11 June the foreign ministers of the EC Nine launched the Euro-Arab dialogue.[116] Soon thereafter, the governments of Arab countries received an aide-mémoire.[117] The first high-level meeting between EC and Arab officials took place in Paris on 31 July.[118]

After his appointment as minister, Sauvagnargues had an easy time dismissing the controversy over consultation as trivial:

> I must say that my first reaction … when I took up office was to say that I did not quite see where the problem lay. Normal diplomatic practice among friends and allies involves fairly permanent exchanges on what the two sides do.
>
> I believe that the pragmatic procedure that we have agreed upon … fully meets everyone's needs and resolves the — largely ungrounded, I must say — difficulties that arose in the past.[119]

However, Sauvagnargues had been highly critical of the U.S. government's call for "organic" consultative arrangements while serving as ambassador in Bonn. His language was designed to provide the French government with a face-saving exit. He may also have been keen to stress Giscard's commitment to change while avoiding criticisms of Giscard's Gaullist predecessor. Giscard indeed depended on Gaullist political backing. He had not dissolved the National Assembly upon assuming power, and his own party, the Independent Republicans (Républicains indépendants, RI), was in a minority within the governing coalition.[120]

Heralding a New Era? The June 1974 NATO Declaration

In June 1974, the fifteen NATO members published a statement that brought the Year of Europe to a close. The shift in political leadership in France facilitated this outcome, as commentators speculated at the time.[121] There is no record of Giscard's conversations with Sauvagnargues, but he most likely instructed him to concede points to the U.S. government in order to hammer through the NATO text. On the eve of the 18–19 June meeting of the North Atlantic Council, the issue of interallied consultation was still pending. Earlier in the year, de Rose had distinguished between "information" and "consultation."[122] His NATO colleagues, however, had not accepted this distinction. Most had pleaded for pledging "close and trust-based consultations." Non-EC NATO members had insisted that internal EC developments should not impact interallied relations.[123] From the outset, Sauvagnargues struck a conciliatory tone. The French government, he stated, did not want to delay agreement on the text.[124] Meeting with his West German counterpart, Hans-Dietrich Genscher, he developed an argument that paved the way for a compromise. Downplaying the controversy, he reiterated that consultation was a normal procedure among allies, albeit a non-compulsory one.[125] At the meeting itself, Kissinger and Sauvagnargues both took a conciliatory stance and quickly reached an agreement.[126] "Much to the surprise of my colleagues," Sauvagnargues reported proudly, "we solved the problem in ten minutes."[127] The compromise involved subtle semantic distinctions. The adjective "committed" was replaced by the phrase "firmly resolved"—a wording that, in French eyes, entailed no binding obligation.[128] In line with U.S. wishes, the text referred to "other areas of the world," but with the caveat that the signatories' interests "as members of the Alliance" had to be at stake for consultation to take place:

> In the spirit of the friendship, equality and solidarity which characterize their relationships, they are firmly resolved to keep each other fully informed and to strengthen the practice of frank and timely consultations by all means which may be appropriate on matters relating to their common interests as members of the Alliance, bearing in mind that these interests can be affected by events in other areas of the world.[129]

Soutou has analyzed the declaration as a "great success" for the French.[130] There is some truth to this claim. The text reasserted the twin pillars of de Gaulle's doctrine on defense, namely, national independence and transatlantic solidarity against the Soviet threat.[131] It recognized the role of French and British nuclear deterrence.[132] It also asserted the indispensability of "North American forces in Europe" and the United States' commitment "to maintain[ing] forces in Europe at the level required to sustain the credibility of the strategy of deterrence." The Quai d'Orsay, moreover, largely got its way in Paragraphs 3 and 4:

> 3. The members of the Alliance reaffirm that their common defence is one and indivisible. An attack on one or more of them in the area of application of the Treaty shall be considered an attack against them all....
> 4. At the same time they realize that the circumstances affecting their common defence have profoundly changed in the last ten years: the strategic relationship between the United States and the Soviet Union has reached a point of near equilibrium. Consequently ... the Alliance's problems in the defence of Europe have thus assumed a different and more distinct character.

The French draft had drawn a distinction between European and U.S. security based on nuclear parity. Kissinger and his staff had argued vigorously against it.[133] Kissinger suspected Pompidou's government of trying to legitimize a future European nuclear force that could be a substitute to America's nuclear umbrella. He insisted that although the United States was not opposed to European nuclear weapons, Atlantic security should be indivisible.[134] In line with a West German compromise formula, the final wording emphasized both elements: the specific situation of Western Europe and the indivisibility of Atlantic defense.[135]

Nonetheless, Soutou's argument is somewhat overdrawn.[136] The final document was based on a British, rather than French, text. On 28 March, Callaghan had offered to table a new NATO draft incorporating U.S. concerns.[137] The FCO did so on 15 May.[138] EC states, and France in particular, moreover, made significant concessions. The Quai d'Orsay largely let the Nixon administration have its way on consultation. It also agreed not to mention the 1973 Agreement on the Prevention of Nuclear War.[139] The Nixon administration still maintained that the agreement had no bearing on interallied relations. Significantly, Jobert lamented to de Rose shortly after the Ottawa meeting that it was not "his" declaration anymore.[140] It should also be stressed that the foreign ministers of the EC Nine—Jobert included—would have preferred to issue both the EC-U.S. and the NATO statements.[141] The Nixon administration, however, decided to publish only the NATO text, based on the assumption that the EC-U.S. text presented almost insuperable difficulties. Any attempt to include a provision on consultation, U.S. officials argued, would cause an "enormous row."[142] They also saw little need for it in light of Britain's and West Germany's renewed commitment to bilateral consultation.[143]

Overall, the Year of Europe had a happy ending for the United States. Kissinger put a very positive spin on it all in his memoirs: "The British took over the drafting.... Key elements of the proposed declaration between the United States and the European Community were incorporated into it; the rest were dropped. The new French government ... dealt with us in a new spirit.... What emerged at Ottawa was the single Declaration we had proposed in the first place."[144] His comments at the time were somewhat less self-congratulatory. He observed that this statement was less than "the far-reaching embodiment of shared purpose and intimate cooperation we had in mind in initiating the Year of Europe."[145] He was nevertheless pleased with the fact that the declaration reaffirmed "the fundamentals" of the transatlantic relationship. Not only did it assert the importance of interallied consultation, but it also endorsed the U.S. line on burden-sharing and issue linkages. Paragraph 11 stated the signatories' commitment to "ensur[ing] that their essential security relationship is supported by harmonious political and economic relations."[146]

Beyond the text of the declaration, the Brussels signing ceremony testified to a new spirit of unity among NATO members and to the United States' leadership of the West. The heads of state or government of NATO countries gathered in the Belgian capital on 26 June. The meeting was carefully orchestrated to keep the spotlight on Nixon. "Your statement will be the centerpiece of the closed NAC meeting," Kissinger had told him.[147] The U.S. president duly carried out his task. He was on his way to Moscow, and despite, or because of, the crescendo of the Watergate scandal, the administration hoped to make his summit with Brezhnev a high-profile event. The context was inauspicious.[148] In 1972, the U.S. Senate had passed an amendment prohibiting any arms control agreements that left the Soviet Union in a position of strength. This amendment would complicate the second round of SALT negotiations. Its promoter, Democratic Senator Henry Jackson, had also led efforts to link the problem of Soviet Jewish emigration to progress in U.S.-Soviet trade. In October 1972, Jackson and Democratic Congressman Charles Vanik had successfully introduced bills tying the granting of most favored nation status to the Soviet lifting of the emigration restrictions. On the eve of Nixon's trip, this issue remained unresolved. The Soviet Union's expulsion of the author Alexander Solzhenitsyn in February 1974 and the hunger strike of nuclear physicist and dissident Andrei Sakharov in June 1974 only fueled U.S. domestic opposition to détente. Against this unfavorable backdrop, Kissinger's advisers pointed to two elements that could strengthen Nixon's hand in his dealings with Brezhnev: Nixon's triumphant June trip to the Arab world in the wake of the U.S.-brokered May 1974 Israeli-Syrian disengagement agreement, and the NATO Declaration.[149] This would turn out to be wishful thinking.

Nevertheless, the NATO Declaration cleared the way for improved transatlantic and Franco-U.S. relations. Giscard still had to be mindful of Gaullist sensibilities. Erring on the side of caution, Sauvagnargues insisted that the text did not impinge on France's and Europe's "independence."[150] Giscard, moreover, did not travel to Brussels, using the planned Paris visit of the shah of Iran as an excuse. He must have had in mind Pompidou's comparison of such a summit to a meeting between Charlemagne and his barons.[151] Sending Prime Minister Jacques Chirac in his stead was a skillful gesture. The U.S. government swallowed it, and the Gaullists warmly approved of it.[152]

An Act of Submission or the Triumph of Reason?
The French Press and the NATO Declaration

The outcome of the Year of Europe divided the French press. The leftist press had harsh words for the declaration. By and large, however, the Year of Europe controversy had run its course in French elite opinion. Outside leftist circles, journalists had grown weary of U.S.- and Euro-French squabbling. Most welcomed the French government's compromise, hoping that it would herald a new era in transatlantic relations.

For both ideological and electoral reasons, leftist commentators assumed an uncompromisingly critical stance. The communists and the Gaullists had long used the same rallying cry, namely, national independence as a sacrosanct principle.[153] They were only too happy to chastise Giscard's government for yielding to U.S. pressure. PCF Secretary-General Georges Marchais argued that the text legitimized the imperialistic designs of the United States and reasserted the Cold War blocs.[154] *L'Humanité* claimed that the provision on consultation would allow the United States to meddle in internal European affairs and to use NATO's resources beyond its treaty-specified boundaries.[155] The communist daily drew no comfort from the United States' reaffirmed commitment to troop maintenance, viewing it instead through the lens of a power struggle. This pledge, it stated, meant asserting U.S. supremacy. Socialist-leaning commentators couched their criticisms in the same language. *Le Nouvel observateur* portrayed the declaration as a symbol of newly strengthened U.S. dominance in Europe.[156] After the Middle East, *Libération* maintained, Kissinger had scored new points "in his struggle to restore the American empire."[157] This "'fresh start' for NATO," it added, fitted with the paradigm of "cooperation/confrontation between the superpowers." Brezhnev would be only too pleased to speak to Nixon as "the undisputed master of the Western bloc." This claim also reflected enduring fears over a U.S.-Soviet condominium that was more imagined than real.

From the center left to the right, press reactions ranged from mild criticism to positive appraisal. *Combat,* the mouthpiece of the noncommunist left, put things into perspective. The declaration, it stated, reasserted the United States' leadership but was still a setback for the Nixon administration, given its original grand design.[158] *Le Monde* pointed to the U.S. willingness to acknowledge the distinct character of European security. This provision, it argued, implied that the Nixon administration had failed to align Western European policies with its own.[159] To *Le Figaro,* the declaration reflected a spirit of compromise.[160] Massip analyzed the U.S. pledge to keep the troops in Europe as "a significant guarantee" —one that should reduce concerns over the appeal of isolationism in the United States.[161] Endorsing the official line, Jacques Ogliastro asserted that France had largely succeeded in safeguarding "the personality of Europe."[162]

Despite such positive appraisals, the symbolism of the NATO ceremony hurt French sensibilities. Many commentators alluded to Pompidou's Charlemagne metaphor. *L'Humanité* sarcastically noted:

> Before meeting the tsar of all the Russias, the emperor of the West is paying a visit today to the king of the Belgians; his fourteen European vassals are pledging allegiance by signing the "Atlantic charter." The count of France will not at-

tend, as he is too busy tasting caviar with the shah of Iran in the splendid palace of Versailles; but he sent his footman, the lord of Corrèze, Chirac.[163]

At one fell swoop, the French daily had condemned the hegemonic intentions of the superpowers, Western Europe's submissiveness, and the French rulers' predilection for luxury. *Le Monde* and *Le Figaro* also elaborated on this theme, albeit more tongue-in-cheek, simply referring to the two summits as an "assembly of barons" and a meeting between "the emperor of the West" and the "tsar of all the Russias," respectively.[164] All commentaries stressed the strengthening of Nixon's position in a Cold War context. *L'Aurore* stressed the significance of this "fresh start" in interallied relations on the eve of Nixon's Moscow trip.[165] *Le Monde* cast it as a face-saving exit, yet one that had its purpose:

> Ultimately, the "Atlantic picture" of Brussels was probably intended for Brezhnev, Nixon's next interlocutor.... From a substantive perspective, the secretary of state may not have succeeded in aligning Europe with U.S. policy through organic arrangements, but he at least wants to save appearances and to establish Nixon as ... the truly undisputed leader of the Atlantic world in the East-West dialogue.[166]

This was an overstatement. Brezhnev was no fool and knew that Nixon had little to offer. There was no breakthrough in the SALT II negotiations, as the Soviets maintained their opposition to the equality of weapon systems.[167] Nixon and Brezhnev agreed to amend the 1972 Anti-Ballistic Missile Treaty by reducing the number of sites granted to each side by one half. They signed a series of other accords on trade, technology, energy, housing, and medical research, but there was nothing groundbreaking in these agreements. Détente had "reached a plateau."[168] Largely because of Nixon's domestic weakness, triangular diplomacy had come to a standstill.

Change is typically a leitmotif of non-incumbent presidential candidates. When such candidates win the elections, friends and foes subject their words and deeds to close critical scrutiny. Giscard's first weeks in office were no exception. Commentators had an easy time using the NATO summit to disparage his proposed reorientation of French policy. Alluding to François Truffaut's 1973 movie *American Night* (*La nuit américaine*), *Libération* stated that Giscard's promised change implied a new trend toward subservience in international affairs:

> Sauvagnargues needed less than a quarter of an hour to change sides and fall back into line. Giscard had promised it: there is change.... France is poised to enter an "American night" ("la France est bien partie pour entrer dans une 'nuit américaine'").[169]

Giscard and his team, it added, had taken an obsequious stance toward U.S. leaders: "Yes, Mr. Kissinger. Very well, Mr. Kissinger. Yes, Mr. Nixon. Very well, Mr. Nixon."[170] Centrist-leaning papers, by contrast, welcomed the change. *L'Aurore* praised the new government for doing away with the "sophisms" and "the aggressive tone" of its predecessor.[171] *L'Aurore* editorialist Roland Faure approved the compromise on consultation, hoping that it would lead to improved transatlantic and intra-European relations.[172] Along similar lines, Jacques Jacquet-Francillon argued in *Le Figaro* that reason had triumphed in both Ottawa and Brussels.[173] Western Europeans, he added, had only themselves to blame for the growing understanding between the United States and the Soviet Union. They had let it happen through their inability to assert their common "identity" and to speak with a single voice on the global stage.[174]

From the center to the right of the political spectrum, the broad consensus on Giscard's move did not mean discarding earlier hopes of the development of an internationally influential European entity. Quite the opposite, *Le Figaro* urged the EC Nine to use their best efforts to foster European political unity. Only by reaching this goal, it stated, could France rightfully claim that it had saved "Europe's personality."[175] Press commentators recognized that France had become increasingly isolated. A change of strategy was therefore in order. Press articles hinted at its main components—improved relations with the United States and reform of the EC institutions. This was the path Giscard would take in the following months.

Explaining France's Policy Reorientation

The emphasis of the French press on the NATO meeting may seem unwarranted. The ceremony in itself did not alter power relations within the Atlantic Alliance. Nonetheless, it held potent symbolic power because it mirrored existing geopolitical power relations. Kissinger later argued that the EC Nine had lost confidence in their ability "to project a distinct European role in world politics."[176] Although this claim is somewhat overstated, EC states had chosen to place renewed emphasis on the transatlantic relationship, be it at the expense of European identity. The outcome of the Year of Europe made this shift in priorities obvious. The highly contentious EC-U.S. declaration, which proclaimed the distinctiveness of a European entity in world affairs, never saw the light of day. Had the procedure enshrined in the Gymnich non-paper been implemented, it would have meant scaling down, if not discarding altogether, ambitions of speaking with an independent voice. Its non-implementation reflected a loss of U.S. interest, given renewed bilateral consultations, rather than a new assertiveness on the EC Nine's part. Last but not least, through the NATO Declaration, EC states lent their support to core tenets of U.S. policy—notably the concept of a "one and indivisible" alliance defense and the Nixon administration's emphasis on consultation.

Three main factors shaped this reorientation: monetary turmoil, the oil shock, and political change in the three main EC countries.[177] Callaghan was a self-proclaimed Atlanticist. The newly elected French president, meanwhile, had long displayed a more pro-Atlantic outlook than his Gaullist colleagues. His academic training and his work experience, moreover, predisposed him to focus on economic issues. Prior to joining the National School of Public Administration, Giscard had studied at the most selective French scientific school, the Ecole Polytechnique, and had spent most of his career working in the General Inspectorate of Finance and as minister of financial and economic affairs.[178] He was all the more inclined to concentrate on economic issues because of their prominence on the West's agenda.[179] This focus meant prioritizing cooperation with the United States rather than asserting Europe's distinctiveness. Change was also taking place in West Germany. Brandt resigned on 6 May after his personal assistant, Günter Guillaume, was found guilty of spying for East Germany. His successor, Schmidt, had built a close relationship with Giscard while working as minister of finance. Most importantly, he shared Giscard's concerns about the world economic situation.

Seen from a French perspective, however, things had not come full circle. "All I did was to get things going [*Mon rôle à moi a été de mettre la machine sur les rails*], I did not do much more," Sauvagnargues claimed in a radio interview on 21 June 1974.[180] He was obviously mindful of Gaullist sensibilities, but he also had a point. The Gymnich non-paper, which had been essentially agreed upon prior to his ministerial appointment, owed little to Giscard's election. Rather, it was meant to allow the start of the Euro-Arab dialogue. As such, this move reflected a new commitment to collective European action on the part of French officials. Their decision to bend stemmed from a realistic assessment of the situation: asserting EPC against the United States was no longer an option. Sauvagnargues spelled this out clearly in a set of handwritten notes he wrote during a vacation in Corsica in August 1974. In trying to accomplish "the gradual assertion of EPC," he warned, care should be taken to avoid "confrontation and rivalry" with the United States.[181] "Europe," he maintained, ought to "speak with a single voice and act through its presidency," particularly in world regions where its interests were at stake: that is, Eastern Europe, the Mediterranean world, North Africa, and the Middle East. But "Jobert-style militancy," he added, could only encourage France's EC partners to push for "entwining the EC more tightly within the 'Atlantic community'" ("l'étroite insertion de la communauté européenne dans la 'communauté atlantique'").[182] Sauvagnargues's hope to conciliate EPC's progress with friendly U.S.-European ties may have been wishful thinking. A U.S.-friendly EPC was likely to maintain a low profile. Nevertheless, this hope was genuine, for Sauvagnargues committed these thoughts to paper for personal use.[183] These handwritten documents thus belie scholarly claims of Sauvagnargues's support for "full bilateralism" and of his skepticism toward a European identity.[184]

Notes

1. Möckli, *European Foreign Policy During the Cold War*, 318.
2. COREU CPE/MUL ETR 29, Bonn, 21 February 1974, MAE, EC files 1971–6, 3811.
3. Robin, *Note pour Monsieur le président de la République : réunion du Comité politique des Neuf*, 20 February 1974, CHAN, 5AG2 1034.
4. FCO, guidance telegram 24, 14 February 1974, doc. 553, in Hamilton, *Documents on British Policy Overseas. The Year of Europe*.
5. Ibid.
6. Van Well, memorandum, 15 February 1974, in Pautsch, *Akten zur Auswärtigen Politik der Bundesrepublik Deutschland 1974*, vol. 1, 200–02.
7. MAE, *Compte-rendu de la réunion ministérielle du 4 mars 1974 au titre de la coopération politique européenne à Bruxelles*, undated, MAE, EC files 1971–6, 3792; MAE, Sous-direction du Levant, circular telegram 161, 5 March 1974, MAE, EC files 1971–6, 3792.
8. On Kissinger's shuttle diplomacy with Egypt and Syria, see Hanhimäki, *The Flawed Architect*, 324–31.
9. Memcon Kissinger/Douglas-Home, 26 February 1974, doc. 560, in Hamilton, *Documents on British Policy Overseas. The Year of Europe*.
10. Memcon Kissinger/Douglas-Home, 10 February 1974, NARA, SD, RG 59, Lot files, Kissinger, 4.
11. Telcon Kissinger/John McCloy, 8 February 1974, 11:10 A.M., NPM, NSC, Kissinger files, Telcons, 24.
12. President's staff meeting, 9 February 1974, NPM, NSC, Presidential memcons, 1028.
13. Telcon Kissinger/Sonnenfeldt, 5 March 1974, 9:06 P.M., NPM, NSC, Kissinger files, Telcons, 25.
14. Memcon Kissinger/Scheel, 4 March 1974, NARA, SD, RG 59, Lot files, Kissinger, 4.
15. American Embassy Bonn, telegram 1452 to Secretary of State, 28 January 1974, NARA, SD, RG 59, Lot files, Kissinger, 3; American Embassy Rome, telegram 1930 to Secretary of State, 8 February 1974, NARA, SD, RG 59, Lot files, Kissinger, 3; FCO, telegram 57 to Washington, 9 January 1974, doc. 497, in Hamilton, *Documents on British Policy Overseas. The Year of Europe*; FCO, letter Brimelow to Cromer, 10 January 1974, doc. 498, ibid.; FCO, telegram 436 to Washington, 20 February 1974, doc. 558, ibid.; Memcon Douglas-Home/Kissinger, 26 February 1974, doc. 560, ibid.
16. Hyland, *Memorandum to the Secretary*, "The EC-Arab initiative of March 4," 5 March 1974, NARA, SD, RG 59, Lot files, Kissinger, 3; Secretary of State, telegram 37780 to

American Embassy Bonn, etc., 25 February 1975, NARA, SD, RG 59, Lot files, Kissinger, 3.

17. Hyland, *Memorandum to the Secretary*, "The EC-Arab initiative of March 4."

18. RM *[74] 1 CP Proche-Orient : Rapport du Comité politique aux ministres des Affaires étrangères en vue de la réunion du 14 février*, 7 February 1974, MAE, EC files 1971–6, 3792.

19. FCO, Memcon Callaghan/Sonnenfeldt, 15 March 1974, doc. 568, in Hamilton, *Documents on British Policy Overseas. The Year of Europe*.

20. On this interpretation, see also Winand, "Loaded Words and Disputed Meanings," 314.

21. FCO, UKDEL NATO telegram 108, 4 March 1974, doc. 563, in Hamilton, *Documents on British Policy Overseas. The Year of Europe*.

22. Telcon Kissinger/Sonnenfeldt, 5 March 1974, 9:06 P.M., NPM, NSC, Kissinger files, Telcons, 25.

23. Möckli, *European Foreign Policy During the Cold War*, 284. Möckli's claim is based on the German memorandum of conversation, which is much more succinct than the U.S. one and does not report Scheel's words on the Euro-Arab ministerial conference.

24. Memcon Kissinger/Scheel, 3 March 1974, NARA, SD, RG 59, Lot files, Kissinger, 7. For the German memorandum, see Pautsch, *Akten zur Auswärtigen Politik der Bundesrepublik Deutschland 1974*, vol. 1, 280.

25. Memcon Brandt/Kissinger, 4 March 1974, in *Akten zur Auswärtigen Politik der Bundesrepublik Deutschland 1974*, 285.

26. FCO, Washington telegram 817, 7 March 1974, doc. 565, in Hamilton, *Documents on British Policy Overseas. The Year of Europe*.

27. Memcon Kissinger/Douglas-Home, 26 February 1974, NARA, SD, RG 59, Lot files, Kissinger, 7 / doc. 560, in Hamilton, *Documents on British Policy Overseas. The Year of Europe*.

28. Sauvagnargues, Bonn telegram 991-7, 7 March 1974, MAE, U.S. files 1970–5, 1138.

29. Quoted in Hanhimäki, *The Flawed Architect*, 188. See also Dallek, *Nixon and Kissinger*, 50–51, 352.

30. Dallek, *Nixon and Kissinger*, 51; Hanhimäki, *The Flawed Architect*, 458.

31. Dallek, *Nixon and Kissinger*, 91, 610.

32. FCO, Washington telegram 817, 7 March 1974, doc. 565, in Hamilton, *Documents on British Policy Overseas. The Year of Europe*.

33. FCO, Memcon Callaghan/Sonnenfeldt, 15 March 1974, doc. 568, ibid.

34. On Kissinger's relationship with the press, see Hanhimäki, *The Flawed Architect*, 26–27.

35. Telcon Kissinger/Sonnenfeldt, 5 March 1974, 9:06 P.M., NPM, NSC, Kissinger files, Telcons, 25.

36. FCO, Washington telegram 817, 7 March 1974, doc. 565, in Hamilton, *Documents on British Policy Overseas. The Year of Europe*.

37. Möckli reaches a similar conclusion, but his claim is only based on the record of a few of Kissinger's telephone conversation and hence is essentially restricted to Kissinger (Möckli, *European Foreign Policy During the Cold War*, 293).

38. President's staff meeting, 9 February 1974, NPM, NSC, Presidential memcons, 1028.

39. Von Staden, Washington telegram 877, 17 March 1974, in Pautsch, *Akten zur Auswärtigen Politik der Bundesrepublik Deutschland 1974*, vol. 1, 404.

40. Telcon Kissinger/Nixon, 15 March 1974, 4:14 P.M., NPM, NSC, Kissinger files, Telcons, 25. On Kissinger's flattery of Nixon, see Dallek, *Nixon and Kissinger*, 92, 616; Hanhimäki, *The Flawed Architect*, 25.

41. Telcon Kissinger/Scowcroft, 15 March 1974, 4:14 P.M., NPM, NSC, Kissinger files, Telcons, 25.

42. Telcon Kissinger/Sonnenfeldt, 16 March 1974, 5:05 P.M., NPM, NSC, Kissinger files, Telcons, 25.

43. Telcon Kissinger/Nixon, 15 March 1974, 11 A.M., NPM, NSC, Kissinger files, Telcons, 25.
44. Ibid.
45. FCO, Washington telegram 817, 7 March 1974, doc. 565, in Hamilton, *Documents on British Policy Overseas. The Year of Europe.*
46. Robin, *Note pour Monsieur le président de la République : réunion du Comité politique des Neuf,* 20 February 1974, CHAN, 5AG2 1034; COREU CPE/MUL ETR 29, Bonn, 21 February 1974, MAE, EC files 1971–6, 3811; MAE, Direction d'Europe, *Note : réunion ministérielle du 4 mars — Europe/Etats-Unis,* 26 February 1974, MAE, EC files 1971–6, 3792.
47. Letter from Nixon to Brandt, 6 March 1974, MAE, U.S. files 1970–5, 1138. See also Telcon Kissinger/Sonnenfeldt, 5 March 1974, 9:06 P.M., NPM, NSC, Kissinger files, Telcons, 25.
48. Secretary's staff meeting, 11 March 1974, NARA, SD, RG 59, Lot files, Sonnenfeldt, 4.
49. Nixon to Brandt, 15 March 1974, MAE, U.S. files 1970–5, 1138.
50. Secretary's staff meeting, 18 March 1974, NARA, SD, RG 59, Lot files, Sonnenfeldt, 4.
51. "Transatlantic Slanging," *The New York Times,* 13 March 1974.
52. André Fontaine, "Le maître d'école," *Le Monde,* 14 March 1974.
53. Jacques Jacquet-Francillon, "M. Kissinger et l'Europe : une escalade verbale soigneusement préparée," *Le Figaro,* 14 March 1974.
54. Hynes, *The Year That Never Was,* 228–29.
55. Telcon Kissinger/Sonnenfeldt, 14 March 1974, 10:25 A.M., NPM, NSC, Kissinger files, Telcons, 25. Kissinger told the same story to Stephen Graubard (Telcon Kissinger/Graubard, 18 March 1974, A.M., NPM, NSC, Kissinger files, Telcons, 25).
56. Memcon Kissinger/Scheel, 24 March 1974, NPM, NSC, Presidential memcons, 1028.
57. Telcon Kissinger/Lawrence Eagleburger, 12 March 1974, 9:17 A.M., NPM, NSC, Kissinger files, Telcons, 25; Telcon Kissinger/Graubard, 18 March 1974, morning, NPM, NSC, Kissinger files, Telcons, 25.
58. Telcon Kissinger/Eagleburger, 12 March 1974, 9:17 A.M., NPM, NSC, Kissinger files, Telcons, 25; Kosciusko-Morizet, Washington telegram 2055-9, 14 March 1974, MAE, U.S. files 1970–5, 1138.
59. FCO, Washington telegram 817, 7 March 1974, doc. 565, in Hamilton, *Documents on British Policy Overseas. The Year of Europe.*
60. Secretary's staff meeting, 11 March 1974, NARA, SD, RG 59, Lot files, Sonnenfeldt, 4.
61. FCO, Washington telegram 817, 7 March 1974, doc. 565, in Hamilton, *Documents on British Policy Overseas. The Year of Europe.*
62. Sonnenfeldt to Kissinger (cover letter), 23 March 1974, NARA, SD, RG 59, Lot files, Sonnenfeldt, 4.
63. Secretary of State, telegram to Scowcroft, 29 March 1974, NPM, NSC, Kissinger files, Trip files, 48.
64. Kissinger used the word "cave" on repeated occasions (Telcon Kissinger/Nixon, 15 March 1974, 11:00 A.M., NPM, NSC, Kissinger files, Telcons, 25; Telcon Kissinger/Scowcroft, 15 March 1974, 9:50 P.M., NPM, NSC, Kissinger files, Telcons, 25).
65. Secretary's staff meeting, 18 March 1974, NARA, SD, RG 59, Lot files, Sonnenfeldt, 4; Telcon Kissinger/Scowcroft, 15 March 1974, 9:50 P.M., NPM, NSC, Kissinger files, Telcons, 25.
66. Von Staden, Washington telegram 877, 17 March 1974, in Pautsch, *Akten zur Auswärtigen Politik der Bundesrepublik Deutschland 1974,* vol. 1, 404.
67. Möckli, *European Foreign Policy During the Cold War,* 300.
68. FCO, Paris telegram 296, 8 March 1974, doc. 567, in Hamilton, *Documents on British Policy Overseas. The Year of Europe.*
69. Kosciusko-Morizet, Washington telegram 1832-42, 7 March 1974, MAE, U.S. files 1970–5, 1138.

70. Memcon Kissinger/Scheel, 3 March 1974, NARA, SD, RG 59, Lot files, Kissinger, 7.
71. Kosciusko-Morizet, Washington telegram 2021-30, 14 March 1974, MAE, U.S. files 1970–5, 1138.
72. Kosciusko-Morizet, Washington telegram 2252-7, 19 March 1974, MAE, U.S. files 1970–5, 1138.
73. See, for example, Sauvagnargues, Bonn telegram 991-7, 7 March 1974, MAE, U.S. files 1970–5, 1138.
74. Pompidou, margin comment on summary document dated 19 March 1974, CHAN, 5AG2 1054.
75. FCO, Bonn telegram 362, 7 March 1974, doc. 566, in Hamilton, *Documents on British Policy Overseas. The Year of Europe.*
76. Ibid.
77. Sauvagnargues, Bonn telegram 1335-45, 26 March 1974, MAE, U.S. files 1970–5, 1138.
78. FCO, Memcon Callaghan/Sonnenfeldt, 15 March 1974, doc. 568, in Hamilton, *Documents on British Policy Overseas. The Year of Europe.*
79. Letter from Brandt to Nixon, 8 March 1974, MAE, U.S. files 1970–5, 1138.
80. Puaux, *Note : réunion des directeurs politiques français et allemand,* 20 March 1974, MAE, U.S. files 1970–5, 1138.
81. Puaux, *Note : consultation entre les Neuf et les Etats-Unis. Echange téléphonique avec M. van Well,* 21 March 1974, CHAN, 5AG2 1021.
82. Gerhard Dohms, circular telegram 34, 3 April 1974, in Pautsch, *Akten zur Auswärtigen Politik der Bundesrepublik Deutschland 1974,* vol. 1, 476–77; *Information et consultation avec les pays alliés et amis. Projet de texte allemand,* MAE, EC files 1971–6, 3792.
83. On the implications of political change in Britain, see Möckli, *European Foreign Policy During the Cold War,* 303–9.
84. Quoted ibid., 307. On the Atlanticist creeds of the new Labour government, see also Hynes, *The Year That Never Was,* 227, 238.
85. Karl-Günther von Hase, London telegram 643, 8 March 1974, in Pautsch, *Akten zur Auswärtigen Politik der Bundesrepublik Deutschland 1974,* vol. 1, 339–40; Secretary of State, telegram to Scowcroft, 29 March 1974, NPM, NSC, Kissinger files, Trip files, 48.
86. FCO, Memcon Callaghan/Sonnenfeldt, 15 March 1974, doc. 568, in Hamilton, *Documents on British Policy Overseas. The Year of Europe.*
87. Ibid.
88. 12–13 March Political Committee, verbatim memorandum, undated, MAE, EC files 1971–6, 3811.
89. Pompidou, margin comment on Puaux, *Note,* 21 March 1974.
90. MAE, record of EPC ministerial meeting, 1 April 1974, MAE, EC files 1971–6, 3792.
91. MAE, record of EPC ministerial meeting, 2 April 1974, MAE, EC files 1971–6, 3792.
92. FCO, minute, Michael Weir to Alan Campbell, 6 March 1974, doc. 564, in Hamilton, *Documents on British Policy Overseas. The Year of Europe.*
93. Dohms, circular telegram 34, 3 April 1974, in Pautsch, *Akten zur Auswärtigen Politik der Bundesrepublik Deutschland 1974,* vol. 1, 478; MAE, Direction d'Europe, *Note : réunion ministérielle de la coopération politique. Luxembourg — 1er-2 avril,* 2 April 1974, MAE, EC files 1971–6, 3792.
94. Dohms, circular telegram 34, 3 April 1974.
95. Puaux, *Note : réunion des directeurs politiques,* 14 March 1974, MAE, U.S. files 1970–5, 1138.
96. FCO, Paris telegram 296, 8 March 1974, doc. 567, in Hamilton, *Documents on British Policy Overseas. The Year of Europe.*
97. Eric Roussel, *Georges Pompidou, 1911–1974,* 2nd ed. (Paris: Perrin, 2004), 625–26.

98. Quoted in Dubois, "La conception de la présidence de Valéry Giscard d'Estaing," 63.
99. Quoted ibid.
100. Vaïsse, *La puissance ou l'influence?* 195.
101. Bozo, *La politique étrangère de la France depuis 1945,* 72.
102. Marie-France Toinet, *Valéry Giscard d'Estaing et les Etats-Unis* (Paris: Association française de sciences politiques, 1983), 3.
103. Arnaud, *Note : Comité politique des 18 et 19 avril,* 19 April 1974, MAE, EC files 1971–6, 3811.
104. MAE, Direction d'Europe, *Note : problème de la consultation entre les Neuf et les Etats-Unis,* 10 May 1974, MAE, EC files 1971–6, 3811.
105. Roussel, *Georges Pompidou, 1911–1974,* 542; Vaïsse, *La puissance ou l'influence?* 35. On the Pompidou-Jobert relationship, see also Weed, *Michel Jobert et la diplomatie française,* 30–47.
106. FCO, Paris telegram 296, 8 March 1974, doc. 567, in Hamilton, *Documents on British Policy Overseas. The Year of Europe.*
107. Arnaud, *Note : Comité politique des 18 et 19 avril,* 19 April 1974, MAE, EC files 1971–6, 3811.
108. Puaux, *Note : entretien des directeurs politiques français et allemand,* 8 May 1974, MAE, EC files 1971–6, 3811.
109. Von der Gablentz, circular telegram 2368, 12 June 1974, in Pautsch, *Akten zur Auswärtigen Politik der Bundesrepublik Deutschland 1974,* vol. 1, 716.
110. Van Well, note, 22 April 1974, in Pautsch, *Akten zur Auswärtigen Politik der Bundesrepublik Deutschland 1974,* vol. 1, 555. The foreign ministers had agreed to meet without their political directors to keep the meeting informal. Callaghan and Moro nevertheless came with their political directors and reported back to them (Klaus Meyer, *Note à l'attention de M. le président Ortoli,* 19 April 1974, HAEU, Fonds Klaus Meyer (KM), 86; Courcel to Ambafrance Bonn, circular telegram 299, 18 April 1974, MAE, EC files 1971–6, 3792).
111. Puaux, *Note : entretien des directeurs politiques français et allemand,* MAE, EC files 1971–6, 3811.
112. The Political Committee worked out a text in French, which other member states then translated into their own language (von der Gablentz, circular telegram 2158, 29 May 1974, in Pautsch, *Akten zur Auswärtigen Politik der Bundesrepublik Deutschland 1974,* vol. 1, 659; von der Gablentz, circular telegram 2368, 12 June 1974, ibid., 717). The French text read: "les ministres se sont entendus pour procéder d'une façon pragmatique et cas par cas. Si l'un des partenaires soulève la question de l'information et de la consultation d'un Etat allié ou ami, les Neuf en discuteront et chargeront, après consensus, la présidence d'y procéder sur la base de celui-ci."
113. MAE, Direction d'Europe, *Note : Comité politique des 27/28 mai,* MAE, EC files 1971–6, 3811.
114. *Department of State, Briefing Paper: Atlantic Relations,* undated [June 1974], NPM, NSC, HAK files, Trip files, 48.
115. Meyer, *Dialogue euro-arabe,* 7 June 1974, HAEU, KM, 39.
116. *Réunion ministérielle Bonn, le 10 juin 1974. Relevé de conclusions. Projet,* 11 June 1974, MAE, EC files 1971–6, 3792.
117. Ibid.
118. The president of the European Commission, Ortoli, and the acting president of the EC Council of Foreign Ministers, Sauvagnargues, met with the designated representatives of the Arab League: Mahmoud Riad, its secretary-general, and the Kuwaiti foreign minister, its council president (MAE, Sous-direction du Levant, circular telegram 536, 2 August 1974, MAE, EC files 1971–6, 3805).

119. *Conférence de presse de M. Genscher, ministre fédéral des Affaires étrangères, en sa qualité de président en exercice de la coopération politique européenne à l'issue de la réunion des ministres des Affaires étrangères des Neuf, à Bonn, le 12 juin 1974. Intervention de M. Jean Sauvagnargues, ministre des Affaires étrangères*, MAE, EC files 1971–6, 3792.

120. Didier Maus, "Les rapports de Valéry Giscard d'Estaing avec ses gouvernements (1974–1981)," in *Les années Giscard. Institutions et pratiques politiques, 1974–1978*, ed. Serge Berstein, Jean-François Sirinelli, and René Rémond (Paris: Fayard, 2003), 116; Dubois, "La conception de la présidence de Valéry Giscard d'Estaing," 67–68. The governing coalition had 298 seats in Parliament: 183 UDR, 55 RI, 30 Réformateurs démocrates sociaux and 30 Union centriste.

121. *Department of State, Briefing Paper: Atlantic Relations*, undated [June 1974], NPM, NSC, HAK files, Office files: Europe, 53. For an interpretation of the connection between the NATO Declaration and change in political leadership, see Hanhimäki, *The Flawed Architect*, 351; Mélandri, "La France et l'Alliance atlantique sous Georges Pompidou et Valéry Giscard d'Estaing," 539. On Giscard d'Estaing's desire to improve Franco-American relations, see ibid.; Soutou, "Le président Pompidou et les relations entre les Etats-Unis et l'Europe"; Toinet, *Valéry Giscard d'Estaing et les Etats-Unis*.

122. Franz Krapf, Brussels telegram 341, 15 March 1974, in Pautsch, *Akten zur Auswärtigen Politik der Bundesrepublik Deutschland 1974*, vol. 1, 380–82.

123. Ibid.

124. Dohms, circular telegram 62, 13 June 1974, in Pautsch, *Akten zur Auswärtigen Politik der Bundesrepublik Deutschland 1974*, vol. 1, 720.

125. Ibid.

126. Ruprecht von Keller, Ottawa telegram 300, 19 June 1974, in Pautsch, *Akten zur Auswärtigen Politik der Bundesrepublik Deutschland 1974*, vol. 1, 793.

127. Sauvagnargues, interview, 11 January 1991, MAE, AO, Sauvagnargues. The French press essentially told the same story (see, for example, Michel Tatu, "A la fin de la session atlantique, MM. Kissinger et Sauvagnargues ont réglé leur différend sur les consultations interalliées," *Le Monde*, 20 June 1974).

128. MAE, Service des pactes et du désarmement, *Note : le point sur la déclaration atlantique au lendemain de la session d'Ottawa*, 21 June 1974, MAE, U.S. files 1970–5, 731.

129. North Atlantic Treaty Organization, "Declaration on Atlantic Relations," http://www.nato.int/cps/en/natolive/official_texts_26902.htm.

130. Soutou, "Georges Pompidou et Valéry Giscard d'Estaing," 312; idem, "La problématique de la détente et le testament stratégique de Georges Pompidou," 103.

131. Bozo, *Deux stratégies pour l'Europe*, 522.

132. North Atlantic Treaty Organization, "Declaration on Atlantic Relations."

133. Von Staden, Washington telegram 187, 19 January 1974, in Pautsch, *Akten zur Auswärtigen Politik der Bundesrepublik Deutschland 1974*, vol. 1, 73–74.

134. Von Staden, Washington telegram 45, 5 January 1974, ibid., 14–15.

135. Von Staden, Washington telegram 187, 19 January 1974, ibid., 72–73.

136. For a similar interpretation, see Möckli, *European Foreign Policy During the Cold War*, 331–33.

137. Secretary of State, telegram to Scowcroft, 29 March 1974, NPM, NSC, Kissinger files, Trip files, 48.

138. Meyer, *Note à l'attention de M. Ortoli, président, Sir Christopher Soames, vice-président, M. Cheysson, membre de la Commission*, 29 May 1974, HAEU, KM, 39; "Ce qui reste de la 'nouvelle charte,'" *Le Monde*, 27 June 1974.

139. "Ce qui reste de la 'nouvelle charte,'" *Le Monde*, 27 June 1974.

140. De Rose, interview with the author, Paris, 30 April 2007.

141. Van Well, note, 22 April 1974, in Pautsch, *Akten zur Auswärtigen Politik der Bundesrepublik Deutschland 1974*, vol. 1, 552–53.
142. Quoted in FCO, Memcon Callaghan/Sonnenfeldt, 15 March 1974, doc. 568, in Hamilton, *Documents on British Policy Overseas. The Year of Europe*.
143. Kosciusko-Morizet, Washington telegram 3679-81, 4 May 1974, MAE, U.S. files 1970–5, 1138; Secretary of State, telegram to Scowcroft, 29 March 1974, NPM, NSC, Kissinger files, Trip files, 48.
144. Kissinger, *Years of Upheaval*, 934.
145. Kissinger, *Memorandum for the President*, "Meeting with NATO heads of government, Wednesday, 26 June 1974," undated [June 1974], NPM, NSC, VIP files, 950.
146. North Atlantic Treaty Organization, "Declaration on Atlantic Relations."
147. Kissinger, *Memorandum for the President*, "Your visit to Brussels, June 25-27, 1974," undated [June 1974], NPM, NSC, VIP files, 950.
148. On domestic opposition to détente, see Schulzinger, "Détente in the Nixon-Ford Years, 1969–1976," 385–86; Hanhimäki, *The Flawed Architect*, 340–42.
149. Hanhimäki, *The Flawed Architect*, 352.
150. Sauvagnargues, interview, 11 January 1991, MAE, AO, Sauvagnargues.
151. Quoted in Jacques Jacquet-Francillon, "Signature demain à Bruxelles de la nouvelle 'charte atlantique': Nixon se fait consacrer leader de l'Occident avant de rencontrer Brejnev à Moscou," *Le Figaro*, 26 June 1974.
152. Jacques de Montalais, "Une absence bienvenue," *La Nation*, 26 June 1974; "Les raisons d'une absence," *Le Figaro*, 26 June 1974.
153. Gilles Richard, "L'élection présidentielle de 1974 : un événement," in *Les années Giscard. Institutions et pratiques politiques, 1974–1978*, ed. Serge Berstein, Jean-François Sirinelli, and René Rémond (Paris: Fayard, 2003), 15–33.
154. "Adoptée par le gouvernement français, la déclaration atlantique d'Ottawa est un mauvais coup contre la détente et l'intérêt de la France, déclare Georges Marchais à l''Humanité,'" *L'Humanité*, 20 June 1974.
155. "La déclaration atlantique adoptée à Ottawa par M. Sauvagnargues consacre la suprématie américaine en Europe," *L'Humanité*, 20 June 1974.
156. Jacques Mornand, "L'empereur d'Occident: exécré dans son pays, Nixon voulait une victoire à Bruxelles et un sacre à Moscou — la puissance de l'Empire américain a permis le tout," *Le Nouvel observateur*, 1 July 1974.
157. "Fin du Conseil atlantique à Ottawa. L'Europe rentre dans 'la nuit américaine,'" *Libération*, 20 June 1974.
158. "Nixon en terrain conquis," *Combat*, 25 June 1974.
159. "Une photo de famille," *Le Monde*, 27 June 1974.
160. Jacques Ogliastro, "'C'est la fin de la dispute la plus inutile du monde,' dit Jean Sauvagnargues," *Le Figaro*, 20 June 1974.
161. Roger Massip, "Souplesse et ambiguïté," *Le Figaro*, 20 June 1974.
162. Jacques Ogliastro, "'C'est la fin de la dispute la plus inutile du monde,' dit Jean Sauvagnargues," *Le Figaro*, 20 June 1974.
163. "Aujourd'hui à Bruxelles : Nixon octroie une charte à l'Europe," *Libération*, 26 June 1974. In a similar vein, see "Bruxelles : blanc-seing au chef de l'exécutif américain," *L'Humanité*, 27 June 1974.
164. "Une photo de famille," *Le Monde*, 27 June 1974; Jacques Jacquet-Francillon, "Signature demain à Bruxelles de la nouvelle 'charte atlantique,'" *Le Figaro*, 25 June 1974.
165. Roland Faure, "Le différend franco-américain aplani, l'Europe peut redémarrer," *L'Aurore*, 20 June 1974.
166. "Une photo de famille," *Le Monde*, 27 June 1974.

167. On Nixon's June 1974 trip to the Soviet Union, see Hanhimäki, *The Flawed Architect*, 352–56; Schulzinger, "Détente in the Nixon-Ford Years, 1969–1976," 388.

168. Hanhimäki, *The Flawed Architect*, 355.

169. "Fin du Conseil atlantique à Ottawa," *Libération*, 20 June 1974.

170. "Fin du Conseil atlantique à Ottawa," "Aujourd'hui à Bruxelles," *Libération*, 26 June 1974.

171. Roland Faure, "Editorial : Nixon en position de force pour rencontrer Brejnev demain à Moscou," *L'Aurore*, 26 June 1974.

172. Roland Faure, "Le différend franco-américain aplani," *L'Aurore*, 20 June 1974.

173. Jacques Jacquet-Francillon, "Signature demain à Bruxelles de la nouvelle 'charte atlantique,'" *Le Figaro*, 25 June 1974.

174. Roger Massip, "L'Europe et les deux grands," *Le Figaro*, 27 June 1974; Jacques Jacquet-Francillon, "Souplesse et ambiguïté," *Le Figaro*, 20 June 1974.

175. Jacques Ogliastro, "'C'est la fin de la dispute la plus inutile du monde,' dit Jean Sauvagnargues," *Le Figaro*, 20 June 1974.

176. Kissinger, *Memorandum for the President*, "Your visit to Brussels, June 25–27, 1974," 24 June 1974, NPM, NSC, HAK files, Office files: Europe, 56.

177. On this interpretation, see also Schulz and Schwartz, "The Superpower and the Union in the Making," 363–64.

178. Conseil constitutionnel, "Les membres du Conseil: Valéry Giscard d'Estaing," http://www.conseil-constitutionnel.fr/conseil-constitutionnel/francais/le-conseil-constitution nel/le-conseil-aujourd-hui/les-membres-du-conseil/liste-des-membres/valery-giscard-d-estaing.222.html.

179. Giscard d'Estaing, interview with the author, 23 May 2008. On Giscard's emphasis on economic affairs, see also Vaïsse, *La puissance ou l'influence?* 22.

180. Sauvagnargues, statement on the radio channel France Inter, 21 June 1974, quoted in "La déclaration atlantique : 'la liberté de décision de la France est intégralement préservée' affirme M. Sauvagnargues," *Le Monde*, 22 June 1974.

181. Sauvagnargues, [*Considérations sur la politique étrangère de la France*], August 1974, MAE, AP, 373.

182. Sauvagnargues, [*Réflexions sur la relance européenne*], August 1974, MAE, AP, 373.

183. Sauvagnargues, interview, 11 January 1991, MAE, AO Sauvagnargues.

184. Möckli, *European Foreign Policy During the Cold War*, 321.

Chapter 6

Building a Political Europe in a Changed International Context

Giscard and the Twin Summits of Paris and Martinique

Seven months after his election, Giscard hosted a Franco-American summit on the French island of Martinique. This summit marked a significant improvement in bilateral relations. Two main factors explain the rapprochement. First, senior U.S. officials changed their tone after Nixon's August resignation over Watergate. This unprecedented event in U.S. history undermined the confidence of U.S. officials, prompting them to think that the U.S. government had lost some of its authority. The new Ford administration assumed a less confrontational stance in international affairs, being more sympathetic to European concerns and less inclined to unilateralism.[1] Second, Giscard encouraged better relations with the United States, as exemplified by the French stance on EPC. In summer 1974, Sauvagnargues went to some lengths to inform the Ford administration of EPC's steps in relation to the Cyprus crisis. U.S. officials acknowledged these efforts. Whereas on 4 July Kissinger was still rehashing complaints about Jobert's 1973 double-dealings with respect to the proposed Atlantic charter,[2] less than two months later he recognized that the resumption of consultation had fostered a better bilateral relationship.[3] At the September 1974 UN General Assembly meeting, there was much talk about Franco-

---

Notes for this section begin on page 187.

American reconciliation.[4] The lull threatened to end on 24 October, when Giscard called for a trilateral energy conference that would gather advanced countries, oil producers, and oil-importing developing countries. Soon thereafter, however, the French and the U.S. governments reached a compromise on international oil policy.

Still, the 1973–1974 French campaign in favor of the assertion of a European identity was not a mere flash in the pan. Giscard's Atlanticism was coupled with a strong European commitment. The main focus in his first months in office was on institutional reform within the EC, that is, on the internal, rather than the external, dimension of a political Europe. He seized the opportunity of France's turn at the rotating EC presidency from July to December 1974 to sponsor a reform blueprint. As Sauvagnargues phrased it, the goal was to "build a confederal Europe—that is, no merging—without any head-on clash with the United States" ("construire l'Europe confédérale, c.f. pas fusion—sans heurts frontaux avec les Etats-Unis").[5] De Gaulle and Pompidou had used the adjective "confederal" as a synonym for "intergovernmental."[6] Sauvagnargues understood it differently. His proposed reforms, which Giscard largely endorsed, included not only institutionalized summitry, but also enhanced supranational decision-making.

Facing the Arab World and the United States: Giscard's Search for New Directions

The U.S. State Department had predicted in May 1974 that Giscard would be "more pragmatic and less idealistic … in his approach to U.S.-French relations" than his predecessors.[7] France's Arab and energy policy during the first months of his presidency spoke of such pragmatism. Giscard took the Franco-Arab rapprochement one step further by refurbishing Jobert's proposal for a world energy conference. But he also toned down the French criticisms of U.S. international energy policy. The French government even acquiesced to the transformation of the ECG into the International Energy Agency (IEA) within the OECD framework.

From the outset, Giscard's government fostered closer ties with the Arab world. On 21 October 1974, Sauvagnargues met with the leader of the Palestine Liberation Organization (PLO), Yasser Arafat. In his press conference of 24 October, Giscard referred to a Palestinian "homeland [*patrie*]."[8] In 1975, the PLO opened an office in Paris. These were significant steps. The international community still largely considered the PLO a terrorist organization, and the United States in particular backed Israel's opposition to its international recognition. The Quai d'Orsay also used its best efforts to rescue the Euro-Arab dialogue when the problem of PLO participation threatened to end it. At its October 1974 summit, the League of Arab States recognized the PLO as the sole legitimate representative of the Palestinian people; then, in mid November, it officially requested PLO participation in the Euro-Arab dialogue as observers,[9] hoping to advance its objective of PLO recognition. On 22 November, the UN General Assembly passed a resolution inviting the PLO to participate in its deliberations.[10] This resolution bolstered the League's resolve; however, all EC states voted against it except France, which abstained.[11] Similarly, the EC states met the Arab League's request for PLO participation in the Euro-Arab dialogue with a blunt refusal. Consequently, the League adjourned sine die the first meeting of the planned Euro-Arab general committee ("commission générale"). It fell upon the Quai d'Orsay to craft a compromise.[12] Sauvagnargues first alluded to a compromise solution during his December 1974 trip to Egypt.[13] The EC Nine's foreign ministers endorsed it in Dublin in February 1975. The so-called "Dublin formula" replaced the planned general committee with an expert committee. European and Arab—including Palestinian—experts would sit on this committee as such, rather than as representatives of a particular nation or organization.[14] The first meeting of the expert committee in June 1975 marked the effective start of the dialogue.[15]

Meanwhile, French officials had yielded to economic self-interest, amending their stance on institutionalized oil cooperation. At its meeting on 8–9 July, the ECG endorsed a U.S. plan for an emergency oil-sharing mechanism.[16] Despite enduring disagreements on the technical aspects of the plan—particularly its trigger level and its automaticity—the ECG agreed on 20 September to create the IEA within the OECD. There were still hard-liners within the Quai d'Orsay. Burin des Roziers stressed the contradiction between "Atlantic solidarity" and the EC countries' declared objective of reducing their energy dependency. His analysis was a familiar tune.[17] The proposed emergency sharing plan, he claimed, implied an "energy community" which would "break up [*dissoudre*]" the EC as such. But this line of argument was losing ground in French governing circles, where officials had become increasingly attuned to the costs of France's self-exclusion. In June 1974, the Quai directorate for economic and financial affairs underscored the negative implications of such exclusion for France's civil nuclear industry.[18] By mid July, most government services— including the prime minister's office, the ministry of economics, the ministry of industry, and Giscard's economic adviser, Jean-Pierre Dutet—had come to recommend a loose form of participation in the ECG.[19]

Giscard listened to the doves. As a member of the OECD, France could have vetoed the creation of the IEA within the OECD. The Quai d'Orsay recommended threatening to veto in order to limit the IEA's powers. Its goal was to exclude all tasks that existing bodies (the OECD Oil and Energy Committees and the Nuclear Energy Agency) already dealt with.[20] This meant limiting the IEA's mission to overseeing the emergency sharing plan. Giscard favored a more conciliatory stance.[21] The Quai's final instructions thus took a milder tone and made no mention of France's veto. The French representative merely abstained from the OECD Council vote on 15 November, even though ECG members had not substantially amended the draft OECD Council Decision to reflect French views.[22]

Giscard was most likely keen to avoid undermining recent efforts to address global challenges through Western cooperation. As minister of finance, in 1973 he had been among the founders of the "library group," named after the ground library of the White House. Established to forge consensus on monetary reform, it was institutionalized as the Group of Five (G5) ministers, including the British, French, Japanese, U.S., and West German finance ministers.[23] Giscard was later to play a central role in the institutionalization of G5 summitry, hosting the first G5 summit in the French castle of Rambouillet in 1975.[24] A hard line on energy would clearly have hampered the progress of this multilateral cooperation.

Giscard probably conceived of his proposal for a trilateral energy conference as a way of counterbalancing the French stance on the IEA. Arab producers remained opposed to what they perceived as a consumer bloc. In June 1975, Quai officials had warned that Arab countries would regard French involvement in the ECG as a policy "shift" in the Arab world. Algeria, Iraq, and Libya, in particular, might retaliate against French interests.[25] A Quai July memorandum recommended that France should participate in the ECG oil-sharing mechanism only if the ECG members reasserted their commitment to a "dialogue" with the producers.[26] Dutet advanced the same argument about the IEA. If France decided to join, it should take a "compelling step [*initiative spectaculaire*]" to launch a consumer-producer dialogue that would balance competing interests ("souci d'équilibre politique").[27] Giscard's proposal of 24 October for a trilateral conference was reminiscent of Jobert's January 1974 call for a world energy conference. Jobert, however, had not distinguished between industrialized and developing countries as consumers.[28] Giscard's triad reflected a growing awareness of the specific woes of oil-importing developing states.

The origins of Giscard's proposal are still largely clouded in mystery. The Quai d'Orsay was most likely left out of the loop. The records of the Quai directorate for economic affairs contain no advance mention of the initiative. A Quai memorandum issued on 24 October even pleaded for talks with the producers within a regional, rather than global, framework.[29] During his December 1974 meeting with U.S. President Gerald

Ford, Giscard suggested that the U.S. visit of Finance Minister Jean-Pierre Fourcade had encouraged him to advance his proposal. Reporting on his trip to Washington, Fourcade had hinted at the U.S. willingness to accept a two-step procedure: first, talks on the guarantees to be given to oil producers, and second, coordinated measures for stopping the price spiral. Giscard, so he himself stated, subsequently decided to "clarify" his stance on energy in his press conference.[30] In any case, Giscard demonstrated his penchant for independent moves. This character trait would come across most vividly in 1980, when he decided to meet with Brezhnev in Warsaw against the advice of his foreign minister.[31]

Giscard had endeavored to reconcile France's Arab policy with a new emphasis on Western cooperation. His proposed energy conference nevertheless met with criticism in both the Arab world and the United States. Since 1973, the Group of Seventy-Seven (G77) had radicalized its stance. Seventy-seven developing countries had established the G77 at the first session of the UN Conference on Trade and Development in 1964. In the wake of the oil shock, the G77 developed an agenda designed to redistribute wealth between the industrialized North and the developing South.[32] Striving to maintain G77 cohesion, Algeria backed the French proposal but argued that the conference should include all raw materials.[33] The Algerian leaders were not a lone voice in the Arab world.[34] In the short run, however, the greatest challenge would be U.S. opposition.

Sealing Franco-American Reconciliation: The 1974 Martinique Summit

Renewed strains in Franco-U.S. relations followed Giscard's energy initiative. The resolution of this crisis highlights the way in which the centrist president sought to chart a new course for French policy. He remained committed to his plan for a consumer-producer dialogue[35] but endeavored to make it compatible with improved transatlantic relations. His tactical flexibility allowed him to succeed in combining these seemingly contradictory objectives.

Giscard's call for a trilateral conference caused unhappiness in Washington, reigniting criticism about the lack of proper consultation;[36] Sauvagnargues had informed Kissinger a mere twenty-four hours beforehand.[37] Senior U.S. officials' qualms went beyond procedural matters. With the memories of the Year of Europe fresh in their mind, they interpreted the French proposal as a reversion to Gaullist obstructionism. The U.S. government was still adamant about strengthened consumer cooperation. A consumer-producer meeting, Kissinger warned, "could accentuate the sense of impotence of the West that could offset all policies."[38] It could also sow division among the industrialized countries: "All it will take is for one producer to say that one position is contrary to the producers' interest to throw a monkey wrench into the consumers' position."[39] The U.S. goal was to put downward pressure on prices and to prevent the enactment of a lasting change in consumer-producer relations. Consequently, the Ford administration was willing to initiate a dialogue with the producers only after the consumers had shown a tangible commitment to solidarity. In July, Giscard had suggested using the library group to discuss energy matters. The U.S. government had thus "embarked on a hopeful course of achieving better cooperation by quiet talks dealing with concrete problems."[40] Giscard's press conference was a wake-up call. U.S. officials warned that it risked "turning us back toward the situation we faced last year when relations between the United States and Europe were at their lowest ebb."[41]

Giscard's proposal reopened old wounds, but Kissinger was not willing to risk another transatlantic row. He wavered between a harsh line and a somewhat conciliatory stance. In early November, he wrote to Sauvagnargues that "a producer-consumer dialogue that is well-prepared" was not incompatible with U.S. policy.[42] Soon thereafter, however, he asserted that consumer cooperation in all its forms—the IEA and the proposed creation of a common loan and guaranty facility to provide a means for recycling petroleum earnings—took absolute priority over a consumer-producer dialogue.[43] His comments to Francophile journalist Pierre Salinger were reminiscent of the verbal escalation of the spring:

> Their people are cutting down ours all over the world. That's the reason why I don't want to go to a producers' conference without all of us, including the French being committed to a certain plan. Otherwise the French will sell us short and undercut us with the producers.[44]

But he softened his tone with Sauvagnargues, "blowing hot and cold."[45] Overall, his statements were mildly accommodating, perhaps reflecting the reduced authority the U.S. government felt it possessed in the aftermath of Nixon's resignation.

The EC states' reactions highlighted the close entwinement of intra-EC and U.S.-European relations. France's EC partners agreed to support the French plan only if the Ford administration did so as well. French officials found the energy talks leading to the December 1974 EC Paris summit "very difficult and occasionally unpleasant."[46] The draft communiqué spoke of deep disagreements. There were competing wordings for all the paragraphs pertaining to international energy issues.[47] On the eve of the summit, Dutet warned that any attempt to go beyond "vague and general" phrasing was doomed to failure.[48] Events proved him right. In Martinique, Giscard would confidently tell his U.S. counterpart that the EC Nine supported his views. All they were saying was that the proposed conference "had to be closely coordinated with the United States."[49] In truth, the communiqué of the EC summit merely stated that the EC heads of state or government had discussed consumer-producer cooperation, and that they attached much importance to the forthcoming Franco-American summit.[50]

The personal relationship between Giscard and Schmidt eased the path toward a compromise, anticipating the role of "personalized diplomacy" during the mid 1970s.[51] The two men had become well acquainted while serving as finance ministers. Once they became the French president and West German chancellor, respectively, they forged close ties resting on trust and mutual appreciation. In his memoirs, Giscard describes their relationship as both "intimate" and "unique" in modern world history.[52] Schmidt paid him back in coin, casting it as a "solid friendship."[53] These statements are perhaps overly rosy. Friendship did not prevent disagreements. Schmidt called Giscard's energy initiative "careless."[54] He also had harsh words for France's policy toward the PLO, which he found "deeply" disturbing. Nonetheless, he tried his best to act as a facilitator. West German officials were anxious to reconcile conflicting priorities, wanting to avoid antagonizing both their oil suppliers and their main security guarantor.[55] On 28 November, Schmidt discussed the matter with Giscard on the phone.[56] With Giscard's assent, he subsequently presented Ford and Kissinger with a three-stage compromise formula: first, a Paris meeting of senior civil servants to set a date for a consumer-producer conference; second, a "consumer caucus"; and, third, a consumer-producer conference.[57] The first step was designed to let everyone "know a conference will happen"[58] and hence that the consumers were not gearing up for confrontation.[59] Ford and Kissinger, however, made a counterproposal that placed greater emphasis on consumer cooperation at this initial stage. Schmidt suggested that if there was any initial confidential consumer meeting, an official consumer-producer meeting should immediately follow.[60]

Giscard's tactical flexibility helped to broker the final agreement. In Sauvagnargues's words, Giscard had come to Martinique "with a sort of mandate to reconcile our [the French and the U.S.] positions."[61] Initially both parties reaffirmed their respective viewpoints, but Giscard soon laid out a four-stage compromise formula. His suggestion provided the basis for the agreement enshrined in the summit communiqué. In line with U.S. wishes, the consumers would first strengthen their cooperation,[62] but then, in March 1975, there would be preparatory talks with the producers. Third, oil-importing countries would pursue "intensive consultations" in order to forge common positions on issues of substance. This process would culminate in the conference advocated by Giscard. No date was set for it, but both parties pledged to carry out all preliminary steps "in the most expeditious manner possible."

Overall, both parties conducted the Martinique talks in a spirit of conciliation. The two presidents quickly settled the issue of U.S.-European consultation, which the State Department's policy planning staff had raised again.[63] Giscard stated that the United States still had to learn how to deal with a united Europe, as opposed to individual nation-states. Kissinger replied that misunderstandings could be avoided "if you would inform us of your views and we would inform you of our discussions with your partners."[64] Neither of them raised the problem of U.S.-EC/EPC consultation per se. Instead, Giscard shared his concerns about European integration:

> Positive things came out of the last [EC] summit, but there was also a negative side to it. On the positive side, it is a good thing to have agreed on regular thrice-yearly meetings of the EC heads of government. ...
>
> But we must say that our [EC] partners did not demonstrate a genuine desire to organize Europe. There was no passion [*feu sacré*], but rather a slight feeling of disappointment. We did not say it to the public, but this is the impression I gathered.[65]

Giscard also took a nuanced position on America's proposed mechanism to recycle petroleum earnings, that is, a common loan and guaranty facility. The Quai d'Orsay viewed it as yet another attempt to curtail European autonomy.[66] Instead of opposing it altogether, Giscard suggested discussing oil-related financial mechanisms in the Group of Ten.[67] The French and the U.S. presidents also resolved a seven-year dispute over U.S. military relocation after France's withdrawal from NATO's command structure. Ford accepted Giscard's offer of 100 million dollars in full settlement—considerably more than the 100 million francs Pompidou had been willing to grant in 1973.[68] Last but not least, Giscard and Ford agreed to resume the nuclear cooperation talks that had ceased in the aftermath of the Year of Europe and the Yom Kippur War. This was an important decision. By February 1974, the French government had understood that in a context of bilateral tensions the Nixon administration no longer wanted to help improve the French nuclear arsenal.[69] That month, Pompidou had issued a military directive reasserting the independence of French nuclear deterrence.[70]

Kissinger sounded upbeat in the aftermath of the summit. "Having attended many similar meetings between French and American leaders," he told the press, "I must say I found this atmosphere the most positive."[71] The summit sealed Franco-U.S. reconciliation.[72] Nonetheless, Giscard did not capitulate to U.S. "diktats," as *L'Humanité* maintained.[73] Rather, the summit testified to both parties' desire to achieve better relations as a prerequisite for strengthened Western cooperation in a changing world. Giscard alluded to it while pleading for a new approach to world monetary reform. The IMF's Committee of Twenty (C20) talks, he stated, had failed. The G5 members should cooperate more closely, possibly at the presidential level, to "reestablish control of the general economic development," by which he probably meant the development of the world.[74] This analysis was largely valid, as the C20 meetings had tended to be ineffectively large.[75] Giscard's statements also reflected his belief in the need for a new form of problem-solving mechanism. He favored talks among the decision makers of a small group of Western countries.[76] Kissinger displayed a similar mindset. "A new set of world rules and interdependencies," he stated at the first 1975 White House cabinet meeting, was in the making.[77] The United States should therefore forge "new political and economic partnerships."

The agreement reached at Martinique, on a trilateral conference on oil, was also important because it paved the way for the North-South dialogue. The planned preparatory consumer-producer meeting was held in April 1975. The talks were unsuccessful because of protracted disagreements between the United States and Algeria over the scope of the conference.[78] The Ford administration was adamant about restricting it to energy-related matters, whereas the Algerian government insisted on including all raw materials. At the Helsinki meeting of the CSCE, Giscard, Ford, Schmidt, and Wilson decided to try again. The Ford administration had embarked on a course of "appeasement" to prevent further radicalization of Third World countries.[79] Its willingness to accommodate Algerian wishes was crucial to the success of the December 1975 Conference on International Economic Cooperation in Paris, which gathered the representatives of eight advanced and nineteen developing countries. It established four committees in charge of discussing energy, raw material trade, development, and finance-related issues. Historians still regard the resulting North-South dialogue as a "success" for Giscard's diplomacy.[80] The centrist leader had indeed been the main Western leader behind this initiative.

France and Europe as Interconnected Entities: The French Blueprint for EC Institutional Reform

Giscard's emphasis on Western cooperation did not mean that he neglected European integration. In his electoral campaign, he had pledged that a first priority of his government would be to resume the drive for European unity. As newly elected president, he matched words with deeds. In July 1974, he instructed Sauvagnargues to make proposals for a European *relance*.[81] The emphasis historians have placed on the European Council suggests that Giscard followed in his predecessors' footsteps, with a focus on intergovernmental cooperation.[82] This is a biased interpretation. The French reform plan also included measures designed to enhance the partly intergovernmental, partly supranational EC institutions.

The full story of the origins of France's institutional *relance* has yet to be told. At best, scholars connect the French proposals to Monnet's 1973 plan for a temporary European government.[83] There was in fact a more direct link. A set of hitherto undiscovered documents elucidate this connection: Sauvagnargues's August 1974 handwritten notes and his September memorandum to Giscard on "how to organize Europe."[84] Sauvagnargues met with Monnet twice, on 28 June and 31 August, respectively. Monnet also sent him copies of two documents: a March 1973 "working document" and his September 1973 Memorandum on a Temporary European Government.[85] Reflecting on French and European policy during his vacation in Corsica, Sauvagnargues found Monnet's views very congenial, borrowing heavily from them.[86] His thinking led to his September memorandum to Giscard. This memorandum, in turn, provided the basis for the reform plan of the French EC presidency of 11 October.[87]

Sauvagnargues's ideas and language owed much to Monnet. Virtually all of Sauvagnargues's proposed reforms were already listed in Monnet's documents and a September 1973 "working document" in particular:[88] a "European Council" consisting of the EC heads of state or government; the election of the European Parliament (EP) by direct universal suffrage; enhanced EP powers, namely, the right to formulate proposals and to legislate in specific fields; discarding strict unanimous decision-making in the EC Council of Ministers; and, finally, new common policies in the fields of energy, industrial development, transportation, the environment, quality of life, civil aviation, and youth.[89] Monnet's and Sauvagnargues's proposals differed on only two counts: the secretariat of the European Council, which Sauvagnargues predictably wanted to have in Paris; and the rotating presidency of the EC, which he wished to restrict to the four largest EC states as smaller ones, he thought, were unable to fill this role "effectively."[90] Sauvagnargues even borrowed from Monnet's wording. Both men stressed the need to use the mixed—supranational and inter-governmental—structure of the EC as a basis for reform. Both portrayed this institutional setup as "unique of its kind [*ensemble sui generis*]."[91] Like Monnet, Sauvagnargues was anxious not to revive the old debate on a federal versus an intergovernmental Europe.[92] Quoting Monnet almost verbatim, he appropriated his definition of "European union" as a work in progress.[93] The basic premise was that "the transformative process" that would result in a "European union" had already started. Sauvagnargues also portrayed this "European union" as an "evolving entity." Like Monnet, he wrote that the process of change would not end in 1980, as the EC heads of state or government had stated at their 1972 Paris summit. Rather, a new treaty would merely endorse the procedures introduced between 1974 and 1980 while leaving room for further reforms.

Sauvagnargues's proposals do not fit with scholarly portrayals in which his role has been reduced to that of an underling.[94] Soutou has also described him as Giscard's most Gaullist foreign minister.[95] In truth, Sauvagnargues was not a hard-line Gaullist.[96] He played an active role in the drafting of the treaty for the ill-fated European Defense Community (EDC) while serving as Quai deputy director for Central European affairs in the early 1950s. He then worked as adviser in charge of German matters to Foreign Minister Antoine Pinay, arranging several meetings between Pinay and Adenauer. When de Gaulle returned to power in 1958, Sauvagnargues's pro-European profile, albeit not fully integrationist, caused suspicion, and he was transferred to the department of African affairs. Commentators interpreted his 1974 appointment as foreign minister as a sign of Giscard's commitment to change. The press cast him as a "pragmatic European." His summer notes and his September memorandum substantiate this claim. Sauvagnargues was "European" because his proposed reforms entailed more than a union of states. He also preferred pragmatic solutions and incremental steps to doctrinal debate.

Sauvagnargues's handwritten notes offer a rare window into the mind of a French policy-maker. They point to the crystallization of an EC-centered ideal within segments of France's governing elites. They also attest to the declining influence of such Gaullist categories as "glory" and "grandeur," which Sauvagnargues depicted as "outdated," as well that of national independence.[97] Sauvagnargues still referred to the concept of French independence, but only to stress its shortcomings. France could not achieve its main policy goals—namely, "security, wealth, influence"—through national independence.[98] The country could not ensure its security by itself. Its economic prosperity was increasingly dependent upon external factors such as energy and European integration. Last, it had to rely largely, "though not exclusively," on "Europe" in order to remain influential on the global stage ("Notre rayonnement passe [mais pas exclusivement] par l'Europe"). Sauvagnargues connected French and European independence. These interrelated objectives, he stated, could only be reached by reducing Europe's "triple dependency": its economic and monetary dependency upon the United States, its oil import dependency, and its security dependency.[99] Sauvagnargue thus still conceived of "Europe" in largely instrumental terms but thought within a broader framework than a strictly national one. His worldview had room for not only the French nation but also a European entity in the making.

By September 1974, Sauvagnargues had devised a far-reaching plan for a European *relance*. Most of his proposals would make their way into the October 1974 blueprint of the French EC presidency.[100] The only exceptions were the right for the EP to make proposals for the implementation of the planned "European union" and new common policies in matters of quality of life, youth, and civil aviation. The proposed introduction of qualified majority voting in the EC Council of Ministers was also more carefully worded. The goal was no longer to list the policy fields to which this procedure would apply. Rather, the EC presidency might suggest applying this procedure to a particular issue during the preliminary meeting held before each EC Council of Ministers. Nevertheless, this blueprint marked a rechartering of France's European policy. French officials certainly perceived it as such. The U.S. embassy in Paris reported that "the French" were describing "their new willingness to consider measures to strengthen supranational institutions as representing a significant change in French policy."[101] Sauvagnargues was instrumental in bringing about this reorientation. So too would Giscard be.

Balancing Intergovernmentalism and Supranationalism: The 1974 Paris Summit Communiqué

Giscard's pledge to give new impetus to European integration owed little to his electoral alliance with Lecanuet's pro-integration centrist party, the Mouvement réformateur.[102] A committed European,[103] the new president had been a member of Monnet's Action Committee for the United States of Europe since 1969.[104] As early as 1966, he portrayed European integration as an important endeavor: "We must invent Europe. It will be the task of our generation to design ... progressively an original construct, leading to the creation of an existential Europe."[105] Giscard's emphasis on *relance* probably reflected circumstances as well. Not only were Western European economies struggling with monetary, energy, and balance-of-payments issues, but the pace of EC reforms had also slowed down. EC countries had failed to create their planned monetary and regional funds.[106] Instead, France had withdrawn from the EC currency float. In tying the franc tightly to the strong West German mark, the "snake" had produced an overvalued currency. By January 1974, Pompidou's government had concluded that the balance-of-payments and economic costs of the "snake" were too high with respect to its short-term benefits, and that it was unlikely to make the U.S. government bend on the reform of the world monetary system.[107] The December 1973 pledge of EC heads of state or government to meet more frequently, moreover, had failed to material-ize. The plan of the West German EC presidency to hold a summit during the first half of 1974 had come to naught due to the Franco-EC split over consultation with the United States.[108] To crown it all, on 1 April, Britain had demanded a renegotiation of its terms of entry into the EC.

In his memoirs, Giscard claims credit for the creation of the European Council.[109] Although this is an exaggeration, Giscard did play an instru-mental role in bringing about this reform. On 14 September, he hosted in Paris a dinner of heads of state or government in order to create a basic agreement on reform. The Paris dinner showed what regular summit meet-ings might be like in the future. Giscard's predilection for institutionalizing summitry reflected in part enduring French prejudices against the Euro-pean Commission. An "act of sabotage [*travail de sape*]," he subsequently stated, had shifted the onus of decision making toward the Commission.[110] The EC Council of Ministers had therefore become "too weak." The estab-lishment of the European Council was designed to redress the balance. But Giscard's approach was not entirely negative; he also wished to provide the EC with stronger leadership. There had been "too few [summit] meetings," he wrote in a set of handwritten notes. In regular Council meetings, techni-cal "details," he added, tended to prevail over "the overall vision."[111]

Despite his bias in favor of personalized diplomacy, Giscard also sup-ported enhanced supranational decision-making. In his letter of 2 May to the European Movement, he had vowed to support the direct election of the EP by universal suffrage.[112] This principle already featured in the 1957 Rome Treaty. Since the late 1950s, many had pleaded for it—notably EP members since the 1960 Dehousse report,[113] federalist organizations, and the main Italian and West German political parties.[114] Intergovern-mentalists had opposed it on the grounds that a democratically elected parliament could be a step toward a federal Europe. Giscard reiterated his 2 May pledge at the Paris dinner, where he also proposed strengthening the EP's powers, introducing limited majority voting in the EC Council of Ministers, and eliminating the watertight divide between the EC and EPC.[115] He reiterated his support for majority voting in a subsequent tele-phone conversation with Schmidt.[116] Giscard's Paris proposals hint at Sau-vagnargues's central role in that all but one—a European passport, which answered the West German plea for a passport union[117]—were already listed in Sauvagnargues's memorandum.

The 11 October document of the French EC presidency initiated lengthy intra-EC talks. Disagreements reflected deeper fears and prejudices. All of France's EC partners except Denmark submitted their own proposals for institutionalized summitry. Some, like those of the British, the Dutch, and the Irish, were quite vague; others, such as those of Italy and Luxembourg, were more in line with the French plan.[118] In language reminiscent of Monnet's, the West German government suggested creating a "European government" building upon a new Council of Ministers for European Affairs. The Dutch and Belgian objective was to limit the influence of institutionalized summitry. The Dutch proposal stipulated that the new council should not make formal decisions or issue communiqués. Rather than create a new institution, the Dutch suggested enlarging the EC Council of Ministers to the heads of state or government and granting them an agenda-setting and coordination role. French officials thought that the "smaller countries" feared possible encroachments onto the Commission's rights.[119] This interpretation held more than a kernel of truth; indeed, such concerns informed the debate over the technicalities of institutionalized summitry. The Benelux countries opposed the creation of a secretariat, which would de facto upgrade institutionalized summitry into a new institution. They were at most willing to use the existing secretariat of the EC Council of Ministers.[120] For similar reasons, the Luxembourger government was against giving a name to institutionalized summitry. There was some irony in Luxembourg's opposition to France's proposed name. This name, "European Council," was "French."[121] But it was only French to the extent that Sauvagnargues had borrowed it from another Frenchman, Monnet, who certainly did not want to weaken the EC institutions. At the Paris dinner, Giscard had referred to a "supreme Council" instead.[122]

Monnet had given the initial impetus for institutional reform in 1973. Did he help to shape the final outcome of the December 1974 Paris summit? There is no clear-cut answer to this question. Records of the preliminary negotiations do not mention him. He most likely did not influence these talks other than indirectly, through the 11 October document of the French EC presidency. Nonetheless, he continued to pull strings behind the scenes, a little-known aspect of Monnet's activism in the twilight of his career.[123] His conversations with EC heads of state or government may have eased the path toward a final compromise. On 17 September, Monnet pressed Giscard to forge ahead with institutional reform. Only France and West Germany, he declared, could take such steps.[124] Less than one month later, he had a long conversation with Schmidt and then persistently tried to speak to Giscard.[125] In a telephone conversation on 21 October, Giscard encouraged Monnet to speak with Elysée Secretary-General Claude Pierre-Brossolette.[126] Monnet immediately presented Pierre-Brossolette with a memorandum that emphasized the importance of Franco-German cooperation for European unity.[127] Pierre-Brossolette was fairly forthcoming and agreed that France had a unique opportunity to foster European integration.[128] Monnet was pleased with the meeting, noting that Pierre-Brossolette understood that "essential decisions" needed to be made sooner rather than later. Monnet's contacts reached beyond Paris and Bonn; he met with Belgian Prime Minister Leo Tindemans, for example. In an attempt to bridge the gap between the French and Belgian positions, Monnet subsequently reported his conversation with Tindemans to Pierre-Brossolette.[129]

A number of issues were still pending on the eve of the Paris summit.[130] On 9–10 December, the EC heads of state or government nevertheless reached an overall agreement on institutional reform. This outcome not only reflected France's tactical flexibility, as has been argued,[131] but also came from Giscard's willingness to endorse supranational decision-making. The final communiqué provided for thrice-yearly summits and gave no name to institutionalized summitry. West German officials thus argued that the French had given up their proposed name.[132] In language reminiscent of the royal oath formula, Giscard, however, referred to a "European Council" after the summit:

> We witnessed the last European summit and took part in the first European Council. The European summit is dead. Long live the European Council![133]

French officials had combined determination with a solid dose of pragmatism. Prior to the summit, Quai d'Orsay officials had accepted a Belgian wording as a basis for discussion, namely, "the heads of state or government would meet in the EC or in the EPC framework, where appropriate."[134] At the summit, Giscard compromised further by agreeing to reduce the number of meetings from four to three per year. He also accepted a convoluted reference to the secretariat: "The administrative secretariat will be provided for in an appropriate manner with due regard for existing practices and procedures."[135] Such flexibility helped to soften opposition to institutionalized summitry. But Giscard's readiness to enhance the EC's institutions played its part too. The far-reaching supranational reforms set forth in the 1974 Paris communiqué included: the EP's election by universal suffrage "in or after 1978," granting the EP "certain powers in the Communities' legislative process," new common policies "in areas to be decided," the end to strict unanimous decision-making in the EC Council of Ministers, and the discarding of the EC/EPC divide Pompidou's government had been so adamant to maintain (the foreign ministers would act as initiators and coordinators between both and hold their EC and EPC meetings in the same city).[136] These provisions certainly reassured the smaller EC states about the meaning of institutionalized summitry: Giscard was not out to sabotage the EC institutions. West German officials, for one, recognized that such measures would "strengthen" them.[137]

Sauvagnargues described Giscard's proposed *relance* as France's "first European initiative in fifteen years."[138] This was an overstatement, but the French initiative was nevertheless important. It signaled a clear departure from Gaullist policy. In 1973, Pompidou had only pleaded for institutionalized summitry and had consistently rejected proposals to enhance supranational governance. Although he favored EC monetary cooperation, he had rejected the 1970 Werner Report on an Economic and Monetary Union due to its strong integrationist bent.[139] That same year, he had only agreed to grant the EP limited budgetary powers in order to put the EC budget and hence the Common Agricultural Policy on a solid footing. Not only did Giscard lift the French veto to the EP's direct election and support this reform in spite of British and Danish opposition, but he also backed a series of supranational reforms. He even pleaded for softening the Luxembourg compromise on unanimity voting, which de Gaulle had imposed in 1966 through the so-called "empty chair crisis." Overall, the French *relance* plan was the French Fifth Republic's first attempt to reconcile the twin pillars—supranational and intergovernmental—of European integration.

A Path Blending Old and New

Like many presidential candidates from François Mitterrand to Sarkozy, Giscard focused his electoral campaign on change. French diplomatic history has tended to stress continuity more than change.[140] In truth, Giscard adjusted the course of French policy, even if he did not fully break with its Gaullist underpinnings. By pursuing a pro-Arab policy, he trod in his predecessors' footsteps. His pleas for a trilateral conference and institutionalized summitry elaborated on earlier proposals. Yet Giscard also took French policy in new directions despite opposition both within and outside his parliamentary majority. Giscard and the Quai d'Orsay labored to improve Franco-American relations. Admittedly, Pompidou had done the same at the beginning of his mandate. What Pompidou had not done, however, was to support a careful move toward strengthened supranational European governance.

Both personal and circumstantial factors egged Giscard along this path of blending old and new. Contemporaries concurred that the new president had a stronger pro-American profile than any French leader since the Fourth Republic.[141] He was also committed to a united Europe. To Giscard's foreign minister from 1978 to 1981, Jean François-Poncet, "the organization of Europe was the main principle guiding his policy [*le fil conducteur principal de son septennat*]."[142] "Europe," Giscard declared at the Paris dinner, "is the most important choice which I could make as president."[143] "In 1920, I would have geared up for war. Today, I am building Europe," he added emphatically. The international context also influenced his government's policy choices. The twin energy and economic crises had created a sense of urgency, driving Western leaders together. Giscard and Schmidt, in particular, believed that the pressing problems of the time called for broader Western and even global solutions. In a 1975 speech, Giscard called for "a new world economic order"—one that would require "global consensus" and prevent the sort of shocks that the West had witnessed since the demise of Bretton Woods.[144] U.S. decision-makers shared this view. "Both presidents seem to me to be convinced of the urgent problems facing their countries and facing the industrialized countries and, indeed, facing the whole world," Kissinger stated in the aftermath of the Martinique summit.[145] This shared sense of urgency and interdependence explains the rise of Western summitry in the mid 1970s, first in the G5 and then, once it was enlarged to Canada and Italy, in the Group of Seven (G7).[146] It also discouraged the French government from asserting further a European identity versus the United States, at least for the time being. Giscard's European path would involve, after institutional reform, monetary integraion.

Notes

1. Schulz and Schwartz, "The Superpower and the Union in the Making," 365.
2. Memcon Kissinger/Sauvagnargues, 4 July 1973, NPM, NSC, Presidential memcons, 1029 / MAE, U.S. files 1970–5, 731.
3. Kosciusko-Morizet, Washington telegram 6791-801, 24 August 1974, MAE, U.S. files 1970–5, 722.
4. Sauvagnargues, interviews on various French television and radio channels, 29 September 1974, MAE, U.S. files 1970–5, 735.
5. Sauvagnargues, [*Notes manuscrites rédigées pendant mes vacances d'août 1974 en Corse. Considérations sur la politique étrangère de la France*], August 1974, MAE, AP, 373.
6. Warlouzet, "Charles de Gaulle's Idea of Europe," 27.
7. State Department, telegram 110560, 25 May 1974, NARA, Central Foreign Policy Files (CFPF) 1973–6, RG 59, electronic telegrams.
8. Quoted in Bozo, *La politique étrangère de la France depuis 1945*, 76. See also Vaïsse, *La puissance ou l'influence?* 381.
9. Bruno de Leusse, Cairo telegram 2023-5, 5 November 1974, MAE, EC files 1971–6, 3807; Leusse, telegramme 2125-31, 16 November 1974, MAE, EC files 1971–6, 3807.
10. Philip Mattar, "Palestine Liberation Organization," in *Encyclopedia of the Modern Middle East*, ed. Reeva S. Simon, Philip Mattar, and Richard W. Bulliet (New York: Macmillan

Reference USA, 1996), 1412; Amy Hackney Blackwell, "Palestine Liberation Organization," in *The Encyclopedia of the Arab-Israeli Conflict: A Political, Social and Military History,* ed. Spencer C. Tucker (Santa Barbara, CA: ABC-CLIO, 2008), 783.

11. Tollys Bebo, "La coopération politique au sein de la Communauté européenne en face des problèmes du Proche-Orient" (Ph.D. thesis, Université Panthéon-Sorbonne, 1987), 260.

12. MAE, European telegram (COREU) 29 to Dublin COREU, 6 February 1975, MAE, EC files 1971–6, 3808.

13. MAE, Direction des Affaires politiques, *Note : dialogue euro-arabe,* 18 February 1975, MAE, U.S. files, 1970–5, 732; Leusse, Cairo telegram 2458-62, 23 December 1974, MAE, EC files 1971–6, 3807.

14. MAE, Direction d'Europe, *Note,* 7 February 1975, MAE, EC files 1971–6, 3810; Irish EC presidency, COREU 862, 28 April 1975, MAE, EC files 1971–6, 3808.

15. MAE, Direction des affaires politiques, *Note,* 23 June 1975, MAE, EC files 1971–6, 3808.

16. *Integrated Emergency Program,* MAE, Economic affairs files, 405; Olivier Wormser, Paris telegram 3239-44, 2 August 1974, MAE, Economic affairs files, 405.

17. Burin des Roziers, Brussels telegram 2883-94, 12 July 1974, MAE, Economic affairs files, 405.

18. MAE, Direction des Affaires économiques et financières, *Note : concertation internationale en matière d'énergie. Groupe des douze,* 29 June 1974, CHAN, 5AG3 51.

19. Jean-Pierre Dutet, *Note : questions énergétiques—plan d'urgence en cours d'élaboration au groupe des douze,* 19 July 1974, CHAN, 5AG3 51.

20. MAE, Direction des Affaires économiques et financières, *Note : tactique à adopter vis-à-vis des projets des douze de création d'une Agence internationale de l'énergie,* 25 October 1974, MAE, Economic affairs files, 412.

21. Ibid.

22. *OCDF. C(74) 203 (final) : Décision du Conseil portant création d'une Agence internationale de l'énergie de l'organisation (adoptée par le Conseil à sa 373ᵉ séance, le 15 novembre 1974),* MAE, Economic affairs files, 406.

23. James, *International Monetary Cooperation since Bretton Woods,* 266.

24. Ibid., 269.

25. MAE, Direction des Affaires économiques et financières, *Note : Groupe des douze—programme intégré en cas de crise énergétique,* 25 June 1974, CHAN, 5AG3 51; MAE, Direction des Affaires économiques et financières, *Note : concertation internationale en matière d'énergie,* 29 June 1974, CHAN, 5AG3 51; Memcon Kissinger/Sauvagnargues, 4 July 1973, NPM, NSC, Presidential memcons, 1029.

26. MAE, Direction des Affaires économiques et financières, *Note : définition de la position française dans les prochaines réunions internationales relatives à l'énergie,* 16 July 1974, CHAN, 5AG3 51.

27. Dutet, *Note pour Monsieur le président de la République,* 11 October 1974, CHAN, 5AG3 51.

28. MAE, Secrétariat général, telegram 52-4, 18 January 1974, MAE, Economic affairs files, 448.

29. MAE, Direction des Affaires économiques et financières, *Note : position française sur la coopération internationale dans le domaine de l'énergie,* 24 October 1974, MAE, Economic affairs files, 412.

30. Memcon Giscard d'Estaing/Gerald Ford, 15 December 1974 (meeting one), CHAN, 5AG3 90.

31. Vaïsse, *La puissance ou l'influence?* 23–24.

32. Garavini, *Dopo gli imperi,* 212–16.

33. Guiringaud, New York telegram 10747-9, 5 December 1974, MAE, Economic affairs files, 265.
34. See, for instance, Paul Martin, Abu Dhabi telegram 273-5, 29 November 1974, MAE United Arab Emirates files 1973–82, 155.
35. Vaïsse, *La puissance ou l'influence?* 209.
36. American Embassy, Paris telegram 25918, 2 November 1974, NARA, CFPF 1973–6, RG 59, electronic telegrams; Kosciusko-Morizet, Washington telegram 9144-9, 30 October 1974, MAE, Economic affairs files, 264; Brunet, circular telegram 743, 9 October 1974, MAE, Economic affairs files, 264.
37. Memcon Giscard d'Estaing/Ford, 15 December 1974 (meeting one), CHAN, 5AG3 90 / Gerald R. Ford Presidential Library (GFPL), National Security Advisor (NSA)'s memcons, 8.
38. Memcon Ford/Schmidt, 5 December 1974, GFPL, NSA's memcons, 7.
39. Memcon Giscard d'Estaing/Ford, 15 December 1974 (meeting one), GFPL, NSA's memcons, 8.
40. American Embassy Bonn, telegram 5926 to American Embassy New Dehli, 27 October 1974, NARA, SD, RG 59, Lot files, Kissinger, 3.
41. American Embassy Bonn, telegram 5926 to American Embassy New Dehli.
42. [*Text of letter from Secretary Kissinger to the minister for foreign affairs delivered November 12, 1974*], MAE, Economic affairs files, 265.
43. Plans for the creation of a petrodollar recycling facility were unveiled at the 28 September G5 meeting (Dutet, *Note pour Monsieur le président de la République. Entretiens avec le président Ford. 'Recyclage' des capitaux pétroliers*, 11 December 1974, CHAN, 5AG3 90). On 14 November, Kissinger sent a letter to Sauvagnargues to inform him of the details of the planned common loan and guaranty facility (Kissinger to Sauvagnargues, MAE, Economic affairs files, 265).
44. *Conversation en tête-à-tête entre Henry Kissinger et Pierre Salinger pendant une heure à bord de l'avion ramenant K. de Bruxelles à Washington* [document submitted to Giscard d'Estaing by Claude Pierre-Brossolette], 15 December 1974, CHAN, 5AG3 90. Pierre Salinger presumably gave this document to a French official, if not to Pierre-Brossolette himself.
45. Rose, Brussels telegram 3771-6, 12 July 1974, MAE, Economic affairs files, 265.
46. Dutet, *Note pour Monsieur le président de la République*, 7 December 1974, CHAN, 5AG3 160.
47. *Préparation de la conférence des chefs de gouvernement. Rapport des ministres des Affaires étrangères*, Brussels, 5 December 1974, CHAN, 5AG3 160.
48. Dutet, *Note pour Monsieur le président de la République*, 7 December 1974, CHAN, 5AG3 160.
49. Memcon Giscard d'Estaing/Ford, 15 December 1974 (meeting one), GFPL, NSA's memcons, 8.
50. "Communiqué of the meeting of heads of Government of the Community (Paris, 10 December 1974)," *Bulletin of the European Communities*, no. 12 (1974): 7–12.
51. James, *International Monetary Cooperation since Bretton Woods*, 264.
52. Valéry Giscard d'Estaing, *Le pouvoir et la vie. [1. La rencontre]*, 3 vols. ([Paris]: Cie 12, 1988), vol. 1, 124.
53. Helmut Schmidt, *Die Deutschen und ihre Nachbarn* (Berlin: Siedler, 1990), 165.
54. Memcon Ford/Schmidt, 5 December 1974, GFPL, NSA's memcons, 7.
55. On the need to avoid confrontation with the United States, see memcon Genscher/Sauvagnargues, 9 November 1974, in Pautsch, *Akten zur Auswärtigen Politik der Bundesrepublik Deutschland 1974*, vol. 2, 1453.

56. Dieter Hiss, summary of Giscard d'Estaing's 28 November phone conversation with Schmidt, 29 November 1974, ibid., 1527–28.
57. Memcon Ford/Schmidt, 5 December 1974, GFPL, NSA's memcons, 7.
58. Memcon Ford/Schmidt, 5 December 1974, GFPL, NSA's memcons, 7.
59. Memcon Ford/Schmidt, 5 December 1974, in Pautsch, *Akten zur Auswärtigen Politik der Bundesrepublik Deutschland 1974*, vol. 2, 1577.
60. Memcon Ford/Schmidt, 6 December 1974, ibid., 1591–92.
61. Memcon Giscard d'Estaing/Ford, 15 December 1974 (meeting one), GFPL, NSA's memcons, 8.
62. Franco-American communiqué, Fort-de-France, Martinique, 16 December 1974, CHAN, 5AG3 90.
63. Kosciusko-Morizet, Washington telegram 9930-40, 25 November 1974, MAE, U.S. files 1970–5, 1138; Beaumarchais, London telegram 3757-8, 26 November 1974, MAE, U.S. files 1970–5, 1138; Kosciusko-Morizet, Washington telegram 10014-6, 27 November 1974, MAE, U.S. files 1970–5, 1138; Courcel to Ambafrance Washington, circular telegram 907, 28 November 1974, MAE, U.S. files 1970–5, 1138; La Gorce to Sauvagnargues, [*Note :*] *consultations Europe-Etats-Unis*, 19 December 1974, MAE, U.S. files 1970–5, 1138; MAE, Direction d'Amérique, *Note : entretiens du président de la République avec M. Ford — relations euro-américaines*, 4 December 1974, MAE, U.S. files 1970–5, 728.
64. Memcon Ford/Giscard d'Estaing, 16 December 1974, NARA, SD, RG 59, Lot files, Kissinger, 22.
65. Memcon Giscard d'Estaing/Ford, 16 December 1974, CHAN, 5AG3 90.
66. MAE, Direction d'Amérique, *Note : rencontre de la Martinique*, 9 December 1974, MAE, U.S. files 1970–5, 728.
67. Belgium, Britain, Canada, France, Italy, Japan, Sweden, the Netherlands, the United States, and West Germany had originally created the Group of Ten in 1961 to provide each other with standby credits. On the Group of Ten, see James, *International Monetary Cooperation since Bretton Woods*, 163–64, 235–38, 43, 46.
68. Mélandri, "La France et l'Alliance atlantique sous Georges Pompidou et Valéry Giscard d'Estaing," 556–57.
69. Trachtenberg, "The French Factor in U.S. Foreign Policy During the Nixon-Pompidou Period, 1969–1974," 40.
70. Giscard d'Estaing/Ford, 15 December 1974 (meeting two), CHAN, 5AG3 90. On Franco-U.S. nuclear cooperation during Giscard d'Estaing's presidency, see Giscard d'Estaing, *Le pouvoir et la vie. 1. La rencontre*, 167, 173; idem, *Le pouvoir et la vie. 2. L'affrontement* ([Paris]: Cie 12, 1991), 186–92.
71. Office of the White House Press Secretary, *Press Conference of Henry A. Kissinger*, Martinique, 16 December 1974, MAE, U.S. files 1970–5, 728.
72. On this interpretation, Mélandri, "La France et l'Alliance atlantique sous Georges Pompidou et Valéry Giscard d'Estaing," 539; Georges-Henri Soutou, "L'anneau et les deux triangles : les rapports franco-allemands dans la politique européenne et mondiale de 1974 à 1981," in Berstein and Sirinelli, *Les années Giscard*, 52.
73. Yves Moreau, "Les capitulations de Fort-de-France," *L'Humanité*, 16 December 1974.
74. Memcon Giscard d'Estaing/Ford, 15 December 1974 (meeting two), GFPL, NSA's memcons, 8.
75. On the C20 talks, see James, *International Monetary Cooperation since Bretton Woods*, 246–51, 255–58.
76. Memcon Giscard d'Estaing/Ford, 15 December 1974 (meeting two), GFPL, NSA's memcons, 8.
77. White House cabinet meeting, 8 January 1975, GFPL, NSA's memcons, 8.

78. Garavini, *Dopo gli imperi*, 233.
79. Ibid., 258–59.
80. Bozo, *La politique étrangère de la France depuis 1945*, 75; Garavini, *Dopo gli imperi*, 264.
81. Sauvagnargues, interview, 11 January 1991, MAE, AO, Sauvagnargues.
82. See in particular Mourlon-Druol, "Filling the EEC Leadership Vacuum?"
83. Bitsch, "Jean Monnet et la création du Conseil européen"; Elisabeth du Réau, "Consolidation et élargissement de la construction européenne," in Berstein and Sirinelli, *Les années Giscard*, 115–32.
84. Sauvagnargues, [*Notes manuscrites rédigées pendant mes vacances d'août 1974 en Corse. Considérations sur la politique étrangère de la France*], August 1974, MAE, AP, 373; Sauvagnargues, [*Notes manuscrites rédigées pendant mes vacances d'août 1974 en Corse. Réflexions sur la relance européenne*], August 1974, MAE, AP, 373; [Sauvagnargues], *Organisation de l'Europe* [*Mémorandum sur le Conseil européen remis au président à mon retour de Corse*], September 1974, MAE, AP, 373.
85. Monnet to Sauvagnargues, *Note confidentielle*, 1 July 1974, FJM, AMK C 14/9/23; Monnet to Sauvagnargues, 5 September 1974, FJM, AMK C 14/9/29; *Document de travail en vue de la prochaine réunion du Comité*, 8 March 1974, FJM, AMK C 14/9/30.
86. Sauvagnargues, [*Considérations sur la politique étrangère de la France*], August 1974, MAE, AP, 373; Sauvagnargues, [*Réflexions sur la relance européenne*], August 1974, MAE, AP, 373.
87. *Document de la Présidence française*, 11 October 1974, MAE, AP, 373.
88. ACUSE, *Document de travail*, undated (filed in between documents dated 16 and 17 September 1973), FJM, AMK 116/2/18. It is unclear how Sauvagnargues obtained a copy of this third document, but its content and wording are most similar to those of Sauvagnargues's September 1974 memorandum. The two documents Monnet sent to Sauvagnargues in summer 1974 did not provide for enhanced EP powers or new common policies (Monnet, *Note confidentielle*, [September 1973], FJM, C 14/9/23; ACUSE, *Document de travail en vue de la prochaine réunion du Comité*, 8 March 1974, FJM, AMK C 14/9/29).
89. The exact same list is found in ACUSE, *Document de travail*, undated [filed in between documents dated 16 and 17 September 1973], FJM, AMK 116/2/18.
90. [Sauvagnargues], [*Mémorandum sur le Conseil européen*], September 1974, MAE, AP, 373.
91. Ibid.; ACUSE, *Document de travail*, undated [filed in between documents dated 16 and 17 September 1973], FJM, AMK 116/2/18.
92. Sauvagnargues, interview, 11 January 1991, MAE, AO, Sauvagnargues.
93. Sauvagnargues's memorandum read: "On peut, dès lors, partir de la constatation que le processus de transformation des Etats membres en une Union européenne a déjà commencé et présenter une conception 'évolutive' de l'Union, dans laquelle l'horizon 80 ne marquerait nullement l'achèvement du processus, mais seulement une de ses étapes ; celle de la consécration par Traité soumis à ratification des procédures suivies de 1974 à 1980" ([Sauvagnargues], [*Mémorandum sur le Conseil européen*], September 1974, MAE, AP, 373). Monnet's working document stated: "Le processus de transformation de l'ensemble des relations entre les Etats membres a déjà commencé. C'est ce que devrait consacrer le prochain sommet. / Dans cette conception évolutive de l'Union, l'horizon 80 serait maintenu—comme une des étapes du processus : celle de la consécration par traité des progrès enregistrés et des procédures suivies de 1974 à 1980" (ACUSE, *Document de travail*, undated (filed in between documents dated 16 and 17 September 1973), FJM, AMK 116/2/18).
94. Möckli, *European Foreign Policy During the Cold War*, 310; Vaïsse, *La puissance ou l'influence?* 37.

95. Soutou, "Georges Pompidou et Valéry Giscard d'Estaing," 52.
96. On Sauvagnargues, see Mathieu Osmont, "Les ambassadeurs de France à Bonn (1955–1999)" (Ph.D. thesis, Institut d'Etudes Politiques, 2011), chap. 5.
97. Sauvagnargues, [*Considérations sur la politique étrangère de la France*], August 1974, MAE, AP, 373.
98. Ibid.
99. Ibid.
100. *Document de la Présidence française,* 11 October 1974, MAE, AP, 373.
101. American Embassy, Paris telegram 25710, 30 October 1974, NARA, CFPF 1973–6, RG 59, electronic telegrams.
102. On Giscard d'Estaing's electoral coalition, Richard, "L'élection présidentielle de 1974," 20–23.
103. Vaïsse, *La puissance ou l'influence?* 121.
104. Du Réau, "Consolidation et élargissement de la construction européenne," 115–16.
105. Quoted in Dulphy and Manigand, *La France au risque de l'Europe,* 132.
106. "Statement from the Paris Summit (October 1972)."
107. Bussière, "Georges Pompidou, les Etats-Unis et la crise du système monétaire international"; idem, "Georges Pompidou et la crise du système monétaire international," 104. On France and the intra-EC currency float, see also Amaury de Saint-Périer, "La France et la sauvegarde du système communautaire de change de 1974 à 1977," in *Milieux économiques et intégration européenne au XXe siècle. La crise des années 1970—De la conférence de La Haye à la veille de la relance des années 1980,* ed. Eric Bussière, Michel Dumoulin, and Sylvain Schirmann (Brussels: P.I.E. Peter Lang, 2006), 51–58.
108. At the Political Committee meeting of 10–11 January, the German delegate announced the German government's intention to convene a summit on 27–28 May (MAE, Direction d'Europe, circular telegram 34, 14 January 1974, MAE, EC files 1971–6, 3792). On 4 March, Scheel confirmed Brandt's intention to send an invitation for 27–28 May (*Compte-rendu de la réunion ministérielle du 4 mars 1974 au titre de la coopération politique européenne à Bruxelles,* MAE, EC files 1971–6, 3796). This plan fell through in March 1974.
109. Giscard d'Estaing, *Le pouvoir et la vie. 1. La rencontre,* 119.
110. Valéry Giscard d'Estaing, interview with the author, 23 May 2007.
111. Giscard d'Estaing, handwritten notes, undated, quoted in Mourlon-Druol, "Filling the EEC Leadership Vacuum?" 318.
112. Thierry Chopin, "Le parlement européen," in Berstein and Sirinelli, *Les années Giscard,* 157.
113. Parlement européen, *Pour l'élection du Parlement européen au suffrage universel direct* (Luxembourg: Office des publications officielles des Communautés européennes, 1969), 27–40.
114. Dinan, *Europe Recast,* 270; Sandro Guerrieri and Maria Sofia Corciulo, "Dall'Assemblea comune della Ceca al Parlamento europeo: la contrastata nomina dei rappresentanti italiani," in *Le istituzioni repubblicane dal centrismo al centro-sinistra, 1953–1968,* ed. Pier Luigi Ballini, Sandro Guerrieri, and Antonio Varsori (Rome: Carocci, 2006), 138; Jean-Marie Palayret, "Il Movimento europeo" in *I movimenti per l'unità europea 1945–1954,* ed. Sergio Pistone (Milan: Jaca Book, 1996), 172–73; Sergio Pistone, "I movimenti per l'unità europea in Italia," in Pistone, *I movimenti per l'unità europea 1945–1954,* 133.
115. Emile Noël (secretary-general of the European Commission), handwritten notes, 14 September 1974, HAEU, EN, 599.
116. Telcon Giscard/Schmidt, 28 November 1974, in Pautsch, *Akten zur Auswärtigen Politik der Bundesrepublik Deutschland 1974,* vol. 2, 1525.
117. Memcon Genscher/Sauvagnargues, 9 November 1974 (second part), ibid., 1454.

118. On the proposals of other EC states, see Mourlon-Druol, "Filling the EEC Leadership Vacuum?" 323–24.
119. Robin, *Note pour Monsieur le président de la République,* 7 November 1974, CHAN, 5AG3 160.
120. Ibid.
121. On the "European Council" as a "French" name, see Mourlon-Druol, "Filling the EEC Leadership Vacuum?" 329.
122. Noël, handwritten notes, 14 September 1974, HAEU, EN, 599.
123. The only mention of Monnet's meetings with EC heads of state or government other than Giscard is in Bitsch, "Jean Monnet et la création du Conseil européen," 409. The discussion is limited to the Monnet-Schmidt meeting.
124. Monnet's office, *Notes pour Jean Monnet* [*Notes emportées par Jean Monnet pour sa conversation avec Valéry Giscard d'Estaing*], September 1974, FJM, AMK C 3/18/107 / FJM, AMK, 151/1/40; Monnet, *Note,* 22 October 1974, FJM, AMK 151/1/46.
125. Christianne Mazerand (secretary of Jean Monnet) to Mrs. Villetelle (secretary of Giscard d'Estaing), 17 October 1974, FJM, AMK C 3/18/111; Mazerand, *Message téléphoné de Bonn par M. Jean Monnet, pour Monsieur le président Giscard d'Estaing,* 17 October 1974, FJM, AMK C 3/18/112.
126. Monnet, *Note,* 22 October 1974, FJM, AMK 151/1/46.
127. Monnet, *Aide-mémoire,* 22 October 1974, FJM, AMK 151/1/48.
128. Monnet, *Conversation avec M. Claude Pierre-Brossolette à l'Elysée — le mardi 22 octobre 1974 à 16h15,* FJM, AMK 151/1/47.
129. Monnet to Pierre-Brossolette, 30 October 1974, FJM, AMK C 3/18/114. Monnet, *Note, 30 octobre 1974 — portée à l'Elysée le 30 octobre 1974 à 19h,* FJM, AMK C 3/18/114.
130. [*Rapport du comité ad hoc, approuvé par les ministres le 25 novembre 1974 — questions institutionnelles*], CHAN, 5AG3 160.
131. Mourlon-Druol, "Filling the EEC Leadership Vacuum?" 328.
132. Dohms, telegram 152, 12 December 1974, in Pautsch, *Akten zur Auswärtigen Politik der Bundesrepublik Deutschland 1974,* vol. 2, 1627. It was therefore not at all "clear ... that all participants had agreed upon it [the name of European Council]" (Mourlon-Druol, "Filling the EEC Leadership Vacuum?" 332).
133. Quoted in du Réau, "Consolidation et élargissement de la construction européenne," 124.
134. Robin, *Note pour Monsieur le président de la République,* 7 November 1974, CHAN, 5AG3 160; Monnet, *Note, 30 octobre 1974,* FJM, AMK C 3/18/114.
135. "Communiqué of the meeting of heads of Government of the Community (Paris, 10 December 1974)"; Robin, *Note pour Monsieur le président de la République,* 7 December 1974, CHAN, 5AG3 160.
136. "Communiqué of the meeting of heads of Government of the Community (Paris, 10 December 1974)."
137. Dohms, telegram 152, 12 December 1974, in Pautsch, *Akten zur Auswärtigen Politik der Bundesrepublik Deutschland 1974,* vol. 2, 1627.
138. Memcon Genscher/Sauvagnargues, 9 November 1974 (first part), ibid., 1449.
139. Bossuat, "Le président Georges Pompidou et les tentatives d'Union économique et monétaire," 413–15.
140. Bozo, *La politique étrangère de la France depuis 1945,* 70, 72; Vaïsse, *La puissance ou l'influence?* 22.
141. American Embassy Paris (Irwin) cable 14541 to Secretary of State, 15 June 1974, NPM, NSC, Country files, 680.
142. Jean François-Poncet, testimony, in Samy Cohen, Marie-Claude Smouts, and Daniel

Bach, *La politique extérieure de Valéry Giscard d'Estaing* (Paris: Presses de la Fondation nationale des sciences politiques, 1985), 424.

143 Giscard d'Estaing, quoted in Noël, handwritten notes, 14 September 1974, HAEU, EN, 599.

144. Giscard d'Estaing, "Le nouvel ordre économique mondial," speech at the Ecole Polytechnique, 28 October 1975, quoted in Marie-Claude Smouts, "Valéry Giscard d'Estaing et le nouvel ordre économique international : une diplomatie plus qu'une politique ?" in Cohen et al., *La politique extérieure de Valéry Giscard d'Estaing*, 266.

145. Office of the White House Press Secretary, *Press Conference of Henry A. Kissinger*, Méridien Hotel, Martinique, 16 September 1974, MAE, U.S. files 1970–5, 728.

146. James, *International Monetary Cooperation since Bretton Woods*, 263–70. See also Schulz and Schwartz, "The Superpower and the Union in the Making," 362.

CONCLUSIONS

Ambivalence has been the hallmark of France's European policy. Since the early days of European integration, French governing elites have been loath to surrender parcels of sovereignty. Nonetheless, successive governments have accepted increasingly greater encroachments on state sovereignty in order to reap the political and economic benefits from closer union. This ambivalence has been particularly strong in foreign policy. As the oldest and historically most powerful founding member of the European Economic Community, France was keen to retain its many worldwide ties accumulated over centuries. The projection of French power was an important component of not only Gaullism, but also, more broadly, the French sense of identity. Postwar geopolitical developments and decolonization in particular, however, made it increasingly obvious that France would never again rank among the great powers. This realization spurred growing acceptance—on an ideological, if not an emotional level—of the need for collective action. It also fostered the rise of a new ideal, *Europe puissance*. By the turn of the twentieth century, the French political elites had ceased trying to "reestablish France's great power status, with Europe acting as its backyard [*arrière-cour*]." Instead, their ideal had shifted to the EU as "a great world power."[1]

This book's central claim is that Pompidou's final year in office and the beginnings of Giscard's presidency were an important moment in this transformation process. Change happened at both a policy and a discursive level. The French political establishment under Pompidou went further than de Gaulle in envisioning and building Europe as an international actor. French officials also invented a new language of European identity. Giscard's 1974 blueprint for EC/EPC institutional reform, in turn, buttressed the new concept of a politically defined European identity. Giscard's cautious move toward enhanced supranational governance implic-

---

Notes for this section begin on page 203.

itly assumed that the nascent European entity could function in the world of states as a unit with political legitimacy.

This argument refines the conventional scholarly paradigm of continuity in French policy between the 1960s and the post–de Gaulle era. Pompidou may have remained essentially "Gaullian [*Gaullien*]" at heart, as Soutou argues—the adjective "Gaullian" referring specifically to de Gaulle's views, as opposed to "Gaullist," which designates a political doctrine that evolved over time.[2] The label "rationalized Gaullism" may subsume Pompidou's political vision.[3] But France's foreign and European policy in 1973–1974, I contend, sowed the seeds for change. By demonstrating an unprecedented commitment to collective European action and fostering the notion of European identity, French officials and some segments of elite opinion indeed went beyond de Gaulle's concept of a "European Europe." This study also highlights lines of continuity between Pompidou's final year in office and Giscard's presidency. The goal of building a political Europe, I argue, remained on the agenda. The thrust shifted from EPC to institutional matters, which were two interrelated dimensions.

The initial trigger for France's new emphasis on EPC in 1973 was Kissinger's Year of Europe initiative. There was perhaps a measure of exaggeration in the French interpretation of this initiative as a scheme to reassert U.S. hegemony in Western Europe. Nonetheless, French officials were right in pointing to conflicting views of power relations between them and their U.S. counterparts. The Nixon administration wished to strengthen transatlantic cohesion under its leadership in order to talk to Soviet (and Chinese) leaders from a position of strength. This view contradicted the French vision of a two-pillar Western world. "Europeanists" in the State Department still shared this vision, but with Kissinger's ascent their influence was on the wane.[4]

Facing this American challenge, French officials took decisive steps to flesh out the ideal of a European world power. They did so reluctantly at first, and then wholeheartedly. In August 1973, the Quai d'Orsay accepted Britain's proposal for a draft EC-U.S. declaration of principles. Quai officials shaped the draft's content both directly and indirectly through their insistence on stressing the distinctiveness of the emerging European political entity.

French officials went on to Europeanize France's Arab policy, which had roots in the nineteenth century. Immediately after the outbreak of the Yom Kippur War, the French government initially discarded a potential EPC Middle East initiative as useless at best. The increasing influence of the United States in the region and Western Europe's sidelining from the peace negotiations prompted a reappraisal. Quai d'Orsay officials were among the main actors behind the November 1973 Declaration on the

Middle East, the first public statement by EC/EU countries on a major foreign policy issue. They also designed the first interregional initiative in which EC/EU states engaged: the Euro-Arab dialogue. These moves had a pro-Arab bent and challenged Kissinger's efforts to assert U.S. supremacy in the Middle East. As such, I argue, they Europeanized France's Middle East and Arab policy.

These steps were remarkable in light of Pompidou's initial skepticism toward EPC. In 1970, Pompidou had emphasized the uncertainties surrounding the planned enlargement of the EC and the risks involved in Brandt's *Ostpolitik*: "With Britain knocking on the door and Germany talking to the East as we know it, what does political cooperation mean? Let us wait first to know who is who," he wrote in the margins of a report.[5] The 1973 enlargement of the EC did not itself change his mind. A series of external events—the Year of Europe, progress in superpower détente, and the course of the Yom Kippur War—proved necessary to trigger a reassessment.

The French reappraisal of EPC was broadly congruent with de Gaulle's early 1960s vision of a European Europe—the vision that had shaped the Fouchet plans. Nonetheless, it hinted at change. In the event, de Gaulle's blueprint never saw the light of day. Not only did French officials in 1973–1974, by contrast, give concrete expression to the notion of an independent European entity, but they also showed a new commitment to common European action. They endorsed a joint EPC démarche in the Arab world on behalf of the Dutch, against their perceived interests. They subsequently made substantial concessions on transatlantic consultation in order to end the stalemate on the Euro-Arab dialogue. This is an important finding. Jobert's plain stubbornness at the Washington Energy Conference was not the whole story.[6] By focusing on a broad range of actors, this book highlights the tactical compromises senior government officials fostered in their efforts to further European political unity.

The Sauvagnargues's notes from summer 1974 testify to this changing mindset among French officials. In Sauvagnargues's eyes, France's "grandeur," a key concept in de Gaulle's vocabulary and policy-thinking,[7] had become "anachronistic."[8] De Gaulle, Sauvagnargues argued, may still have been able to play a role on the world stage ("rôle mondial") due to his historic stature. But France now had to rely on "Europe" to exert an "influence [*rayonnement*]."

On a discursive level, French officials pushed the groundbreaking concept of European identity to the forefront of political discourse. The existing scholarship on the Year of Europe has largely overlooked this discursive shift, but it had great significance. The broad cultural meaning of the term "European identity" that prevailed through the early 1970s referred to a geographically circumscribed cultural heritage. In 1973, French officials both played an essential role in shaping the Declaration on European Identity and popularized the concept of a politically defined European identity. The Declaration on European Identity was a landmark statement. The first EC document to use the term "European identity," it also affirmed the building blocks of a united Europe, including its cultural distinctiveness and its core political values. As such, it posited the notion of a European political community. Further statements and treaties, including the ill-fated Constitution for Europe and the 2007 Lisbon Treaty, would elaborate this notion.

In spurring efforts to construct a political European identity, French officials struck a chord with wider segments of French elite opinion, and the new concept quickly rose to prominence in political discourse. Like de Gaulle's "European Europe," it was essentially construed in opposition to the United States. Both terms were rooted in a long tradition of positioning America as a mirror and foil to European societies, stretching back to Tocqueville's *Democracy in America*.[9] But the concept of European identity, I contend, had farther-reaching implications: it subsumed the notion of a supranational locus of allegiance, possibly competing with the nation-state. So long as the term "European identity" had referred to a shared cultural legacy, it had coexisted, rather than challenged, the concept of French identity. The popularization of this new notion of European identity brought an added layer of complexity to French political discourse.

With the exceptions of EPC's involvement in the Conference on Security and Cooperation in Europe, all studies of EPC's early history end with the February 1974 Washington Energy Conference or the June 1974 NATO Declaration. This endpoint mirrors the view of a policy shift in all three major EC countries—that is, Britain, France, and West Germany—due to a change of political personal.[10] It is my contention that the shift was only partial in France. Giscard certainly had a more U.S.-friendly profile than his predecessor. As a former minister of finance, he was acutely aware of the need to meet the challenge of the oil shock and of the collapse of the Bretton Woods monetary order. His international economic priorities explain his insistence on enhanced Western cooperation and friendly Franco-U.S. ties. But his emphasis on transatlantic cooperation went hand in hand with a strong European commitment. Significantly, he purposely used France's EC presidency from July to December 1974 to foster European political unity. To be sure, the main emphasis was no longer on EPC: the 1974 French reform plan dealt with another essential aspect of a political Europe, that is, its institutional framework. Sauvagnargues, as one of its main architects, certainly viewed foreign policy cooperation and institutional engineering as closely interconnected. Institutional reform, he argued, was crucial for building an internally cohesive and internationally influential Europe.[11]

The main elements of the French reform plan, moreover, included not only institutionalized summitry but also supranational provisions: namely, the election of the EP through direct universal suffrage, limited legislative powers for the EP, new EC common policies, and the introduction of majority voting in the EC Council of Ministers. A year earlier, Pompidou's government had endorsed Monnet's proposal for a temporary European government but stripped it of its (comparatively modest) supranational element, that is, the direct election of the EP.[12] There is no evidence that Giscard proposed these supranational measures as a "quid pro quo"[13] for the creation of the European Council. We know now that Sauvagnargues, for one, suggested them to him without thinking in terms of a trade-off. Rather, such proposals meant that by 1974, some (if not all) French political actors were ready to substantiate the new concept of a European identity by fleshing out the European Union in institutional terms.

Toward a Political Europe

The French political establishment had passed an important milestone in acknowledging EPC's value in 1973–1974. Giscard would build upon this *acquis* while trying to reassert European influence in the international arena in 1980. On repeated occasions, Giscard called for an end to what he dubbed a "historical anomaly," that is, the decline of "Europe" on the global stage.[14] He also pleaded for restoration of the European Council's "original purpose," namely, to give the EC and EPC strengthened leadership.[15] Renewed Franco-American antagonisms were again an important background factor. U.S. President Jimmy Carter's commitment to a human rights–focused foreign policy met with suspicion in Paris. Giscard also criticized the June 1979 SALT II agreement for decoupling Western European from U.S. defense. The Carter administration's policies toward Central Asia and the Middle East added fuel to the fire. The Soviet invasion of Afghanistan in December 1979 prompted tough U.S. measures— including the severing of diplomatic ties with Moscow, the withdrawal of SALT II, and a grain embargo.[16] Giscard's priority, by contrast, was to safeguard détente. He acted alone, meeting Brezhnev in Warsaw, and within the Franco-German framework.[17] But he also supported collective European statements that condemned the invasion while simultaneously asserting the EC Nine's continued commitment to détente.[18]

Likewise, the French government fostered renewed EPC action on the Middle East. In June 1980, the Venice European Council issued a declaration calling for an overall peace settlement. The Venice Declaration explicitly acknowledged the Palestinians' "right to self-determination" and also granted recognition to the PLO, requesting "the involvement and support of all the parties concerned in the peace settlement," including "the Palestinian people" and "the PLO."[19] Such provisions further Europeanized France's Middle East policy while challenging U.S. policy. The United States had sponsored a separate peace treaty between Egypt and Israel in 1979. The Reagan administration's 1982 peace plan excluded PLO participation,[20] and the U.S. government did not open a dialogue with the PLO until Arafat's 1988 recognition of Israel's right to exist and his renunciation of terrorism.[21]

Giscard's policy toward the EC institutions was another example of continuity with the 1973–1974 years. He threw his weight behind the proposed reform of EP elections. Direct elections strengthened the EP's legitimacy and hence "the democratic legitimacy of the whole European institutional apparatus," as Belgian Prime Minister Tindemans argued in his 1975 Report on European Union.[22] The Gaullists logically opposed this reform. Michel Debré, a prominent figure of the Gaullist party, challenged the constitutionality of the 1976 EC Act on Direct Elections. Giscard, however, stood his ground. In an unusual step, he referred the case to the Constitutional Council, France's highest constitutional court, which declared the act to be constitutional while arguing that direct elections did not entail a transfer of sovereignty. It also reaffirmed traditional principles of state sovereignty such as the notion of "indivisibility."[23] Such statements did not silence Giscard's opponents. His Gaullist coalition partners and the communists attempted to defeat the bill translating the act into French law. During a parliamentary debate, Debré warned that the election of the EP via universal suffrage implied the existence of "a European people." As such, it involved "a hypocritical alienation of sovereignty."[24] Giscard applied a rarely used constitutional provision to push the bill through: instead of the French National Assembly voting on it, the prime minister sought the National Assembly's confidence. Since no censure vote was tabled within twenty-four hours, the law was deemed passed.[25]

Giscard adopted a more cautious stance on the other supranational reforms enshrined in the 1974 Paris summit communiqué, but political pragmatism could easily explain this. In 1974, France rejected the Tindemans Report, which set forth measures to improve EC and EPC decision-making—including majority voting, a right for the EP to propose legislation, and a legal obligation to adopt joint foreign policy positions, by a majority vote where necessary.[26] In 1977, Giscard retracted his 1974 pledge on strengthened EP powers.[27] Whatever his personal preferences may have been, any proposed strengthening of the EC's institutions would have threatened his governing coalition. During the 1978–1979 EP electoral campaign, former Prime Minister Chirac cast Giscard's Union pour la démocratie française as "the party from abroad [*le parti de l'étranger*]."[28] Had Giscard had more room to maneuver, he would probably have been willing to strengthen European supranational governance,[29] but during his presidency he did not break with the Gaullist principle of "confederation."[30] "Confederation," however, is a broad concept. Evidence suggests that Giscard's confederal vision entailed more supranational governance than his predecessors deemed acceptable. "The European confederation," he stated in 1979 to the West German weekly *Der Spiegel*, will rest on "three pillars": an executive arm (derived from the European Council), an administrative arm in charge of EC matters (derived from the European Commission), and a legislative arm (derived from the EP).[31] This meant granting the EP legislative powers. After 1981, Giscard would clearly stand in favor of a mixed form of supranational and intergovernmental governance, which he called "a federative Europe."[32]

Giscard's caution on supranational reform notwithstanding, the 1974 reform program laid the basis for a reconfigured approach to European institution-building. This new paradigm meant balancing the French preference for intergovernmentalism against the need to strengthen supranational governance. Giscard cautiously alluded to it in his press conference of 24 October 1974. He calculated that "a confederal" Europe would require "another decision-making mechanism on a wider scale" ("une autre technique de décision à l'échelon d'un plus grand ensemble").[33] The election of the EP through direct universal suffrage in June 1979 was no minor achievement for the integrationists. As such, it was a concrete sign of change. It fell to Giscard's successors to help implement the other supranational provisions of the 1974 Paris summit communiqué. In a famous speech to the EP in 1984, President Mitterrand renounced the 1966 Luxembourg compromise on unanimity voting within the EC Council of Ministers. Under the 1986 Single European Act, nearly all the measures required to complete the single market were subjected to qualified majority voting. The 1992 Maastricht Treaty extended the scope of qualified majority voting. It also introduced the co-decision procedure, which granted the EP limited legislative powers. Most recently, the Lisbon Treaty has extended co-decision to 90 percent of EU legislation. The EU, as it now stands, is a far cry from de Gaulle's proposed "union of states."

Toward a European Foreign Policy

A final word about EPC is in order. The story of its rapid rise in 1973 and decline in 1974 is appealing, but what this argument misses is the longer-term perspective. EPC's work during the mid and late 1970s should not be compared only to its 1973 achievements, but also to the protracted efforts from the 1950s to the early 1970s to foster a political Europe. The EC Nine may have demonstrated in 1973 "a degree of ambition and enthusiasm" that would remain unmatched during the Cold War.[34] Nevertheless, it is taking the argument too far to state that many of EPC's achievements "were undone again in 1974." EC countries continued to try to harmonize their foreign policies. That they did so was in itself a significant achievement. EPC's early 1970s beginnings had been painstaking. Moreover, after the French National Assembly's rejection of the EDC in 1954 it took sixteen years to establish this framework for political, that is, foreign policy cooperation; the EDC Treaty, had it been implemented, would have created an EDC Assembly in charge of drafting a blueprint for a European political authority. Granted, during the mid and late 1970s, the EC Nine no longer endeavored to assert themselves against the United States or to challenge its Middle East diplomacy head-on. But they held on to the Euro-Arab dialogue and became involved, if only at a rhetorical level, in other regions. They issued a series of statements over Cyprus, for instance, advocating a "negotiated" outcome that would safeguard the territorial unity of the island.[35] They also used EPC to coordinate a joint démarche to Athens and Ankara.[36] Seeing the glass half full, I would argue that the steps taken vis-à-vis the United States and the Arab world in 1973–1974 helped to consolidate EPC at a critical early stage. They also established the Arab world as a key focus area of the emerging European diplomacy.

This reinterpretation of EPC's early history fits nicely with the ongoing reappraisal of the 1970s in European integration history. New scholarship presents these years as a decade of transition marked by new dynamics,[37] rather than a period of "disillusionment" and "eurosclerosis."[38] EPC was an example of this new development, which subsequently expanded. In 1980, a changing geopolitical context gave EPC a new lease on life. The 1980–1981 initiatives of the now ten EC countries often differed from U.S. policy.[39] Regarding Afghanistan, the EC Ten advanced the concept of a "neutral" status to assuage the Soviet Union. Neutrality would ensure that a withdrawal of Soviet troops would not result in a change of camp.[40] Over Iran, they condemned the November 1979 seizure as hostages of U.S. embassy staff, but they also stressed "the right of the Iranian people to determine their own future."[41] The Venice Declaration on the Middle East recognized the PLO's rights eight years before the United States did. In Poland, the EC Ten went beyond declaratory diplomacy: following the December 1981 imposition of martial law, they decided on joint economic sanctions.[42] They did the same in Iran. Admittedly, these sanctions were a response to U.S. pressure. On occasion, however, the EC Ten took concrete steps proactively. In 1981, the British EC presidency used EPC to coordinate an attempt at mediation in Moscow over Afghanistan.[43] These various statements and actions were all steps toward an objective that remains high on the agenda of EU policy-makers: namely, a common European foreign and security policy.

In both 1973–1974 and 1980–1981, France played an active role in forging a common European voice in the international arena. Its 1973–1974 dynamism was particularly significant because it was connected to a reorientation of French policy in rhetorical and institutional terms. Cracks began to appear in the Gaullist mold as officials and press commentators fostered the notion of a political European identity and Giscard endorsed several EC supranational reforms. These cracks foreshadowed the stance the French elites would adopt in subsequent decades. Governing officials would gradually recognize the need to vest greater authority in a European entity mustering a distinct identity. Public voices would increasingly extol European, rather than French, power. *Europe puissance* has now become a central notion of French political imagery, even if it remains an elusive objective. And the reconfigured ideal of many French political actors includes multiple identities—not only local, regional, and national, but also European.

Notes

1. Bossuat, *Faire l'Europe sans défaire la France,* 217.
2. Soutou, "Le président Pompidou et les relations entre les Etats-Unis et l'Europe," 112.
3. Ibid. For an endorsement of Soutou's interpretation, see Marc Trachtenberg, "The French Factor in U.S. Foreign Policy During the Nixon-Pompidou Period, 1969–1974" (paper presented at the conference on Georges Pompidou et les Etats-Unis, "une relation spéciale," 1969–1974, Paris, 26–27 June 2009), 4.
4. Weisbrode, *The Atlantic Century,* 209–19.
5. Pompidou, margin comment on Raimond, *Note pour Monsieur le président de la République,* 26 June 1970, CHAN, 5AG2 1035. On Pompidou's stance on Ostpolitik, see Soutou, "President Pompidou, Ostpolitik, and the Strategy of Détente"; idem, "The Linkage between European Integration and Détente," 28–29.
6. Möckli, *European Foreign Policy During the Cold War,* 368.
7. Vaïsse, *La grandeur,* 32.

8. Sauvagnargues, [*Notes manuscrites rédigées pendant mes vacances d'août 1974 en Corse. Considérations sur la politique étrangère de la France*], August 1974, MAE, AP, 373.

9. Tocqueville, *De la démocratie en Amérique*.

10. See in particular Möckli, *European Foreign Policy During the Cold War*.

11. Sauvagnargues, [*Notes manuscrites rédigées pendant mes vacances d'août 1974 en Corse. Réflexions sur la relance européenne*], August 1974, MAE, AP, 373.

12. *Entretien avec Michel Jobert aux Affaires étrangères à 11h30*, 8 September 1973, FJM, AMK 116/1/28.

13. Gabriel Robin, testimony, in Cohen et al., *La politique extérieure de Valéry Giscard d'Estaing*, 118.

14. Giscard d'Estaing, trip to West Germany, speeches, 7, 8 and 11 July 1980, CHAN, 5AG3 72; Giscard d'Estaing, Franco-British summit, concluding speech, 19 September 1980, CHAN, 5AG3 99; Giscard d'Estaing, Franco-German summit, concluding speech, 10 November 1980, CHAN, 5AG3 94.

15. Giscard d'Estaing, press conference following the European Council held on 28 April 1980, CHAN, 5AG3 169.

16. Joe Renouard and D. Nathan Vigil, "The Quest for Leadership in a Time of Peace: Jimmy Carter and Western Europe, 1977–1981," in Schulz and Schwartz, *The Strained Alliance*, 328–31.

17. Soutou, "L'anneau et les deux triangles," 72–73; Vaïsse, *La puissance ou l'influence?* 202.

18. "Declaration by the Nine on political cooperation (15 January 1980)," *Bulletin of the European Communities*, no. 1 (1980): 7–8; *Déclaration du conseil européen sur l'Afghanistan, Venise, 12–13 juin 1980*, CHAN, 5AG3 169; "Declaration on Afghanistan (29–30 June 1981)," *Bulletin of the European Communities*, no. 6 (1981): 9.

·19. *Déclaration du Conseil européen sur le Moyen-Orient, Venise, 12–13 juin 1980*, CHAN, 5AG3 169; "Statement by the European Council on the Situation in the Middle East (Venice Declaration), Venice, 12–13 June 1980," in Christopher Hill and Karen Elizabeth Smith, eds., *European Foreign Policy Key Documents* (London and New York: Routledge, 2000), 302–04.

20. Mattar, "Palestine Liberation Organization," 1413. On the Reagan plan, see Quandt, *Peace Process*, 254–56.

21. Quandt, *Peace Process*, 282–85.

22. Léo Tindemans, "Rapport sur l'Union européenne," *Bulletin des Communautés européennes, Supplément*, no. 1/76 (1976): 11–36.

23. Chopin, "Le parlement européen," 173.

24. Quoted ibid., 178–79.

25. Ibid., 176–77.

26. Jürgen Nielsen-Sikora, "The Idea of a European Union and a Citizen's Europe: The 1975 Tindemans Report and Its Impact on Today's Europe," in van der Harst, *Beyond the Customs Union*, 377–89; Tindemans, "Rapport sur l'Union européenne."

27. Chopin, "Le parlement européen," 161.

28. Quoted ibid., 183, note 1.

29. For this interpretation, see also Michèle Weinachter, *Valéry Giscard d'Estaing et l'Allemagne. Le double rêve inachevé* (Paris: L'Harmattan, 2004), 345–46.

30. Ibid., 101.

31. Quoted in Chopin, "Le parlement européen," 186.

32. Quoted in Weinachter, *Valéry Giscard d'Estaing et l'Allemagne*, 101.

33. Giscard d'Estaing, press conference, quoted in Toinet, *Valéry Giscard d'Estaing et les Etats-Unis*, 18.

34. Möckli, *European Foreign Policy During the Cold War*, 363.

35. MAE, Europe directorate, *Note*, 29 November 1974, MAE, EC files 1971–6, 3793; EPC, ministerial meeting, statement of conclusions, 13 February 1975, MAE, EC files 1971–6, 3793; EPC, ministerial meeting, press statement guidelines, 13 September 1975, MAE, EC files 1971–6, 3794.
36. EPC, ministerial meeting, statement of conclusions, 13 September 1975, MAE, EC files 1971–6, 3793.
37. Van der Harst, *Beyond the Customs Union.*
38. Möckli, *European Foreign Policy During the Cold War*, 250.
39. N. Piers Ludlow, "Who Speaks for Europe? Evolving Transatlantic Dialogues During the 1980s" (paper presented at the conference on Europe and America in the 1980s: Old Barriers, New Openings, European University Institute, Florence, 14–15 May 2010).
40. Italian EC presidency, COREU, 29 April 1980, CHAN, 5AG3 169; "Declaration by the Nine on political cooperation (15 January 1980)"; "Declaration on Afghanistan (29–30 June 1981)"; Simon J. Nuttall, *European Political Co-Operation* (Oxford and New York: Clarendon Press and Oxford University Press, 1992), 156–57.
41. "Statement by the European Council on Iran, Dublin, 30 November 1979," in Hill and Smith, *European Foreign Policy Key Documents*, 317–18.
42. On Poland, see Ludlow, "Who Speaks for Europe?"
43. Christopher Hill, "National Interests—the Insuperable Obstacles?" in *National Foreign Policies and European Political Cooperation*, ed. Christopher Hill (London and Winchester, MA: G. Allen & Unwin, 1983), 189.

BIBLIOGRAPHY

Primary Sources

Centre historique des archives nationales (CHAN), Paris, France

Archives de Georges Pompidou, Série 5AG2

Archives de Valéry Giscard d'Estaing, Série 5AG3

Ministère des affaires étrangères (MAE), Paris France

Archives orales (AO): Etienne Burin des Roziers, Michel Jobert, Jacques Kosciusko-Morizet, Charles Lucet, Jean Sauvagnargues, François de Tricornot de Rose

Archives privées (AP): Jean Sauvagnargues

Direction des affaires économiques et financières, Sous-direction des affaires générales (Economic affairs files)

Direction d'Afrique du nord et du Moyen-Orient, Sous-direction du Levant, Série Proche-Orient (Middle East files)

Direction d'Afrique du nord et du Moyen-Orient, Sous-direction du Levant, Série Syrie (Syria files)

Direction d'Afrique du nord et du Moyen-Orient, Sous-direction du Levant, Série Tunisie (Tunisia files)

Direction d'Amérique, Sous-direction d'Amérique du nord, Série Etats-Unis (U.S. files)

Direction d'Europe, Sous-direction d'Europe occidentale, Série Communautés économiques européennes (EC files)

Direction d'Europe, Sous-direction d'Europe orientale, Série Union des républiques socialistes soviétiques (SU files)

Secrétariat général

Fondation Jean Monnet pour l'Europe (FJM), Lausanne, Switzerland

Action Committee for the United States of Europe (AMK)

Action Committee for the United States of Europe, Correspondence (AMK/C)

Historical Archives of the European Union (HAEU), Florence, Italy

Fonds Emile Noël (EN)

Fonds Klaus Meyer (KM)

Nixon Presidential Materials (NPM), National Archives and Records Administration (NARA) II, College Park, MD

National Security Council (NSC):

— Country files: France

— Name files

— Presidential Memorandums of Conversations (Memcons)

— Subject files

— VIP files

National Security Council, Henry A. Kissinger (HAK) and Staff Files:

— Office files: Europe

— Telephone Conversations (Telcons)

— Trip files

National Security Council Institutional Files:

— National Security Study Memorandums (NSSMs)

— National Security Decision Memorandums (NSDMs)

White House Central Files, Subject Numeric Files

Gerald R. Ford Presidential Library (GFPL), Ann Arbor, MI

National Security Advisor, Memorandums of conversation

Records of the State Department (SD), National Archives and Records Administration (NARA) II, College Park, MD

Central Files (Record Group 59), Subject Numeric Files:

— Europe

— France

Central Foreign Policy Files

Lot files (Record Group 59):

— Henry A. Kissinger

— Helmut Sonnenfeldt

Newspapers and Periodical Reviews

Bulletin des Communautés européennes

Bulletin of the European Communities

Combat

Documents d'actualité internationale

Europe Documents

L'Aurore

La Nation

Le Figaro

Le Monde

Le Nouvel observateur

L'Humanité

Libération

Official Journal of the European Communities

Official Journal of the European Union

USA documents

Published Governmental Sources

Council on Foreign Relations, ed. *American Foreign Relations*. New York: New York University Press, 1976.

[European Parliament], ed. *Selection of Texts Concerning Institutional Matters of the Community from 1950 to 1982*. Luxembourg: European Parliament, 1982.

GATT. *GATT Activities in 1973*. Geneva: GATT Secretariat, 1974.

Hamilton, Keith A., ed. *Documents on British Policy Overseas. The Year of Europe: America, Europe and the Energy Crisis, 1972–1974*. Vol. III.4. London: Whitehall History Publishing, 2006.

Hill, Christopher, and Karen Elizabeth Smith, eds. *European Foreign Policy Key Documents*. London and New York: Routledge, 2000.

International Energy Agency and Organisation for Economic Cooperation and Development. *Energy Balances of OECD Countries, 1971–1981*. Paris: International Energy Agency and Organisation for Economic Cooperation and Development, 1983.

[Irish government]. *Membership of the European Communities: Implications for Ireland, Laid by the Government before Each House of the Oireachtas*. Dublin: The Stationery Office, 1970.

Medzini, Meron, ed. *Israel's Foreign Relations: Selected Documents 1947–1974*. Vol. 2 of 3 vols. Jerusalem: Ministry for Foreign Affairs, 1976.

Parlement européen. *Pour l'élection du Parlement européen au suffrage universel direct*. Luxembourg: Office des publications officielles des Communautés européennes, 1969.

Pautsch, Ilse Dorothee, ed. *Akten zur Auswärtigen Politik der Bundesrepublik Deutschland 1973*. 3 vols. Munich: Oldenbourg, 2004.

———, ed. *Akten zur Auswärtigen Politik der Bundesrepublik Deutschland 1974*. 2 vols. Munich: Oldenbourg, 2005.

Press and Information Office of the Government of the Federal Republic of Germany, ed. *Texts Relating to the European Political Cooperation*. Bonn: Press and Information Office of the Government of the Federal Republic of Germany, 1974.

Memoirs, Pamphlets, and Essays

Aron, Raymond. *Les articles de politique internationale dans Le Figaro de 1947 à 1977*. Edited by Georges-Henri Soutou. Vol. 3 of 3 vols. Paris: Editions de Fallois, 1990–1997.

———. *Plaidoyer pour l'Europe décadente*. Paris: Robert Laffont, 1977.

Benoist, Alain de. *Vu de droite. Anthologie critique des idées contemporaines*. Paris: Copernic, 1977.

Benoist, Jean-Marie. *Pavane pour une Europe défunte. L'adieu aux technocrates*. Paris: Denoël-Gonthier, 1978.

Gaulle, Charles de. *Discours et messages*. Vols. 4 and 5 of 5 vols. Paris: Plon, 1970.

Giscard d'Estaing, Valéry. *Le pouvoir et la vie. 2. L'affrontement*. [Paris]: Cie 12, 1991.

———. *Le pouvoir et la vie. 1. La rencontre*. [Paris]: Cie 12, 1988.

Gobard, Henri. *La guerre culturelle. Logique du désastre*. Paris: Copernic, 1979.

Jobert, Michel. *L'autre regard*. Paris: Grasset, 1976.

———. *Mémoires d'avenir*. Paris: Grasset, 1974.

Kissinger, Henry. *Diplomacy*. New York: Simon & Schuster, 1994.

———. *Years of Upheaval*. Boston, MA: Little, Brown, 1982.

———. *The Troubled Partnership: A Re-Appraisal of the Atlantic Alliance*. Garden City, NY: Doubleday, 1966.

Monnet, Jean. *Mémoires*. Paris: Fayard, 1976.

Revel, Jean-François. *Ni Marx, ni Jésus. De la seconde révolution américaine à la seconde révolution mondiale*. Paris: Robert Laffont, 1970.

Schmidt, Helmut. *Die Deutschen und ihre Nachbarn*. Berlin: Siedler, 1990.

Servan-Schreiber, Jean-Jacques. *Le défi américain*. Paris: Denoël, 1967.

Thibau, Jacques. *La France colonisée*. Paris: Flammarion, 1980.

Tocqueville, Alexis de. *De la démocratie en Amérique*. Paris: C. Gosselin, 1835–1840.

Valéry, Paul. *Regards sur le monde actuel*. Paris: Stock, 1931.

Sources Available Online

"The Future Tasks of the Alliance ("The Harmel Report")." http://www.nato.int/docu/basic txt/b671213a.htm.

"Mutual and Balanced Force Reductions: Declaration adopted by Foreign Ministers and Representatives of Countries participating in the NATO Defence Program." http://www.nato.int/docu/comm/49-95/c680624b.htm.

"Treaty Establishing the European Economic Community." http://eur-lex.europa.eu/en/treaties/index.htm#founding.

Conseil constitutionnel. "Les membres du Conseil: Valéry Giscard d'Estaing." http://www.conseil-constitutionnel.fr/conseil-constitutionnel/francais/le-conseil-constitutionnel/le-conseil-aujourd-hui/les-membres-du-conseil/liste-des-membres/valery-giscard-d-estaing.222.html.

European Commission. "COM(74) 1090 final, Report on the tariff negotiations which it conducted under Article XXIV(6) of the General Agreement on Tariffs and Trade (GATT), 11 July 1974." http://aei.pitt.edu/8897/01/31735055278927_1.pdf.

Kennedy, John F. "Address at Independence Hall, Philadelphia, July 4, 1962." http://www
.jfklibrary.org/Historical+Resources/Archives/Reference+Desk/Speeches/JFK/003POF
03IndependenceHall07041962.htm.

North Atlantic Treaty Organization. "Declaration on Atlantic Relations." http://www.nato
.int/cps/en/natolive/official_texts_26902.htm.

Sarkozy, Nicolas. "Allocution prononcée le 16 décembre 2008 au Parlement européen de
Strasbourg à l'occasion de la fin de la présidence française de l'Union européenne." http://
www.ambafrance-cn.org/Discours-de-Nicolas-Sarkozy-au-Parlement-Europeen.html.

United Nations General Assembly. "The Universal Declaration of Human Rights." http://
www.un.org/en/documents/udhr/index.shtml.

———. "Resolution 2628 of 4 November 1970: The Situation in the Middle East." http://unis
pal.un.org/UNISPAL.NSF/0/8A68B2315AF81AED852560DE006E2BEB.

———. "Resolution 2949 of 8 December 1972: The Situation in the Middle East." http://
daccess-dds-ny.un.org/doc/RESOLUTION/GEN/NR0/269/79/IMG/NR026979.pdf?Open
Element.

United Nations Security Council. "Resolution 242 of 22 November 1967: The Situation in the
Middle East." http://daccess-dds-ny.un.org/doc/RESOLUTION/GEN/NR0/240/94/IMG/
NR024094.pdf?OpenElement.

———. "Resolution 338: Cease-Fire in the Middle East (22 Oct)." http://daccess-dds-ny.un
.org/doc/RESOLUTION/GEN/NR0/288/65/IMG/NR028865.pdf?OpenElement.

Secondary Literature

Allen, David, and Alfred Pijpers. *European Foreign Policy-Making and the Arab-Israeli Conflict.*
The Hague and Hingham, MA: Martinus Nijhoff Publishers, 1984.

Allen, David, Reinhardt Rummel, and Wolfgang Wessels, eds. *European Political Cooperation:
Towards a Foreign Policy for Western Europe.* London and Boston: Butterworth Scientific,
1982.

Allen, Peter. *The Yom Kippur War.* New York: Scribner, 1982.

Association Georges Pompidou, ed. *Action et pensée sociales chez Georges Pompidou.* Paris:
Presses universitaires de France, 2004.

———, ed. *Culture et action chez Georges Pompidou.* Paris: Presses universitaires de France,
2000.

———, ed. *Georges Pompidou et l'Europe.* Brussels: Editions Complexe, 1995.

———, ed. *Georges Pompidou face à la mutation économique de l'Occident, 1969–1974.* Paris: Presses universitaires de France, 2003.

———, ed. *Un politique : Georges Pompidou.* Paris: Presses universitaires de France, 2001.

Association Georges Pompidou, and Eric Bussière, eds. *Georges Pompidou face à la mutation
économique de l'Occident, 1969–1974.* Paris: PUF, 2003.

Aubourg, Valérie, Gérard Bossuat, and Giles Scott-Smith, eds. *European Community, Atlantic
Community?* Paris: Editions Soleb, 2008.

Balta, Paul, and Claudine Rulleau. *La politique arabe de la France. De de Gaulle à Pompidou.*
Paris: Sindbad, 1973.

Bange, Oliver. *The EEC Crisis of 1963: Kennedy, Macmillan, De Gaulle and Adenauer in Conflict.* New York: St. Martin's Press, 2000.

Barnhart, Michael A. "From Hershey Bars to Motor Cars: America's Economic Policy toward Japan, 1945–1976." In *Partnership: The United States and Japan, 1951–2001,* edited by Akira Iriye and Robert A. Wampler, 201–22. Tokyo and New York: Kodansha International, 2001.

Bass, Warren. *Support Any Friend: Kennedy's Middle East and the Making of the U.S.-Israel Alliance.* Oxford and New York: Oxford University Press, 2003.

Beale, Marjorie A. *The Modernist Enterprise: French Elites and the Threat of Modernity, 1900–1940.* Stanford, CA: Stanford University Press, 1999.

Bebo, Tollys. "La coopération politique au sein de la Communauté européenne en face des problèmes du Proche-Orient." Ph.D. thesis, Université Panthéon-Sorbonne, 1987.

Ben-Ghiat, Ruth. *Fascist Modernities: Italy, 1922–1945.* Berkeley: University of California Press, 2001.

Ben-Zvi, Abraham. *Decade of Transition: Eisenhower, Kennedy, and the Origins of the American-Israeli Alliance.* New York: Columbia University Press, 1998.

Berstein, Serge. "De la nation à l'Europe." *Historiens et géographes,* no. 366 (1999): 360–70.

Berstein, Serge, Jean-Marie Mayeur, and Pierre Milza, eds. *Le MRP et la construction européenne.* Brussels: Editions Complexe, 1993.

Berstein, Serge, and Jean-François Sirinelli, eds. *Les années Giscard. Valéry Giscard d'Estaing et l'Europe, 1974–1981.* Paris: Armand Colin, 2006.

Bitsch, Marie-Thérèse. *Histoire de la construction européenne de 1945 à nos jours.* 5th ed. Brussels: Editions Complexe, 2008.

———. "Jean Monnet et la création du Conseil européen." In *Jean Monnet, l'Europe et les chemins de la paix,* edited by Gérard Bossuat and Andreas Wilkens, 399–410. Paris: Publications de la Sorbonne, 1999.

Bitsch, Marie-Thérèse, and Gérard Bossuat, eds. *L'Europe unie et l'Afrique : de l'idée d'Eurafrique à la convention de Lomé I.* Brussels, Paris, and Baden-Baden: Bruylant, L.G.D.J., and Nomos Verlag, 2005.

Bitsch, Marie-Thérèse, Wilfried Loth, and Raymond Poidevin. "Institutions européennes et identités européennes." In *Les identités européennes au XXe siècle. Diversités, convergences et solidarités,* edited by Robert Frank and Gérard Bossuat, 125–44. Paris: Publications de la Sorbonne, 2004.

Blackwell, Amy Hackney. "Palestine Liberation Organization." In *The Encyclopedia of the Arab-Israeli Conflict: A Political, Social and Military History,* edited by Spencer C. Tucker, 781–85. Santa Barbara, CA: ABC-CLIO, 2008.

Bonvicini, Gianni. "Out-of-Area Issues: A New Challenge to the Atlantic Alliance." In *The Atlantic Alliance and the Middle East,* edited by Joseph I. Coffey and Gianni Bonvicini, 1–16. Pittsburgh, PA: University of Pittsburgh Press, 1989.

Bossuat, Gérard. *Faire l'Europe sans défaire la France. 60 ans de politique d'unité européenne des gouvernements et des présidents de la République française (1943–2003).* Brussels: P.I.E. Peter Lang, 2005.

———. "Histoire d'une controverse. La référence aux héritages spirituels dans la Constitution européenne." *Matériaux pour l'histoire de notre temps,* no. 78 (2005): 68–82.

———. "Jean Monnet et le partenariat atlantique des années soixante." *Relations internationales,* no. 119 (2004): 285–301.

————. "Jean Monnet, le Département d'Etat et l'intégration européenne (1952–1959)." In *Europe brisée, Europe retrouvée. Nouvelles réflexions sur l'unité européenne au XXe siècle*, edited by René Girault and Gérard Bossuat, 307–45. Paris: Publications de la Sorbonne, 1994.

————. "La quête d'une identité européenne." In *La culture et l'Europe. Du rêve européen aux réalités*, edited by Antoine Mares, 19–43. Paris: Institut d'études slaves, 2005.

————. "Le président Georges Pompidou et les tentatives d'Union économique et monétaire." In *Georges Pompidou et l'Europe*, edited by Association Georges Pompidou, 405–46. Brussels: Editions Complexe, 1995.

Bozo, Frédéric. *Deux stratégies pour l'Europe. De Gaulle, les Etats-Unis et l'Alliance atlantique, 1958–1969*. Paris: Plon, 1996.

————. *La politique étrangère de la France depuis 1945*. Paris: Editions La Découverte, 1997.

Brinkley, Douglas, and David R. Facey-Crowther, eds. *The Atlantic Charter*. New York: St. Martin's Press, 1994.

Brondino, Michel. "Bourguiba, *Policy Maker* entre mondialisation et tunisianité : une approche systémique et interculturelle." In *Habib Bourguiba. La trace et l'héritage*, edited by Michel Camau and Vincent Geisser, 463–73. Paris: Editions Karthala, 2004.

Bundy, William P. *A Tangled Web: The Making of Foreign Policy in the Nixon Presidency*. New York: Hill and Wang, 1998.

Bussière, Eric. "Georges Pompidou et la crise du système monétaire international : intérêt national, solidarité européenne et enjeux internationaux." In *Georges Pompidou face à la mutation économique de l'Occident, 1969–1974*, edited by Eric Bussière, 69–106. Paris: Presses universitaires de France, 2003.

————. "Georges Pompidou, les Etats-Unis et la crise du système monétaire international." In *Georges Pompidou et les Etats-Unis, « une relation spéciale », 1969–1974*, edited by Eric Bussière and François Dubasque. Brussels: Peter Lang, forthcoming.

————, ed. *Georges Pompidou et la modernité, les tensions de l'innovation, 1962–1974*. Brussels: Peter Lang, 2006.

————, ed. *Georges Pompidou et le monde des campagnes, 1962–1974*. Brussels: Peter Lang, 2007.

Bussière, Eric, and François Dubasque, eds. *Georges Pompidou et les Etats-Unis, "une relation spéciale," 1969–1974*. Brussels: Peter Lang, forthcoming.

Bussière, Eric, and Emilie Willaert, eds. *Un projet pour l'Europe. Georges Pompidou et la construction européenne, Georges Pompidou. Archives No. 4*. Brussels: Peter Lang, 2010.

Caviglia, Daniele, and Massimiliano Cricco, eds. *La diplomazia italiana e gli equilibri mediterranei. La politica mediorientale dell'Italia dalla guerra dei Sei Giorni al conflitto dello Yom Kippur*. Soveria Mannelli: Rubbettino Editore, 2006.

Checkel, Jeffrey T. "International Institutions and Socialization in Europe: Introduction and Framework." *International Organization* 59, no. 4 (2005): 801–26.

Checkel, Jeffrey T., and Peter J. Katzenstein. *European Identity*. Cambridge, UK, and New York: Cambridge University Press, 2009.

Chehdan-Kalifé, Michel. *Les relations entre la France et le Liban (1958–1978)*. Paris: Presses universitaires de France, 1983.

Chopin, Thierry. "Le parlement européen." In *Les années Giscard. Valéry Giscard d'Estaing et l'Europe, 1974–1981*, edited by Serge Berstein and Jean-François Sirinelli, 153–89. Paris: Armand Colin, 2006.

Cogan, Charles. *Oldest Allies, Guarded Friend: The United States and France since 1940*. Westport, CT: Praeger, 1994.

Cohen, Avner. *Israel and the Bomb*. New York: Columbia University Press, 1998.

Cohen, Bernard. *Habib Bourguiba. Le pouvoir d'un seul*. Paris: Flammarion, 1986.

Cohen, Samy. "De Gaulle et Israël. Le sens d'une rupture." In *La Politique étrangère du général de Gaulle*, edited by Elie Barnavi and Saul Friedländer, 192–202. Paris: Presses universitaires de France, 1985.

———. *De Gaulle, les gaullistes et Israël*. Paris: A. Moreau, 1974.

Cohen, Samy, Marie-Claude Smouts, and Daniel Bach. *La politique extérieure de Valéry Giscard d'Estaing*. Paris: Presses de la Fondation nationale des sciences politiques, 1985.

Constantinesco, Vlad. "Le rôle du Conseil européen dans la formation d'une identité européenne." In *Institutions européennes et identités européennes*, edited by Marie-Thérèse Bitsch, Wilfried Loth, and Raymond Poidevin, 435–47. Brussels: Bruylant, 1998.

Coppolani, Antoine. "La France et les Etats-Unis dans les négociations quadripartites sur le Moyen-Orient (1969–1971)." In *Les relations franco-américaines au XXe siècle*, edited by Pierre Mélandri and Serge Ricard, 193–207. Paris: L'Harmattan, 2004.

Coppolaro, Lucia. "The United States and EEC Enlargement (1969–1973): Reaffirming the Atlantic Framework." In *Beyond the Customs Union: The European Community's Quest for Deepening, Widening and Completion, 1969–1975*, edited by Jan van der Harst, 135–62. Brussels: Bruylant, 2007.

Costigliola, Frank. *France and the United States: The Cold Alliance since World War II*. New York and Toronto: Twayne Publishers and Maxwell Macmillan, 1992.

Curli, Barbara. "Le origini della politica energetica comunitaria, 1958–1964." In *Diplomazia delle risorse. Le materie prime e il sistema internazionale nel Novecento*, edited by Massimiliano Guderzo and Matteo Luigi Napolitano, 95–118. Florence: Polistampa, 2004.

Dallek, Robert. *Nixon and Kissinger: Partners in Power*. New York: Harper Collins Publishers, 2007.

Dawn, C. Ernest. "The Foreign Policy of Syria." In *Diplomacy in the Middle East: The International Relations of Regional and Outside Powers*, edited by L. Carl Brown, 159–78. London and New York: I.B. Tauris, 2001.

Del Pero, Mario, Victor Gavín, Fernando Guirao, and Antonio Varsori. *Democrazie. L'Europa meridionale e la fine delle dittature* (Florence: Le Monnier, 2010).

Defrance, Corinne. "La culture dans les projets d'union politique de l'Europe (1961–1962)." *Revue d'Allemagne et des pays de langue allemande* 29, no. 2 (1997): 289–302.

De Grazia, Victoria. *Irresistible Empire: America's Advance through Twentieth-Century Europe*. Cambridge, MA: Belknap Press of Harvard University Press, 2005.

Deighton, Anne, and Elisabeth du Réau. "Elites, opinions et constructions européennes." In *Les identités européennes au XXe siècle. Diversités, convergences et solidarités*, edited by Robert Frank and Gérard Bossuat, 47–68. Paris: Publications de la Sorbonne, 2004.

Deighton, Anne, and Alan S. Milward, eds. *Widening, Deepening and Acceleration: The European Economic Community 1957–1963*. Baden-Baden: Nomos, 1999.

Demagny-Van Eyseren, Armelle. "Les réactions de la présidence française face au choc pétrolier." In *Milieux économiques et intégration européenne au XXe siècle. La crise des années 1970—De la conférence de La Haye à la veille de la relance des années 1980*, edited by Eric

Bussière, Michel Dumoulin, and Sylvain Schirmann, 105–17. Brussels: P.I.E. Peter Lang, 2006.

Dietl, Ralph. "Kontinuität und Wandel—Zur Geschichte der europäischen Zusammenarbeit auf dem Gebiet der Sicherheits- und Verteidigungspolitik 1948–2003." In *Gemeinsam sicher? Vision und Realität europäischer Sicherheitspolitik,* edited by Reinhard C. Meier-Walser, 19–86. Neuried: Ars una, 2004.

Dinan, Desmond. *Europe Recast: A History of European Union.* Basingstoke: Palgrave Macmillan, 2004.

Di Sarcina, Federica. "Une assemblée pour l'égalité des chances. Origines de la Commission des droits de la femme du Parlement européen, 1979–1984." In *The Road to a United Europe: Interpretations of the Process of European Integration,* edited by Ann-Christina L. Knudsen and Morten Rasmussen, 365–80. Brussels: P.I.E. Peter Lang, 2009.

Drysdale, Alasdair, and Raymond A. Hinnebusch. *Syria and the Middle East Peace Process.* New York: Council on Foreign Relations Press, 1991.

Dubois, Jean-Pierre. "La conception de la présidence de Valéry Giscard d'Estaing." In *Les années Giscard. Institutions et pratiques politiques, 1974–1978,* edited by Serge Berstein, Jean-François Sirinelli, and René Rémond, 59–75. Paris: Fayard, 2003.

Dubosclard, Alain, Laurent Grison, Dominique Trimbur, Pierre Journoud, and Laurent Jean-Pierre. *Entre rayonnement et réciprocité. Contributions à l'histoire de la diplomatie culturelle.* Paris: Publications de la Sorbonne, 2002.

Dulphy, Anne, and Christine Manigand. *La France au risque de l'Europe.* Paris: Armand Colin, 2006.

Dunstan, Simon. *The Yom Kippur War 1973.* Oxford: Osprey, 2003.

du Réau, Elisabeth. "Consolidation et élargissement de la construction européenne." In *Les années Giscard. Valéry Giscard d'Estaing et l'Europe, 1974–1981,* edited by Serge Berstein and Jean-François Sirinelli, 115–32. Paris: Armand Colin, 2006.

du Réau, Elisabeth, and Christine Manigand, eds. *Vers la réunification de l'Europe. Apports et limites du processus d'Helsinki de 1975 à nos jours.* Paris: L'Harmattan, 2005.

Eichengreen, Barry J. *The European Economy since 1945: Coordinated Capitalism and Beyond.* Princeton, NJ: Princeton University Press, 2007.

———. *Globalizing Capital: A History of the International Monetary System.* Princeton, NJ: Princeton University Press, 1996.

El Ganari, Ali. *Bourguiba, le combattant suprême.* Paris: Plon, 1985.

Ferraris, Luigi Vittorio. *Manuale della politica estera italiana, 1947–1993.* Rome: Laterza, 1996.

Findlay, Ronald, and Kevin H. O'Rourke. *Power and Plenty: Trade, War, and the World Economy in the Second Millennium.* Princeton, NJ: Princeton University Press, 2007.

Fontaine, Pascal. "Le rôle de Jean Monnet dans la genèse du Conseil européen." *Revue du marché commun,* no. 229 (1979): 357–65.

Frank, Robert. "Introduction." In *Les identités européennes au XXe siècle. Diversités, convergences et solidarités,* edited by Robert Frank and Gérard Bossuat. Paris: Publications de la Sorbonne, 2004.

Fraser, T. G. *The Arab-Israeli Conflict.* 3rd ed. Basingstoke and New York: Palgrave Macmillan, 2008.

Frémeaux, Jacques. *Le monde arabe et la sécurité de la France depuis 1958.* Paris: Presses universitaires de France, 1995.

Gaddis, John Lewis. *Strategies of Containment: A Critical Appraisal of American National Security Policy During the Cold War.* 2nd ed. New York: Oxford University Press, 2005.

Garavini, Giuliano. "The Colonies Strike Back: The Impact of the Third World on Western Europe, 1968–1975." *Contemporary European History* 16, no. 3 (2007): 299–319.

———. *Dopo gli imperi. L'integrazione europea nello scontro Nord-Sud.* Florence: Le Monnier Università, 2009.

Gavin, Francis J. *Gold, Dollars, and Power: The Politics of International Monetary Relations, 1958–1971.* Chapel Hill and London: University of North Carolina Press, 2004.

Gentile, Emilio. "Modernity: Fascism and the Ambivalent Image of the United States." *Journal of Contemporary History* 28, no. 1 (1993): 7–29.

Gerbet, Pierre. *La construction de l'Europe.* Paris: Imprimerie Nationale, 1983.

Gerbet, Pierre, Gérard Bossuat, and Thierry Grosbois, eds. *Dictionnaire historique de l'Europe unie.* Alost and Paris: André Versaille éditeur, 2009.

Geyer, David C., and Bernd Schaefer. "American Détente and German Ostpolitik, 1969–1972: Preface." *German Historical Institute, Washington, D.C., Bulletin Supplement* (2004): 143–46.

Goldman, Zachary K. "The Cold War and Israel. Ties That Bind: John F. Kennedy and the Foundations of the American–Israeli Alliance." *Cold War History* 9, no. 1 (2009): 23–58.

Goren, Haim. *Germany and the Middle East: Past, Present, and Future.* Jerusalem: Hebrew University Magnes Press, 2003.

Grebing, Helga, Gregor Schoellgen, and Heinrich August Winkler, eds. *Willy Brandt. Berliner Ausgabe.* Edited by Gregor Schoellgen and Heinrich August Winkler. Vol. 6 of 10 vols. Bonn: Dietz, 2000–2009.

Greilsammer, Alain, and Joseph Weiler. *Europe's Middle East Dilemma: The Quest for a Unified Stance.* Boulder, CO: Westview Press, 1987.

Griffiths, R.T. "A Dismal Decade? European Integration in the 1970s." In *Origins and Evolution of the European Union,* edited by Desmond Dinan, 169–90. Oxford and New York: Oxford University Press, 2006.

Guerrieri, Sandro, and Maria Sofia Corciulo. "Dall'Assemblea comune della Ceca al Parlamento europeo: la contrastata nomina dei rappresentanti italiani." In *Le istituzioni repubblicane dal centrismo al centro-sinistra, 1953–1968,* edited by Pier Luigi Ballini, Sandro Guerrieri, and Antonio Varsori, 124–41. Roma: Carocci, 2006.

Hackett, Clifford P., ed. *Monnet and the Americans: The Father of a United Europe and His U.S. Supporters.* Washington, D.C.: Jean Monnet Council, 1995.

Hahn, Peter. "Conflict and Cooperation: Pompidou, Nixon and the Arab-Israeli Conflict, 1969–1974." In *Georges Pompidou et les Etats-Unis, « une relation spéciale », 1969–1974,* edited by Eric Bussière and François Dubasque. Brussels: Peter Lang, forthcoming.

Hamilton, Keith. "Britain, France, and America's Year of Europe, 1973." *Diplomacy & Statecraft* 17, no. 4 (2006): 871–95.

Hanhimäki, Jussi M. "Détente: A Three-Way Discussion. Conservative Goals, Revolutionary Outcomes: The Paradox of Détente." *Cold War History* 8, no. 4 (2008): 503–12.

———. *The Flawed Architect: Henry Kissinger and American Foreign Policy.* New York: Oxford University Press, 2004.

———. "Kissinger et l'Europe : entre intégration et autonomie." *Relations internationales,* no. 119 (2004): 319–32.

Hellema, Duco, Cees Wiebes, and Toby White. *The Netherlands and the Oil Crisis: Business as Usual*. Chicago: University of Chicago Press, 2004.

Hiepel, Claudia. "Kissinger's 'Year of Europe'—a Challenge for the EC and the Franco-German Relationship." In *Beyond the Customs Union: The European Community's Quest for Deepening, Widening and Completion, 1969–1975,* edited by Jan van der Harst, 277–96. Brussels: Bruylant, 2007.

Hilfrich, Fabian. "West Germany's Long Year of Europe: Bonn between Europe and the United States." In *The Strained Alliance: U.S.-European Relations from Nixon to Carter,* edited by Matthias Schulz and Thomas A. Schwartz, 237–56. New York: Cambridge University Press, 2009.

Hill, Christopher. "Changing Gear in Political Co-Operation." *The Political Quarterly* 53, no. 1 (1982): 47–60.

———. "National Interests—the Insuperable Obstacles?" In *National Foreign Policies and European Political Cooperation,* edited by Christopher Hill, 185–202. London and Winchester, MA: G. Allen & Unwin, 1983.

Hill, Christopher, and William Wallace. "Diplomatic Trends in the European Community." *International Affairs* 55, no. 5 (1979): 47–66.

Hitchcock, William I. *The Struggle for Europe: The Turbulent History of a Divided Continent, 1945–2002.* New York: Doubleday, 2003.

Hoffmann, Stanley. "Towards a Common European Foreign and Security Policy." *Journal of Common Market Studies* 38, no. 2 (2000): 189–98.

Hohensee, Jens. *Der erste Ölpreisschock 1973/74. Die politischen und gesellschaftlichen Auswirkungen der arabischen Erdölpolitik auf die Bundesrepublik Deutschland und Westeuropa.* Stuttgart: Steiner, 1996.

Hopwood, Derek. *Habib Bourguiba of Tunisia: The Tragedy of Longevity.* Houndmills, UK: Macmillan, 1992.

Hubel, Helmut. "Germany and the Middle East Conflict." In *Germany and the Middle East: Patterns and Prospects,* edited by Shahram Chubin, 41–54. London: Pinter, 1992.

Hurd, Douglas. "Political Co-Operation." *International Affairs* 57, no. 3 (1981): 383–93.

Hynes, Catherine. *The Year That Never Was: Heath, the Nixon Administration and the Year of Europe.* Dublin: University College Dublin Press, 2009.

Hynes, Catherine, and Sandra Scanlon, eds. *Reform and Renewal: Transatlantic Relations during the 1960s and 1970s.* London: Cambridge Scholars Publishing, 2010.

Ifestos, Panayiotis. *European Political Cooperation: Towards a Framework of Supranational Diplomacy?* Aldershot, UK: Avebury, 1987.

Ikenberry, G. John. "The Irony of State Strength: Comparative Responses to the Oil Shocks in the 1970s." *International Organization* 40, no. 1 (1986): 105–37.

James, Harold. *International Monetary Cooperation since Bretton Woods.* Washington, D.C., and New York: International Monetary Fund and Oxford University Press, 1996.

Jawad, H. A. *Euro-Arab Relations: A Study in Collective Diplomacy.* Reading, UK: Ithaca Press, 1992.

Joffe, Josef. "Reflections on German Policy in the Middle East." In *Germany and the Middle East: Patterns and Prospects,* edited by Shahram Chubin, 195–209. London: Pinter, 1992.

Judt, Tony. *Postwar: A History of Europe since 1945.* London: William Heinemann, 2005.

Kaiser, Wolfram, and Antonio Varsori, eds. *European Union History: Themes and Debates.* Basingstoke: Palgrave Macmillan, 2010.

Karamouzi, Eirini. "Telling the Whole Story: America, the EEC and Greece, 1972–1974." In *Europe in the International Arena During the 1970s: Entering a Different World,* edited by Antonio Varsori and Guia Migani, 355–374. Brussels: Peter Lang, 2011.

Keohane, Robert O., and Joseph S. Nye. *Power and Interdependence: World Politics in Transition.* 3rd ed. New York: Longman, 2001.

Khalidi, Rashid. *Sowing Crisis: The Cold War and American Dominance in the Middle East.* Boston: Beacon Press, 2009.

Kieninger, Stephan. "Transformation or Status Quo: The Conflict of Stratagems in Washington over the Meaning and Purpose of the CSCE and MBFR, 1969–1973." In *Helsinki 1975 and the Transformation of Europe,* edited by Oliver Bange and Gottfried Niedhart, 67–82. New York: Berghahn Books, 2008.

Klitzing, Holger. "To Grin and Bear It: The Nixon Administration and *Ostpolitik.*" In *Ostpolitik, 1969–1974: European and Global Responses,* edited by Carole Fink and Bernd Schaefer, 80–110. Cambridge and New York: Cambridge University Press, 2009.

Kohl, Wilfrid L. "Energy Policy in the Communities." *Annals of the American Academy of Political and Social Science* 440 (1978): 111–21.

Kroes, Rob. *If You've Seen One, You've Seen the Mall: Europeans and American Mass Culture.* Urbana: University of Illinois Press, 1996.

Kuisel, Richard F. *Seducing the French: The Dilemma of Americanization.* Berkeley and Los Angeles: University of California Press, 1993.

Kunz, Diane B. "Cold War Diplomacy: The Other Side of Containment." In *The Diplomacy of the Crucial Decade: American Foreign Relations During the 1960s,* edited by Diane B. Kunz, 80–114. New York: Columbia University Press, 1994.

Labbate, Silvio. "L'Italia e lo shock petrolifero del '73 tra interesse nazionale e vincoli europei." Paper presented at the Seminario di Storia Internazionale dell'Età Contemporanea (SSIEC–SISSCO), Università degli Studi di Padova, 28–29 January 2010.

Lacorne, Denis, Jacques Rupnik, and Marie-France Toinet, eds. *L'Amérique dans les têtes. Un siècle de fascinations et d'aversions.* Paris: Hachette, 1986.

La Gorce, Paul-Marie de. "La politique arabe du Général de Gaulle." In *La Politique étrangère du général de Gaulle,* edited by Elie Barnavi and Saul Friedländer, 179–91. Paris: Presses universitaires de France, 1985.

Lapparent, Olivier de. *Raymond Aron et l'Europe. Itinéraire d'un Européen dans le siècle.* Brussels: Peter Lang, 2010.

Laskier, Michael M. "Israeli-Tunisian Relations between Bourguibism and Nasserism." In *Israel and the Maghreb: From Statehood to Oslo,* 187–217. Gainesville: University Press of Florida, 2004.

Laurens, Henry. *Le royaume impossible. La France et la genèse du monde arabe.* Paris: Armand Colin, 1990.

Laursen, Johnny, ed. *From Crisis to New Dynamics: The European Community 1974–83.* Brussels: Bruylant, forthcoming.

Leveau, Rémy. "France's Arab Policy." In *Diplomacy in the Middle East: The International Relations of Regional and Outside Powers,* edited by L. Carl Brown, 3–21. London and New York: I.B. Tauris, 2001.

Lieber, Robert J. *The Oil Decade: Conflict and Cooperation in the West.* New York: Praeger, 1983.

Link, Werner. "Aussen- und Deutschlandpolitik in der Ära Brandt, 1960–1974." In *Republik im Wandel, 1969–1974. Die Ära Brandt,* edited by Karl Dietrich Bracher, Wolfgang Jäger, and Werner Link, 163–282. Stuttgart and Mannheim: Deutsche Verlags-Anstalt and F.A. Brockhaus, 1986–1987.

————. "Ostpolitik: Détente German-Style and Adapting to America." In *The United States and Germany in the Era of the Cold War, 1945–1990: A Handbook,* edited by Detlef Junker, Philipp Gassert, Wilfried Mausbach, and David B. Morris, 33–39. New York: Cambridge University Press, 2004.

Logevall, Fredrik, and Andrew Preston, eds. *Nixon in the World: American Foreign Relations, 1969–1977.* Oxford and New York: Oxford University Press, 2008.

Loth, Wilfried. "Europäische Identität und europäisches Bewusstsein." In *Nationale Identität und transnationale Einflüsse. Amerikanisierung, Europäisierung und Globalisierung in Frankreich nach dem Zweiten Weltkrieg,* 35–52. Munich: Oldenburg, 2007.

————. "Willy Brandt, Georges Pompidou und die Entspannungspolitik." In *Willy Brandt und Frankreich,* edited by Horst Möller and Maurice Vaïsse, 167–80. Munich: Oldenburg, 2005.

Louis, William Roger. "Britain and the Middle East after 1945." In *Diplomacy in the Middle East: The International Relations of Regional and Outside Powers,* edited by L. Carl Brown, 21–58. London and New York: I.B. Tauris, 2001.

Ludlow, N. Piers. *European Integration and the Cold War: Ostpolitik-Westpolitik, 1965–1973.* London and New York: Routledge, 2007.

————. "Who Speaks for Europe? Evolving Transatlantic Dialogues During the 1980s." Paper presented at the conference on Europe and America in the 1980s: Old Barriers, New Openings, European University Institute, Florence, 14–15 May 2010.

Lundestad, Geir. *The United States and Western Europe since 1945: From "Empire" By Invitation to Transatlantic Drift.* Oxford and New York: Oxford University Press, 2003.

Maddison, Angus. *Dynamic Forces in Capitalist Development: A Long-Run Comparative View.* Oxford: Oxford University Press, 1991.

Mahan, Erin R. *Kennedy, de Gaulle and Western Europe.* Houndmills, UK, and New York: Palgrave Macmillan, 2002.

Ma'oz, Moshe. *Syria and Israel: From War to Peacemaking.* Oxford and New York: Clarendon Press, 1995.

Mario Del Pero, Victor Gavín, Fernando Guirao, and Antonio Varsori. *Democrazie. L'Europa meridionale e la fine delle dittature.* Florence: Le Monnier, 2010.

Mattar, Philip. "Palestine Liberation Organization." In *Encyclopedia of the Modern Middle East,* edited by Reeva S. Simon, Philip Mattar, and Richard W. Bulliet, 1411–13. New York: Macmillan Reference USA, 1996.

Maus, Didier. "Les rapports de Valéry Giscard d'Estaing avec ses gouvernements (1974–1981)." In *Les années Giscard. Institutions et pratiques politiques, 1974–1978,* edited by Serge Berstein, Jean-François Sirinelli, and René Rémond, 113–35. Paris: Fayard, 2003.

Mazower, Mark. *Dark Continent: Europe's Twentieth Century.* New York: A.A. Knopf, 1999.

Megens, Ine. "The December 1973 Declaration on European Identity as the Result of Team Spirit among European Diplomats." In *Beyond the Customs Union: The European Communi-*

ty's Quest for Deepening, Widening and Completion, 1969–1975, edited by Jan van der Harst, 317–38. Brussels: Bruylant, 2007.

Mélandri, Pierre. "Aux origines de la coopération nucléaire franco-américaine." In *La France et l'atome,* edited by Maurice Vaïsse, 235–54. Brussels: Bruylant, 1994.

———. "La France et l'Alliance atlantique sous Georges Pompidou et Valéry Giscard d'Estaing." In *La France et l'OTAN, 1949–1996,* edited by Maurice Vaïsse, Pierre Mélandri, and Frédéric Bozo, 519–58. Brussels: Editions Complexe, 1996.

———. "Une relation très spéciale. La France, les Etats-Unis et l'année de l'Europe, 1973–1974." In *Georges Pompidou et l'Europe,* edited by Association Georges Pompidou, 89–131. Brussels: Editions Complexe, 1995.

Migani, Guia. "Gli Stati Uniti e le relazione eurafricane da Kennedy a Nixon." In *Dollari, petrolio e aiuti allo sviluppo. Il confronto Nord-Sud negli anni '60–70,* edited by Daniele Caviglia and Antonio Varsori, 47–64. Milan: Franco Angeli, 2008.

———. "Un nuovo modello di cooperazione Nord-Sud? Lomé, la CEE ed i paesi ACP." In *La Comunità europea e le relazioni esterne, 1957–1992,* edited by Alessandra Bitumi, Gabriele D'Ottavio, and Giuliana Laschi, 173–92. Bologna: Clueb, 2008.

Möckli, Daniel. *European Foreign Policy During the Cold War: Heath, Brandt, Pompidou and the Dream of Political Unity.* London: I.B. Tauris, 2009.

Moravcsik, Andrew. *The Choice for Europe: Social Purpose and State Power from Messina to Maastricht.* Ithaca, NY: Cornell University Press, 1998.

Morgan, Michael Cotey. "The United States and the Making of the Helsinki Final Act." In *Nixon in the World: American Foreign Relations, 1969–1977,* edited by Fredrik Logevall and Andrew Preston, 164–82. Oxford and New York: Oxford University Press, 2008.

Mourlon-Druol, Emmanuel. "Economist or Monetarist? The Difficult Creation of an Internal French Consensus About European Monetary Integration (1974–1976)." In *Les deux Europes / The Two Europes,* edited by Michele Affinito, Guia Migani, and Christian Wenkel, 213–24. Brussels: P.I.E. Lang, 2009.

———. "The Emergence of a European Bloc? A Trans-and Supranational History of European Monetary Cooperation, from the Failure of the Werner Plan to the Creation of the European Monetary System, 1974–1979." Ph.D. thesis, European University Institute, 2010.

———. "Filling the EEC Leadership Vacuum? The Creation of the European Council in 1974." *Cold War History* 10, no. 3 (2010): 315–339.

Nichter, Luke A. "Nixon and Europe: Transatlantic Policy in the Shadow of Other Priorities." In *A Companion to Richard M. Nixon,* edited by Melvin Small, 444–59. Malden, MA: Blackwell Publishers, 2011.

Niedhart, Gottfried. "Frankreich und die USA im Dialog über Détente und Ostpolitik, 1969–1970." *Francia: Forschungen zur westeuropäischen Geschichte* 31, no. 3 (2004): 65–85.

———. "Ostpolitik: The Role of the Federal Republic of Germany in the Process of Détente." In *1968, The World Transformed,* edited by Carole Fink, Philipp Gassert, and Detlef Junker, 173–92. Cambridge, UK, and New York: Cambridge University Press, 1998.

———. "Revisionistische Elemente und die Initiierung friedlichen. Wandels in der neuen Ostpolitik 1967-1974." *Geschichte und Gesellschaft,* no. 28 (2002): 233–66.

———. "U.S. Détente and West German *Ostpolitik.*" In *The Strained Alliance: U.S.-European Relations from Nixon to Carter,* edited by Matthias Schulz and Thomas A. Schwartz, 23–44. New York: Cambridge University Press, 2009.

Nielsen-Sikora, Jürgen. "The Idea of a European Union and a Citizen's Europe: The 1975 Tindemans Report and Its Impact on Today's Europe." In *Beyond the Customs Union: The European Community's Quest for Deepening, Widening and Completion, 1969–1975*, edited by Jan van der Harst, 377–89. Brussels: Bruylant, 2007.

Noble, Alastair. "Kissinger's Year of Europe, Britain's Year of Choice." In *The Strained Alliance: U.S.-European Relations from Nixon to Carter*, edited by Matthias Schulz and Thomas A. Schwartz, 221–35. New York: Cambridge University Press, 2009.

Nolan, Mary. *Visions of Modernity: American Business and the Modernization of Germany*. New York: Oxford University Press, 1994.

Nouailhat, Yves-Henri. "Les divergences entre la France et les Etats-Unis face au conflit israélo-arabe de 1967 à 1973." *Relations internationales*, no. 119 (2004): 334–44.

Nouschi, André. *La France et le monde arabe. Depuis 1962, mythes et réalités d'une ambition*. Paris: Vuibert, 1994.

Nuttall, Simon J. *European Political Co-Operation*. Oxford and New York: Clarendon Press and Oxford University Press, 1992.

Nye, Joseph S. "Independence and Interdependence." *Foreign Policy*, no. 22 (1976): 130–61.

Olivi, Bino, and Alessandro Giacone. *L'Europe difficile. La construction européenne*. Paris: Editions Gallimard, 2007.

Osmont, Mathieu. "Les ambassadeurs de France à Bonn (1955–1999)." Ph.D. thesis, Institut d'Etudes Politiques, 2011.

Palayret, Jean-Marie. "Il Movimento europeo." In *I movimenti per l'unità europea 1945–1954*, edited by Sergio Pistone, 151–78. Milan: Jaca Book, 1996.

———. "Mondialisme contre régionalisme : CEE et ACP dans les négociations de la convention de Lomé, 1970–75." In *Inside the European Community: Actors and Policies in the European Integration*, edited by Antonio Varsori, 369–97. Baden-Baden and Brussels: Nomos and Bruylant, 2006.

Paoli, Simone. *Il sogno di Erasmo. La questione educativa nel processo di integrazione europea*. Milan: Franco Angeli, 2010.

Parker, Richard B. *The October War: A Retrospective*. Gainesville: University Press of Florida, 2001.

Passerini, Luisa, and Hartmut Kaelble. "European Identity, the European Public Sphere, and the Future of 'Europe.'" In *Les identités européennes au XXe siècle. Diversités, convergences et solidarités*, edited by Robert Frank and Gérard Bossuat, 91–100. Paris: Publications de la Sorbonne, 2004.

Pells, Richard H. *Not Like Us: How Europeans Have Loved, Hated and Transformed American Culture since World War II*. New York: Basic Books, 1997.

Perkins, Kenneth J. *Tunisia: Crossroads of the Islamic and European Worlds*. Boulder, CO, and London: Westview Press and C. Helm, 1986.

Petrini, Francesco. "L'arma del petrolio: lo 'shock' petrolifero e il confronto Nord-Sud. Parte prima. L'Europa alla ricerca di un' alternativa: la Communità tra dipendenza energetica ed egemonia statunitense." In *Dollari, petrolio e aiuti allo sviluppo. Il confronto Nord-Sud negli anni '60-70*, edited by Daniele Caviglia and Antonio Varsori, 79–107. Milan: Franco Angeli, 2008.

Pfetsch, Frank. "La problématique de l'identité européenne." *The Tocqueville Review*, no. 2 (1998): 87–103.

Pistone, Sergio. "I movimenti per l'unità europea in Italia." In *I movimenti per l'unità europea 1945–1954*, edited by Sergio Pistone, 17–53. Milan: Jaca Book, 1992.

Primakov, E. M. *Russia and the Arabs: Behind the Scenes in the Middle East From the Cold War to the Present*. New York: Basic Books, 2009.

Prodi, Romano, and Alberto Clô. "Europe." In *The Oil Crisis*, edited by Raymond Vernon, 91–112. New York: Norton, 1976.

Quandt, William B. *Peace Process: American Diplomacy and the Arab-Israeli Conflict since 1967*. 3rd ed. Washington, D.C., and Berkeley: Brookings Institution Press and University of California Press, 2005.

Rabinovich, Abraham. *Yom Kippur War: The Epic Encounter That Transformed the Middle East*. New York: Schocken Books, 2004.

Renouard, Joe, and D. Nathan Vigil. "The Quest for Leadership in a Time of Peace: Jimmy Carter and Western Europe, 1977–1981." In *The Strained Alliance: U.S.-European Relations from Nixon to Carter*, edited by Matthias Schulz and Thomas A. Schwartz, 309–32. New York: Cambridge University Press, 2009.

Rey, Marie-Pierre. "Chancellor Brandt's *Ostpolitik*, France, and the Soviet Union." In *Ostpolitik, 1969–1974: European and Global Responses*, edited by Carole Fink and Bernd Schaefer, 111–25. Cambridge and New York: Cambridge University Press, 2009.

———. "France and the German Question in the Context of Ostpolitik and the CSCE, 1969–1974." In *Helsinki 1975 and the Transformation of Europe*, edited by Oliver Bange and Gottfried Niedhart, 53–66. New York: Berghahn Books, 2008.

———. *La tentation du rapprochement. France et URSS à l'heure de la détente (1964–1974)*. Paris: Publications de la Sorbonne, 1991.

Riccardi, Luca. *Il problema Israele. Diplomazia italiana e PCI di fronte allo stato ebraico (1948–1973)*. Milan: Guerini studio, 2006.

Richard, Gilles. "L'élection présidentielle de 1974 : un événement." In *Les années Giscard. Institutions et pratiques politiques, 1974–1978*, edited by Serge Berstein, Jean-François Sirinelli, and René Rémond, 15–33. Paris: Fayard, 2003.

Roche, François, and Bernard Piniau. *Histoires de diplomatie culturelle des origines à 1995*. Paris: La documentation française, 1995.

Roger, Philippe. *L'ennemi américain. Généalogie de l'antiaméricanisme français*. Paris: Editions du Seuil, 2002.

Romano, Angela. *From Détente in Europe to European Détente: How the West Shaped the Helsinki CSCE*. Brussels: P.I.E. Peter Lang, 2009.

Rossbach, Niklas H. *Heath, Nixon and the Rebirth of the Special Relationship: Britain, the US and the EC, 1969–74*. Basingstoke: Palgrave Macmillan, 2009.

Roussel, Eric. *Georges Pompidou, 1911–1974*. 2nd ed. Paris: Perrin, 2004.

———. *Jean Monnet, 1888–1979*. Paris: Fayard, 1996.

Rubin, Barry M., J. Ginat, and Moshe Ma'oz, eds. *From War to Peace: Arab-Israeli Relations, 1973–1993*. New York: New York University Press, 1994.

Saint-Périer, Amaury de. "La France et la sauvegarde du système communautaire de change de 1974 à 1977." In *Milieux économiques et intégration européenne au XXe siècle. La crise des années 1970—De la conférence de La Haye à la veille de la relance des années 1980*, edited by Eric Bussière, Michel Dumoulin, and Sylvain Schirmann, 51–58. Brussels: P.I.E. Peter Lang, 2006.

Schaefer, Bernd. "The Nixon Administration and West German *Ostpolitik, 1969–1973.*" In *The Strained Alliance: U.S.-European Relations from Nixon to Carter,* edited by Matthias Schulz and Thomas A. Schwartz, 45–64. New York: Cambridge University Press, 2009.

Schillo, Frédérique. *France-Israël, 1948–1959.* Paris: André Versaille, 2012.

Schulz, Matthias. "The Reluctant European: Helmut Schmidt, the European Community, and Transatlantic Relations." In *The Strained Alliance: U.S.-European Relations from Nixon to Carter,* edited by Matthias Schulz and Thomas A. Schwartz, 279–307. New York: Cambridge University Press, 2009.

Schulz, Matthias, and Thomas A. Schwartz. "The Superpower and the Union in the Making: U.S.-European Relations, 1969–1980." In *The Strained Alliance: U.S.-European Relations from Nixon to Carter,* edited by Matthias Schulz and Thomas A. Schwartz, 355–73. New York: Cambridge University Press, 2009.

Schulz, Matthias, and Thomas A. Schwartz, eds. *The Strained Alliance: U.S.-European Relations from Nixon to Carter.* Cambridge, UK: Cambridge University Press, 2009.

Schulzinger, Robert D. "Détente in the Nixon-Ford Years, 1969–1976." In *The Cambridge History of the Cold War,* edited by Melvyn P. Leffler and Odd Arne Westad, 373–94. Cambridge and New York: Cambridge University Press, 2010.

Schwabe, Klaus. "Jean Monnet, les Etats-Unis et le rôle de l'Europe au sein de la Communauté atlantique." In *Jean Monnet, l'Europe et les chemins de la paix,* edited by Gérard Bossuat and Andreas Wilkens, 275–93. Paris: Publications de la Sorbonne, 1999.

Schwartz, Hans-Peter. "Willy Brandt, Georges Pompidou und die Ostpolitik." In *Willy Brandt und Frankreich,* edited by Horst Möller and Maurice Vaïsse, 155–65. Munich: Oldenburg, 2005.

Schwartz, Thomas A. *Lyndon Johnson and Europe: In the Shadow of Vietnam.* Cambridge, MA, and London: Harvard University Press, 2003.

Scichilone, Laura. *L'Europa e la sfida ecologica. Storia della politica ambientale europea, 1969–1998.* Bologna: Il Mulino, 2008.

Shannon, Vaughn P. *Balancing Act: US Foreign Policy and the Arab-Israeli Conflict.* Aldershot, UK, and Burlington, VT: Ashgate, 2003.

Smouts, Marie-Claude. "Valéry Giscard d'Estaing et le nouvel ordre économique international : une diplomatie plus qu'une politique ?" In *La politique extérieure de Valéry Giscard d'Estaing,* edited by Samy Cohen, Marie-Claude Smouts, and Daniel Bach, 263–83. Paris: Presses de la Fondation nationale des sciences politiques, 1985.

Soutou, Georges-Henri. "Georges Pompidou et Valéry Giscard d'Estaing : deux réconciliations et deux ruptures avec les Etats-Unis." *Relations internationales,* no. 119 (2004): 303–18.

———. *La guerre de cinquante ans. Le conflit Est-Ouest, 1943–1990.* Paris: Fayard, 2001.

———. "La problématique de la détente et le testament stratégique de Georges Pompidou." *Cahiers du Centre d'études d'histoire de la défense,* no. 22 (2004): 79–107.

———. *L'alliance incertaine. Les rapports stratégiques franco-allemands, 1954–1996.* Paris: Fayard, 1996.

———. "L'anneau et les deux triangles : les rapports franco-allemands dans la politique européenne et mondiale de 1974 à 1981." In *Les années Giscard. Valéry Giscard d'Estaing et l'Europe, 1974–1981,* edited by Serge Berstein and Jean-François Sirinelli, 45–79. Paris: Armand Colin, 2006.

———. "Le général de Gaulle et le Plan Fouchet d'union politique européenne : un projet stratégique." *Revue d'Allemagne et des pays de langue allemande* 29, no. 2 (1997): 211–20.

———. "Le président Pompidou et les relations entre les Etats-Unis et l'Europe." *Journal of European Integration History* 6, no. 2 (2000): 111–46.

———. "The Linkage between European Integration and Détente: The Contrasting Approaches of De Gaulle and Pompidou, 1965–1974." In *European Integration and the Cold War: Ostpolitik-Westpolitik, 1965–1973*, edited by N. Piers Ludlow, 11–35. London: Routledge, 2007.

———. "President Pompidou, Ostpolitik, and the Strategy of Détente." In *The Strategic Triangle: France, Germany, and the United States in the Shaping of the New Europe*, edited by Helga Haftendorn, Georges-Henri Soutou, Stephen F. Szabo, and Samuel F. Wells, 229–57. Baltimore, MD: Johns Hopkins University Press and the Woodrow Wilson Center Press, 2007.

Styan, David. *France and Iraq: Oil, Arms and French Policy Making in the Middle East.* London and New York: I.B. Tauris, 2006.

Szulc, Tad. *The Illusion of Peace: Foreign Policy in the Nixon Years.* New York: Viking Press, 1978.

Thornton, Richard C. *Nixon-Kissinger Years: Reshaping America's Foreign Policy.* 2nd ed. St. Paul, MN: Paragon House Publishers, 2001.

Thune, Christian. "Denmark." In *European Foreign Policy-Making and the Arab-Israeli Conflict*, edited by David Allen and Alfred Pijpers. The Hague and Hingham, MA: Martinus Nijhoff Publishers, 1984.

Toinet, Marie-France. *Valéry Giscard d'Estaing et les Etats-Unis.* Paris: Association française de sciences politiques, 1983.

Trachtenberg, Marc. "The French Factor in U.S. Foreign Policy During the Nixon-Pompidou Period, 1969–1974." Paper presented at the conference on Georges Pompidou et les Etats-Unis, "une relation spéciale," 1969–1974, Paris, 26–27 June 2009.

———. "The French Factor in U.S. Foreign Policy During the Nixon-Pompidou Period, 1969–1974." *Journal of Cold War Studies* 13, no. 1 (2011): 4–59.

———. "The Structure of Great Power Politics, 1963–1975." In *The Cambridge History of the Cold War*, edited by Melvyn P. Leffler and Odd Arne Westad, 482–502. Cambridge and New York: Cambridge University Press, 2010.

Turner, Louis. "The Politics of the Energy Crisis." *International Affairs* 50, no. 3 (1974): 404–15.

Vaïsse, Maurice. "Changement et continuité dans la politique européenne de la France." In *Georges Pompidou et l'Europe*, edited by Association Georges Pompidou, 29–42. Brussels: Editions Complexe, 1995.

———. *La grandeur. Politique étrangère du général de Gaulle, 1958–1969.* Paris: Fayard, 1998.

———. *La puissance ou l'influence? La France dans le monde depuis 1958.* [Paris]: Libraire Arthème Fayard, 2009.

———. "Les 'relations spéciales' franco-américaines au temps de Richard Nixon et Georges Pompidou." *Relations internationales*, no. 119 (2004): 345–62.

———. "Valéry Giscard d'Estaing de la défense de l'Europe à la défense européenne." In *Les années Giscard. Valéry Giscard d'Estaing et l'Europe, 1974–1981*, edited by Serge Berstein and Jean-François Sirinelli, 207–29. Paris: Armand Colin, 2006.

———, ed. *De Gaulle et la Russie.* Paris: CNRS Editions, 2006.

van der Harst, Jan, ed. *Beyond the Customs Union: The European Community's Quest for Deepening, Widening and Completion, 1969–1975*. Brussels: Bruylant, 2007.

Varsori, Antonio, ed. *Alle origini del presente. L'Europa occidentale nella crisi degli anni Settanta.* Milan: Franco Angeli, 2008.

———. "Les mers, frontières de l'Europe et leur rôle dans la formation de l'identité européenne." In *Identité et conscience européennes au XXe siècle,* edited by René Girault, 157–67. Paris: Hachette, 1994.

Varsori, Antonio, and Lorenzo Mechi. "At the Origins of the European Structural Policy: The Community's Social and Regional Policies from the Late 1960s to the Mid-1970s." In *Beyond the Customs Union: The European Community's Quest for Deepening, Widening and Completion, 1969–1975,* edited by Jan van der Harst, 223–50. Brussels: Bruylant, 2007.

Varsori, Antonio, and Maria Petricioli. "Europe, Its Borders, and the Others." In *Les identités européennes au XXe siècle. Diversités, convergences et solidarités,* edited by Robert Frank and Gérard Bossuat, 81–90. Paris: Publications de la Sorbonne, 2004.

Venn, Fiona. "International Cooperation Versus National Self-Interest: The United States and Europe During the 1973–1974 Oil Crisis." In *The United States and the European Alliance since 1945,* edited by Kathleen Burk and Melvyn Stokes, 71–98. Oxford and New York: Berg Publishers, 1999.

———. *The Oil Crisis.* London and New York: Longman, 2002.

———. *Oil Diplomacy in the Twentieth Century.* Basingstoke: Macmillan, 1986.

Vernon, Raymond, ed. *The Oil Crisis.* New York: Norton, 1976.

Visintin, Giorgia. "Il 'dialogo Euro-Arabo' (1974/1982): un tentativo di politica estera comune della CEE." MA thesis, Università degli studi di Padova, 2010.

Walton, Ann-Margaret. "Atlantic Bargaining Over Energy." *International Affairs* 52, no. 2 (1976): 180–96.

Waltz, Kenneth N. *Theory of International Politics.* New York: McGraw-Hill, Inc, 1979.

Warlouzet, Laurent. "Charles de Gaulle's Idea of Europe. The Lasting Legacy." *Kontur,* no. 19 (2010): 21–31.

Weed, Mary Kathleen. *Michel Jobert et la diplomatie française. L'image publique d'un homme secret.* Paris: Editions F. Lanore, 1988.

Weinachter, Michèle. *Valéry Giscard d'Estaing et l'Allemagne. Le double rêve inachevé.* Paris: L'Harmattan, 2004.

Weingardt, Markus A. *Deutsche Israel- und Nahostpolitik. Die Geschichte einer Gratwanderung seit 1949.* Frankfurt and New York: Campus, 2002.

Weisbrode, Kenneth. *The Atlantic Century: Four Generations of Extraordinary Diplomats who Forged America's Vital Alliance with Europe.* Cambridge, MA: Da Capo Press, 2009.

Winand, Pascaline. "De l'usage de l'Amérique par Jean Monnet pour la construction européenne." In *Jean Monnet, l'Europe et les chemins de la paix,* edited by Gérard Bossuat and Andreas Wilkens, 252–71. Paris: Publications de la Sorbonne, 1999.

———. *Eisenhower, Kennedy, and the United States of Europe.* New York: St. Martin's Press, 1993.

———. "Loaded Words and Disputed Meanings: The Year of Europe Speech and Its Genesis from an American Perspective." In *Beyond the Customs Union: The European Community's Quest for Deepening, Widening and Completion, 1969–1975,* edited by Jan van der Harst, 297–315. Brussels: Bruylant, 2007.

Winand, Pascaline, and Fondation Jean Monnet pour l'Europe. "20 ans d'action du Comité Jean Monnet (1955–1975)." *Problématiques européennes,* no. 8 (2001): 1–11.

Yergin, Daniel. *The Prize: The Epic Quest for Oil, Money, and Power.* New York: Simon & Schuster, 1991.

Zampoli, Davide. "I primi passi della Cooperazione politica europea: problematiche ed evoluzione instituzionale." In *Alle origini del presente. L'Europa occidentale nella crisi degli anni Settanta,* edited by Antonio Varsori, 169–92. Milan: Franco Angeli, 2008.

———. "Verso una political estera comune: problemi di coordinamento tra i lavori della Cooperazione Politica e della Communità negli anni Settanta." In *La Comunità europea e le relazioni esterne, 1957–1992,* edited by Alessandra Bitumi, Gabriele D'Ottavio, and Giuliana Laschi, 41–63. Bologna: Clueb, 2008.

Zeiler, Thomas W. "Nixon Shocks Japan, Inc." In *Nixon in the World: American Foreign Relations, 1969–1977,* edited by Fredrik Logevall and Andrew Preston, 289–308. Oxford and New York: Oxford University Press, 2008.

INDEX